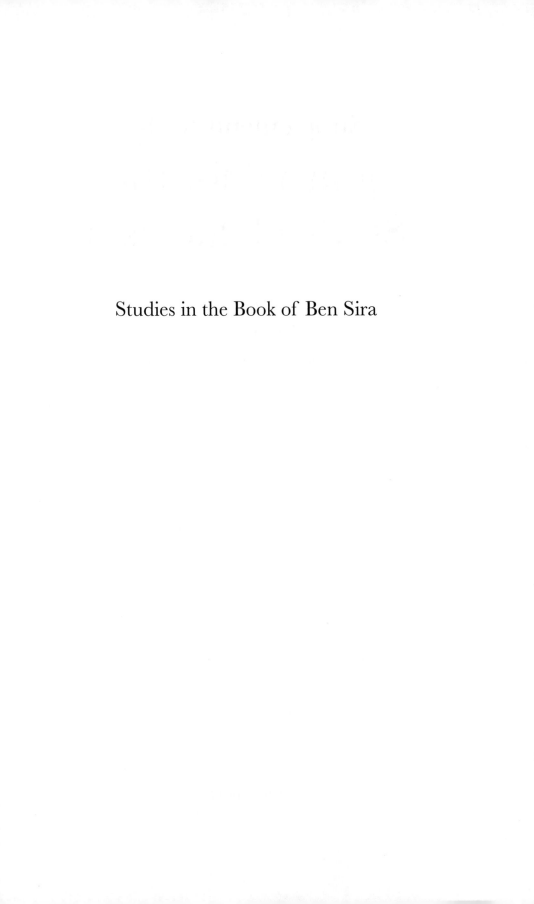

Studies in the Book of Ben Sira

Supplements to the
Journal for the
Study of Judaism

Editor

John J. Collins

The Divinity School, Yale University

Associate Editors

Florentino García Martínez

Qumran Institute, University of Groningen

Hindy Najman

Department of Near and Middle Eastern Civilizations,

University of Toronto

Advisory Board

J. DUHAIME — A. HILHORST — P.W. VAN DER HORST

A. KLOSTERGAARD PETERSEN — M.A. KNIBB

J.T.A.G.M. VAN RUTTEN — J. SIEVERS — G. STEMBERGER

E.J.C. TIGCHELAAR — J. TROMP

VOLUME 127

Studies in the Book of Ben Sira

Papers of the Third International Conference on
the Deuterocanonical Books, Shime'on Centre, Pápa,
Hungary, 18-20 May, 2006

Edited by

Géza G. Xeravits
József Zsengellér

BRILL

LEIDEN • BOSTON
2008

This book is printed on acid-free paper.

Library of Congress Cataloging-in Publication data

International Conference on the Deuterocanonical Books (3nd : 2006 : Pápa, Hungary)
    Studies in the book of Ben Sira : papers of the Third International Conference on the
Deuterocanonical books, Shime'on Centre, Pápa, Hungary, 18-20 May 2006 / edited by
Géza G. Xeravits, József Zsengellér.
        p. cm. — (Supplements to the journal for the study of Judaism ; v. 127)
    Includes index.
ISBN 978-90-04-16906-7 (hardback : alk. paper)
    1. Bible. O.T. Apocrypha. Ecclesiasticus—Criticism, interpretation, etc.—Congresses.
I. Xeravits, Géza G. II. Zsengellér, József. III. Title. IV. Series.

BS1765.52.I58 2006
229'.406—dc22

                                                                                    2008015444

BS
1765.52
.I58
2006

ISSN: 1384-2161
ISBN: 978 90 04 16906 7

THE PRESENT VOLUME IS DEDICATED TO
THE TALENTED HUNGARIAN JEWISH SCHOLARS OF ANCIENT JUDAISM
OF THE LAST TWO CENTURIES

ESPECIALLY TO THE MEMORY OF
PROF. DR. ALEXANDER SCHEIBER
(1913-1985)

CONTENTS

PREFACE

The present volume contains papers read at the Third International Conference on the Deuterocanonical Books, organised by the Shime'on Centre for the Study of Hellenistic and Roman Age Judaism and Christianity of the Reformed Theological Academy, Pápa, Hungary. The topic of the conference was the Book of Ben Sira. This book, on the one hand, is an early Jewish document with crucial importance; and, on the other hand, has a "Hungarian relationship." It is well known, that an important fragment of an unknown manuscript of the Hebrew text of Ben Sira was discovered by the rabbi and professor Alexander Scheiber in the Taylor-Schechter Collection (Cambridge) in the early eighties. It is thus appropriate to dedicate this volume to those Hungarian Jewish scholars of the last two centuries, who actively and creatively participated the study of various aspects of ancient Judaism.

The material of this volume can be divided in three main parts. In the first, the authors deal with introductory problems of the complex oeuvre of Ben Sira. The first two essays focus on rarely investigated ancient versions of the book; then its intellectual background is studied. The first part is finished by two complementary articles, touching certain aspects of the question of canon. The second main part of the volume focuses primarily on the wisdom part of Ben Sira. Here we read a treatment of a particular theme (divorce); a methodological and lexicographical essay on the possibility of the identification of the concepts of wisdom and law in Ben Sira; finally, an analysis of the relationship between wisdom thought and the Temple. At the end of the present volume, the reader will find four papers dealing with particular pericopae of the Praise of the Fathers section of the book.

The editors express their deep gratitude to series editors John J. Collins, Florentino García Martínez, and Hindy Najman, who kindly accepted this book for publication in the series of JSJ Supplements; and also to Ms. E. Kekk, who prepared the indices.

Pápa, Hungary
25. February 2008

the editors

LIST OF ABBREVIATIONS

AB	Anchor Bible
ABD	*The Anchor Bible Dictionary*
AGAJU	Arbeiten zur Geschichte des antiken Judentums und des Urchristentums
AOAT	Alter Orient und Altes Testament
APOT	*Apocrypha and Pseudepigrapha of the Old Testament* (ed. R.H. Charles)
ATD	Das Alte Testament Deutsch
BA	*Biblical Archeologist*
BBB	Bonner Biblischer Beiträge
BBET	Beiträge zur biblischen Exegese und Theologie
BETL	Bibliotheca Ephemeridum Theologicarum Lovaniensium
Bib	*Biblica*
BibInt	*Biblical Interpretation*
BIFAO	*Bulletin de l'Institut Français d'Archéologie Orientale*
BJS	Brown Judaic Studies
BKAT	Biblischer Kommentar Altes Testament
BN	*Biblische Notizen*
BS	The Biblical Seminar
BZ	*Biblische Zeitschrift*
BZAW	Beihefte zur Zeitschrift für die alttestamentliche Wissenschaft
BZRGG	Beihefte zur Zeitschrift für Religions- und Geistesgeschichte
CBQ	*Catholic Biblical Quarterly*
CBQMS	Catholic Biblical Quarterly Monograph Series
CCSL	Corpus Christianorum Series Latina
ConBNT	Coniectanea Biblica New Testament
CRINT	Compendia rerum iudaicarum ad novum testamentum
CSCO	Corpus Scriptorum Christianorum Orientalium
CSEL	Corpus Scriptorum Ecclesiasticorum Latinorum
DCLY	Deuterocanonical and Cognate Literature Yearbook
DJD	Discoveries in the Judaean Desert
EDSS	*The Encyclopedia of the Dead Sea Scrolls*
EtBib	Etudes Bibliques
ETR	*Etudes theologiques et religieuses*
EvTh	*Evangelische Theologie*
FAT	Forschungen zum Alten Testament
FRLANT	Forschungen zur Religion und Literatur des Alten und Neuen Testament
FzB	Forschung zur Bibel
GCS	Griechischen Christlichen Schriftsteller
HdO	Handbuch der Orientalistik
Hen	*Henoch*
HSM	Harvard Semitic Monographs
HTR	*Harvard Theological Review*

HUCA	Hebrew Union College Annual
HUCM	Monographs of the Hebrew Union College
IDB	Interpreters Dictionary of the Bible
IEJ	Israel Exploration Journal
JANES	The Journal of the Ancient Near Eastern Society of Columbia University
JBL	Journal of Biblical Literature
JCS	Journal of Cuneiform Studies
JDS	Judaean Desert Studies
JEA	Journal of Egyptian Archaeology
JECS	Journal of Early Christian Studies
JJS	Journal of Jewish Studies
JNES	Journal of Near Eastern Studies
JNSL	Journal of Northwest Semitic Languages
JQR	Jewish Quarterly Review
JSHRZ	Jüdische Schriften aus hellenistisch-römischer Zeit
JSJ	Journal for the Study of Judaism
JSJSup	Journal for the Study of Judaism Supplements
JSNTSup	Journal for the Study of the New Testament Supplements
JSOTSup	Journal for the Study of the Old Testament Supplements
JSP	Journal for the Study of the Pseudepigrapha
JSPSup	Journal for the Study of the Pseudepigrapha Supplements
JThS	Journal for Theological Studies
LCL	Loeb Classical Library
LeDiv	Lectio Divina
LThK	Lexikon für Theologie und Kirche
MEFRA	Mélanges de l'École française de Rome
MSU	Mitteilungen des Septuaginta-Unternehmens
NEB	Neue Echter Bibel
NEBAT	Neue Echter Bibel. Altes Testament
NIB	New Interpreter's Bible
NSKAT	Neue Stuttgarter Kommentar. Altes Testament
NTS	New Testament Studies
OBO	Orbis Biblicus et Orientalis
OLA	Orientalia Lovaniensia Analecta
OTL	Old Testament Library
OTP	The Old Testament Pseudepigrapha (ed. J.H. Charlesworth)
PAAJR	Proceedings of the American Academy of Jewish Research
PEQ	Palestine Exploration Quarterly
PG	Patrologia Graeca (ed. Migne)
PL	Patrologia Latina (ed. Migne)
PTSDSSP	The Princeton Theological Seminary Dead Sea Scrolls Project
PWSup	Paulys Realencyclopädie der classischen Altertumswissenschaft Supplement
RAC	Reallexikon für Antike und Christentum
RB	Revue biblique
RBén	Revue bénédictine
REG	Revue des études grecques
RevQ	Revue de Qumrân
RGG	Religion in Geschichte und Gegenwart
RGVV	Religionsgeschichtliche Versuche und Vorarbeiten
RHR	Revue de l'histoire des religions
SBLDS	Society of Biblical Literature Dissertation Series

SBLEJL	Society of Biblical Literature Early Judaism and its Literature
SBLMS	Society of Biblical Literature Monograph Series
SBLSCS	Society of Biblical Literature Septuagint and Cognate Studies
SBLSP	*Society of Biblical Literature Seminar Papers*
SBS	Stuttgarter Bibelstudien
SC	Sources Chrétiennes
SFSHJ	South Florida Studies in the History of Judaism
SNTSMS	Society for New Testament Studies Monograph Series
STDJ	Studies on the Texts of the Desert of Judah
SPB	Studia Post-Biblica
SVTP	Studia Veteris Testamenti Pseudepigrapha
TANZ	Texte und Arbeiten zum neutestamentlichen Zeitalter
TCAAS	Transactions of the Connecticut Academy of Arts and Sciences
TDNT	*Theological Dictionary of the New Testament*
TRE	Theologische Realenzyklopädie
TSAJ	Texte und Studien zum Antiken Judentum
TU	Texte und Untersuchungen
TUAT	*Texte aus der Umwelt des Alten Testaments*
TWNT	*Theologiches Wörterbuch zum Neuen Testament*
VC	*Vigiliae Christianae*
VT	*Vetus Testamentum*
VTSup	Supplements to Vetus Testamentum
WdF	Wege der Forschung
WMANT	Wissenschaftliche Monographien zum Alten und Neuen Testament
WUNT	Wissenschaftliche Untersuchungen zum Neuen Testament
ZÄS	*Zeitschrift für ägyptische Sprache und Altertumskunde*
ZAW	*Zeitschrift für die alttestamentliche Wissenschaft*
ZDPV	*Zeitschrift des Deutschen Palästina-Vereins*
ZNW	*Zeitschrift für die neutestamentliche Wissenschaft*

THE VETUS LATINA OF ECCLESIASTICUS

Maurice Gilbert, S.J.
(Pontifical Biblical Institute, Rome)

Scholarly research on the Old Latin Version of the book called Ecclesiasticus is rare. From the end of the 19th century, the main publications are these.

First, two articles of Ph. Thielmann deserves mentioning.[1] His study—it must be noted—is previous to the discovery of the first Hebrew fragment of the book of Ben Sira, made by S. Schechter in May 1896. According to Thielmann, the original Latin version of Ecclesiasticus only comprised chapters 1-43 and 51, and it was done by an African at the beginning of the 3rd century. The *Laus Patrum* was translated later by a European.

The second study was published in Leipzig by H. Herkenne.[2] In fact, Herkenne also used the Syriac Peshitta version and the Hebrew fragments already published, those discovered in Cambridge by Schechter and in Oxford by A. Neubauer. In 1897, A.E. Cowley and A. Neubauer had published all of the fragments discovered up till then, but these covered only nine chapters of the book, from 39:15 to 49:11, all of them from the manuscript called B. The opinion of Herkenne is that the Vetus Latina of Ecclesiasticus was done on the basis of a Greek version—which had been corrected in the light of a Hebrew text of Ben Sira—and of which the Latin version of Ecclesiasticus remains the only witness.

The third study is that by R. Smend in his commentary on Ben Sira.[3] On pages cxviii-cxxix, he suggested that the Old Latin version of Ecclesiasticus was done on the basis of a manuscript of the short text of Sirach, Greek I, but "a ms which retains far more traces of the influence of Gr II than any of the surviving Gr mss," as C. Kearns puts it, in his dissertation.[4]

---

[1] "Die lateinische Übersetzung des Buches Sirach," *Archiv für lateinische Lexicographie und Grammatik* 8 (1893) 511-61; "Die europäischen Bestandteile des lateinischen Sirach," *ibid.* 9 (1894) 247-84.

[2] *De Veteris Latinae Ecclesiastici capitibus I-XLIII una cum notis ex eiusdem libri translationibus aethiopica, armeniaca, copticis, latina altera, syro-hexaplari depromptis* (Leipzig: Hinrichs 1899, vii+268 pages).

[3] *Die Weisheit des Jesus Sirach erklärt* (Berlin: Reimer 1906).

[4] *The Expanded Text of Ecclesiasticus* (Rome: Pontifical Biblical Institute 1951, viii+309 pages), especially on page 21, where he refers to Smend's pages cxviii and cxxiv.

This thesis of Smend was discussed by the Benedictine D. de Bruyne,[5] who was preparing the Roman edition of the Vulgate of Ecclesiasticus. He was able to use many more manuscripts than Thielemann and Herkenne, and he thought that the Vetus Latina of Ecclesiasticus was done during the second half of the 2nd century, earlier than the date proposed by Herkenne. De Bruyne considered that the Old Latin version of Ecclesiasticus

> is based *directly* on a ms of Gr II; that the opposing readings of Gr I entered it only subsequently; and that it is thus the only known direct representative of Gr II, since fam. 248 merely represents Gr I with *interpolations* from Gr II,

as Kearns summarized it on his page 21, referring to de Bruyne's pages 41-43 and 46.

Then we have to wait till 1964 for the edition of the *Liber Iesu Filii Sirach* in the Roman publication by the Benedictine Fathers.[6] For my purpose in this paper, I quote here in an English translation a few sentences written by P.-M. Bogaert in his recension of this Roman edition:

> The original Latin version of *Sir.* depends on a Greek text revised in accordance with the Hebrew one. Long before the Vulgate recension, this Latin text had already been disturbed by a revision done on the basis of the Alexandrian text, purer and not revised on the Hebrew one. The readings that are also found in Hebrew, in Syriac, in Clement of Alexandria, in the Origenian recension of the Septuagint, and in Cyprian, may go back to the primeval Latin version. The others are peculiar to the Vulgate recension or are still later than it. In this latter case, they must be rejected.[7]

Keeping in mind this global vision of the Latin text of Ecclesiasticus, we have to point out that the Roman edition offers the text of Ecclesiasticus as it was when it was inserted into the Vulgate, probably at the end of the 5th century or at the beginning of the 6th.

One year after the Roman edition of the Vulgate text of Ecclesiasticus, J. Ziegler published his Greek version of Sirach.[8] Here I will make two points. First Ziegler insisted on the necessity to keeping an eye on the variant readings of the Vetus Latina (p. 23). Secondly, in his critical apparatus, he noted the numerous occasions where the Vetus Latina has a text similar to the Hebrew one instead of the Greek.

In 1977, O. Wahl published the first critical edition of the Sirach Greek text quoted in the *Sacra Parallela*.[9] Smend already knew the importance of

---

[5] "Étude sur le texte latin de l'Ecclésiastique," *RBén* 40 (1928) 5-48.

[6] *Liber Iesu Filii Sirach* (Biblia Sacra iuxta latinam Vulgatam versionem, vol. XII, Roma: Typis polyglottis Vaticanis 1964, 105-375 pages).

[7] *Bulletin de la Bible latine (1955-1973)*, n. 143, p. [34].

[8] *Sapientia Iesu Filii Sirach* (Septuaginta. Vetus Testamentum Graecum XII/2, Göttingen: Vandenhoeck & Ruprecht 1965, 368 pages)

[9] *Der Sirach-Text der Sacra Parallela* (FzB 16, Würzburg: Echter, 172 pages).

these witnesses. But, for the Vetus Latina version of Ecclesiasticus, this edition by Wahl brought something unknown up to now: seventeen stichs of the Greek version with additions, Greek II, transmitted only in Latin. This is the list of these texts: 1:3b; 2:6c, 14b; 3:26c; *4:30b*; 5:12c; *6:1c*; *8:7b*; 9:17c; 14:16b; *15:8bc, 10b*; 20:28b; *21:28b*; *25:23c*; *30:22b*. Those printed in cursive are mentioned by Ziegler in his critical apparatus, but he ignored the eight others.

During recent decades, W. Thiele published the first half of the Vetus Latina version of Ecclesiasticus.[10] From 1987 to 2005, he gave a long introduction of 162 pages, followed by the edition of chapters 1-24, with the Prologue. Thiele does not agree with the main thesis of Thielmann about a later Latin version of the *Laus Patrum*, but P.-M. Bogaert is not convinced by Thiele's new proposal.[11] Against de Bruyne, Thiele considers that all the doublets in the Latin Ecclesiasticus go back to a Greek text, and on this point Bogaert agrees.[12]

❧❧❧

Now, using various passages from the book of Ecclesiasticus, it is possible to make some points.

1. *The Vetus Latina of Ecclesiasticus was done on the basis of a Greek version.*

It is well known that in the Hebrew MS A and in the Peshitta, Sir 4:11-19 is divided into two different ways of speaking: in 4:11-14, the author speaks in a neutral way, but in 4:15-19, he makes Wisdom herself speak. Now, in Greek and in Latin, these two steps are not distinguished and only the author speaks till the end of the passage. Besides, in 4:15a, Hebrew and Peshitta read: "he will judge truly," when Greek and Latin have: "he judges the nations." These two different readings reveal a confusion between *'emet* and *'ummôt*, and the latter may be the correct one.

In 51:1-12, there is a similar situation. In this prayer of thanksgiving, Ben Sira starts speaking directly to God in 51:1-6a, according to the Hebrew MS B. It is the same in the Peshitta 51:1-4, even if the Syriac version abridges the text, especially omitting any allusion to the calumny for which Ben Sira was put on trial. But in the second half of this prayer, mainly in 51:8-10aα, 11c-12 in Hebrew, Ben Sira speaks no more to God, but about him and about the

---

[10] *Sirach (Ecclesiasticus)* (Vetus Latina. Die Reste der altlateinischen Bibel, vol. XI/2, Freiburg: Herder 1987-2001, 9 fascicules, 726 pages).

[11] *Bulletin de la Bible latine (1974-1999)*, n. 673, p. [241-42].

[12] Cf. W. Thiele, "Die lateinische Sirachtexte als Zeugnis der griechischen Sirachüberlieferung," in *Evangelium. Schriftauslegung. Kirche* (FS P. Stuhlmacher, eds. J. Ådna, *et al.*, Göttingen: Vandenhoeck & Ruprecht, 1997) 394-402. As regards the study by L. Schrader, *Verwandtschaft der Peschitta mit der (alt)lateinischen Übersetzung in Sirachbuch? Ein Beitrag zur Methodik textgeschichtlicher Forschung* (BN 11, München: Görg 1998) 75, it does not concern the problem analysed in this paper.

rescue he received from God after calling upon him: 51:10aβ-11b properly quoted the prayer Ben Sira addressed to God at the time of his distress. In the Peshitta, it is exactly the same for 51:8-12.

On the contrary, in Greek and in Latin, the difference between the two sections of the prayer disappears: there is no more a first section addressed to God with "You" and a second one with "He," but the whole text is directly addressed to God—"You"—except in 51:10aα, 12d in Greek, and in Latin 51:8a (Greek 6b), 14a (Greek 10), 17b (Greek 12d).

Moreover, in this prayer, two strange readings of the Greek, which are not in Hebrew or in Syriac, are reproduced in Latin. The first one is the mention of a king in 51:6a, according to the manuscripts (Ziegler made here a conjectural proposal according to the Hebrew).[13] The second is in 51:10a: "I called the Lord father of my Lord," an obscure reading literally translated into Latin.

2. *The Greek text translated in the Vetus Latina of Ecclesiasticus was different from the one transmitted by all the Greek manuscripts still extant.*

It is also well known that all the manuscripts of the Greek version, both Greek I and Greek II, have inverted Sir 30:25-33:16a and 33:16b-36:13a.[14] In the modern editions of Rahlfs (1935) and of Ziegler (1965), the normal order of these chapters has been restored according to the Hebrew, the Syriac and also the Latin order.

After the discovery of the Hebrew MS E in 1931 by J. Marcus, it became possible to prove that the Greek order of these chapters was wrong.[15] An accurate demonstration of this was done in 1963 by A.A. Di Lella.[16]

It is therefore very astonishing to observe that an edition of the Hebrew text of Ben Sira now available thanks to the various manuscripts discovered since 1896, except the sixth one, maintains the wrong order of these chapters as it is found only in the Greek manuscripts.[17]

But, if the Latin version of Ecclesiasticus has the same order of these chapters as in Hebrew and in Syriac, it must be concluded that the Greek manuscript which was used by the Latin translator was different from the archetype of all the Greek manuscripts still extant. What was the date of this archetype with the inversion of some chapters? It is impossible to answer

[13] Therefore the proposal made by P. McKechnie, "The Career of Joshua Ben Sira," *JThS* 51 (2000) 1-26, esp. 15, based on this strange reading of the Greek 51:6a, is unacceptable.

[14] For a recent explanation, cf. F. Böhmisch, "Die Blattvertauschung (Lage 12 und 13) im griechischen Sirachbuch," *Protokolle zur Bibel* 14 (2005) 17-22.

[15] "A Fifth Ms of Ben Sira," *JQR* 21 (1931) 223-40.

[16] "Authenticity of the Geniza Fragments of Sirach," *Bib* 44 (1963) 171-200, esp. 173-79.

[17] This is the case of *The Book of Ben Sira* (Jerusalem: Academy of the Hebrew Language and the Shrine of the Book 1973) 26-34. This edition does not follow the order of verses present in MSS B and E of Ben Sira's Hebrew text.

this question with certainty. It was certainly done before the first half of the 4th century, because the uncial manuscripts *Vaticanus* and *Sinaiticus* already have the inversion. It is impossible to give an earlier date, because today we do not yet have any previous Greek papyrus comprising the chapters in question. It is generally accepted that the inversion was done during the 3rd century. Then the Greek manuscripts used by the Latin translator were anterior, and if the Latin version was done, as de Bruyne suggested, during the second half of the 2nd century, this Greek manuscript used by the Latin translator has to be dated earlier (see below).

Let us have a look at another passage where the order of the text is not the same in Greek as it is in Latin: Sir 22:27-23:6 is a double prayer requesting God's help in order to control tongue and passions. Both P. Beentjes and F. Reiterer made an excellent stylistic analysis of these two prayers according to the Greek version.[18] But their analysis does not take account of a textual critical problem which arises when the Greek version is compared with both the Latin version and the Peshitta. The Hebrew text is still lacking.

In the Vetus Latina version, according to the Pseudo-Augustine *Speculum*, 51, Sir 23:1b is omitted and, according to the Vulgate text, this stich is inserted after 23:4a.[19] In the Peshitta, it is exactly the same. Many translators and commentators consider that, when one wants to reach the original text written by Ben Sira, it is necessary to follow the reading of the Vetus Latina and the Peshitta versions.[20] These authors form the majority of scholars and I agree with them. The main reason is of course the witness of the Latin and the Syriac against the Greek version, but their evidence has also the

---

[18] P.C. Beentjes, "Sirach 22:27-23:6 in zijn context," *Bijdragen* 39 (1978) 144-51, esp. 145; F.V. Reiterer, "Gott, Vater und Herr meines Leben. Ein poetisch-stilistische Analyse von Sir 22,27-23,6 als Verständnisgrundlage des Gebetes," in *Prayer from Tobit to Qumran* (eds. R. Egger-Wenzel and J. Corley, DCLY 2004, Berlin: de Gruyter 2004) 137-70.

[19] See Thiele, *Sirach (Ecclesiasticus)*, 633 and 637-38.

[20] Herkenne, *De Veteris Latinae Ecclesiastici*, 185. Smend, *Die Weisheit des Jesus Sirach erklärt*, 203-05; *idem*, *Die Weisheit des Jesus Sirach hebräisch und deutsch* (Berlin: Reimer 1906) 38. W.O.E. Oesterley, *The Wisdom of Jesus the Son of Sirach or Ecclesiasticus* (The Cambridge Bible for Schools and Colleges, Cambridge: Cambridge University Press 1912) 150-51. N. Peters, *Das Buch Jesus Sirach oder Ecclesiasticus* (EHAT 25, Münster: Aschendorff 1913) 184-85. A. Vaccari, *I libri sapienziali* (La Sacra Bibbia V/2, Firenze: Salani 1949) 224. M.Z. Segal, *Spr bn-syr' hšlm* (2nd ed., Jerusalem: Bialik 1958) 136. J. Vella, "Eclesiastico", in *La Sagrada Escritura, Antiguo Testamento* (vol. 5, BAC 312, Madrid: B.A.C. 1970) 90-91. H. Duesberg and I. Fransen, *Ecclesiastico* (La Sacra Bibbia, Antico Testamento, Torino: Marietti 1966) 190 and 192. L. Alonso Schökel, *Proverbios y Eclesiastico* (Los Libros Sagrados VIII/1, Madrid: Cristiandad 1968) 222-23. *Die Bibel. Altes und Neues Testament Einheitsübersetzung* (Freiburg: Herder 1980) 776. *The New American Bible* (Nashville: Nelson 1983) 743. P.W. Skehan and A.A. Di Lella, *The Wisdom of Ben Sira* (AB 39, New York: Doubleday 1987) 318 and 320-21. *La Bible de Jérusalem* (3rd ed., Paris: Cerf 1999) 1206 (M. Gilbert). O. Kaiser, *Weisheit für Leben. Das Buch Jesus Sirach übersetzt und eingeleitet* (Stuttgart: Radius 2005) 54.

advantage of showing that normally and even here, Ben Sira used to write bicolon verses.

Therefore, even if for this passage the Hebrew text is lacking, one can be sure that the Vetus Latina version of this text was done on the basis of a Greek version different from the classical one, an earlier one of which we have no witness except in the Vetus Latina. How do we explain the change in the classical Greek version? Probably by appeal to reasons of style, to emphasise the two direct invocations to God, as Beentjes and Reiterer pointed out.

3. *The additions peculiar to the Vetus Latina version of Ecclesiasticus are normally of Jewish origin and they translate Greek texts which were in the manuscript used by the Latin translator.*

Concerning the first assertion, it has to be acknowledged that the Latin additions which do not have a similar Greek text, Greek II, are not to be considered as Christian additions. It is extremely rare to find a Christian addition in the Vetus Latina of Ecclesiasticus. This is perhaps the case in Sir 2:10cVL: *qui timetis Deum diligite illum...*, where the third theological virtue, charity, is mentioned after faith and hope. This is the opinion of N. Calduch Benages.[21] But G.L. Prato has some doubts about such a Christian origin ("difficilement").[22] My opinion is that when we speak of a Christian addition, it needs to be proved that the text in question cannot be understood as a Jewish assertion. This is exactly the question in Sir 24:45VL, as we shall see below.

Concerning the second assertion, let us concede that, even if there is no witness of a Greek text corresponding to a Vetus Latina addition, it is wiser to consider that there was one in the Greek manuscript used by the Latin translator. The main question is whether there have been some corrections of the Vetus Latina of Ecclesiasticus on the basis of the Hebrew text of Ben Sira. That question arises, because, in his edition of the classical Greek text of Sirach, Ziegler mentioned many passages where there is agreement between the Vetus Latina of Ecclesiasticus and the text offered by Ben Sira's manuscripts in Hebrew.

As a matter of fact, there is no agreement among scholars on a possible correction of the Vetus Latina translation of the Bible on the basis of the text of the Hebrew Bible. According to J. Cantera "it is enough to suppose that the translator had known a Greek text which was different from the one we

---

[21] *En el crisol de la prueba. Estudio exégetico de Sir 2,1-18* (Associación Bíblica Española 32, Estella: Verbo Divino 1997) 104, and note 24.

[22] "La lumière interprète de la Sagesse dans la tradition textuelle de Ben Sira," *La Sagesse de l'Ancien Testament* (2nd ed., ed. M. Gilbert, BETL 51, Leuven: Peeters 1990) 340, note 77.

know."[23] On the other side, some recent scholars, for instance M. Kraus, affirm that there has been a secondary Hebrew influence on the Vetus Latina text transmission since Jerome's time.[24] In any case, these two contradictory positions only concern the books which are in the Hebrew Bible. What may we say about the Vetus Latina of Ecclesiasticus, which is not in the Hebrew Bible?

In a recent paper, I wrote in French what I now give here in translation:

> Does the Vetus Latina always rely on a Greek text, even when that is lacking? Is it impossible that the Vetus Latina of Ecclesiasticus ever gives in Latin a Hebrew text that had not been translated in the meantime into Greek? Were not some additions, while being of Jewish origin, born in the Hellenistic diaspora, therefore without having a Hebrew substratum?[25]

Today, it is not possible to give a positive answer to these questions. At least, it seems that the discussion of a correction of the Vetus Latina on the basis of the Massoretic text does not concern the book of Ecclesiasticus, which is not in the Hebrew Bible. Secondly, the theory of Kraus and others affirms that a Hebrew influence on the Vetus Latina appears only after Jerome's time, and our questions about Ecclesiasticus in Latin have to do with a period of time earlier than Jerome. Finally, it seems difficult to assert that, during the 2nd century, in Christian North Africa, a Hebrew influence on the Vetus Latina version of Ecclesiasticus was possible.

Therefore it is wiser to suppose that these additions in the Vetus Latina of Ecclesiasticus were translated from the Greek text, Greek II, which was at the disposal of the Latin translator. It is also wiser to assume that these additions were first translated into Greek from a Hebrew text, Hb II. These assertions seem at least correct for a majority of the Vetus Latina additions in Ecclesiasticus, which are not in the classical Greek text of that book.

Let me take here two examples in Sir 24, which Thiele very accurately published in 2005 in his Vetus Latina text.

The first example is taken from Sir 24:31VL, a Latin addition at the end of the discourse by Wisdom: *qui elucidant me vitam æternam habebunt*, which means: "they who throw light on me shall have eternal life." There is no witness of this text, neither in Hebrew, in Greek nor in Syriac. Thiele writes: "ex textu graeco interpretis latini" ("from the Greek text used by the Latin translator").[26] Commentators see in this Latin addition a reference to Dan

---

[23] "La Vetus Latina y el texto masorético. Hipótesis de una revisión de la Vetus Latina a base del texto hebreo," *Sefarad* 23 (1963) 252-64, as Bogaert assumed in his *Bulletin de la Bible latine (1955-1973)* n. 301, p. [73].

[24] "Hebraisms in the Old Latin Version of the Bible," *VT* 53 (2003) 487-513.

[25] M. Gilbert, "Les additions grecques et latines à Siracide 24," *Lectures et relectures de la Bible* (FS P.-M. Bogaert, eds. J.-M. Auwers and A. Wénin, BETL 144, Leuven: Peeters 1999) 207.

[26] *Sirach (Ecclesiasticus)* 699.

12:2-3, and Kearns agrees:[27] the theme of an eschatological afterlife is the main one in many additions to the different versions of the book of Ben Sira.

The second example comes from Sir 24:45VL, inserted after Sir 24:32Gr:

> *penetrabo inferiores partes terræ*
> *et inspiciam omnes dormientes*
> *et illuminabo sperantes in Deo*

In this verse of three stichs, Wisdom speaks, as in Sir 24:30 MS 248, which corresponds to Sir 24:40VL. An English translation would be:

> I will penetrate to the nether parts of the earth, and will visit all those who sleep, and will bring to the light those who hope in the Lord.

In his edition, Thiele notes:

> Satis adsunt lectiones similes (sumptae sive ex traditione graeca sive ex veteri versione latina), quae conferri possunt. Mihi persuasum est sententiam Sir 24,45 V partem versionis latinae primigeniae esse (contra eos, quibus insertum christianum veri simile est).[28]

In this note, Thiele follows the opinion of Kearns[29] against Peters,[30] but in agreement with Smend,[31] who thought this addition had a Hebrew origin.

In his dissertation, Kearns offered a long analysis of this addition, with many parallels taken from Biblical or Jewish sources.[32] For instance, he quoted two passages from *1 Enoch*: "And the righteous shall arise from their sleep, And wisdom shall arise and be given unto them" (91:10) and "Fear not, ye, souls of the righteous, And be hopeful, ye, that have died in righteousness" (102:4). Kearns also showed that the three stichs of this addition mentioned three steps of the eschatological "visit" of Wisdom to the dead. My own analysis—in a shorter form—is along the same lines.[33] Also Prato denies any Christian influence on this text of Ecclesiasticus.[34]

---

[27] *The Expanded Text*, 146-47:

[28] *Sirach (Ecclesiasticus)*, 710: "There are enough similar readings (taken either from the Greek translation or from the Vetus Latina version), which can be collected. I am convinced that the sentence of Sir 24:45 Vulgate is a part of the original Latin version (against those for whom it is probably a Christian insertion)."

[29] *The Expanded Text*, 145.

[30] *Das Buch Jesus Sirach*, 205-06.

[31] *Die Weisheit des Jesus Sirach erklärt*, cxvii.

[32] *The Expanded Text*, 149-73.

[33] "Les additions," 205-07.

[34] "La lumière," 338, note 70.

4. Therefore, the Vetus Latina of Ecclesiasticus was done on the basis of a Greek text already enlarged. This was partially closer to the Hebrew text of Ben Sira than to the classical Greek version, and partially with early mistakes of translation.

There seems to be no other way to explain so many agreements in this Vetus Latina text with the Hebrew fragments, which Ziegler mentioned in his edition. On the other side, this hypothesis may also explain many discrepancies between the Hebrew texts, sometimes in agreement with the Peshitta, and both the Greek and the Vetus Latina versions.

As regards the date of the Greek manuscript used by the Latin translator, it must be assigned to that of the enlarged edition of the Greek version, Greek II, while also bearing in mind that the additions come from different hands, during a period of time ranging from 80 BC to 80 AD.

THE COPTIC VERSION(S) OF THE BOOK OF JESUS SIRACH

Frank Feder
(Berlin — Brandenburgische Akademie der Wissenschaften
Altägyptisches Wörterbuch)

The Coptic translations of the Old and New Testaments are well known as important witnesses for the textual history of the Christian Bible. Since there are already a number of manuscripts from the third and fourth centuries, the Coptic versions are among the oldest known Bible manuscripts which can shed light on the earliest history of the transmission of the Biblical text.[1] The Biblical text of the Old Testament from which the Coptic version was translated was not, as we well know today,[2] the Bible in Hebrew but the Septuagint. This is already obvious from the fact that the Book of Sirach— among other deuterocanonical writings—is part of the canon of the Coptic Bible.

But the Coptic translation of the Bible shows a certain variety in its character and its transmission because there were apparently different attempts to translate the Scriptures from the third century onwards. Moreover, the Bible had been translated into the different dialects of Coptic. Only the Sahidic and Bohairic dialects, however, attained a widespread diffusion over space and time. A complete translation of the Bible exists only in Sahidic which was the language of classical Christian literature of Egypt (gradually replaced by Bohairic from the 11th century onwards) and yielded the first and most of the Coptic Bible translations that have survived.[3]

In spite of the importance of the Coptic version of the Old and New Testaments for the textual criticism of the Septuagint and New Testament studies its reconstruction, analysis, and interpretation is still far from being completed. The monumental edition of the Bohairic and Sahidic New

---

[1] Cf. F. Feder, *Biblia Sahidica: Ieremias, Lamentationes (Threni), Epistula Ieremiae et Baruch* (TU 147, Berlin: de Gruyter 2002) 1-10.

[2] Cf. P. Nagel, "Old Testament, Coptic Translations of," in *The Coptic Encyclopedia* (ed. A.S. Atiya, New York: Macmillan 1991) 6: 1836-40.

[3] Cf. note 1 and 2; furthermore: G. Mink, "5.1. Neues Testament" and S.P. Brock, "5.2. Altes Testament," *TRE* 6: 196-99; 199-200; B.M. Metzger, "New Testament, Coptic Versions of the," in *The Coptic Encyclopedia*, 6: 1787-89.

Testaments[4] from the beginning of the last century is nowadays completely
outdated. But, this is still a favourable state of research regarding that there
is no critical edition of the Coptic Old Testament so far. There is no critical
edition of the Coptic Old Testament so far. The ambitious attempt of the
project *Koptische Septuaginta* at the *Institut für Orientalistik* of the *Martin-
Luther-Universität Halle-Wittenberg* which gathered a lot of material and
prepared the first editions between 1994 and 2000 had to be stopped in 2000
due to the lack of support in Germany. The work of this project resulted, at
least, in the critical edition of the *Corpus Ieremiae* in the Sahidic Dialect, the
only critical edition of the Coptic Bible until now noting consequently the
different readings in comparison to the Greek text (LXX).[5]

The reconstruction and editing of the Coptic Bible is a difficult enterprise
since no complete Bible manuscript has come down to us. The transmission
of one complete book or even more than one book is a rare case at all. There
are, in general, more good manuscripts of the New Testament and the New
Testament is, therefore, preserved as a whole in the Sahidic and Bohairic
dialects. As for the Old Testament, there has been a complete translation
only in Sahidic. But many books are only known from fragments. From the
other dialects—including Bohairic—only individual (often fragmentary)
books survived. However, it is not very likely that in those dialects existed a
complete Bible translation at all.[6]

For the most part, Coptic Bible manuscripts have come to us in a very
fragmentary state. Many formerly more or less complete manuscripts or
collections of manuscripts (e.g. from abandoned monasteries) were divided
and sometimes single leaves or fragments were sold in small portions to
European and American collections (from the 18th to 20th centuries). Thus, it
is indispensable for anyone who wants to work with the Coptic Bible to
reassemble beforehand as far as possible the preserved manuscripts.
Although the published Coptic Bible texts have been regularly compiled in
lists over the last century[7] a record of the numerous unpublished manuscripts and a systematic attempt to reconstitute the codices which once belonged together is still missing. One recent project seems to fulfil this task to
a satisfying extent for the Sahidic Bible texts: the "Biblia Coptica" catalogue
by Karlheinz Schüssler.[8]

---

[4] G. Horner, *The Coptic Version of the New Testament in the Northern Dialect* (4 vols.,
Oxford: Clarendon Press 1898-1904); *idem, The Coptic Version of the New Testament in the
Southern Dialect* (7 vols., Oxford: Clarendon Press 1911-1924).

[5] Feder, *Biblia Sahidica.*

[6] For references see notes 1-3.

[7] Last update: P. Nagel, "Editionen koptischer Bibeltexte seit Till 1960," *Archiv für
Papyrusforschung* 35 (1989/90) 43-100.

[8] K. Schüssler, *Biblia Coptica: Die koptischen Bibeltexte: Das sahidische Alte und Neue
Testament* (Wiesbaden: Harrassowitz, from 1995, already published: vol. 1 [fasc. 1-4]
and vol. 3 [fasc. 1-4]).

1. THE COPTIC MANUSCRIPTS OF THE BOOK OF SIRACH

The number of manuscripts transmitting a certain Biblical book in Coptic can be quite different. This is often influenced by the extreme dispersion of the leaves of the manuscripts. However, it is evident that some Biblical books were more frequently copied than others. This is, above all, true for the Book of Psalms which is by far the best preserved book of the Coptic Bible.[9] This predominance of the Psalms depended on their importance in the liturgy of the Coptic Church. On the other hand, there are several Biblical books that are poorly recorded, sometimes only in fragments.[10] As for the Book of Sirach, we possess only two Sahidic codices which transmit the Book of Sirach together nearly completely, although they themselves have lacunae in many passages of the text, and a number of fragmentary manuscripts. Finally, certain verses are present in very late liturgical manuscripts (Lectionaries) for the Holy Week and as citations, for example, in the hagiographic literature. These will be presented below after an overview of the extant manuscripts of the different Coptic dialects.

1.1. *Sahidic Manuscripts*

1. Ms Turin, Museo Egizio Cat. 7117 (Parchment codex from the 6th or 7th century, Sir Prologus 30-33; Sir 1:1.3-51:30 [with many lacunae] followed by Sap 1:1-19.22.)

In spite of the lacunae, this manuscript preserved most of the text of Sir compared to the other witnesses. The text was published already in 1883 by Paul de Lagarde and is still the most important source for the Coptic text of Sir besides the following manuscript.[11]

2. Ms London, British Library Or 5984 (Papyrus Codex from the 6th or 7th century [see fig. 1].)

This papyrus manuscript was originally a large volume of the poetical books. Unfortunately, the papyrus leaves are often damaged and bear many lacunae. The sequence of the books in the codex is: Job, Proverbs, Ecclesias-

---

[9] Cf. Schüssler, *Biblia Coptica*, passim; P. Nagel, "Der sahidische Psalter: seine Erschließung und Erforschung 90 Jahre nach Alfred Rahlfs' Studien zum Text des Septuaginta-Psalters," in *Der Septuagina-Psalter und seine Tochterübersetzungen* (eds. A. Aejmelaeus and U. Quast, MSU 25, Göttingen: Vandenhoeck & Ruprecht 2000) 82-96; J. Horn, "Die koptische (sahidische) Überlieferung des alttestamentlichen Psalmenbuches—Versuch einer Gruppierung der Textzeugen für die Herstellung des Textes," *ibid.* 97-106.

[10] For instance, the Books of the Maccabees; cf. Schüssler, *Biblia Coptica*, vol. 1 fasc. 4, (Gesamtregister) 157.

[11] For all relevant information to the manuscript, see: Schüssler, *Biblia Coptica*, vol. 1 fasc. 4, 21-22 (98).

tes, Canticle of Canticles, Wisdom, Sirach; the book of Sir is extant from the
Prologue to 40:18, but the text is incomplete.[12]

3. Ms Turin, Museo Egizio Cat 7117, f. 1-3 (Parchment codex from the 6th
century, Sir Prol. 1-22.24-35, 1:1-2. The text is still unpublished.[13])

This fragmentary leaf and two other fragments had been wrongly attached
to the Ms quoted under 1. They belonged, as Schüssler could recognise, to a
separate manuscript.

4. Ms John Rylands Library Manchster Suppl. 6

According to the editor, W.C. Till,[14] a fragmentary parchment leaf from the
5th century containing Sir 1:5-13, 16-20; no further information is given. The
pagination conserved upon the leaf (pages 3 and 4 respectively) indicates
that it was part of a codex beginning the text of Sir with a new pagination.

5. Ms John Rylands Library Manchster Suppl. 7

From the same collection and published together with 4.[15] According to Till:
"bottom of a vellum double leaf," 4th or 5th century, certainly from a codex:
Sir 18:18-20, 28-31 and 23:19-20, 28-30.

6. Ms Vienna Papyrussammlung der Nationalbibliothek K 8689

Fragment of the middle of a parchment leaf.[16] In the catalogue of the Coptic
manuscripts of the collection Till dates the manuscript to the 7th century.[17] It
contains Sir 45:9-10, 13-15.

7. Ms Cairo Coptic Museum inv. 12761 (= 6635 in the Manuscripts' section)

This is a very interesting case of a palimpsest, for some leaves of an old
parchment codex from the 4th-5th centuries containing poetical books were
reused, approximately in the 9th century, to write upon them a prayer of

---

[12] For all relevant information to the manuscript, see: Schüssler, *Biblia Coptica*, vol.
1 fasc. 3, 71-73 (75). Publication: H. Thompsen, *The Coptic (Sahidic) Version of Certain
Books of the Old Testament from a Papyrus in The British Museum* (Oxford: University
Press 1908).

[13] For all relevant information to the manuscript, see: Schüssler, *Biblia Coptica*, vol.
1 fasc. 4, 24 (100).

[14] W.C. Till, "Coptic Biblical Fragments in the John Rylands Library," *BJRL* 34
(1951-52) 438-40.

[15] *Ibid*. 441-42.

[16] *Idem* "Sahidische Fragmente des Alten Testamentes," *Le Muséon* 50 (1937) 216.

[17] *Idem* "Papyrussammlung der Nationalbibliothek in Wien: Katalog der koptischen Bibelbruchstücke, Die Pergamente," *ZNW* 39 (1940) 15 (Nr. 46).

Shenoute. From the old manuscript passages of Ecclesiastes and of Sir 8:19-9:8, 9:10-14, 10:30-11:6, 11:8-14 are still readable.[18]

8. Ms Berlin Papyrussammlung P 10586 (see fig. 2)

5 leaves and one fragment of a parchment codex with poetical books from Hermupolis 4th-5th centuries, containing Prov 31:26-31 followed by Sir Prol. and 4:2-6:4.[19]

9. Ms Berlin Papyrussammlung P 15869

Fragmentary double leaf from a parchment codex, 4th-5th centuries (slightly older than the one quoted under 8.) with Sir 7:10-19.25-29, 9:14-18, 10:5-11.[20]

10. Ms Berlin Staatsbibliothek Cod. Or. Berol. in 8. 409 fol.1-2 + London British Museum Or. 3579 (29)

Three pages of a late paper codex; neither in the catalogue[21] nor in the publication[22] is a date or a description of the manuscript given. Paper manuscripts were not in use before the 12th century. These pages contain Sir 6:36-7:18, 18:17-31, 21:8-23.

If we take into account the already mentioned dispersion of the Coptic manuscripts it is more than likely that we will have to complete the list above with new findings. That the quest for new manuscripts in the collections can be successful is demonstrated by Hans-Gebhard Bethge who recently detected further manuscripts from the book of Sirach in the *British Library* at London. He indicates passages from Sir 13-26 in the papyrus lot Or. 13825 (1-37) and the parchment lot Or. 6201 C containing, among other biblical texts, Sir 23:11f and 15ff as well as Sir 23:12.17.[23]

---

[18] N. Bosson, "Un palimpseste du Musée Copte du Caire, » *Le Muséon* 104 (1991) 5-37; for Sir cf. 23-27.

[19] F. Feder, "Koptische Bibelfragmente der Berliner Papyrussammlung I," *Archiv für Papyrusforschung* 48/1 (2002) 159-74.

[20] F. Feder, "Koptische Bibelfragmente der Berliner Papyrussammlung II," *Archiv für Papyrusforschung* 50/1 (2004) 99-104.

[21] W.E. Crum, *Catalogue of the Coptic Manuscripts in the British Museum* (London: BM press 1905) 13 (42).

[22] O. von Lemm, "Sahidische Bibelfragmente III," in *Bulletin de l'Académie Impériale des Sciences de St.-Pétersbourg* 25/4 (1906) 095, 0115-0120.

[23] H.G. Bethge, "Neue Bibelfragmente: Ein Überblick," in *Coptic Studies on the Threshold of a New Millenium: Proceedings of the Seventh International Congress of Coptic Studies Leiden 2000* (eds. M. Immerzeel and J. Van Der Vliet, OLA 133, Leuven: Peeters 2004) 1: 195-207; cf. 197.

1.2. *The Bohairic Transmission of Sirach*

It seems very unlikely that the Book of Sirach was ever translated into Bohairic. The only available Bohairic passages of Sir are the pericopae in the Lectionary for the Holy Week. These are read—together with other pericopae of other Biblical texts—on several days of the week at a certain time. According to the sequence of the Sirach text, these are:

Sir 1:1-19	Monday, Morning Office
Sir 1:20-30	Monday, 11th hour
Sir 2:1-9	Tuesday, 3rd hour
Sir 4:20-5:2	Tuesday, 6th hour
Sir 12:13-13:1	Thursday, 6th hour
Sir 22:7-18	Wednesday, 3rd hour
Sir 23:7-14	Wednesday, 6th hour
Sir 24:1-11	Thursday, 3rd hour

These pericopae were thoroughly studied by Burmester[24] and revealed that they are completely dependent on the Sahidic text. This supports the assumption that there was no Bohairic translation of Sirach. For the use of Sirach in the Lectionaries see 2 below.

1.3. *The Akhmimic Transmission of Sirach*

There is only one other Coptic dialect which preserved a manuscript of a Sirach text: the Akhmimic. Only one papyrus leaf has been discovered to date from the Akhmimic text of Sirach. This was acquired by a French mission to Akhmim in Middle Egypt in 1885. The papyrus leaf belonged to a lot of papyrus manuscripts with passages from Biblical books in Sahidic and Akhmimic. Since the text was written on a reused papyrus and not in the usual stichometric disposition of the verses (cf. fig. 1 and 2), it is very improbable that the leaf with the text of Sirach belonged once to a codex. The extant text is Sir 22:17-23:6.[25] The manuscript dates to the 4th century.

2. THE PRESENCE OF THE BOOK OF SIRACH IN THE LITURGICAL BOOKS AND THE COPTIC CHRISTIAN LITERATURE (WITH AN EXAMPLE FROM THE HAGIOGRAPHIC LITERATURE)

We have already seen that pericopae of Sirach were read during the liturgy of the Holy Week from the Bohairic Lectionary for the Holy Week. The Sahidic manuscripts of Lectionaries suffered from the division and disper-

---

[24] O.H.E. Burmester, "The Bohairic Pericopae of Wisdom and Sirach," *Biblica* 15 (1934) 451-65 and 16 (1935) 25-174; all manuscripts are of very late date.

[25] P. Lacau, "Textes Coptes en Dialectes Akhmimique et Sahidique," *BIFAO* 8 (1911) 3-67, Sir: 24-27.

sion of their leaves. There is still a lot of work to do until we have clearer insight into their composition and the sequence of the lessons of the Biblical texts within them. But, studies in this field are gaining ground and it seems highly probable that the Sahidic Lectionaries had much in common with the Bohairic.[26] Indeed, if we consult what is perhaps the best preserved Sahidic Lectionary—a Coptic/Arabic manuscript (paper) from the Withe Monastery near Sohag (ca. 13th century or slightly later)—we discover that this is also a Lectionary for the Holy Week (Pascha-Lectionary). K. Schüssler was able to reconstruct this manuscript so that we are informed for the first time in detail about the sequence of the lessons from Scripture during the Holy Week's daily service in a Sahidic Lectionary.[27] In the extant pages of the manuscript (the first three quires are nearly lost), lessons from Sirach are to be read on Wednesday at the first hour of the day (after lessons from Exodus, Proverbs, Hosea and followed by lessons from Colossians, Psalms, Gospel of John): Sir 1:14.19.22-26.28-30; 2:1.5.7.10. Compared to the Bohairic Lectionary of the Holy Week it is obvious that approximately the same passages from Sir were used in the service, though not at the same time. But further progress in the study of the Sahidic Lectionaries may reveal more common features between them.

The presence of the Book of Sirach also as citation in the Christian Coptic literature may be exemplified by an example of the hagiographic literature. In the two Encomia on the martyr Victor, son of Romanos, the General, which were very popular in the Coptic Church and read on the memorial day of the martyr, the following verses of Sirach are present: (in the first Encomium) Sir 10:3; 16:4; 21:3 (in the second Encomium) Sir 2:14; 14:18; 20:28; 22:9. We have to thank Jürgen Horn for the reexamination of the citations from the Bible in these Encomia which were not always correctly and not completely indicated in the publications of the text.[28] Although citations from Sirach may not be as frequent as, for example, citations from the Prophets or the Psalms, they appear, nevertheless, regularly in the Coptic literature quoting the Bible.

3. THE COPTIC VERSION OF SIRACH
IN THE TEXTUAL HISTORY OF THE SEPTUAGINT

Only few can be said about the position of the Coptic version of the Book of Sirach within the textual history of the Septuagint (we have to rely here, as

---

[26] For the most recent studies and an overview over the literature cf.: D. Atanassowa, "Zu den Sahidischen Pascha-Lektionaren," in *Coptic Studies on the Threshold of a New Millenium*, 1: 607-20.

[27] Schüssler, *Biblia Coptica*, vol. 1 fasc. 4, 49-69 (108^L).

[28] J. Horn, "Die Präsenz des Alten Testamentes in der ägyptischen christlichen Frömmigkeit, aufgewiesen an zwei Werken der koptisch-sahidischen hagiographischen Literatur," in *Sprache, Mythen, Mythizismen: Festschrift Walter Beltz zum 65. Geburtstag* (eds. A. Drost-Abgarian and Jürgen Tubach, Hallesche Beiträge zur Orientwissenschaft 32, Halle: Druckerei der Universität 2004 [2001]) 2: 355-82.

noted above, only on the Sahidic text). But this concerns the Coptic version of the LXX in general. The edition of the Book of Sirach by the Septuagint project at Göttingen made also use,[29] as usual, also of the Coptic version. But the publications and also the first study evaluating the Coptic text for the textual history of the Greek text quoted there do not correspond to the actual state of knowledge.[30] Nevertheless, the short evaluation of the character of the Coptic text given here is apparently on the right way. The author of these lines when publishing the above mentioned fragments of Sirach from the papyrus collection in Berlin (cf. 1.2 and number 8. and 9.) was able to confirm the assumption that the Coptic (Sahidic) witnesses show very little variants among each other and that the Coptic (Sahidic) text seems clearly to belong to the old Greek text represented by the Greek (majuscule) manuscripts B S and A.

All in all, a definite evaluation of the textual character of the Coptic version of Sirach will only be possible via a critical edition of the Sahidic text of the book.

The two following figures are meant to give an impression of typical Coptic Bible manuscripts.

---

[29] J. Ziegler, *Sapientia Iesu Filii Sirach: Septuaginta Vetus Testamentum Graecum Auctoritate Societas Litterarum Gottingensis editum* vol. XII,2 (Göttingen: Vandenhoeck & Ruprecht 1965).

[30] *Ibid.* 29-30.

Fig. 1.: Thompson, *Coptic (Sahidic) Version of Certain Books of the Old Testament* (1908)
Cf. number 2. under the heading 1.1.

TAFEL XIV

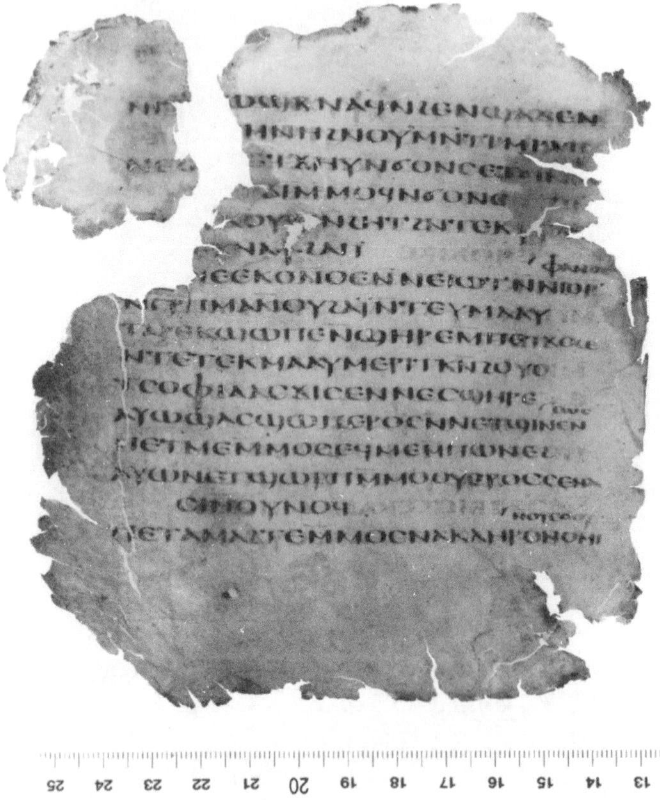

Sirach 4,8-13 (P.Berol. 10586 B – Haarseite S. 18);
zu F. Feder, S. 168

Fig. 2.: Feder, *Archiv für Papyrusforschung* 48/1 (2002)
Cf. number 8. under the heading 1.1.

WHERE DOES BEN SIRA BELONG?
THE CANON, LITERARY GENRE, INTELLECTUAL MOVEMENT, AND SOCIAL GROUP OF A ZADOKITE DOCUMENT

Gabriele Boccaccini
(University of Michigan)

1. THE BOOK OF SIRACH
AS AN APOCRYPHAL OR DEUTERO-CANONICAL DOCUMENT

The major obstacle to the study of ancient Jewish thought is ironically not the lack of documentation but the way in which sources have come down to us, grouped into denominationally determined corpora, or canons (the Hebrew Bible or Old Testament, the New Testament, the Apocrypha or Deuterocanonical books, the Pseudepigrapha, the Dead Sea Scrolls, etc.). Such denominational division has given birth to a denominationally divided scholarship with clear boundaries between Christian and Judaic studies, and a very confusing fragmentation of canonical and non-canonical corpora. To a large extent, each corpus still lives its own separate, self-sufficient existence, with its own specialists, journals, bibliographies, and audience. The canonical status of a document, more than any intrinsic historical value, is still the best warranty of success: it secures a high frequency of editions and commentaries, the presence in the programs of universities and seminaries, and a predictable and consolidated degree of popularity among readers.

The Book of Ben Sira is a case in point. Its study has greatly suffered by its marginal location (especially in Protestant countries) as an apocryphal or deuterocanonical document.

It is true that contemporary critical scholarship is no longer bound by canonical or denominational division. In the last century, we have seen a proliferation of introductions specifically devoted to the Apocrypha, from the pioneering work of W.O.E. Oesterley to the classical work of Bruce Metzger in the fifties to the recent introductions of Daniel Harrington, David DeSilva, and Otto Kaiser.[1] Any attempt to revive interest in this neglected

---

[1] W.O.E. Oesterley, *An Introduction to the Books of the Apocrypha* (New York: Macmillan 1935); B.M. Metzger, *An Introduction to the Apocrypha* (New York: Oxford University Press 1957); D. J. Harrington, *Invitation to the Apocrypha* (Grand Rapids: Eerdmans 1999); D.A. DeSilva, *Introducing the Apocrypha: Message, Context, and*

body of literature, such as lately the successful series of seminars on Deuterocanonical texts launched in 2004 by the Shimeon Center under the leadership of Géza Xeravits and József Zsengellér, is an important and much welcome contribution to our comprehension of Second Temple Judaism. Yet, so serious a problem as the existence of canons cannot be solved by simply balancing the specific weight of each corpus and giving an introduction, distinct research tools (journals, conferences, publications, etc.) and even the dignity of a theology to each and every collection.

Canons and corpora only make sense in relation to the epoch and ideology in which they were born, and tell us the fascinating history of how ancient texts were collected, selected and handed down to us, and how religious groups found identity and legitimacy in the process. Canons and corpora, however, are misleading in their interposition between the sources (their author, their age, their worldview) and modern interpreters. What is the point of studying and teaching sources within an anachronistic framework that gives a false illusion of unity and homogeneity while only creating artificial, a posteriori affinities and separates originally related texts? A denominational criterion for collecting sources is not a criterion for understanding their original content.

An introduction to the Old Testament Apocrypha may serve practical purposes, but superimposes on the text an anachronistic and misleading category. A definition of Ben Sira as an apocryphal or deuterocanonical document tells us a lot about the history of the text and its fortune (and misfortune) over the centuries but tell us nothing about where the document belonged. The sooner we abandon the categories of apocryphal or deuterocanonical in our scholarly discussions and publications on the book of Ben Sira, the better.

2. BEN SIRA AS A SECOND-CENTURY BC JEWISH DOCUMENT

Freeing Second Temple Jewish texts from the cages of their anachronistic corpora and canons is the first, necessary and fascinating step. By simply reintroducing a simple, obvious historical criterion, the interpreter finds forgotten connections and unexpected distances, new hierarchies or unsettling marginalities, supporting roles elevated to protagonists and protagonists reduced to supporting roles. Chronologically, Ben Sira is, yes, very close to two of its apocryphal companions, Tobit and Baruch, but much closer to texts like the "canonical" Daniel or the "pseudepigraphical" Dream Visions than to any other deuterocanonical documents. A chronological outlook immediately gives us a much better understanding of the literary and historical context in which the book of Ben Sira was composed.

Yet shifting the focus of attention from the traditional corpora to the time of composition of the documents themselves is not enough. A purely chro-

Significance (Grand Rapids: Baker 2002); and O. Kaiser, The Old Testament Apocrypha: An Introduction (Peabody, Mass.: Hendrickson 2004).

nological approach, like the one even advocated by George Nickelsburg already in 1981 and recently re-proposed in the revised edition of his survey of Second Temple Jewish literature,[2] has great advantages compared to the "canonical" approach and yet does not solve the problem of the ideological identification of a document. If Judaism is not the monolith suggested by the canons, it also has never been a single incremental tradition, but always a set of contemporarily diverse and sometimes competing forms of Judaism. Documents written in the same period are expressions of different intellectual movements and were authored by different social groups. A definition of Ben Sira as an early second-century BC Jewish document is historically correct but is very generic and still tells us very little about where the document originally belonged.

3. BEN SIRA: A SAPIENTIAL TEXT?

In order to narrow the search for the original ideological setting of ancient Jewish documents, scholars have turned from canons to the identification and study of some common features that seems to unite similar texts in Second Temple Judaism according to trans-canonical lines—the literary genres. The mapping and study of ancient texts according to their literary genre has contributed significantly to our understanding of the role these literary genres and their respective worldviews played in ancient Judaism, and has shown that the traditional canons are not the only way in which the literature can be grouped. Many documents have been given a universally recognized double citizenship that has created new and dynamic links among them: the same collection of apocalyptic literature includes the pseudepigraphical *1 Enoch*, the OT Daniel, and the NT Revelation, while the pseudepigraphical *Ahiqar*, the OT Qoheleth, and the apocryphal Ben Sira belong to the same collection of wisdom literature.

Furthermore, the recognition of a literary connection has often been the first step in the rediscovery of ideological affinities among documents. However, classifying and analyzing the history and worldview of literary genres is not the same as identifying systems of thought. The fact that two documents share the same worldview does not mean that they belong to the same form of Judaism. Conversely, documents belonging to the same form of Judaism expressed the same system of thought by using different literary genres.

In the case of Ben Sira, there is no doubt that from the literary point of view, this is a sapiential text, but by the end of the third century BC, the sapiential genre that originally denoted a distinctive form of Judaism (Proverbs, Job, Jonah, Qohelet), had spread and so-to-speak "contaminated" other forms of Judaism, so much so that it can no longer be taken as a clear

---

[2] G.W.E. Nickelsburg, *Jewish Literature between the Bible and the Mishnah* (Minneapolis: Fortress Press 1981; 2nd edition 2005).

marker of the ideology of the texts.[3] While from the literary point of view, Ben Sira and Baruch, the later Enochic literature, the *Letter of Aristeas* and the sapiential texts preserved among the Dead Sea Scrolls can all be described (at least to a certain extent) as second-century BC sapiential texts, yet they hardly can be seen as expressions of the same intellectual movement, even less of a single social group.

As witnessed by both Jeremiah (18:18) and Ezekiel (7:26), the wisdom tradition originated already in pre-exilic times as a distinctive variety of Judaism autonomously from the priesthood and the Torah, on one hand, and the prophets and their divinely given "word," on the other. The heavenly and preexistent nature of Wisdom is a concept that the Jews inherited from the polytheistic world of the ancient Near East, as witnessed by the sayings of Ahiqar:[4]

> From Shamayn the peoples are favored; Wisdom is of the gods. Indeed she is precious to the gods, her kingdom is et[er]nal. She has been established by Shamayn; yea, the Holy Lord has exalted her (Ahiqar 6:13).

Wisdom is a goddess ("of the gods"); she is "precious to the gods" and inaccessible to human beings. Her special relationship with Baal Shamayn, the Canaanite Lord of Heaven, seems to allude to divine marriage; her enthronement is a sign of Shamayn's benevolence toward humankind. The divine Wisdom rules forever as the queen (and mother) of the created universe.

The language of post-exilic Jewish texts, such as Job 28 and Proverbs 1-9, is still largely polytheistic, although now in the context of a henotheistic exaltation of the God of Israel, who is not seen yet as the only God but as the most powerful of all gods, the only one capable of "acquiring" Wisdom and using her to give order to the universe.[5] In Job 28, four former gods of the Canaanite pantheon (Tehom, Yam, Abaddon and Mot) are summoned to testify to the inaccessibility of Wisdom. What people and other gods cannot do, the God of Israel can: Elohim/YHWH found her and "established" her and made her beneficial to humankind. Proverbs 1-9 emphasized the role that Wisdom played in creation. She "was set up, at the first, before the beginning of the earth" (Prov 8:23), and through her God gave order to the primordial chaos (Prov 8:30). Through creation, God made the inaccessible Wisdom close to humans, desirable to their eyes, necessary to their well-being (Prov 8:31). The key verse is Prov 8:22a: "YHWH acquired [Wisdom] as the beginning (ראשית) of His work" (Prov 8:22). Not only does Proverbs

---

[3] See G. Boccaccini, *Roots of Rabbinic Judaism: An Intellectual History, from Ezekiel to Daniel* (Grand Rapids: Eerdmans 2002); J.J. Collins, *Jewish Wisdom in the Hellenistic Age* (OTL, Louisville: Westminster John Knox Press 1997).

[4] On the Book of Ahiqar, see J.M. Lindenberger, "Ahiqar," in *OTP* 2: 479-507.

[5] On the emergence of Jewish monotheism from polytheism through henotheism, see *The Triumph of Elohim: From Yahwisms to Judaisms* (ed. D.V. Edelman, Grand Rapids: Eerdmans 1996).

confirm that Wisdom is divine and uncreated, but by calling Wisdom "the beginning" (ראשית; Gk. ἀρχή), it also reinterprets the *incipit* of Gen 1:1 (בראשית; Gk. ἐν ἀρχῇ) in light of the principles of Sapiential Judaism: God created the heavens and the earth not "in" the beginning but "by means of" the beginning, that is, Wisdom.[6]

In short: in pre-Hellenistic Jewish literature, Wisdom (חכמה; Gk. σοφία) is essentially a (female) divine being. Nobody possesses Wisdom; no human being, no rival god but the God of Israel alone "acquired" her and used her to create the universe. The language itself betrays the ancient polytheistic concept of marriage among gods, the very same language that we find also in Genesis where the creation narrative is introduced as "the generations (תולדות) of Heaven and Earth" (Gen 2:4), to which "the book of the generations (ספר תולדות) of Adam" would follow (Gen 5:1). In pre-Hellenistic Jewish literature, nothing is said about the origin of Wisdom; her existence is simply taken for granted. Seeking wisdom and conforming to wisdom is the essence and the goal of religious life, for all those who "fear God." And as the universe is an orderly cosmos shaped by God through Wisdom, experience is the main tool to understand God's will, and the wise are the elders, or those who hand down their teachings. The result was a rich legacy of parental and traditional teaching passed on from one generation to the next, from parents to children and from teachers to disciples, in families and in schools, outside the religious boundaries of the Mosaic covenant (and the ethnic boundaries of the Jewish people) and outside the control of the priesthood. It is no surprise therefore that nothing is said about the relation between Wisdom and the Mosaic Torah, a problem that is completely ignored in the ancient wisdom literature.

While the ancient Wisdom tradition seems to have its unity and distinctive identity, in the Jewish literature of the second century BC we now encounter at least three parallel developments, three different understanddings of the nature (either heavenly or divine) of Wisdom and of her relationship with the Torah.

(a) The first trend is that represented by Ben Sira and Baruch. In the Ptolemaic period, the wisdom tradition gradually penetrated the priestly circles where the idea of the Mosaic Torah had first developed.[7] At the end of the third century BC, the book of Tobit[8] was the first to state that the faithful Jew should live according to both the teaching of the Mosaic Torah and the sayings of the wisdom tradition. The sapiential document re-

---

[6] On the concept of Wisdom in Second Temple Judaism and its cultural environment, see U. Wilckens and G. Fohrer, "σοφία," *TWNT* 7: 466-528. On Job 28, Proverbs 1-9 and the early wisdom tradition, see *The Sages in Israel and the Ancient Near East* (eds. J.G. Gammie and L.G. Perdue, Winona Lake: Eisenbrauns 1990); R.E. Murphy, *The Tree of Life: An Exploration of Biblical Wisdom Literature* (2nd ed., Grand Rapids: Eerdmans, 1996); G. Boccaccini, *Roots of Rabbinic Judaism*, 103-11.

[7] G. Boccaccini, *Roots of Rabbinic Judaism*, 113-50; Collins, *Jewish Wisdom*.

[8] Cf. C.A. Moore, *Tobit* (AB 40A, Garden City: Doubleday 1996).

peatedly appeals to the authority of the Jerusalem priesthood and to the authority of the Zadokite Torah (Tob 1:8; 6:13; 7:11-13). Even more striking-ly, the wise Tobit claims that his righteousness is based on both "the ordi-nance decreed concerning it in the Law of Moses and according to the instructions of Deborah, the mother of my father Tobiel" (Tob 1:8). This is the first time that the two sets of traditions, the priestly and the familial, are put on the same level, so opening the path to a more sophisticated under-standing of the relation between Wisdom and Torah.

A few decades later, the book of Ben Sira[9] proposed what would prove to be an ingenious and fortunate solution. According to Ben Sira, Wisdom is not a goddess or a divine attribute, but a heavenly being created by God (Sir 1:4) and used by God as a tool in creation (1:7-8). Wisdom lived in heaven with the angels, but asked God for a dwelling place on earth (24:1-7). This dwelling place is Israel, more specifically the Temple (24:8-12). There, she manifested herself in an embodied form, namely, "the book of the covenant of the Most High God, the Law that Moses commanded us as an inheritance for the congregations of Jacob" (Sir 24:23). The concept would later be reiterated in similar terms by the Book of Baruch (3:9-4:4).[10]

The implications of this concept are remarkable. Not only is there no wisdom without the practice of the Torah (as in Tobit), but observance of the Torah is also the propaedeutically indispensable condition by which people become worthy of receiving the gift of wisdom. The Torah gains a solid link with the order of creation, but Wisdom loses her divine status and much of her cosmopolitan dimension of being accessible to human experience, even outside the boundaries of the covenantal community of Israel, and experi-ence loses much of its non-conformist and autonomous power of revelation and criticism towards and even against the Torah, which we see so power-fully in action in the books of Job, Jonah and Qohelet.

(b) Ben Sira's and Baruch's understanding of the relation between Wisdom and the Torah, and their reduction of Wisdom from the divine to the heavenly realm, or from a goddess to a created angelic being, did not be-come commonplace in Second Temple Judaism. The nature of Wisdom re-mained a highly controversial issue, among texts which accepted the sapiential worldview or were affected by it. The covenantal understanding of the relationship between Wisdom and Torah was explicitly rejected by yet another ancient movement of Second Temple Judaism, the so-called Enochic Judaism.[11] Already in the *Book of Dream Visions* (second century BC) the

---

[9] Cf. P.W. Shekan and A.A. Di Lella, *The Wisdom of Ben Sira* (AB 39, Garden City, Doubleday 1987).

[10] Cf. C.A. Moore, *Daniel, Esther and Jeremias: The Additions* (AB 44, Garden City: Doubleday 1977) 255-316.

[11] On Enochic Judaism as one of Second Temple Judaisms, see P. Sacchi, *Jewish Apocalyptic and Its History* (JSPSup 20, Sheffield: Academic Press 1997); G.W.E. Nickelsburg, *1 Enoch: A Commentary* (Hermeneia, Minneapolis: Fortress Press 2001); and the Proceedings of the Enoch Seminar that biennially gathers the specialists of the

anxiety about Wisdom leaving her divine status is already apparent, symbolized by this declaration of her enthronement: "Wisdom does not escape you, and she does not turn away from your throne, nor from your presence" (*1 Enoch* 84:3). One century later, at the end of the first century BC, in the *Book of the Parables*, Enochic Judaism gave the most direct attack on the priestly conception of Wisdom:

> Wisdom could not find a place in which she could dwell; but a place was found for her in the heavens. Then Wisdom went out to dwell with the children of the people, but she found no dwelling place. So Wisdom returned to her place and she settled permanently among the angels. Then Iniquity went out of her rooms... and dwelt with them (*1 Enoch* 42).

The text is an explicit rebuttal of Ben Sira and Baruch. It takes up the myth that Wisdom searched for a dwelling place but denies its happy ending. The disappointing outcome of Wisdom's search fits the Enochic idea that the world has become the place of evil as a consequence of a cosmic rebellion of angels. Only at the end of times, Wisdom would be revealed on earth by the eschatological Messiah, the Son of Man, a creature who shares the same heavenly nature as Wisdom and with whom Wisdom is closely associated in heaven ("in him dwells the spirit of Wisdom," *1 Enoch* 49:3):[12] "In those days, the Elect One shall sit on my throne, from the conscience of his mouth shall come out all the secrets of Wisdom, for the Lord of the Spirits has given them to him and glorified him" (*1 Enoch* 51:3). But in this world there is no room for the salvific role of Wisdom or the Law.

The implications of this view are equally remarkable. Wisdom does not dwell in this world, which is the place of Iniquity, and there is nothing resembling an embodiment of her in this world. God rules unchallenged in heaven, but not as much on earth—at least not since the angelic sin—and won't again until the end of times. The heavenly Wisdom is an eschatological gift, and the Mosaic Law no more that a feeble image of God's will on earth.

(c) The Enochians were not the only ones to remain unconvinced by the transformation of the divine Wisdom into a heavenly being created by God, and by the view that the Mosaic Torah is the embodiment of Wisdom on earth. While sharing the priestly idea of the universe as an orderly cosmos, a series of Second Temple Jewish texts testifies to the existence of a trend of thought which preferred to keep Wisdom unambiguously connected with the divine. Here Wisdom is an attribute or hypostasis of God and not one of

---

Enoch literature: *The Origins of Enochic Judaism* (= *Henoch* 24 [2002], ed. G. Boccaccini, Turin: Zamorani 2002), *Enoch and Qumran Origins* (ed. G. Boccaccini, Grand Rapids: Eerdmans 2005).

[12] Cf. S. Chialà, *Il libro delle Parabole di Enoc* (Brescia: Paideia 1997); G.W.E. Nickelsburg, "Son of Man," in *ABD* 6: 137-50; *Enoch and the Messiah Son of Man* (ed. G. Boccaccini, Grand Rapids: Eerdmans 2007).

his creatures, is generated rather than created by God, and shares the same divine nature. This is the position that is consistently expressed in the documents of the so-called Hellenistic Judaism, starting with the *Letter of Aristeas*, with which the prologue of the Greek Sirach seems to engage an open debate.

Like the Enochic tradition and contrary to Ben Sira and Baruch, the Jewish-Hellenistic tradition speaks of the divine *sophia*, but unlike the tradition of Enoch, however, Wisdom in not relegated to heaven, nor is an eschatological gift, but is rather a constant salvific presence in the history of Israel and of the entire humankind.

The transcendence of God's *sophia* clearly makes it impossible in the Jewish-Hellenistic tradition to identify Wisdom with Torah. Contrary to the ancient wisdom tradition, however, Hellenistic Judaism recognized an important role to the Torah, although not in the terms articulated by Ben Sira and Baruch. While the natural order of Wisdom is pre-existent and eternal, the Law neither equals nor embodies Wisdom. Rather, the Law was created, as Philo would say, "in harmony with the cosmos..."

> The man who observes the Law is constituted thereby a loyal citizen of the cosmos, regulating his doings by the purpose and will of nature, in accordance with which the entire cosmos itself is administered (*Op.* 3),

and remains subordinated to her as the perfect education (παιδεία) which leads the faithful Jews to the supreme goal of understanding wisdom.

The implications of this concept of Wisdom (and of her relation with the Torah) are, once again, remarkable. In this view, Judaism is not a Temple-centered or Torah-centered religion but a Wisdom-centered religion. As such, Judaism is not simply the religion of the Jewish people but more properly the religion of the universe, and the Jews, who are taught by the Torah to live according to the order of the universe, are by education a philosophical nation. Philo would call them the priests of humankind. "A priest has the same relation to a city that the nation of the Jews has to the entire inhabited world" (*Spec.Leg.* II 163).

The stated primacy of hearing over the reading of the Law is part of this new attitude of mind: "the good life consists in observing the law and this aim is achieved by hearing much more than by reading" (*Aristeas* 127). To the self-sufficient model of the scribe (the "reader" of the Prologue to the Greek Sirach) the *Letter of Aristeas* opposes the ideal of a sage who is expert in both Jewish and Greek culture, ready for dialogue, and free from every prejudice, every idea of presumption or contempt for the others (*Aristeas* 121-22).

In sum: talking of Wisdom literature in the second-century BC as a single intellectual movement is improper and misleading. By the same term "sapiential" we label documents that belong to at least three distinctive forms of Judaism. What John Collins says about apocalypticism, that "neither was it peculiar to a particular sect nor the product of a single movement,"[13] applies also to Wisdom literature. Literary genres are not Judaisms, but worldviews that shaped, influenced, or were used by, differrent varieties of Judaisms. The definition of Ben Sira as a sapiential text tells us a lot about the spreading and pervasiveness of this literary genre and worldview, but does not clearly locate the document within a determined intellectual movement or theology, or social group.

4. BEN SIRA'S SYNTHESIS OF ZADOKITE AND SAPIENTIAL JUDAISM

In order to identify where Ben Sira belongs we need to compare his attitude toward the major institution of the early Seleucid period: the power of the ruling high priesthood of the House of Zadok.

At the beginning of the second century BC, before the Maccabean crisis, Ben Sira is an enthusiastic witness of the golden age of the Zadokite priesthood. He salutes the late Simon II as the ideal high priest, who gloriously ministered in the Temple, and the ideal leader of a time of peace and prosperity, who "took care for his people against brigands and strengthened his city against the enemy" (Sir 50:1-24).

This eulogy was neither nostalgic memory of years gone by, nor the personal and occasional tribute to a charismatic leader. Scholars such as Ellis Rivkin, Saul Olyan and Ben Wright have convincingly stressed the attitude of Ben Sira as a faithful and zealous supporter of the priestly establishment of Jerusalem.[14]

In Ben Sira's view, Jerusalem is the "holy city" that God "loves" (Sir 24:11; 36:18; 49:6), and "the foundation for [God's] throne" (36:18-19). There is an unbroken continuity from "the holy tent" of the desert (Sir 24:10) to "the lasting sanctuary" established by Solomon (47:13), to the Second Temple rebuilt by "Jeshua, son of Jozadak" (49:12) and renovated by "Simon son of Jochanan" (50:1). The Jerusalem sanctuary is, and always will be, "the holy Temple destined for everlasting glory" (49:12). Ben Sira shows his deepest contempt for the Samaritans, who did not recognize the holiness of Jerusalem and worshipped YHWH in the rival temple on Mount Gerizim; "the foolish folk who dwell in Shechem" are "not even a people" (50:25-26).[15]

The Jerusalem Temple is the legitimate sanctuary, ruled by the legitimate priesthood. In his review of the Mosaic revelation, Ben Sira repeats and shares the interpretation of the Priestly Writing. The first step was the gift of the divine revelation, which needed a prophet, Moses, as the mediator. "[God] gave into his hands the commandments, the law of life and under-

---

[13] J.J. Collins, *Apocalypticism in the Dead Sea Scrolls* (London: Routledge 1997) 8.

[14] B.G. Wright, "Fear the Lord and Honor the Priest: Ben Sira as Defender of the Jerusalem Priesthood," in *The Book of Ben Sira in Modern Research* (ed. P.C. Beentjes, BZAW 255, Berlin: de Gruyter 1997) 189-222; S.M. Olyan, "Ben Sira's Relationship to the Priesthood," *HTR* 80 (1987) 261-86; E. Rivkin, "Ben Sira and Aaronite Hegemony," *A Hidden Revolution* (Nashville: Abingdon 1978) 191-207.

[15] Cf. J.D. Purvis, "Ben Sira and the Foolish People of Shechem," *JNES* 24 (1965) 88-94.

standing, that he might teach his precepts to Jacob, his covenant decrees to Israel" (45:5). Moses in turn was instrumental to the establishment of the priestly order by virtue of his relationship with his brother Aaron (45:6-22). The divine covenant made the "sons of Aaron" the legitimate priests forever. "Moses ordained him and anointed him with the holy oil, in a lasting covenant with him and with his family, as permanent as the heavens, that they should serve God in his priesthood and bless his people in his name" (45:15). Thus the Mosaic Torah became the priestly Torah. "[Moses] gave to him his laws, and authority to prescribe and to judge, to teach the precepts to his people, and the norms to the descendants of Israel" (45:17). The final step was the establishment of the high priesthood, which God granted to one branch of the sons of Aaron, that is, Phinehas and his descendants. "On him God conferred the right, in a covenant of friendship, to provide for the sanctuary, so that he and his descendants should possess the high priesthood forever" (44:24).

The lack of any reference to the "sons of Zadok" has (mis)led Saul Olyan to see in Sirach evidence of a "pan-Aaronid," anti-Zadokite attitude.

> Though Ben Sira praises Simon greatly, presenting him as a priestly ideal, his Zadokite heritage is ignored and the occasion is used to make pan-Aaronid claims.[16]

In a recent contribution, Benjamin Wright "accepts" Olyan's view maintaining that "by skipping any reference to Zadok, Ben Sira may well be looking beyond him to the broader number of Phinehas's descendants, both Zadokites and non-Zadokites."[17] The problem is that ancient priestly genealogies do not know "other" descendants of Phinehas. The Zadokites are the only descendants of Phinehas (1 Chr 6:1-15); all the other twenty-four priestly families descend from either Eleazar or Ithamar (1 Chr 24).

If Ben Sira intended to promote a pan-Aaronid attitude, he would have avoided any reference to Phinehas and stressed in his stead the role of Eleazar and Ithamar, the common ancestors of all the Aaronid priestly classes. On the contrary, he advisedly skips the two sons of Aaron to focus on the grandson of Aaron from whom the Zadokites claimed exclusive descent and praises him as the founder of the "high priesthood," in even more explicit terms than Numbers 25. In Ben Sira's view, Phinehas (not Zadok) is "third in line" after Moses and Aaron as the ancestor of the Zadokite high priests: "a covenant of peace was established with him [i.e. Phinehas] that he should be leader of the sanctuary of his people, that he and his descendants should have the dignity of the priesthood forever" (Sir 46:23-24). Consistently, Ben Sira shows Phinehas' descendant, Simon II, surrounded by the "sons of Aaron" (50:13,16) and the levitical "singers" (50:18) as a king surrounded by his officers and honored by his "people," the

[16] Olyan, "Ben Sira's Relationship," 276.

[17] B.G. Wright, "Ben Sira and the Book of the Watchers on the Legitimate Priesthood," in *Intertextual Studies in Ben Sira and Tobit* (eds. J. Corley and V. Skemp, CBQMS 38, Washington: Catholic Biblical Association 2005) 241-54 (here 245-46).

"whole congregation of Israel"(50:13,20). Contrary to what claimed by Olyan and Wright, Ben Sira does indeed mention and single out Simon's special lineage, even though he does it by referring not to Zadok but to Phinehas. So ends the eulogy of the Zadokite high priest Simon II in the original Hebrew text: "May [God's] kindness toward Simon be lasting; may he fulfill for him the covenant with Phinehas, so that it ay be not abrogated for him or for his descendants while the heavens last" (Sir 50:24 [Heb]).

The reference to Phinehas, not to Zadok, as well as the lack of interest in highlighting any relationship between the two, is no surprise. By the time in which Sirach was written the Jerusalem priesthood (that we modern interpreters call "Zadokites") had long ceased to define themselves as "sons of Zadok." Such identification had been superseded, already in the early period of the Second Temple period, by the Priestly edition of the Torah (Num 25) and by Chronicles (5:30-41; 6:35-48) through the reference to a new Sinaitic ancestor, the grandson of Aaron, "Phinehas," who with his "zeal" gained the right "for himself and for his descendants" to "a covenant of perpetual priesthood" (Num 25:10-13). Consistently, in the book of Ezra, the "Zadokite" protagonist is a descendant of Phinehas (7:1-5) and the "sons of Phinehas" are the first and most distinguished group of priests who came back from Babylon (8:2). Like Sirach, Psalm 106 praises Phinehas, not Zadok, as the new hero of the priesthood, third in line after Moses and Aaron. Ironically, the centuries in which the descendants of Zadok were in power, are also the ones in which the term "sons of Zadok" became obsolete and the memory itself of Zadok as the founding father of the high priesthood vanished.

In a Hebrew manuscript of Sirach, there is indeed an addition (at Sir 51:12) that contains a reference to the "sons of Zadok." This psalm of praise is conspicuous for being the only reference to the "sons of Zadok" in the entire literature of the post-exilic "Zadokite" period. But as recognized by all interpreters, the text certainly was neither composed by Ben Sira nor belonged to the original text.[18] The praise to God "who rebuilt his city and sanctuary... makes a horn to sprout for the House of David... and has chosen the sons of Zadok to be priests" evokes the climate of the early years of return under the diarchy of Zerubbabel and Jeshua, when the prophecy of Ezekiel seemed to be fulfilled with the Davidic king and the "sons of Zadok" as "priests," *before* the Priestly Author created the character of Phinehas and Chronicles made the genealogical connection between Phinehas and Zadok.

That by the second century BC the covenant with Phinehas was now seen as the foundation of the Zadokite high priesthood is shown by the later Maccabaean propaganda, and by the indifference of the Hasmonaeans toward the character of Zadok, compared to their insistence in transforming their father Mattathias into a Phinehas *redivivus*. In their struggle to demonstrate that their line was not less legitimate than that of the Zadokites,

---

[18] See S.C. Reif, "The Discovery of the Cambridge Genizah Fragments of Ben Sira: Scholars and Texts," in *The Book of Ben Sira in Modern Research*, 1-22.

the Maccabees compared Mattathias' zeal to Phinehas' (1 Macc 2:26), and by calling the latter "our father," applied typologically to themselves "the covenant of everlasting priesthood" (1 Macc 2:54).

The idea that the zeal of Mattathias preempted the covenant with Phinehas for him and his descendants was a bold and controversial move by an Aaronid family which was descended from Eleazar only. While largely supporting the new Hasmonaean high priesthood, the other Aaronid families were obviously quite reluctant to grant to one of their peers a distinctive status and more inclined to support a "democratic" position that would grant all of them the right to, and the hope for, the high priesthood. The Maccabaean propaganda, subtly aimed not only to replace the Zadokites but also to prevent the challenge by rival Aaronid families, did not gain general consensus. The embarrassment for the end of the Zadokite line but also the resistance to the Maccabaean claim is apparent at the end of the second century BC in the Greek version of the Book of Ben Sira. The translator turned the prayer to Simon II and his descendants into a generic wish of prosperity on behalf of the entire people of Israel ("May [God's] kindness remain constantly with us and may he save us in our days"), rather than repeating a promise that failed, or applying the covenant of Phinehas to the new Hasmonaean priesthood (what the new high priesthood in power would have certainly appreciated but would also have doomed the other Aaronids to "eternal" submission).

Eventually, the idea that all "sons of Aaron" are eligible for the high priesthood became normative in Roman times, certainly facilitated by the demise of the Hasmonaeans. Flavius Josephus drops any connection (either direct or indirect) between the covenant of Phinehas and the high priesthood, as if it were not part of the priestly Sinaitic order and the hereditary Zadokite high priesthood never existed: "it is a custom of our country, that no one should take the high priesthood of God, but he who is of the blood of Aaron" (*AJ* 20:226). Were the omission of Zadok and the reference to Phinehas already evidence of a pan-Aaronid claim as Olyan and Wright have claimed, why did the Greek translator of Sirach and Flavius Josephus censor both names in connection with the high priesthood? Since Sirach mentioned Phinehas as the ancestor of the high priest Simon, the omission of Zadok is totally irrelevant; it was the connection between Phinehas and the high priesthood that had to be eradicated in order to promote a "pan-Aaronid" perspective.

That the term "sons of Zadok" did not denote the Zadokite priests "sons of Phinehas" of the second century BC is also confirmed, although indirectly, by the literature of Qumran. The *Damascus Document* uses the term "sons of Zadok" not as a genealogical reference to the Zadokite dynasty (whose power the Qumranites had no intention of restoring) but as a typological reference to the prophecy of Ezekiel, which in their view was not historically fulfilled by the rising to power of the descendant of Zadok (that is, the sons of Phinehas) in the Second Temple but would only be fulfilled by the new Qumran priesthood.[19] Had the Qumranites been Zadokites (that is, former members of the ruling high priesthood deposed by the Hasmonaeans), they would have reclaimed for themselves the title of "sons of Phinehas," and appeal to their Sinaitic right to the high priesthood. Instead, the Qumranites went back to Ezekiel claiming that his prophecy did not refer to the actual "Jerusalem priests" (the "sons of Phinehas," as well as the other "sons of Aaron") but to a forthcoming priesthood (their priesthood "at the end of times"). In this way the Qumranites were dismissing the very foundation of the Zadokite (and Aaronid) legitimacy by making themselves (not the actual Jerusalem priesthood) the true and exclusive fulfillment of Ezekiel's prophecy, twisting the foundational passage of Zadokite authority into an anti-Zadokite statement. After all did Ezekiel himself not present his prophecy as a modification of the Sinaitic order, an unfortunate consequence of the sin of the priests? Where the Aaronids fit in this picture posed no problem for the prophet-priest; he did not know of the existence of "sons of Aaron" and the distinction between "sons of Aaron" and "sons of Levi," as he followed the Deuteronomic stance that "the Lord your God has chosen [Levi] out of all your tribes, to stand and minister in the name of the Lord, him and his sons for all time" (Deut 18:5; cf. 17:9; 21:5; 31:9).[20] The point of the *Damascus Document* is that Ezekiel's prophecy was not historically fulfilled after the exile by the rise to power of the "sons of Phinehas" as the promise of Ezekiel refers to the eschatological "sons of Zadok"—hardly a Zadokite statement.

Ben Sira belongs to a generation who is not yet troubled by conflicts within the Aaronid priesthood, or between Aaronids and Zadokites. His admiration for the Jerusalem priesthood is unreserved. He does not hesitate to compare the honor due to the priests to the honor due to God.

> With all your heart, fear God and treat as holy his priests. With all your might, love your Maker and do not forsake his servants. Honor God and honor the priest, and give their portion as you are commanded: the trespass offering, and (voluntary) offering, the sacrifices of righteousness, and the holy offering (Sir 7:29-31).

No Jewish document had ever gone so far. As Ellis Rivkin has effectively summarized,

> Ben Sira spreads before us a hierocratic society. A priesthood consisting exclusively of the "sons of Aaron" formed its ruling class, and a high priest, a direct descendent of Aaron, Eleazar, Phinehas, and Zadok, exercised ultimate authority... Undergirding this system was the Pentateuch, which (so it was believed) had been revealed by God to Moses... [who] bestowed upon Aaron and his des-

---

[19] P.R. Davies, *Behind the Essenes: History and Ideology in the Dead Sea Scrolls* (BJS 94, Atlanta: Scholars Press 1987) 51-72

[20] J. Blenkinsopp, *Sage, Priest, Prophet: Religious and Intellectual Leadership in Ancient Israel* (Louisville: Westminster John Knox Press 1997).

cendants not only an everlasting priesthood but also the ongoing authority over the law.[21]

5. SIRACH AS AN ANTI-ENOCHIC TEXT

Ben Sira is more than a witness of the Zadokite power; he is an apologist against their opponents. Their enemies are his enemies. Under the calm and asystematic style of the document smolders a bitter, often acrimonious controversy which divided Jewish society behind the apparent quiet of the early Seleucid period. Ben Sira was aware that there were some Jews who did not recognize the legitimacy of the Second Temple and of the Jerusalem priesthood, and did not spare them his most polemical arrows.

That the Enochians were his target, is apparent by the strength with which he not only defends the present and future rights of the sons of Aaron but also dismisses the existence of a pre-Aaronid priesthood:

> before [Aaron] no one was adorned with [the sacred vestments], nor may they ever be worn by any except his sons and them alone, generation after generation, for all time (44:13).[22]

He does not even miss an explicit reference to the "followers of Dathan and Abiram and the band of Korah" as an eternal warning that God's "wrath" protects the sons of Aaron against whoever, priests or laypeople, dare challenge their authority (45:18-19).

Ben Sira also rejects a knowledge acquired by the unveiling of heavenly secrets, apart from the authoritative teaching of the Zadokite Torah. Once again, his vocabulary brings Enochic Judaism to mind. In a passionate speech, Ben Sira dismisses the reliability of dreams,

> for dreams have led many astray, and those who base their hopes on them have perished. Without deceit the law is fulfilled, and well-rounded wisdom is the discourse of the faithful (34:1-8).

Ben Sira warns against those who claim the human capability to understand the secrets of heaven. "For wonderful are the works of the Lord, yet they remain hidden from men his works" (Sir 11:4b). What is needed for humans

---

[21] Rivkin, *A Hidden Revolution*, 191 and 195.

[22] On Ben Sira as an anti-Enochic document, see G. Boccaccini, *Roots of Rabbinic Judaism*; Idem, *Middle Judaism: Jewish Thought, 300 BCE to 200 CE* (Minneapolis: Fortress Press 1991) 77-125; Idem, "Origine del male, libertà dell'uomo e retribuzione nella Sapienza di Ben Sira," *Hen* 8 (1986) 1-37; R.A. Argall, *1 Enoch and Sirach: A Comparative Literary and Conceptual Analysis of the Themes of Revelation, Creation, and Judgment* (SBLEJL 8, Atlanta: Scholars Press 1995); Wright, "Fear the Lord and Honor the Priest;" and, "Ben Sira and the Book of the Watchers."

to know, has been already revealed. The search of "hidden things" is super-
fluous and unnecessary; besides, it is a sinful presumption.

> Don't look for things that are too difficult, and don't investigate things that are too
> obscure. What is commanded to you, attend to; for you have no need of the
> hidden things [Gk. κρυπτά]. With what is superfluous to your works, meddle not;
> for what is beyond man's intelligence was shown to you. Presumption, in fact has
> misled many, an evil illusion seduced their thoughts (Sir 3:21-24).

With the same decision, Ben Sira rejects any theory of corruption. In line
with the Priestly Writing, he describes creation as a process of setting boundaries that produces a series of opposites. This is the reason why "all the
works of the Most High… come in pairs, the one the opposite of the other"
(33:15). Sacred days and ordinary days, priests and laypeople, Jews and
Gentiles, sinners and just (33:7-14), "good and evil, life and death, poverty
and riches, are from the Lord" (Sir 11:4; cf. 33:14-15; 42:24)

The presence of opposites does not disrupt the goodness and unity of
God's creation. "All things come in twos, one corresponding the other; yet
none of them has he made in vain" (42:14). Everything is ultimately good, as
everything has been made for a purpose. "The works of God are all of them
good, for every need in its own time He provides. No cause to say: This is
not as good as that; for each shows its worth at the proper time" (Sir 39:33-
35). Good for the good and evil for the wicked, is Ben Sira's general rule.
"For the good [God] provided good things from the beginning" (39:25). "For
the wicked evil was created" (Sir 40:10), and even "good things… turn out
evil" (Sir 39:27).

Ben Sira makes a strong case that the supreme authority of God is not
challenged by any rebellious power. Even the most destructive forces of
nature, such as "storm winds… fire and hail, famine, disease… ravenous
beasts, scorpions, vipers and the avenging sword… were created to meet a
need"—punishment of the wicked—and are unleashed according to God's
will: "When [God] commands them, they rejoice, and in their assignments
they do not disobey his bidding" (Sir 39:28-35).

The immutability and obedience of creation are underscored with
particular emphasis in reference to the heavenly beings God created before
humankind.

> When God created the first of His works and, as He made them, assigned their
> tasks, He ordered for all time what they were to do and their domains from gene-
> ration to generation… They do not crowd one another, and they never disobey
> His word (Sir 16:26-28).

The insistence is anything but random. Ben Sira is not ready to provide any
pretext for the Enochic claim that evil is a consequence of a disorder that
generated in the heavenly domain among the angels. In referring to Gen 6:1-
4, Ben Sira consciously avoids any mythological overtone; the "giants" are
"princes of old who were rebellious in their might" (Sir 16:7) and were

punished by God as all other sinners. In Ben Sira's worldview, there is no room for devils, fallen angels, or evil spirits, not even for a mischievous officer of the divine court as the satan of Job, or for a domesticated demon as the Asmodeus of Tobit. The only reference to "the satan" in Sirach is in a context (21:1-22:18) that emphasizes personal responsibility and the capability of "whoever keeps the law to control his impulses" (21:11). The satan of Sir 21:17 is primarily the personal adversary, but the skillful ambiguity of the saying is aimed also to stigmatize the "impious" belief in the existence of the heavenly enemy. "When an impious man curses the satan, he really curses himself" (Sir 21:27).

Ben Sira is aware of the ambivalence of human nature, even of people's apparent attitude to sin: "the flesh and body have evil thoughts... the Lord alone is righteous," (Sir 17:31-8:2). Yet, he excludes the idea that evil should be attributed to an agent external to human beings, either to an angelic rebellion in heaven or even to God. Sirach is an unshakable champion of human free will and responsibility:

> From the first, when [God] created humankind, He made them subject to their own free choice. If you choose you can keep the commandments... Before each person are life and death; whichever he chooses shall be given him (Sir 15:11-20).[23]

Since this world is (and always will be) the good and uncorrupted universe created by God, Ben Sira rejects any hypothesis of an afterlife retribution as well as any perspectives of a "new" creation; from death "there is no return... once the breath of life has left" (Sir 38:21-23). After death, there is only the *sheol*, the netherworld, the common destiny of all and the eternal and joyless resting place of the dead, righteous and sinners alike (Sir 14:16; 17:27-28; 21:10; 22:11; cf. Ps 88:4-7).

For the same reasons, God's creation will not be overthrown to leave room to a new creation; a perfect work does not need to be redone. Rather, Ben Sira shares the primary concern of Zadokite Judaism that humans must cooperate to preserve the stability of this world, as it has been promised from God's part through the covenant with Noah: "A lasting sign sealed the assurance to him that never should all flesh be destroyed" (Sir 44:18).

Worship is the major guarantee of stability of the universe, as people continuously remind their Maker and Ruler of the engagements and responsibilities of the covenant. This is the goal of the "sweet odor" of perpetual sacrifices (35:8), and the ultimate function of worship. Ben Sira singles out three cultic elements as "a memorial before the Most High for the children of His people," and all of them are associated with the Jerusalem priesthood: the ringing of the golden bells of Aaron's robe (Sir 45:9), the precious stones with seal engraving in golden settings on the ephod (45:11), and the sounding of the trumpets (50:16).

[23] J. Hadot, *Penchant mauvais et volonté libre dans la sagesse de Ben Sira* (Bruxelles: Presses universitaires 1970); G. Maier, *Mensch und freier Wille, nach den jüdischen Religionsparteien zwischen Ben Sira and Paulus* (Tübingen: Mohr Siebeck 1971).

The cycle is now completed. This world, and this world only, is the good and uncorrupted universe created by God, and the place of God's retribution. This priesthood, and this priesthood only, is the guarantee of the stability of the universe. As the world will last forever, so will the priesthood.

6. SIRACH AS AN ANTI-SAPIENTIAL TEXT

Ironically, the Book of Ben Sira, which from the literary point of view is undoubtedly a sapiential text, could be properly defined (from the ideological point of view) as an anti-sapiential text as well. The same determination and strength he shows in defending the Mosaic covenant against its Enochic opponents is apparent in Ben Sira's revisionist approach to skeptical wisdom. Ben Sira tries hard to react to any sense of despair and frustration and make people cope with the manifest absence of justice in this world. He will neither deny the evidence, nor the right of submitting reality to the scrutiny of experience, but is ready to fight back. Unlike Job, Jonah and Qohelet, he accepts that the answer comes before the inquiry and is the one given by the covenant:

> The sinner will not escape with [his] plunder, and the righteous man's perseverance will not be disappointed. [The Lord] will hold every righteous deed in account, each will receive according to his own deeds (Sir 16:13-14; cf. 2:8-10; 16:6-23; 35:10-23).

Ben Sira is not open to accept the possibility of a different answer; his search is only for the rationale. Human skill and the sophisticated techniques of sapiential inquiry are twisted and put out to service, not to criticize but to prove the soundness of the Mosaic revelation. There must be some explanation, even when humans are unable to find it at once and all evidence seems to point to a different conclusion.

God's patience can explain the delay in punishing sinners and silence, at least for a while, those who doubt the validity of the covenant: "Say not: I have sinned, yet what has befallen me?, for the Lord is patient" (5:4). God knows how frail humans are, and continually renews the offer of salvation, delaying the moment of punishment and giving more and more opportunities for repentance. "That is why the Lord is patient with human beings and shows his mercy upon them" (18:11).

The testing of the righteous, which in Job was an (occasional) act of obstinacy by a heavenly adversary, "the satan," and in Tobit an (occasional) delay in the unfolding of God's retribution, is now a providential, almost ordinary aspect of the divine pedagogy. Just as God corrects and admonishes the sinners, so God also tests the righteous to reinforce and confirm their righteousness.

> When you come to serve the Lord, prepare your soul for trial... Accept whatever
> befalls you, in crushing misfortune be patient, for in fire gold is tested and worthy
> men in the crucible of humiliation (Sir 2:1-5).

These arguments cannot be stretched too far, however, to the point that
God's mercy nullifies God's justice. Ben Sira has to warn "not to be
overconfident of forgiveness, adding sin upon sin, and saying: Great is His
mercy; many sins He will forgive" (5:5-6). Certainly, the God of Israel is "a
merciful God, who forgives sins and saves in time of trouble" (2:11). This
aspect of God, however, does not cancel the reality of judgment and the
covenant. God's merciful and parental affection is reserved to "those who
accept His guidance, and are diligent in His precepts" (Sir 18:14). At the end,
God's mercy cannot prevail over God's justice, which remains the measure
of God's mercy. "Mercy and wrath are with [God], mighty when He forgives
and when he alights His wrath. Great as His mercy is His justice, He will
judge men, each according to his deeds" (16:11-12; cf. 5:6).

After engaging the enemy in some skirmish, Ben Sira is back to the initial
front of defense. The covenant requires God to reward the righteous and
punish the sinners in this world. How does this happen? Ben Sira believes in
what the covenant promises, yet he is also a wise man who, enlightened by
experience, knows how things go in this world. He dramatically feels that
the boundaries of individual existence, so uncertain and fleeting, have
become too narrow for divine retribution to fulfill. He retreats to the day of
death as the decisive, mysterious and only remaining time in which the
individual may meet God and fully experience the power of God's judgment. That "only when man's life comes to its end in prosperity can one call
that man happy" was a wide-spread maxim of popular wisdom.[24] In the
religious world of Ben Sira, it is turned into a theological statement about
God's retribution.

> For it is easy for the Lord on the day of death to repay a person according to his
> deeds... A moment's affliction brings forgetfulness of past delights; when a man
> dies, his life is revealed. Call no one happy before his death, for by how he ends, a
> person is truly known (Sir 11:26-28; cf. 9:11-12).

The *memento mori*—the recurring reminder, You must die!—becomes one of
the most characteristic elements in Ben Sira's parenesis, placing him at the
beginning of a long and successful tradition of preaching. "In whatever you
do, remember your end, and you will never sin" (Sir 7:36; cf. 14:12; 18:24;
28:6).

As strong as they may be, these arguments also are far from being con-
clusive against the burden of evidence. Ben Sira keeps promising a happy
life and a good death (1:13) to the righteous, but at the very end, the only
thing that he can plausibly offer, besides an uncertain experience of happy

---

[24] See Aeschylus, *Agamennon*, 1:928; Herodotus, *Histories*, 1:32; and Sophocles,
Oedipus Rex, 1:1529.

life and an equally uncertain hope of good death, is the perspective of everlasting memory. In this way, in his discussion of retribution, he can go decidedly beyond the boundaries of death, while remaining anchored to a system that excludes any hypothesis of afterlife.

The conservation of one's name for the righteous, corresponding to the *damnatio memoriae* for the wicked, is certainly not a new theme in Jewish thought (and in foreign wisdom).[25] However, in Ben Sira it receives singular emphasis, being affirmed as the truest and most authentic reward for the righteous, better than any riches or even a long and happy life.

> Have a care for your name, for it will endure for you better than a thousand great precious treasures. The days of a happy life are limited, but a good name will endure forever (Sir 41:12-13).

In his criticism, Qoheleth had not spared even this traditional assumption: "there is no enduring remembrance of the wise or of fools, seeing that in the days to come all will have been long forgotten" (Qoh 2:16). Among the objections put forward by skeptical wisdom in the name of experience, this is the only one for which Ben Sira denies all evidence. He is aware that the memory of the righteous is the last trench, that cannot be lost, and his only remaining chance to shake off the skeptical inquiry of experience.

It was not an easy task, indeed. The righteous count on the blessing of children (30:4-5; 40:19); however, experience shows that their birth and righteousness are not at all guaranteed, so much so that "it is better to die childless than to have wicked children" (Sir 16:1-3). Ben Sira had to hold the name of the righteous to a more solid and less volatile anchorage, which only could be provided by the collective memory of Israel. "Limited are the days of one man's life, but the days of Israel are without number. The wise man will be honored among his people and his name will live forever" (37:25-26). The *Praise of the Fathers* that ends the book of Ben Sira (Sir 44-49) is a grandiose celebration of the collective memory of Israel, of its capability of keeping alive the name and legacy of the righteous, generation after generation. The wide-angle picture has the effect to put out of focus the details of individual life and remove reward and punishment from experience's critical eye. As evil fades and comes to nothing in the divine economy of the cosmos (Sir 42:15--43:33), so does any contradiction to the principle of covenantal retribution in the larger historical perspective of the history of Israel.

---

[25] P.A.H. de Boer, *Gedenken und Gedachtnis in der Welt des Altes Testaments* (Stuttgart: Kohlhammer 1962); W. Schottroff, *Gedenken im Alten Orient und im Alten Testament* (WMANT 15, Neukirchen-Vluyn: Neukirchener Verlag 1964); J.H. Yerushalmi, *Zakhor: Jewish History and Jewish Memory* (Seattle: University of Washington, 1982); G. Boccaccini, "Il tema della memoria nell'ebraismo e nel giudaismo antico," *Hen* 7 (1985) 164-92.

7. INTELLECTUAL MOVEMENT AND SOCIAL GROUP

In a comprehensive map of intellectual movements in Second Temple Judaism, Ben Sira should be seen as a Zadokite document. An intellectual movement, however, is never a single social group, but rather a constellation of groups and individuals, and Zadokite Judaism is no exception.

Because Ben Sira was a supporter of the Zadokite order, we should not argue that Ben Sira himself was necessarily a member of the Zadokite family or, more likely, an Aaronite priest or levite; even though he might well have been.[26] He takes pride in being an honored member of the ruling class, not a farmer or artisan who has to work (38:24-34). Being a priest or levite, however, is not Ben Sira's primary self-identity. He portrays himself as a scribe (39:1-11), who imparts wisdom in his school (51:23).

The Zadokite Torah has a place of honor in his teaching; he pronounces "woe to the wicked people, who forsake the law of the Most High" (41:8). He rejects the stance of Enochic Judaism and denounces the excesses of skeptical wisdom. Yet, "Ben Sira remains a wisdom teacher, not an exegete or expositor of the Torah."[27] The teachings of Ben Sira are largely those traditional of Sapiential Judaism, based on Proverbs in particular, and on the popular wisdom of the Near East. Using the usual formula of wisdom literature, Ben Sira addresses his readers as "my son" (2:1; passim), or "my children" (3:1; passim). With great emphasis, he praises the role and teaching of the wise.

> Do not spurn the discourse of the wise, but acquaint yourself with the proverbs; from them you will acquire instruction and learn how to serve great men. Do not disregard the tradition of old men, for they themselves learned from their fathers; from them you will obtain understanding and learn how to give an answer in time of need (Sir 8:8-9).

Despite the emphasis of the priesthood and cultic obligations, Ben Sira's primary concerns are those of Sapiential Judaism—"harmony among kindred, friendship among neighbors, and the mutual love of husband and wife" (Sir 25:2).

As in the case of Tobit, we meet in Ben Sira a representative of a new generation of sages, who openly supports the priesthood and the Zadokite order and does so with much greater sophistication than Tobit.

Had the Zadokites kept their leadership over the Jewish society, the merging of Sapiential and Zadokite traditions would have ultimately resulted in the strengthening of the priestly power with an acknowledged role for the sage subordinate to the priest. While building up a fine reputation for himself as a sage, Ben Sira served the priest as well. He confirmed the centrality of the covenant and the retributive principle, opposing the challenge

---

[26] See H. Stadelmann, *Ben Sira als Schriftgelehrter* (WUNT 6, Tübingen: Mohr Siebeck 1980).

[27] Collins, *Jewish Wisdom*, 56.

of Enochic Judaism and putting an end to the doubts of skeptical wisdom. Furthermore, Ben Sira offered to Zadokite Judaism a sophisticated theological system in which there was a harmony between the order of the universe (Wisdom) and the priestly order (Torah), as well as a balance between revelation and experience—notions that Job, Jonah and Qoheleth had deemed contradictory, and Tobit had only juxtaposed.

8. CONCLUSION

We can now conclude that the now apocryphal or deuterocanonical Ben Sira was a sapiential text, a second-century BC Jewish document, written by a supporter of Zadokite Judaism, and the product of a social group of scribes who enthusiastically backed the Zadokite order.

Ben Sira fully recognized the legitimacy of the high priesthood of the "sons of Phinehas" (the Zadokites of modern scholarship) and contrary to what argued by Olyan and Wright, did not articulate a view that the priesthood should belong to all the sons of Aaron. The emphasis in Sirach, however, was not on the House of Phinehas in itself but rather on the priestly order of high priests ("sons of Phinehas), priests ("sons of Aaron") and levites ("sons of Levi") they created and supported. This allowed the synthesis created by Sirach to survive even after the collapse of the Zadokite priesthood, as proved by the Book of Baruch, the Greek translation of Sirach itself, and Flavius Josephus. Historical circumstances led to extend to all the "sons of Aaron" God's promises to the "sons of Phinehas." The solidity of the system, however, was not affected, laying the foundation for that priestly movement that Flavius Josephus would call "Sadducean," and is nothing else than the Zadokite ideology successfully surviving the demise of the House of Phinehas. Even before the destruction of the Second Temple and the collapse of the order that the Zadokites had created, the memory of the covenant with Phinehas faded, to never recover again, surprisingly even in modern scholarship.

THE PRE-EMINENCE OF THE HEBREW LANGUAGE
AND THE EMERGING CONCEPT OF THE "IDEAL TEXT"
IN LATE SECOND TEMPLE JUDAISM

Stefan Schorch
(Kirchliche Hochschule Bethel, Bielefeld)

The prologue to the Book of Ben Sira is one of the most important testimonies to the intellectual culture of Judaism in the 2nd century BCE, specifically in its second half.[1] It reflects the concepts that were crucial for that milieu and may therefore serve as a starting point for its reconstruction. The following paper will focus on some of these concepts, especially regarding the pre-eminence of the Hebrew language as well as the "ideal text."

1. THE PRE-EMINENCE OF THE HEBREW LANGUAGE

From the perspective of the Masoretic text, Hebrew is of course the language in which the sacred scriptures of Israel were composed, apart from only a few passages which are written in Aramaic. We may expect, therefore, that the Hebrew language has been an important marker of Jewish identity throughout the late second temple period, at least in Palestinian Jewry. Unfortunately, explicit and unambiguous statements regarding the Hebrew language coming from that very time are rare and seem not to cover the whole period.

One of the most important testimonies is preserved in the prologue to the Book of Ben Sira, line 6, containing one of the earliest testimonies of the language name "Hebrew." Before we consider it, however, the question may

---

[1] It has been suggested by Veltri that the prologue dates to the 1st century CE and not, as the dates given by the text itself seem to indicate, to the 2nd century BCE, see G. Veltri, *Eine Tora für den König Talmai: Untersuchungen zum Übersetzungsverständnis in der jüdisch-hellenistischen Literatur* (TSAJ 41, Tübingen: Mohr Siebeck 1994) 139. However, the basis for Veltri's suggestion seems narrow, being formed only by a small number of lexical parallels between the prologue and Greek texts from the 1st century CE, as the writings of Josephus and the New Testament. Moreover, as will be demonstrated below, the concepts of language (especially with regard to the Hebrew language) and translation one encounters in the prologue fit a 2nd century BCE context but much less the 1st century CE. Therefore, the date provided by the prologue itself still seems the most probable and should be followed unless evidence comes to light which prooves the contrary.

be asked, whether the passage "things originally said in Hebrew" (αὐτὰ ἐν ἑαυτοῖς Ἑβραϊστὶ λεγόμενα) does indeed refer to the Hebrew language as apart from the Aramaic. In many similar cases it is not easy to know whether a given ancient Jewish source refers to the Hebrew or rather to the Aramaic language, and often there seems to have been made no clear-cut difference in the designation of the two.

This situation is especially problematic with regard to sources composed in Hebrew or Aramaic: So far, the oldest known testimony which is written in Hebrew and attests the designation עברית ("Hebrew") comes from the Babylonian Talmud and thus dates only to the period of the 3rd-5th centuries CE. Even in Talmudic times, however, the name עברית does not specifically refer to the Hebrew language in the modern linguistic sense, but may be applied to the Aramaic language as well, at least to the Aramaic dialect used by Jews.[2]

If we look at the Greek sources from the first century CE, the situation is essentially the same: Both the New Testament writings and Josephus apply the adverb Ἑβραϊστί and the adjective Ἑβραΐς to the Hebrew as well as to the Aramaic language (e.g. John 5:2; Acts 21:40).[3] Philo, on the other hand, seems to mix up the two as well, when he applies the word χαλδαῖος not a few times to designate the Hebrew tongue, as has been shown by Wong.[4]

It may be surprising, therefore, that the situation is different if we look into sources from the 2nd century BCE, since they are obviously based on a clear distinction of Aramaic and Hebrew. Most prominently, this distinction appears in the Letter of Aristeas, composed probably in the second half of the 2nd century BCE:[5]

LetAris 11:4-6: ἑρμενείας προσδεῖται χαρακτῆρσι γὰρ ἰδίοις κατὰ τὴν 'ιουδαίαν χρῶνται……καὶ φωνὴν ἰδίαν ἔχουσιν. ὑπολαμβάνονται Συριακῇ χρῆσθαι τὸ δ' οὐκ ἔστιν ἀλλ' ἕτερος τρόπος ("Translation is needed. They use letters characteristic of the language of the Jews […] They are supposed to use Aramaic [Syriac] language, but this is not so, for it is another language.")

LetAris 30:1-3: τοῦ νόμου τῶν Ἰουδαίων βιβλία σὺν ἑτέροις ὀλίγοις τισὶν ἀπολείπει τυγχάνει γὰρ Ἑβραϊκοῖς γράμμασι καὶ φωνῇ λεγόμενα ("Books of the law of the Jews, together with few others, are missing [from the library], for these works are written in Hebrew characters and language.")

---

[2] See e.g. M. Jastrow, A Dictionary of the Targumim, the Talmud Babli and Yerushalmi, and the Midrashic Literature (Jerusalem: Horeb [reprint of the edition from 1903]) 1040 s.v. עברי and J. Blau, "Hebrew Language. Biblical. The Names," in Encyclopaedia Judaica (CD-Rom Edition Version 1.0).

[3] See E. Schürer, The History of the Jewish People in the Age of Jesus Christ (175 B.C.-A.D. 135) (3 vols., rev. and ed. by Geza Vermes, et al., Edinburgh: T&T Clark 1973-1987) 2: 28, note 118, and compare W. Bauer, Griechisch-Deutsches Wörterbuch zu den Schriften des Neuen Testaments und der übrigen urchristlichen Literatur (5th edition, Berlin: de Gruyter 1971) 422.

[4] For details see C.K. Wong, "Philo's use of Chaldaioi," The Studia Philonica Annual 4 (1992) 1-14.

[5] Translation from R.J.H. Shutt, "Letter of Aristeas," in OTP 2: 7-34.

The use of Συριστί and ἡ Συριακή φωνή for "Aramaic" is widespread and especially well attested in the Septuagint.[6] Referring to the fact that the Aramaic language had been the Semitic *lingua franca* of Palestine and beyond, the author tells the king that it is neither the language of the Jews nor of their laws which are instead written in Hebrew script and language (Ἑβραϊκός).

Thus, the cited references allows for two observations:

1. The anonymous author of the *Letter of Aristeas* makes a clear distinction between Hebrew and Aramaic, and
2. The Hebrew language is referred to as "Hebrew" (Ἑβραϊκός).

A similar distinction, although without using the term "Hebrew," may be found in 2 Maccabees:[7]

2 Macc 15:36: [...] ἔχειν δὲ ἐπίσημον τὴν τρισκαιδεκάτην τοῦ δωδεκάτου μηνὸς Αδαρ λέγεται τῇ Συριακῇ φωνῇ [...] ("[...] but to celebrate the thirteenth day of the twelfth month—which is called Adar in the Aramaic language [...]")

In this indication of date, the month is given according to two different systems: First according to the system which is known from the Torah and seems to have been generally followed in Palestinian Judaism throughout the late Second Temple period in religious contexts,[8] namely the numbering of months (τοῦ δωδεκάτου μηνός, "of the twelfth month"). Subsequently, the author mentions the name of the respective month according to the Aramaic system of month names, which had its origin in Mesopotamia, seems to have been adopted by Judaism in the Persian period[9] and remained in use mainly for secular purposes.[10]

As in the *Letter of Aristeas*, the Aramaic language is referred to as "Syriac language" (ἡ Συριακή φωνή).[11] The way the author uses the Aramaic name of the month as a kind of explanation ("which is called Adar in the Aramaic language") indicates that the Aramaic month names must have been in use

---

[6] In the Septuagint, Συριστι as the counterpart to אֲרָמִית in the Masoretic text occurs in 2 Kgs 18:26//Isa 36:11; Ezra 4:7; Dan 2:4.

[7] The translation of Biblical texts mostly follows the NRSV, but deviates where it seemed necessary in the context of the present study.

[8] This system is attested in *1 Enoch*, *Jubilees*, the *Temple Scroll* and further writings, see J.C. VanderKam, "Calendars, Ancient Israelite and Early Jewish," in *ABD* (CD-Rom version).

[9] Thus, it is attested in Ezra, Nehemiah, Esther, and Zechariah.

[10] It is followed by the Elephantine Papyri and the Wâdi ed-Daliyeh Papyri, see VanderKam, "Calendars."

[11] Van Henten ponders the possibility that ἡ Συριακή φωνή could refer to the (Neo-) Babylonian language, compare J.W. van Henten, "The ancestral languageof the Jews in 2 Maccabees," in *Hebrew study from Ezra to Ben-Yehuda* ed. W. Horbury, Edinburgh: T&T Clark 1999) 61. This, however, seems quite impossible within the context of Palestine in the 2nd century BC.

at that time, otherwise the author perhaps would not have mentioned it. Obviously, however, he regarded the first system—the Hebrew numbering of months—as the regular and normal way. Thus, he makes a distinction between the "foreign" Aramaic (Συριακή) and the "indigenous" Hebrew terminology.

Other than in the *Letter of Aristeas*, however, the term "Hebrew" is not attested in 2 Maccabees. Instead, it uses the designation "ancestral language" (ἡ πάτριος φωνή): in chapter 7, both the mother and their sons use this language when being pressed to abandon their Jewish religion or to be put into torture and death. Judas raises the battle cry (12,37), and he and his soldiers praise God in that language (15,29). The passages are as follows:

> 2 Macc 7:8: ὁ δὲ ἀποκριθεὶς τῇ πατρίῳ φωνῇ προσεῖπεν οὐχί ("He replied in the ancestral language and said to them, 'No.'")
>
> 2 Macc 7:21: ἕκαστον δὲ αὐτῶν παρεκάλει τῇ πατρίῳ φωνῇ ("She encouraged each of them in the ancestral language.")
>
> 2 Macc 7:27: προσκύψασα δὲ αὐτῷ χλευάσασα τὸν ὠμὸν τύραννον οὕτως ἔφησεν τῇ πατρίῳ φωνῇ ("But, leaning close to him, she spoke in their ancestral language as follows, deriding the cruel tyrant.")
>
> 2 Macc 12:37: (Ιουδας...) καταρξάμενος τῇ πατρίῳ φωνῇ τὴν μεθ᾽ ὕμνων κραυγήν ("In the ancestral language he (i.e. Judas) raised the battle cry, with hymns.")
>
> 2 Macc 15:29: γενομένης δὲ κραυγῆς καὶ ταραχῆς εὐλόγουν τὸν δυνάστηντῇ πατρίῳ φωνῇ ("Then there was shouting and tumult, and they blessed the Sovereign Lord in the ancestral language.")

That the expression "ancestral language" refers to the Hebrew language can hardly be doubted,[12] although it has been explained as referring to Aramaic by generations of scholars who took it for granted that Hebrew died out after the exile.[13] Today we know that this was not the case and that Hebrew at the time of 2 Maccabees even survived as a spoken language.[14] The distinction standing behind the introduction of the two systems of month names discussed above makes it entirely clear that the author indeed intended to present the seven brothers, their mother and Judas as speaking Hebrew. As to the equation of the attribute πάτριος and the Hebrew language, it is attested in a similar way in the prologue to the Book of Ben Sira pointing out that the "ancestral books" (line 10: τὰ πάτρια βιβλία) are composed in the Hebrew language (line 22).

If we look at these citations in their respective contexts it becomes obvious that the author of 2 Maccabbees regarded the Hebrew language as a very important marker of Jewish identity. This is well in line with the observation that during the Hasmonaean period, Hebrew seems to have become a

---

[12] Similarly D.R. Schwartz, *The Second Book of Maccabees. Introduction, Hebrew Translation, and Commentary* (Jerusalem: Yad Ben-Tzvi 2004) (in Hebrew) 167.

[13] For details, see van Henten, "The Ancestral Language," 65-66.

[14] See A. Sáenz-Badillos, *A History of the Hebrew Language* (Cambridge: University Press 1993) 170f.

Judean national symbol as is suggested by its use on the coins of that period.[15]

However, the high status ascribed at that time to the Hebrew language was not confined to its being a national symbol but extended to its pre-eminent religious importance. This is most clearly expressed in a further Jewish literary composition from the 2nd century BCE, the *Book of Jubilees*. In chapter 12, the angel who came to dictate the Torah to Moses tells about Abraham learning Hebrew, which has been the language of creation but has been forgotten over generations:

> Then the Lord God said to me: 'Open his mouth and his ears to hear and speak with his tongue in the revealed language.' For from the day of the collapse[16] it had disappeared from the mouth(s) of all mankind. I opened his mouth, ears and lips, and began to speak Hebrew with him—in the language of the creation. He took his fathers' books (they were written in Hebrew), and copied them. From that time he began to study them, while I was telling him everything that he was unable (to understand).[17]

According to this passage, Hebrew is the language in which the world had been created by God, it is the language of creation, spoken and revealed by God himself, used for the holy writings and spoken by mankind until the fall of the tower of Babylon. It was re-revealed to Abraham when he was chosen by God and, therefore, the use of the Hebrew language is a sign of belonging to the children of Abraham, of belonging to the chosen ones. Thus Hebrew had been considered as the sacred language, even if the first occurrence of the term לשון הקודש is attested only in the 1st century BC, in a fragment from Qumran.[18]

The translation of the Book of Ben Sira and the composition of its prologue was carried out at around the same time in which the compositions cited above were written. We should suppose, therefore, that the grandson of Ben Sira by using the term Ἑβραϊστι was aware not only of the clear-cut distinction between the Hebrew and the Aramaic language, but of the high

---

[15] See M. Rubin, "The Language of Creation or the Primordial Language: a Case of Cultural Polemics in Antiquity," *JJS* 49 (1998) 313.

[16] I.e., of the tower of Babel, see J.C. VanderKam, *The Book of Jubilees. A Critical Text* (CSCO Sc.Aeth. 87-88, Louvain: Peeters 1989) 73.

[17] *Jub* 12:25-27; translation from VanderKam, *The Book of Jubilees*, 73-74; Ethiopic text according to the critical edition of VanderKam. For detailed treatments of this passage see especially K. Müller, "Die hebräische Sprache der Halacha als Textur der Schöpfung: Beobachtungen zum Verhältnis von Tora und Halacha im Buch der Jubiläen," in *Bibel in jüdischer und christlicher Tradition: Festschrift für Johann Maier zum 60. Geburtstag* (eds. H. Merklein, *et al.*, Frankfurt: Anton Hain 1993) 157-62 and Rubin, "The Language of Creation," 310.

[18] 4Q464, which, although altogether in a poor state of preservation leaving the context in a high degree of uncertainty, clearly preserves these words, see Eshel, Esther and Stone, Michael, "The Holy Language at the End of the Days in Light of a New Fragment Found at Qumran," *Tarbiz* 62 (1992/93) 170-71 and 174 (in Hebrew).

national and religious importance ascribed by his contemporaries to the Hebrew language as well.

2. THE PRE-EMINENCE OF THE HEBREW TEXT

It is within this context that the reflections of the grandson of Ben Sira about the difficulties of his own translation project in particular as well as the difficulties of translating from Hebrew into Greek in general should be interpreted. In lines 15-20 of the prologue he writes as follows:[19]

> Παρακέκλησθε οὖν μετ' εὐνοίας καὶ προσοχῆς τὴν ἀνάγνωσιν ποεῖσθαι καὶ συγγνώμην ἔχειν ἐφ' οἷς ἂν δοκῶμεν τῶν κατὰ τὴν ἑρμηνείαν πεφιλοπονημένων τισὶν τῶν λέξεων ἀδυναμεῖν·("You are invited, therefore, to give a reading with goodwill and attention, and to have forbearance for those things where we may seem to lack ability in certain phrases, despite having labored diligently in the translation.")

Obviously, this passage, especially the last three lines (18-20), refers to possible criticism with regard to the good quality of the text which is in front of the reader. The question is only in which regard the of the text may be questioned: regarding the right rendering of the Hebrew original into the Greek language or regarding the right use of the Greek language? In other words, does the grandson of Ben Sira excuse himself for possibly not translating the original Hebrew correctly into Greek, or rather for not meeting the standards of good Greek?

The first understanding, although often followed,[20] seems to be difficult to accept, since we cannot assume that the readers of the Greek Book of Ben Sira had access to the Hebrew original and were able to compare the former with the latter.[21]

The second understanding has been recently elaborated by Benjamin Wright: "[...] the grandson in this passage appears to be asking the reader to

---

[19] The English text of the prologue follows the translation of Benjamin Wright for the "New English Translation of the Septuagint" (NETS), see B.G. Wright, "Why a Prologue? Ben Sira's Grandson and his Greek Translation," in *Emanuel. Studies in Hebrew Bible, Septuagint and Dead Sea Scrolls in Honor of Emanuel Tov* (eds. S. Paul, *et al.*, VTSup 94, Leiden: Brill 2003) 637.

[20] E.g., this understanding forms the basis for the German translation of Georg Sauer: "Laßt euch nun ermahnen, [...] Nachsicht zu haben dort, wo es scheinen könnte, daß wir trotz fleißigen Bemühens bei der Übersetzung in gewissen Fällen nicht ganz den richtigen Sinn getroffen haben." (Sauer, *Jesus Sirach [Ben Sira]* [JSHRZ 3, Gütersloh: Gütersloher Verlagshaus 1981] 505). Compare Wright, "Why a Prologue," 637.

[21] Generally speaking, the knowledge of Hebrew in Hellenistic Egyptian Jewry seems to have been rather poor, and the Prologue itself seems to support the view that the readers did not know Hebrew, since it says (lines 34f) that the translation has been made "for those living abroad who wish to gain learning", supposing that without translation they would not have been able to read Ben Sira's book, see B.G. Wright, "Access to the Source: Cicero, Ben Sira, the Septuagint and their Audiences," *JSJ* 34 (2003) 14 and compare the explanations of lines 23f of the prologue given below.

forgive any perceived inability of his *in the way he expresses things in Greek*."[22] In his interpretation, Wright stresses the understanding of the word ἑρμηνεία as "expression" over against "translation" or "interpretation." It should be added, however, that an ἑρμηνεία always stands in close connection with the message to be expressed. The term ἑρμηνεία refers to an expression insofar as it is related to a certain content, be it by way of translation, by way of interpretation, or by way of mediating a certain thought in speech or writing. Thus, although ἑρμηνεία in the prologue does indeed refer to the Greek text which lies in front of the reader, this text is clearly conceived as the result of a translation (or interpretation) of the original Hebrew. Most obviously, the translator asks the reader to forgive possible weaknesses of the Greek text which follows the prologue. At the same time, however, he seems to remind him that he had been committed not only to the rules of Greek language and style, but, as a translator, had been obliged to the original as well.

In the following two lines (21-22), the grandson of Ben Sira further develops this argument:

οὐ γὰρ ἰσοδυναμεῖ αὐτὰ ἐν ἑαυτοῖς Ἑβραϊστὶ λεγόμενα καὶ ὅταν μεταχθῇ εἰς ἑτέραν γλῶσσαν ("For those things originally in Hebrew do not have the same force when rendered into another language.")

This sentence has been understood as a critical view towards translation in general. For instance, Alexander di Lella in his commentary to Ben Sira explains the text as follows:

[T]he grandson articulates the anguish of translators throughout history: how to render one language into another in an idiomatic and accurate way and to capture at least some of the elegance of the original.[23]

The passage in question, however, is not a general statement about translation, but is rather a statement about the translation of Hebrew texts, or more specifically: It is a statement about the fundamental difference between a Hebrew text and its translation. According to the grandson of Ben Sira, there is no ἰσοδυναμία "equal force" between the two. Since this argument appears in the context of the grandson's apology for his Greek translation, it is obvious that he believes the Greek to have *less* force than the original Hebrew. It is, therefore, not he as the translator who is "lacking ability" (line 20: ἀδυναμεῖν), but it is the Greek language when used in the translation of a Hebrew text that lacks ability. In order to firmly establish this link, the grandson uses the wordplay between δοκῶμεν...ἀδυναμεῖν "we may seem to lack ability" (line 20) and the immediately following οὐ γὰρ ἰσοδυναμεῖ... "for [they, i.e. the Hebrew original and the Greek translation] do not have the same force" (line 21).

---

[22] Wright, "Why a Prologue," 639 (italics quoted from the original).
[23] P.W. Skehan and A.A. Di Lella, *The Wisdom of Ben Sira* (AB 39, New York: Doubleday 1987) 134.

Wagner in his analysis of the *hapax legomena* in the Book of Ben Sira successfully demonstrated that the meaning of ἰσοδυναμεῖν cannot be restricted to either the semantic or the stylistic dimension. Rather, it means "to have equal effective force in terms of content and form."[24] Thus, according to the grandson of Ben Sira, the translation of a Hebrew text into another language *a priori* does have less effective force on the reader than the Hebrew original.[25]

What the translator seems to promote here is the view that the content of a given Hebrew text cannot be separated from its being composed in the Hebrew language, since the message is inseparably intertwined with the Hebrew language itself. This view is reminiscent of the semiotic theory of language as advocated in Plato's *Kratylos* by Kratylos and Sokrates. According to this theory, a very close connection exists between the phonetic appearance of a given word and the thing—or rather the idea of the thing—the word refers to.[26] Plato's *Kratylos*, and specifically the part about etymology in which this theory of language as a naturalistic imitation of the world is developed in detail, was a favourite reading in the Hellenistic period[27] and deeply influenced the theory of language current among the Stoics.[28]

Of course, we cannot know whether or not the grandson of Ben Sira was aware of Plato's Kratylos or the philosophy of the Stoa, be it due to direct or indirect influence. We especially do not know, whether or not the grandson of Ben Sira would have been prepared to extend his view to texts in other languages as well, since the text of the prologue refers to Hebrew texts only. It seems, however, not impossible or even improbable that he was aware of the Platonic and Stoic theories of language,[29] and at least he seems to argue in a similar way.

What is certain, however, is that the translator's theory of mutual dependency of the content and the language of a given Hebrew text fits well with the contemporary views of Hebrew as a sacred language. Due to this high status of the Hebrew language, a text written in Hebrew must have been regarded as in itself more important than a Greek text. The prologue to the

---

[24] "Der Hauptakzent der Aussage liegt bei ἰσοδυναμεῖν zweifellos auf der δύναμις d.h. der (inhaltlichen und ästhetischen) Wirkkraft eines Textes auf seinen Leser," C. Wagner, *Die Septuaginta-Hapaxlegomena im Buch Ben Sira. Untersuchungen zur Wortwahl und Wortbildung unter besonderer Berücksichtigung des textkritischen und übersetzungstechnischen Aspekts* (BZAW 282, Berlin: de Gruyter 1999) 125.

[25] Compare G. Stemberger, "Hermeneutik der Jüdischen Bibel," in C. Dohmen and G. Stemberger, *Hermeneutik der Jüdischen Bibel und des Alten Testaments* (Stuttgart: Kohlhammer 1996) 52.

[26] See M. Kraus, "Platon (428/27-348/47 v. Chr.)," in *Klassiker der Sprachphilosophie: von Platon bis Noam Chomsky* (ed. T. Borsche, München: C.H. Beck 1996) 24-26.

[27] See Kraus, "Platon," 31.

[28] According to the Stoics, a given utterance is not just a reference to a certain thing, but it rather bears the thing in itself, cp. „Stoa (Beginn ca. 300 v. Chr.)," in *Klassiker der Sprachphilosophie*, 59.

[29] As to Ben Sira himself, influence of the Stoa seems probable, see R. Pautrel, "Ben Sira et le Stoïcisme," *RSR* 51 (1963) 535-49.

Book of Ben Sira, however, adds a further detail to the pre-eminence of Hebrew: Although a Hebrew text is not exactly untranslatable, it loses a lot of its power during translation. Any translation of a Hebrew text is much less important and less meaningful than the Hebrew original, and it will never have the same impact on the reader. Of course, this is quite different from the view of Aristeas, as we will later see.

3. THE EMERGENCE OF THE ORIGINAL

It seems that this view is closely connected to yet another development: The emergence of the concept of an authoritative "original text." Most obviously, if no translation will succeed to entirely reproduce a given Hebrew text, the Hebrew version always owning a significantly higher rank of authority than the translation, it will be the original against which the translation has to be held and which remains more important anyway.

In lines 23-24, immediately following the passage quoted above, the grandson of Ben Sira brings the Biblical books as an example for the differrence between original and translation:

οὐ μόνον δὲ ταῦτα ἀλλὰ καὶ αὐτὸς ὁ νόμος καὶ αἱ προφητεῖαι καὶ τὰ λοιπὰ τῶν βιβλίων οὐ μικρὰν ἔχει τὴν διαφορὰν ἐν ἑαυτοῖς λεγόμενα ("That is true not only for this book, but also the Law itself, the Prophets, and the rest of the books differ no little in the original.")

The way the Hebrew original is introduced at the end of the argument shows that the comparison proceeds from the Greek and not from the Hebrew version of the Law, the Prophecies and the remaining books. This proves, that the grandson of Ben Sira believed his Greek readers to be familiar with the Greek version of these books, but ignorant of the Hebrew text. In light of the preceding lines the "no little difference" obviously refers to the effective force on the reader, supposing that the Greek versions have less of it than the Hebrew original. Thus, the grandson of Ben Sira claims that the reader who really wants to know what is written in these books would have to read the Hebrew original.[30]

This attitude towards translations seems to have been by no means self-evident in the second half of the 2nd century BCE. The *Letter of Aristeas*, trying to answer the very same question about the authority of the translation, even contradicts the prologue in claiming equal authority for both the Hebrew and the Greek versions of the Torah.[31] On the other hand, the coincidence that both the *Letter of Aristeas* and the prologue to the Book of Ben Sira

---

[30] Compare Boccaccini's conclusion that for the grandson of Ben Sira, the original Hebrew had primacy "over any translation, whose worth is limited to a didactic role," G. Boccaccini, *Middle Judaism: Jewish Thought, 300 B.C.E. to 200 C.E.* (Minneapolis: Fortress Press 1991) 162.

[31] See H. Orlinsky, "The Septuagint as Holy Writ and the Philosophy of the Translators," *HUCA* 46(1975) 96-97.

deal with the subject of the original and its authority suggests that this question was being virulent at that time.

Although the grandson of Ben Sira and the *Letter of Aristeas* do not touch the question of the original in general, but rather focus on the original of a translation, the contemporary discussion of the problem does not seem to have been restricted to that field. This conclusion may be drawn if we look on the concepts of the "Heavenly Tablets" and primordial writing contained in the *Book of Jubilees*. As García Martínez has demonstrated, the Heavenly Tablets referred to in this book time and again were ascribed different functions. Most importantly, the Heavenly Tablets are said to record prescriptions running parallel to the text of the Torah[32] along with prescriptions not contained in the Torah.[33] In terms of their function, the latter should be compared to the Rabbinic concept of Oral Torah (תורה שבעל פה), as Florentino García Martínez suggests:

> The H[eavenly] T[ablets] constitute a hermeneutical recourse which permits the presentation of the "correct" interpretation of the Law, adapting it to the changing situations of life.[34]

In difference to תורה שבעל פה, however, the prescriptions of the Heavenly Tablets are essentially in writing, as has been pointed out by Hindy Najman.[35] It seems, therefore, that the expression "Heavenly Tablets" refers to the concept of a pre-existent written Torah, comprising both the Law as submitted to Moses on Mount Sinai as well as additional written prescriptions. Therefore, the Torah written on the Heavenly Tablets is the "original" as against the Sinaitic Torah known to the reader, and the latter may be interpreted, expanded and possibly even modified with reference to the former, the pre-existent Torah.[36]

Obviously, the concept of the original facilitates and even creates a critical distance with regard to the actual text which lies in front of the reader. This distance seems to have been something new in the 2nd century BCE,[37] and at least it is, to the best of my knowledge, unknown to the books

---

[32] F. García Martínez, "The Heavenly Tablets in the Book of Jubilees," in *Studies in the Book of Jubilees* (eds. M. Albani, *et al.*, TSAJ 65, Tübingen: Mohr Siebeck 1997) 243-46.

[33] García Martínez, "The Heavenly Tablets," 251-58.

[34] García Martínez, "The Heavenly Tablets," 258.

[35] H. Najman, "Interpretation as Primordial Writing: Jubilees and Its Authority Conferring Strategies," *JSJ* 30 (1999) 410.

[36] The concept of a pre-existent Torah is well known in Rabbinic Judaism, e.g. SifDev 37: קדם מפעליו מאז תורה לפי שחביבה מכל נבראת קודם לכל שנאמר [משלי ח כב] ה' קנני ראשית דרכו see N.M. Samuelson and G. Stemberger, "Schöpfer/Schöpfung, IV. Judentum," in *TRE* 30: 292.

[37] According to Albert Pietersma and Benjamin Wright III, the intention of the Septuagint translators was from the very beginning "bringing the reader to the original," which would imply that already these Greek translators denied their translation any independence from the original, see Wright, "Access," 24. However, the fact that the Greek translations include numerous exegetical elements, actualizations

of the Hebrew bible. Thus for instance, although the Ten Commandments had been revealed to Moses, the Torah itself suggests that the actual text of the Ten Commandments in Exod 20 and Deut 5 is identical with this early revelation. In other passages, the distance between the reader and the text even seems to be purposefully levelled out. A good example for the latter device is Deut 28:58:

אם לא תשמר לעשות את כל דברי התורה הזאת הכתובים הספר הזה ("If you do not dili-gently observe all the words of this law that are written in *this book* [...]")

Most obviously, the reader of this passage is supposed to connect the deictic reference "in this book" (בספר הזה) with the book he currently holds in his hands, thus ignoring any possible distance. By contrast to the concept of the "original" versus the actual text, this concept found in Deuteronomy may be called the concept of "ritual presence" of the text,[38] the text being present in the course of reading.

The concept of the "original text" seems to be unattested in Judaism prior to the 2nd century BCE. Therefore, the evidence of the prologue to the Book of Ben Sira, the *Letter of Aristeas* and the *Book of Jubilees* suggests that it has been developed as an innovation in the second half of the 2nd century BC. Although the focus of the prologue to Ben Sira and the *Letter of Aristeas*, on the one hand, and of the Book of Jubilees, on the other, seems to be quite different—the latter being focused on the pre-existent Torah, the former on the *Vorlage* of a translation—the essence seems basically identical: The emergence of a distinction between the "original" (or "ideal") and the "actual" text.

As to this distinction, the prologue to the Book of Ben Sira even seems to provide an illuminating Greek terminology which may give the modern reader more insights: The "original" of the translation is called τὰ ἐν ἑαυτοῖς λεγόμενα, which may be literally translated as "the things said in themselves". Since "things" refers to the content, the expression "in themselves" obviously refers to the form, supposing that the "original" is where the content finds its appropriate form and both, content and form, create an ideal union.

The possible counterpart of the terminus τὰ ἐν ἑαυτοῖς λεγόμενα "ideal text" may be found in line 29 of the Book of Ben Sira, although it is not used with regard to a text, but with regard to the measure of Jewish education in Egypt: The grandson of Ben Sira writes as follows (lines 25-29):

---

as well as adaptations to the world of the translators, seems to stand against this claim, although the perspective of "Übersetzung als Vollendung der Auslegung," as proposed by Martin Rösel with regard to Genesis-LXX, seems to be too extreme in the opposite direction: *Übersetzung als Vollendung der Auslegung. Studien zur Genesis-Septuaginta* (BZAW 223, Berlin: de Gruyter 1994).

[38] Compare J.W. Watts, "Ritual Legitimacy and Scriptural Authority," *JBL* 124 (2005) 410-12.

> I arrived in Egypt in the thirty-eighth year of the reign of King Euergetes, and during my stay I came across the similarity (ἀφόμοιον) of a good deal of instruction.

The meaning of the word ἀφόμοιον is much disputed and not entirely clear. It seems me, however, that Wagner has successfully demonstrated that ἀφόμοιον should be understood as "similarity."[39]

Thus, the grandson of Ben Sira expresses his surprise that the Jewish education in Egypt is very similar to the standards he is used to, that is in Palestine, although it is not and will not be identical. It seems to me that this term ἀφόμοιον is the counterpart to the "original" or "ideal" and similarly could have said with regard to a text, all the more so since the Jewish education in Egypt has been based on a translation.

According to the grandson of Ben Sira, Jewish education in Egypt is only an ἀφόμοιον, because it is based on an ἀφόμοιον.

CONCLUSION

In 2nd century BC Judaism, Hebrew and Aramaic were commonly recognized as different languages, the former being a national and a religious identity marker of highest importance. When referring to the Hebrew language and the translation of Hebrew texts, the prologue to the Book of Ben Sira most probably proceeds from this notion of the Hebrew language. The translator adds, however, a further thought: A Hebrew text, when translated, has less effect on the reader than the original. The reason is that the ideal union between form and content which characterizes the original has been destroyed. The theory of language which stands behind this theory of translation has parallels in the theories of language as developed in Plato's *Kratylos* and among the Stoics.

The prologue's reflections about the restricted translatability of Hebrew texts should be seen in the context of the concept of the "ideal text" versus the "actual text," which seems to have been an innovation in 2nd century BCE Judaism.

This concept of the "ideal text," it seems to me, was an important step towards the creation of the concept of "canon," leading to the stabilization of the wording of Hebrew texts from the 1st century BCE onwards.

---

[39] "[…D]as substantivierte Adjektiv ἀφόμοιον (bezeichnet) in positiver Konnotation eine relativierende Ähnlichkeit (nicht jedoch Gleichheit bzw. -rangigkeit!) gegenüber einem Original […]," Wagner, *Die Septuaginta-Hapaxlegomena*, 120.

"THE LAW, THE PROPHETS, AND THE OTHER BOOKS OF THE FATHERS" (SIR, PROLOGUE) CANONICAL LISTS IN BEN SIRA AND ELSEWHERE?

Armin Lange
(University of Vienna)

Since the beginnings of critical research in the book of Ecclesiasticus, scholars understood its Greek prologue as referring to the three parts of the later Hebrew canon[1] or to a comparable tripartite collection of scriptures.[2]

---

[1] See e.g H.B. Swete, *An Introduction to the Old Testament in Greek* (ed. R.R. Ottley, with an Appendix Containing the Letter of Aristeas by H.S.T. Thackeray, Cambridge: Cambridge University Press 1902) 24; A. Eberharter, *Der Kanon des Alten Testaments zur Zeit des Ben Sira: Auf Grund der Beziehungen des Sirachbuches zu den Schriften des A. T. dargestellt* (ATA 3.3, Münster: Aschendorff 1911) 2-4, 52-54; O. Eissfeldt, *Einleitung in das Alte Testament unter Einschluß der Apokryphen und Pseudepigraphen sowie der apokryphen- und pseudepigraphenarten Qumrānschriften: Entstehungsgeschichte des Alten Testaments* (3rd ed., Neue theologische Grundrisse, Tübingen: Mohr Siebeck 1964) 766-67; J.C.H. Lebram, "Aspekte der alttestamentlichen Kanonbildung," *VT* 18 (1968) 173-89, 175; J.G. Snaith, *Ecclesiasticus or the Wisdom of Jesus Son of Sirach* (CBC, Cambridge: Cambridge University Press 1974) 8; S.Z. Leiman, *The Canonization of Hebrew Scripture: The Talmudic and Midrashic Evidence* (TCAAS 47, Hamden: Archon Books 1976) 29; R.A.F. MacKenzie, *Sirach* (OTM 19, Wilmington: Glazier 1983) 20-21; R.T. Beckwith, *The Old Testament Canon of the New Testament Church and its Background in Early Judaism* (London: SPCK 1985) 110-11; idem, "The Formation of the Hebrew Bible," in *Mikra: Text, Translation, Reading and Interpretation of the Hebrew Bible in Ancient Judaism and Early Christianity* (eds. M.J. Mulder and H. Sysling, CRINT 2.1, Assen: Van Gorcum 1988) 39-86, 52; H. Burkhardt, *Die Inspiration heiliger Schriften bei Philo von Alexandrien* (2nd ed., Giessen: Brunnenverlag 1992), 138-39; H.M. Orlinsky, "Some Terms in the Prologue to Ben Sira and the Hebrew Canon," *JBL* 110 (1991) 483-90; L.H. Schiffman, *Reclaiming the Dead Sea Scrolls: The History of Judaism, the Background of Christianity, the Lost Library of Qumran* (Philadelphia: JPS 1994) 164; H.-J. Fabry, "Die Qumrantexte und das biblische Kanonproblem," in *Recht und Ethos im Alten Testament—Gestalt und Wirkung: Festschrift für Horst Seebass zum 65. Geburtstag* (Neukirchen-Vluyn: Neukirchener Verlag 1999) 251-71, 252, 266; P. Brandt, *Endgestalten des Kanons: Das Arrangement der Schriften Israels in der jüdischen und christlichen Bibel* (BBB 131, Berlin: Philo 2001) 69-70, 121; G. Steins, *Die Chronik als kanonisches Abschlußphänomen: Studien zur Entstehung und Theologie von 1/2Chronik* (BBB 93, Weinheim: Beltz Athenäum 1995) 512; G. Sauer, *Jesus Sirach / Ben Sira: Übersetzt und erklärt* (ATD Apokryphen 1, Göttingen: Vandenhoeck & Ruprecht 2000) 37-38; J. Marböck, "Text und Übersetzung—Horizonte einer Ausle-

Good examples are the commentary of Patrick W. Skehan and Alexander A. Di Lella and the remarks of James C. VanderKam:

> Here for the first time mention is made of the threefold division of the OT: the Law, Heb *tôrâ*, the Prophets, Heb *nĕbî'îm*, and "the later authors," or the other books of our ancestors"..., or "the rest of the books"... The third division, referred to in a somewhat general way by the grandson, came to be known later as the Writings, Heb *kĕtûbîm*. The Jews today still use these three divisions, calling the OT as a whole *Tanak*...[3]

> These statements show that the grandson was obviously familiar with a threefold division of the ancestral books, a division not dissimilar from the later law-pro-phets-writings arrangement of the Hebrew Bible.[4]

Alternatively, the prologue to Ecclesiasticus was read as referring to a bipartite canon of law and prophets (sometimes regarded as not closed) while the other books mentioned would designate non-canonical Jewish texts.[5]

---

gung im Prolog zum Griechischen Sirach," in *Horizonte biblischer Texte, FS J.M. Oesch* (OBO 196, Fribourg: Academic Press Fribourg 2003) 109-11.

[2] A.G. Sundberg, "The Septuagint: The Bible of Hellenistic Judaism," in *The Canon Debate* (eds. L.M. McDonald and J.A. Sanders, Peabody: Hendrickson 2002) 68-90, 80-81; idem, *The Old Testament of the Early Church* (HTS 20, Cambridge: Harvard University Press 1964) 67-69; A. van der Kooij, "Canonization of Ancient Hebrew Books and Hasmonean Politics," in *The Biblical Canons* (eds. J.-M. Auwers and H.J. de Jonge, BETL 163, Leuven: Peeters 2003) 27-38; cf. idem, "The Canonization of Ancient Books Kept in the Temple of Jerusalem," in *Canonization and Decanonization: Papers Presented to the International Conference of the Leiden Institute for the Study of Religions (LISOR), Held at Leiden 9-10 January 1997* (eds. A. van der Kooij and K. van der Toorn, SHR 82, Leiden: Brill 1998) 17-40, 23-24.

[3] P.W. Skehan and A.A. Di Lella, *The Wisdom of Ben Sira: A New Translation with Notes* (AB 39, New York: Doubleday 1987) 133.

[4] J.C. VanderKam, "Revealed Literature in the Second Temple Period," in idem, *From Revelation to Canon: Studies in the Hebrew Bible and Second Temple Literature* (JSJSup 62, Leiden: Brill 2000) 1-30, 6; cf. also idem, *The Dead Sea Scrolls Today* (Grand Rapids: Eerdmans 1994) 143-44.

[5] See e.g. H. Graetz, *Kohelet* קהלת *oder der Salomonische Prediger: Übersetzt und Kritisch Erläutert* (Leipzig: Winter 1871) 151-52; T.N. Swanson, *The Closing of the Collection of Holy Scriptures: A Study in the History of the Canonization of the Old Testament* (Ph.D. diss., Nashville: Vanderbilt University 1970) 125-31; J. Barton, *Oracles of God: Perceptions of Ancient Prophecy in Israel after the* Exile (New York: Oxford University Press 1986) 47-48; J.G. Campbell, "4QMMT[d] and the Tripartite Canon," *JSJ* 51 (2000) 181-90, 187: J.C. Trebolle Barrera, "Origins of a Tripartite Old Testament Canon," in *The Canon Debate*, 128-45, 129; P. Flint, "Scriptures in the Dead Sea Scrolls: The Evidence from Qumran," in *Emanuel: Studies in Hebrew Bible, Septuagint, and Dead Sea Scrolls in Honor of Emanuel Tov* (eds. S.M. Paul *et al.*, VTSup 94, Leiden: Brill 2003) 269-304, 280; E. Ulrich, "The Non-attestation of a Tripartite Canon in 4QMMT," *CBQ* 65 (2003) 202-14, 211-13; idem, "Qumran and the Canon of the Old Testament," in *The Biblical Canons*, 57-80, 71.

Only rarely was this scholarly common opinion of the prologue's importance for the canonical history of the Hebrew Bible questioned. An example is David M. Carr.

> Contrary to the typical interpretation of this passage, I would argue that this prologue emphasizing Ben Sira's broader studies is not endorsing a category of Scripture like the later "Writings" of the rabbinic Tanach. Instead, he is prefacing his translation of Ben Sira with an endorsement of the ongoing worth of study of Hellenistic-period works *like the Book of Ben Sira itself.* This endorsement, made around 130 B.C.E., would have been particularly urgent in the wake of the recent ascendance of the Hasmonean monarchy in Palestine and their early promotion of an emergent "Torah and Prophets" Hebrew scriptural collection, one that excluded Hellenistic period works by "father"-teachers like Ben Sira because they were postprophetic. In other words, the prologue to Ben Sira is not an endorsement of a proto-rabbinic canon of "Torah, Prophets and [Writings]." Rather, it is one of the first testimonies of Jewish resistance to a Hebrew collection of Scripture promoted by the Hasmoneans and (much like the one) used by the rabbis.[6]

But does the scholarly common opinion of a tripartite canon in the prologue to Ecclesiasticus stand scrutiny or are the few critical voices entitled to be heard?

To answer this question, I will discuss some terminological issues and survey the lists of Jewish authorities and Jewish literature from the 2nd and early 1st cent. BCE. Afterwards, I will analyze the three lists of Jewish literature in the prologue to Ecclesiasticus and its reception by the *Letter of Aristeas.* A second survey will study the lists of Jewish authorities in later Jewish literature. At the end of this paper, I will draw some conclusions.

TERMINOLOGY

The earliest use of the Greek word κανών as a designation of a list of books is Athanasius' thirty-ninth Easter letter dated to 367 CE. Hence, to use the term "canon" in modern scholarship on ancient Judaism runs the danger of cross-cultural misconceptions. I therefore use a more nuanced terminology which was introduced into the study of the Hebrew Bible's canonical history by Eugene Ulrich.[7] Ulrich distinguishes between an "authoritative text," "that a community, secular or religious, acknowledges to hold authority" and "a book of scripture" as "a sacred authoritative text which, in the Jewish or Christian context, the community acknowledges as having authority over

---

[6] D.M. Carr, *Writing on the Tablet of Heart: Origins of Scripture and Literature* (Oxford: Oxford University Press 2005) 265.

[7] E. Ulrich, "The Canonical Process, Textual Criticism, and Latter Stages in the Composition of the Bible," in *Sha'arei Talmon: Studies in the Bible, Qumran, and the Ancient Near East Presented to Shemaryahu Talmon* (eds. M. Fishbane *et al.*, Winona Lake: Eisenbrauns 1992) 267-91, esp. 269-76; idem, "Canon," in *Encyclopedia of the Dead Sea Scrolls* (eds. L.H. Schiffman and J.C. VanderKam, Oxford: Oxford University Press 2000) 1: 117-20, esp. 117.

the faith and practice of its members." The term "canon" refers to "the established and exclusive list of books that hold supreme authoritative status for a community." Finally, the term "canonical process" or canonical history designates the process beginning with the recognition of authoritative texts and ending in an exclusive canonical list of books having binding authority.

LISTS OF JEWISH AUTHORITIES IN THE 2ND AND EARLY 1ST CENTURY BCE

From the non-Essene literature of the 2nd and early 1st century BCE only bipartite lists of Jewish literature are preserved.

Although *Non-Canonical Psalms B* might predate the prologue to Ecclesiasticus significantly,[8] a canonical list preserved in this text would be of great importance for its interpretation. H.-J. Fabry[9] wants to find such a reference to a bipartite canon in the mention of both prophets and Moses in 4QNon-*Canonical Psalms B* (4Q381) 69 4, 5. In this canon the prophets would be of higher authority than Moses because they are mentioned first.

4   ]בכם ויתתם לכם ברוחו נביאים להשכיל וללמד אתכם

5sup   ]°כם מן שמים ירד וידברעמכם להשכיל אתכם ולהשיב ממעשי ישבי

5   נתן חֻקים תורות ומצות בברית העמיד בידֻן משהן °°°

4]*bkm*, and he gave them to you by his spirit, prophets to instruct and to teach you
5sup].*km* from heaven he came down, and he spoke with you to instruct you and to turn (you) away from the deeds of the inhabitants of
5 He gave la]ws, instructions and commandments by the covenant he established through[Moses]...[10]

But lines 4 and 5 of fragment 69 are divided by an extensive supralinear correction of a haplography by the original scribe[11] which puts considerable textual distance between the mention of the prophets and the reference to Moses. Furthermore, as in deuteronomistic literature, Moses seems to be understood by 4QNon-*Canonical Psalms B* (4Q381) 69 4, 5sup, 5 as a prophet[12] who was preceded by other prophets such as Abraham, Isaac, and Jacob. Such an understanding of the patriarchs as prophets is also attested in Ps 105:15. And Tob 4:12 describes Noah, Abraham, Isaac, and Jacob as prophets.[13] 4QNon-*Canonical Psalms B* (4Q381) 69 4, 5 lists thus neither the two

---

[8] For a dating of *Non-Canonical Psalms B* in Persian or Early Hellenistic times, see E. Schuller, *Non-Canonical Psalms from Qumran: A Pseudepigraphic Collection* (HSS 28, Atlanta: Scholars Press 1986) 21-23.

[9] Fabry, "Qumrantexte," 266.

[10] Transcription and translation according to E. Schuller, "Non-Canonical Psalms," *DJD* 11 (1998) 75-172, 149, 150.

[11] Cf. Schuller, "Non-Canonical Psalms," 151.

[12] See below.

[13] For a similar interpretation, see Schuller, *Non-Canonical Psalms from Qumran*, 206; cf. also idem, "Non-Canonical Psalms," 151.

parts of a bipartite canon nor two categories of Jewish literature but puts Moses in line with earlier patriarchal prophets.

In the 2nd century BCE, 4QapocrJer Cᵉ (4Q390) 2 i 5 speaks of Moses and the prophets.[14]

וּבַ֗יוֹבֵל ההוא יהיו מפרים את כול חקותי ואת כל מצותי אשר אצוה בני֯ד
מושה ובי֯ד עבדי הנביאים

> And] in that jubilee they will be annulling all my laws and all my commandments which I commanded thr[ough Moses and throu]gh my servants the prophets (4QapocrJer Cᵉ (4Q390) 2 i 4-5)[15]

In this heavily damaged passage of the *Apocryphon of Jeremiah*, the prophet Jeremiah predicts a jubilee of lawlessness connected with the Hellenistic religious reforms of the years 175-164 BCE. Israel is accused of abandoning the laws and commandments which God gave through Moses and through the prophets. In 4QapocrJer Cᵉ (4Q390) 2 i 5, the *Apocryphon of Jeremiah* does not provide an exclusive list of canonical literature but a historical retrospect. The text specifies through which authorities God revealed the laws neglected by Judah during the Hellenistic religious reforms, i.e. through Moses and the prophets. This pairing of Moses and the prophets reflects a deuteronnomistic idea of prophecy, which is expressed in Deut 18:15-19.[16]

> 15 The Lord your God will raise up for you a prophet like me from among your own people; you shall heed such a prophet. 16 This is what you requested of the Lord your God at Horeb on the day of the assembly when you said: "If I hear the voice of the Lord my God any more, or ever again see this great fire, I will die." 17 Then the Lord replied to me: "They are right in what they have said. 18 I will raise up for them a prophet like you from among their own people; I will put my words in the mouth of the prophet, who shall speak to them everything that I command. 19 Anyone who does not heed the words that the prophet shall speak in my name, I myself will hold accountable..."

---

[14] For the *Apocryphon of Jeremiah* as non-Essene text, see S. White Crawford, "Jeremiah, Book of: Pseudo-Jeremiah," in *Encyclopedia of the Dead Sea Scrolls* 1: 400-02, 401. D. Dimant, *Qumran Cave 4.XXI: Parabiblical Texts, Part 4: Pseudo-Prophetic Texts* (DJD 30, Oxford: Clarendon Press 2001) 112, classifies the *Apocryphon of Jeremiah* as intermediate between sectarian and non-sectarian literature. Dimant dates the *Apocryphon of Jeremiah* to the last quarter of the 2nd cent. BCE (ibid., 116).

[15] My reconstruction is based on 1QS i 3. The *dalet* before עבדי suggests ובי֯ד which would in turn recommend בני֯ד מושה in the *lacuna*. Guided by 2 Kgs 17:13, Dimant (*Pseudo-Prophetic Texts*, 245, 247) reconstructs אשר אצוה או֯ותם ואשלח בי֯ד עבדי הנביא֯ים "which I commanded them and (which) I sent through my servants, the prophets."

[16] For Deut 18:15-19 as part of a more extensive deuteronomistic addition to Deuteronomy (Deut 18:9-22), see A. Lange, *Vom prophetischen Wort zur Prophetischen Tradition: Studien zur Traditions- und Redaktionsgeschichte innerprophetischer Konflikte in der Hebräischen Bibel* (FAT 34, Tübingen: Mohr Siebeck 2002) 169-75.

In this passage, Moses is understood as the supreme prophet. All other prophets are his successors. God commanded laws not only through Moses but also through his prophetic successors. Moses is at the beginning of a long line of prophetic lawgivers.[17]

Such a bipartite list of Moses and the prophets seems also to occur in the *Words of the Heavenly Luminaries (Dibre HaMe'orot)*[18] — a non-Essene text from the middle of the 2nd century BCE.[19] 4QDibHam[a] (4Q504) 1-2 iii 12-14 reads:

את כול אל[ות]יכה אשר כתב מושה ועבדיכה הנביאים אש[ר
ש]לחתה ל[נקר]תנו הרעה באחרית הימים

all]your[execrat]ions[20] which Moses wrote and your servants, the prophets, whic[h] you [s]ent so that the evil may [befa]ll us in the last days (4QDibHam[a] (4Q504) 1-2 iii 12-14)

But unlike the formula employed in 4QapocrJer C[e] (4Q390) 2 i 5, Moses and the prophets are connected with two different verbal acts. Moses writes execrations (כתב; cf. Deut 28:15-68) and the prophets are sent by God to assure that evil will befall Israel in the last days. 4QDibHam[a] (4Q504) 1-2 iii 12-14 can thus neither be regarded as a list of Hebrew scriptures nor as a list of authorities through which God communicated his law.

The mention of the law and the prophets in 2 Macc 15:9 has sometimes been understood as attesting to a bipartite canon.[21] Written almost at the same time as the prologue to Ecclesiasticus,[22] the verse describes how Judah Maccabee tries to boost the morale of his men.

---

[17] For the idea that god commands his laws through the prophets, see 2 Kgs 17:13; Zech 7:12; Ezra 9:10-11; 2 Chr 29:25; 4Q*Non-Canonical Psalms B* 69 4; Dan 9:10; 4QpHos[a] ii 5.

[18] Cf. the references of M. Baillet to 1QS viii 15-16; Luke 16:29; 24:27; Acts 26:22 (*Qumrân grotte 4.III (4Q482-4Q520)* [DJD 7, Oxford: Clarendon Press 1982] 143) and the reference of J.R. Davila to 1QS i 3 in his commentary on 4QDibHam[a] (4Q504) 1-2 iii 12-13 (*Liturgical Works* [ECDSS 6, Grand Rapids: Eerdmans 2000] 258).

[19] For *Words of the Heavenly Luminaries* as a non-Essene text, see D.K. Falk, *Daily, Sabbath, and Festival Prayers in the Dead Sea Scrolls* (STDJ 27, Leiden: Brill 1998) 61-94, and E. Chazon, "Words of the Luminaries," in *Encyclopedia of the Dead Sea Scrolls* 2: 989-90, 989. For a date of this text in the early or middle 2nd cent. BCE, see eadem, *A Liturgical Document from Qumran and Its Implications: "Words of the Luminaries" (4QDib Ham)* (Ph.D. diss., Jerusalem: Hebrew University, 1991) 81-85.

[20] For this reconstruction, see Davila, *Liturgical Works*, 257.

[21] See e.g. J.A. Goldstein, *II Maccabees: A New Translation with Introduction and Commentary* (AB 41A, New York: Doubleday 1983) 497; Sundberg, "Septuagint," 80; Trebolle Barrera, "Origins," 130.

[22] The epitome of Jason of Cyrene perserved in 2 Maccabees was produced shortly after 124 BCE (see H. Engel, "Die Bücher der Makkabäer," in E. Zenger *et al., Einleitung in das Alte Testament* [5th ed., Stuttgart: Kohlhammer 2004] 312-28, 326-27).

Encouraging them from the law and the prophets, and reminding them also of the struggles they had won, he made them the more eager.[23]

Although read in light of the later Hebrew Bible the phrase "from the law and the prophets" (ἐκ τοῦ νόμου καὶ τῶν προφητῶν) raises the impression of a dual canon, this is not what 2 Maccabees relates. It emphasizes that Judah Maccabee referred his fighters to stories out of the law and prophetic books which illustrate how God would support his people in a military conflict. There are no delimitations for which books constitute the law, which texts belong to the prophetic books, and which do not. As with the other bipartite lists discussed below, 2 Macc 15:9 characterizes just the categories of literature Judah Maccabee referred to. It does not even imply that only the two literary categories—i.e. of law and prophets—exist. The only thing stressed is that books belonging to these two categories were quoted by Judah Maccabee.

In Essene literature, the pairing of Moses and the prophets occurs several times. The collective manuscript 1QS[24] attests to such a pairing of Moses and the prophets in two of its community rules, i.e. in 1QS i 2-3 and in 1QS viii 15-16. 1QS i 2-3 is part of a long chain of infinitive-constructions (1QS i 1-11) which defines the purpose of the first community rule (1QS i-iv).

ל[עשות הטוב והישר לפניו כאשר צוה ביד מושה וביד כול עבדיו הנביאים

to do the good and the right before him according to what he commanded through Moses and through his servants the prophets (1QS i 2-3)[25].

1QS i 2-3 employs deuteronomistic language and deuteronomistic ideas. The formula לעשות הטוב והישר לפניו recalls similar formulae in the book of Deuteronomy (e.g. Deut 6:18). In the case of 1QS i 3, God has revealed "what is good and right before him" by way of Moses and the prophets, i.e. God has given his commands through them. As argued before, the pairing of Moses and the prophets reflects a deuteronomistic idea of prophecy which understands Moses as the first in a long line of prophetic lawgivers (cf. Deut 18:15-19). Similarly, in 1QS i 3, the pairing of Moses and the prophets does

---

[23] Translation according to the RSV.

[24] For 1QS as a collective manuscript and its various community rules see H. Stegemann, "Zu Textbestand und Grundgedanken von 1QS III,13-IV,26," *RevQ* 13 (1988) 95-131, 96-100; A. Lange, *Weisheit und Prädestination: Weisheitliche Urordnung und Prädestination in den Textfunden von Qumran* (STDJ 18, Leiden: Brill 1995) 124-26. For the complicated literary growth of the material collected in 1QS, see S. Metso, *The Textual Development of the Qumran Community Rule* (STDJ 21, Leiden: Brill 1997).

[25] In 1QS i 2-3, no textual deviations from 4QpapSᵃ 1 2-4 and 4QpapSᶜ I 2 can be observed.

not designate two different literary entities which could be construed as a dual canon,[26] but one chain of halakhic authorities which follow each other.

As halakhic authorities, Moses and the prophets are also mentioned in 1QS viii 14 and its parallels in the 4QS-manuscripts.[27]

הואה]מד[ר[ש התורה אש]ר[צֻוה ביד מֹשה

This is the [stu]d[y of the law, whic]h he commanded through Moses (4QS^e iii 6).

היאה מדרש התורה צוה ביד מושה לעשות ככול הנגלה עת בעת וכאשר גלו
הנביאים ברוח קודשו

This is the study of the law, (which) he commanded through Moses, so that one acts according to everything that was revealed from age to age and according to what the prophets revealed by way of his holy spirit (1QS viii 15-16).

היאה מדרש התור]ה אשר צוה בי]ד מושה לע]ש[ות כל[הנגל[ה] ע[ת בעת
28וא]שר גלו הנב[יאים ברוח קודשו

This is the study of the la]w which he commanded thro[ugh Moses, so that one d]oes everything [which is revealed] from a[ge to age and what the prophets revealed by way of his holy spirit (4QS^d vi 7-8).

In 1QS viii 14 and 4QS^e iii 6, the preceding quotation of Isa 40:3—to prepare a way for the Lord in the wilderness—is interpreted as the study of the law. Although Isa 40:3 is alluded to in 4QS^d vi 6-7, an explicit quotation of it is missing in 4QS^d.[29] Hence, in 4QS^d the quotation of Isa 40:3 itself seems to have been lost due to scribal error.

The earliest version of the community rule attested in 1QS v-xi is preserved in manuscript 4QS^e.[30] In the text of 1QS viii 15, this manuscript speaks only of the study of the Torah, which God commanded through Moses. In 4QS^e iii 6, the precepts for the Maskil (1QS ix 12ff.) follow the interpretation of Isa 40:3 immediately. 1QS viii 15-ix 11 is thus a later addition to the community rule attested in 1QS v-xi.[31]

---

[26] For an interpretation of this passage as a mention of a dual canon, see Schiffman, *Reclaiming*, 165; Fabry, "Qumrantexte," 256; Trebolle Barrera, "Origins," 131; Flint, "Scriptures," 290.

[27] For an interpretation of this passage as a mention of a dual canon, see Trebolle Barrera, "Origins," 131.

[28] P. Alexander and G. Vermes (*Qumran Cave 4.XIX: Serekh Ha-Yahad and Two Related Texts* [DJD 26, Oxford: Clarendon Press 1998] 105) and Metso (*Textual Development*, 44) reconstruct with 1QS viii 16 וכאשר. But in my opinion the parallel construction with הנגלה כל] (1QS viii 15 reads הנגלה ככול) suggests that the preposition כ should be excluded from the reconstruction of this line.

[29] Cf. Metso, *Textual Development*, 85.

[30] Cf. e.g. Metso, *Textual Development*, 143-49.

[31] Cf. Metso, *Textual Development*, 71-73, 118.

While in 4QS^e, the study of the Torah seems to be exemplified by precepts for the Maskil, in the later versions of this community rule attested by 1QS and 4QS^d, the purpose of the study of the Torah is specified, i.e. to act according to everything which is revealed and according to what the prophets revealed. The word הנגלה ("that what is revealed") is a technical term which stands in opposition to הנסתר ("that what is hidden") in Essene texts. While נסתר designates a special hidden interpretation of the law to which only the Essenes had access, נגלה identifies the meaning of law which was open to a broader Jewish public.[32] When 1QS viii 15-16 and 4QS^d vi 7-8 link this publicly accessible meaning of the law with the prophets they create a bipartite structure which resembles 1QS i 3. As in 1QS i 3, in 1QS viii 15-16 both prophets and Moses are of interest only as channels through which God commanded the law. As before, we encounter the deuteronomistic understanding of the prophets as lawgivers and successors of the lawgiving prophet Moses. And as before, in 1QS viii 15-16 and 4QS^d vi 7-8, the bipartite formulation "everything what is revealed and what is revealed through the prophets" does not describe a bipartite canon[33] but a group of halakhic authorities through which God revealed his laws in different times.

A reference in the *Damascus Document*[34] which suffered from scribal error in manuscript CD A (CD v 21-vi 1), seems to argue in a similar way as 1QS i 3 and 1QS viii 15-16 do.

כי דברו עצה סרה על[מצוות אל ב׳׳ד]מושה וגם במשיחי הקודש

for they spoke rebellious counsel against] the precepts of God through [Moses and also through the anointed ones of the holy one (4QD^a 3 ii 8-9).

כי דברו עצה סרה על מצוות אל בן֯ד]מושה[*vac* וגם במשיחי הקודש

for they spoke rebellious counsel against the precepts of God th[r]ough M[oses] *vac* and also through the anointed ones of the holy one (4QD^b 2 5-6).

כי דברו סרה על מצות אל ביד משה וגם במשיחו הקודש

for they spoke rebellion against the precepts of God through Moses and also through his anointed[35] the holy one (CD v 21-vi 1).

Crucial for the understanding of this reference is the phrase "through the anointed ones of the holy one" (במשיחי הקודש). The parallel placement of Moses and the anointed ones in 4QD^b 2 5-6 (cf. CD v 21-vi 1) argues for the

[32] See L.H. Schiffman, *The Halakhah at Qumran* (SJLA 16, Leiden: Brill 1975) 22-32.

[33] Thus e.g. Schiffman, *Reclaiming*, 165.

[34] CD vii 15, 17 mention "the books of the law" and "the books of the prophets" but in a pesher like exegesis the reference identifies "the books of the law" and "the books of the prophets" with certain phrases of Amos 5:26-27. An exclusive list of a bipartite canon is not implied. Contra Schiffman, *Reclaiming*, 165.

[35] For במשיחו as a miscopying of במשיחי, see Lange, *Weisheit und Prädestination*, 265 n. 119.

interpretation of the anointed ones as prophets.[36] Hence, it is again the halakhic authorities of Moses and the prophets through which God commanded his laws. No bipartite canonical list is implied.

In this context CD xvi 2-3 might be of interest, too. This reference attributes a Mosaic quality to the book of *Jubilees*.[37] Adhering to it is synonymous with returning to the law of Moses.

> (For God made) xvi 1 a Covenant with you and all Israel; therefore a man shall bind himself by oath to return to 2 the Law of Moses, for in it all things are strictly defined. As for the determination of their times to which Israel turns a blind eye, 3 behold it is strictly defined in the *Book of the Divisions of the Times into their* 4 *Jubilees and Weeks.* And on the day that a man swears to return to 5 the Law of Moses, the Angel of the Presence shall cease to follow him provided that he fulfils his word: 6 for this reason Abraham circumcised himself on the day that he knew. (CD xvi 1-6)[38]

Hence, CD xvi 2-3 shows that for the Essenes Mosaic texts were not limited to the Pentateuch. Moses does not designate a closed part of an Essene canon but a category of literature to which e.g. the Pentateuch and the book of *Jubilees* belong.

In the literature found in the Qumran caves in general and in the Essene literature from Qumran in particular, only one tripartite or to be more precise quadripartite list of Jewish authorities can be found, i.e. MMT C 10-11 (4QMMT[d] [4Q397] 14-21 10-11). In this text the authors of MMT[39] advise the letter's addressee

כתבנ̇ו אליכה שתבין בספר מושה̇ [ו]בספר̇י הנ̇ב̇יאים ובדוי̇ד [במעשי]
דור ודור

> we [have written] to you that you may study the book of Moses [and] the books[of the p]rophets and Davi[d   the acts of] the generations.

MMT C 10 is all the more exceptional as it is also the only list of texts from the Qumran library which refers explicitly to books, i.e. the book of Moses and the book of the prophets.

Since the publication of MMT in 1994, MMT C 10 has been understood as "the earliest tripartite list" of the Hebrew canon with David referring to the

---

[36] Cf. e.g. J. Zimmermann, *Messianische Texte aus Qumran: Königliche, priesterliche und prophetische Messiasvorstellungen in den Schriftfunden von Qumran* (WUNT 2.104, Tübingen: Mohr Siebeck 1998) 326.

[37] See also the adaption of *Jub.* 23:11 in CD x 8-10. For the authoritative status of *Jubilees* in the *Damascus Document*, cf. e.g. Fabry, "Qumrantexte," 256; J.C. VanderKam, "Authoritative Literature in the Dead Sea Scrolls," *DSD* 3 (1998) 382-402, 399.

[38] Translation according to G. Vermes, *The Complete Dead Sea Scrolls in English* (New York: Penguin Press 1997) 137. Line counting inserted by A.L.

[39] For the Essene character of MMT, see E. Qimron and J. Strugnell, *Qumran Cave 4.V: Miqṣat Maʿaśe Ha-Torah* (DJD 10, Oxford: Clarendon Press 1994) 109-21.

book of psalms.[40] Only rarely MMT C 10 has been interpreted as referring to a bi-partite collection of texts.[41] Against such far reaching conclusions, it needs to be emphasized, that MMT C 10-11 mentions not three but four authorities, i.e. the book of Moses, the books of the prophets, David, and—after a lacuna—the acts of the generations.[42] Further caution is asked for, as Ulrich doubts that fragment 4QMMT[d] 17 is placed correctly in the *DJD* 10 edition. If he is right this would remove the word בספר from the phrase [ובספר]י הנביאים and would thus question whether MMT C 10-11 gives any kind of list at all. But Ulrich grants that his reconstruction is based on printed photographs only and requires thus verification with the original manuscript as well as reference to photographs of better quality.[43]

Furthermore, only seven lines later, in MMT C 17 (4Q397 14-21 15), MMT mentions another list of authoritative literature:[44]

[כתוב בספר]מושה ובס[פרי הנביאי]ם שיבואו[ן

It is written in the book of]Moses and the bo[oks of the prophet]s that they will come[

This time, MMT speaks about the past and future blessings and curses of Israel and invokes only the authority of the book of Moses and the books of the prophets. Neither David nor the acts of the generations are mentioned.

What is included in a list of authorities by MMT depends on the subject matter involved. For the past and future blessings and curses of Israel, MMT C 17 refers to the books of Moses and the prophets. Only the books of Moses and the prophets are referred to because only they are relevant when it comes to issue of blessings and curses. MMT C 10-11 assures MMT's addressee that study of the books of Moses and the prophets as well as David and

---

[40] See Qimron and Strugnell, *Miqṣat Maʿaśe Ha-Torah*, 112, 132-33. This interpretation by the *editio princeps* has found widespread acceptance. For similar interpretations of MMT C 10-11 see e.g. VanderKam, *Dead Sea Scrolls Today*, 149; idem, "Authoritative Literature," 387; H. Eshel, "4QMMT and the History of the Hasmonean Period," in *Reading 4QMMT: New Perspectives on Qumran Law and History* (eds. J. Kampen and M. Bernstein, SBLSS 2, Atlanta: Scholars Press 1996) 53-65, 59; Schiffman, *Reclaiming*, 165-66; idem, "The Place of 4QMMT in the Corpus of Qumran Manuscripts," in *Reading 4QMMT*, 81-98, 95; P. Flint, *The Dead Sea Psalms Scrolls and the Book of Psalms* (STDJ 17, Leiden: Brill 1997) 219; idem, "Scriptures," 290-92; van der Kooij, "The Canonization of Ancient Books Kept in the Temple of Jerusalem," 26-31; idem, "Canonization of Ancient Hebrew Books and Hasmonean Politics," 32; Fabry, "Qumrantexte," 256, 266; Trebolle Barrera, "Origins," 130.

[41] Campbell, "4QMMT[d]," 189-90; T. Lim, "The Alleged Reference to the Tripartite Division of the Hebrew Bible," *RevQ* 20 (2001-2002) 23-37.

[42] Cf. e.g. Ulrich, "Canon," 118-19.

[43] See Ulrich, "Non-attestation," 208-11; idem, "Qumran and the Canon of the Old Testament," 66-71.

[44] For the reconstruction of MMT C 17, see Qimron and Strugnell, *Miqṣat Maʿaśe Ha-Torah*, 28, 60.

the acts of the generations will convince him of the letter's halakhic arguments; i.e. for purposes of halakhah the books of Moses and the prophets as
well as David and the acts of the generations are of interest.

MMT C 10-11 mixes two literary categories with two other categories not
explicitly connected with books; i.e. MMT C 10-11 mentions the book of
Moses and the books of the prophets on the one hand as well as David and
the acts of the generations on the other hand. As MMT C 10 speaks of David
and not the book or books of David,[45] David should be understood as a reference to Israel's hymnic tradition in general and not to the book of psalms in
particular.[46] This would also exclude an understanding of the designation
David as describing the whole "Writings"-part of the later Hebrew canon. [47]
This interpretation is supported by the 4050 songs composed by David
according to 11QPs^a XXVII 2-11. This number of songs is far too large to be
included in just one collection of liturgical poetry. Hence, David denotes a
certain type of Jewish literature and not a specific book. "The acts of the
generations" would then refer to Israel's historical traditions.[48] This could be
supported by the mention of this phrase in 4QD^e (4Q270) 2 ii 21: In the
context of an admonition to understand "the law of God" (תורת אל; 4QD^e
[4Q270] 2 ii 19), the reader is advised to consider "the acts of the generations" (ובהבינכם במעשי דור ודור) for a better understanding of God's law.

As in the bipartite lists of other Essene and non-Essene Jewish literature,
canonical exclusivity is not in the interest of MMT C 10-11, 17. MMT C 10-11
and 17 do not argue that only these texts are sacred and that only in these
texts the addressees will find MMT's arguments confirmed. In MMT C 10-
11, the mentioning of David and the acts of the generations demonstrates
further an effort for inclusiveness and comprehensiveness.

The most extensive list of categories of ancient Jewish literature is attested in Sir 38:34b-39:3. As part of his praise of the scribe, Ben Sira describes
the different forms of literature studied by him.

> 34b How different the person who devotes himself to the fear of God and to the
> study of the Law of the Most High!
> 39:1 He studies the wisdom of all the ancients and occupies himself with the pro-
> phecies;
> 2 He treasures the discourses of the famous, and goes to the heart of involved
> sayings;

---

[45] Cf. M. Bernstein, "The Employment and Interpretation of Scripture in 4QMMT:
Preliminary Observations," in *Reading 4QMMT*, 29-51, 50-51 n. 49.

[46] Against Ulrich, "Canon," 118-19; Flint, "Scriptures," 291.

[47] Against Qimron and Strugnell who interpret David as a reference to the writings section of the canon (*Miqṣat Ma'aśe Ha-Torah*, 59 [esp. n. 10], 112; for further literature, see above n. 40).

[48] Cf. similarly Flint, "Scriptures," 292.

3 He studies the hidden meaning of proverbs, and is busied with the enigmas found in parables.[49]

In this description of the scribe's interpretative efforts, Ben Sira does not list the three parts of the Hebrew canon.[50] On the contrary, Ben Sira describes not three but seven different forms of literature the scribe is concerned with, i.e. the law of the most high, the wisdom of the ancients, the prophecies, the discourses of the famous, involved sayings, proverbs, and parables. Especially the later items of Ben Sira's list establish beyond a reasonable doubt that law and prophecies are not understood as two parts of a tripartite canon. Ben Sira designates with the terms law and prophets as much literary categories as he does with the other parts of his list, i.e. the wisdom of the ancients, the prophecies, the discourses of the famous, involved sayings, proverbs, and parables.[51]

To summarize: Neither the bipartite, nor the quadripartite lists of Jewish authorities in the Qumran library refer to canons. The bipartite lists describe Moses and the prophets as a group through which God revealed his law. In the case of MMT C 17 the dual list is due to the line's subject matter. Only the books of Moses and the prophets are referred to because only they are relevant when it comes to blessings and curses. And the quadripartite list from MMT C 10-11 recommends the study of all Jewish literary authorities. How does this evidence relate to the three lists mentioned in the prologue to Ecclesiasticus?

THE LAW, THE PROPHETS, AND THE OTHER BOOKS OF THE FATHERS IN THE PROLOGUE TO BEN SIRA

In the prologue to his translation, Ben Sira's grandson employs three tripartite lists of Jewish authorities. Each of these lists is phrased differently.

1-2 τοῦ νόμου καὶ τῶν προφητῶν καὶ τῶν ἄλλων τῶν κατ᾽ αὐτοὺς ἠκολουθηκότων
the law, the prophets, and the others, which followed them.

---

[49] Translation according to Skehan and DiLella, *Wisdom of Ben Sira*, 446.

[50] Thus e.g. Lebram, "Aspekte," 180; Snaith, *Ecclesiasticus*, 191-92; H. Stadelmann, *Ben Sira als Schriftgelehrter: Eine Untersuchung zum Berufsbild des vor-makkabäischen Sōfēr unter Berücksichtigung seines Verhältnisses zu Priester-, Propheten- und Weisheitslehrertum* (WUNT 2.6, Tübingen: Mohr Siebeck 1980) 223-24; MacKenzie, *Sirach*, 148; Skehan and Di Lella, *Wisdom of Ben Sira*, 451-52; Burkhardt, *Inspiration*, 139; Schiffman, *Reclaiming*, 164; E. Zenger, "Der Pentateuch als Tora und als Kanon," in *Die Tora als Kanon für Juden und Christen* (ed. E. Zenger, HBS 10, Freiburg: Herder 1996) 5-34, 5 n. 1.

[51] For similar interpretations of Sir 38:34b-30:3, cf. Swanson, *Closing*, 99-104; Fabry, "Qumrantexte," 252; van der Kooij, "The Canonization of Ancient Books Kept in the Temple of Jerusalem," 33-36; idem, "Canonization of Ancient Hebrew Books and Hasmonean Politics," 35-36; C.A. Evans, "The Scriptures of Jesus and His Earliest Followers," in *The Canon Debate*, 185-95, 187; Flint, "Scriptures," 279.

8-10 τὴν τοῦ νόμου καὶ τῶν προφητῶν καὶ τῶν ἄλλων πατρίων βιβλίων ἀνάγνωσιν
the reading of the law, the prophets, and the other books of the fathers.

24-25 ὁ νόμος καὶ αἱ προφητεῖαι καὶ τὰ λοιπὰ τῶν βιβλίων
the law and the prophecies and the remainder of the books.

The different wordings of the three lists mentioned in such close proximity to each other argue against interpreting the grandson's tripartite descriptions of Hebrew literature as one canonical formula listing the three parts of the TaNaKH. But beyond the different wordings, other observations confirm that the grandson is not speaking of a tripartite canonical collection of Jewish literature which excludes all other Jewish texts.

Just the opposite! The grandson's phrasing strives for comprehensiveness and openness. A good example are lines 21-26.

> For they, which have in themselves been phrased in Hebrew, are not equally powerful when they are transferred into another tongue. And not only these, but also the law, and the prophecies, and the remainder of the books are not a little different, when they speak on their own.

Ben Sira's grandson apologizes to his readers for the inadequateness of his translation. Because of the differences between two given languages every translation falls necessarily short of its *Vorlage*. This is amply demonstrated by the translations of the law, the prophecies, and the rest of the books.[52] The formulation of the last category makes an effort to include everything which is not law or prophecy by describing it as the remainder of Jewish literature, i.e. τὰ λοιπὰ τῶν βιβλίων. No canonical exclusivity is implied. Everything that was translated from Hebrew into Greek is as inadequate as the grandson's translation. The grandson does not describe three parts of a corpus of canonical scriptures but three different categories of Jewish literature. This becomes all the more evident, when it is recognized that Ben Sira's grandson does not speak of Moses or the prophets but of the law (ὁ νόμος) and the prophecies (αἱ προφητεῖαι). Not only the translation of his grandfather's book is difficult; translating any Hebrew book into another language results in a loss of meaning and expressiveness.

The prologue's first two tripartite lists of Jewish writings are part of one rather long sentence (lines 1-15). In this sentence the grandson explains, why his grandfather wrote the book of Ecclesiasticus.

Lines 7-11 specify how the grandfather's education qualified him to write a book which entices people to benefit from living according to the law: because the grandfather had given himself to

---

[52] For a discussion of the grandson's deliberations of the quality of his translation, see B.G. Wright III, "Why a Prologue? Ben Sira's Grandson and His Greek Translation," in *Emanuel: Studies in Hebrew Bible, Septuagint, and Dead Sea Scrolls in Honor of Emanuel Tov*, 633-44.

the reading of the law, the prophets, and the other books of the fathers and after acquiring considerable proficiency in these.

In this passage of his prologue, the grandson makes an effort to demonstrate the comprehensiveness of his grandfather's education. Next to the law and the prophets he studied also all the other books of the fathers. As the τὰ λοιπὰ τῶν βιβλίων of line 25, the phrase τῶν ἄλλων πατρίων βιβλίων of line 10 names all Jewish books which cannot be described as law or prophets. As in line 24, the grandson speaks of the law and not Moses. Again, the grandson does not imply the tripartite canon of the later Hebrew Bible but three different categories of Jewish literature. The phrase "the law, the prophets, and the other books of the fathers" comprises the whole of Jewish literature. That Ben Sira studied it all enabled him to write the book of Ecclesiasticus.

The first tripartite categorization of Hebrew literature in the prologue to Ecclesiasticus (lines 1-2), serves a similar purpose. It is part of a *genetivus absolutus* whose function becomes evident when most of the other *participia coniuncta* and subclauses are deleted from lines 1-15.

Πολλῶν καὶ μεγάλων ἡμῖν διὰ τοῦ νόμου καὶ τῶν προφητῶν καὶ τῶν ἄλλων τῶν κατ᾽ αὐτοὺς ἠκολουθηκότων δεδομένων (lines 1-2) ...ὁ πάππος μου Ἰησοῦς (line 7) ...προήχθη καὶ αὐτὸς συγγράψαι τι τῶν εἰς παιδείαν καὶ σοφίαν ἀνηκόντων (line 12)

In as much as many and great things were given to us by the law, the prophets, and the others which followed them (lines 1-2) ...my grandfather Jesus (line 7) ... was induced also himself to write something of the things which pertain to education and wisdom (line 12).

The grandson compares the writing of his grandfather Jesus with "the law, the prophets, and the others, which followed them." As was the case with these books, the grandfather was induced by God (προήχθη is phrased in the divine passive[53]) to write his own book. And as Israel gained many and great things "by the law, the prophets, and the others which followed them," the reader of the grandfather's book will benefit from its study by way of a life according to the law (διὰ τῆς ἐννόμου βιώσεως, line 14).[54]

---

[53] Cf. L. Perdue, "Ben Sira and the Prophets," in *Intertextual Studies in Ben Sira and Tobit: Essays in Honor of Alexander A. DiLella* (eds. J. Corley and V. Skemp, CBQMS 38, Washington: CBA 2005) 132-54, 135.

[54] Perdue (ibid., 135) argues that the passive participle δεδομένων (line 2) lacks a logical subject and should be understood as a divine passive. In this way, the grandson would indicate the inspired character of the books in question. Perdue's observation would strengthen the case for tripartite categorization of scriptures in the prologue to Ben Sira. But contrary to Perdue, a logical subject of δεδομένων is mentioned in line 1-2: διὰ τοῦ νόμου καὶ τῶν προφητῶν καὶ τῶν ἄλλων τῶν κατ᾽ αὐτοὺς ἠκολουθηκότων ("by the law, the prophets, and the others which followed them"). For διά as marking the logical subject of a passive, see e.g. Plato, *Phileb.* 58b; cf. LSJ, 389.

The prologue's first tripartite categorization of Jewish literature could thus indeed put Ben Sira's book in line with an exclusive collection of sacred Jewish literature. However, the phrase τῶν ἄλλων τῶν κατ' αὐτοὺς ἠκολουθηκότων ("the others, which followed them") is not exclusive but inclusive in its meaning. It refers to all other Jewish books created after the law and the prophets were written. Furthermore, the grandson uses again the designation ὁ νόμος ("the law") and does not speak of Moses. Hence, it is more likely that in lines 1-2 of the prologue the grandson describes three categories of Jewish literature and not a tripartite canon. In this way, he puts the book of Ecclesiasticus in line with the whole of Jewish literature.

To summarize: In the prologue to Ecclesiasticus, the tripartite segmentation of Jewish literature refers not to the tripartite canon of the later Hebrew Bible. The three tripartite enumerations are not canonical lists which exclude other Jewish literature. On the contrary, they describe the whole of Jewish literature in a comprehensive way by segmenting it into three different categories, i.e. law, prophets, and others.

READING "THE LAW, THE PROPHETS, AND THE OTHER BOOKS OF THE FATHERS" — THE *LETTER OF ARISTEAS* 121

In the case of the phrase τοῦ νόμου καὶ τῶν προφητῶν καὶ τῶν ἄλλων πατρίων βιβλίων (lines 8-10 of the prologue to Ecclesiasticus), my interpretation is confirmed by an allusion to it in the *Letter of Aristeas*. The *Letter of Aristeas* describes the Septuagint-translators as follows.

Ἐπιλέξας γὰρ τοὺς ἀρίστους ἄνδρας καὶ παιδείᾳ διαφέροντας, ἅτε δὴ γονέων τετευχότας ἐνδόξων οἵτινες οὐ μόνον τὴν τῶν Ἰουδαϊκῶν γραμμάτων ἕξιν περιεποίησαν αὐτοῖς, ἀλλὰ καὶ τῆς τῶν Ἑλληνικῶν ἐφρόντισαν οὐ παρέργως κατασκευῆς

For he selected the best men, which were also excelling in education, in as much as they were also decorated with the honor of their parents, (men) which had acquired not only proficiency in the Jewish writings for themselves but considered not to a small extent the nature of the Greek writings as well (*Let. Aris.* 121).

According to the *Letter of Aristeas*, the Septuagint translators are thus well versed both in Jewish and Greek literature. The phrase ἕξιν περιποιέω which the *Letter of Aristeas* employs to emphasize the Jewish education of the LXX translators can also be found in line 11 of the prologue to Ecclesiasticus:

ἐν τούτοις ἱκανὴν ἕξιν περιποιησάμενος
acquiring considerable proficiency in these (Prologue to Ecclesiasticus 11).

Whether this use of the locution ἕξιν περιποιέω both in the *Letter or Aristeas* and the prologue to Ecclesiasticus points to an intertextual relation between the two can only be decided in light of the overall use of the idiom ἕξιν περιποιέω in Greek literature.

The earliest reference to the phrase ἕξιν περιποιέω can be found in Aristophanes of Byzantium's (257- ca. 180 BCE) work περὶ ζῴων (II 50). Aristophanes of Byzantium became head of the Alexandrian library around 200 BCE. Although a rather important figure in Greek literature, it seems hardly plausible that the *Letter of Aristeas* or the prologue to Ecclesiasticus would allude to the history of animals by Aristophanes and thus compare the excelling education of the LXX translators or Ben Sira with the practical wisdom of a particular type of herbivores who feed on trees (ἐκ τοῦ παντὸς βίου περιπεποίηνται τὴν ἕξιν ["out of the whole life they gained proficiency"]). Furthermore, Aristophanes of Byzantium construes the expression ἕξιν περιποιέω slightly differently from both the prologue to Ecclesiasticus and the *Letter of Aristeas* by prefixing the adverbial phrase ἐκ τοῦ παντὸς βίου. And the *Letter of Aristeas* displays faulty knowledge about the history of the library of Alexandria. It claims that Demetrius of Phaleron, who died very early in the reign of Ptolemy II, founded the library of Alexandria (*Let. Aris.* 9).[55] Not knowing even the most basic facts about the Alexandrian librarians, it seems unlikely that the *Letter of Aristeas* would have had in depth knowledge about the work of Aristophanes of Byzantium. Hence, it seems unlikely that in their use of the phrase ἕξιν περιποιέω either the prologue to Ecclesiasticus or the *Letter of Aristeas* are influenced by the rhetoric of Aristophanes of Byzantium.

From the late 2nd century BCE to the early 1st century CE, the phrase ἕξιν περιποιέω is attested almost exclusively in Jewish literature: Prologue to Ecclesiasticus 11; *Letter of Aristeas* 121; Philo of Alexandria, *Alleg. Interp.* I 10.3 and Περὶ ἀριθμῶν *sive* Ἀριθματικά Fragment 62c line 3. The only exception to the rule is the *Library of History* (II 29.4) by Diodorus Siculus written in the years 56-36 BCE. Hence, it seems likely that Diodorus absorbed the phrase during his visit to Egypt (60-56 BCE), probably out of the *Letter of Aristeas* itself.

The *Letter of Aristeas* and the prologue to Ecclesiasticus were written in the same period. Based on its use of formal administrative language, Bickermann dated the *Letter of Aristeas* to the years 145-127 BCE.[56] The Prologue to Ecclesiasticus was written shortly after 117 BCE.[57]

---

[55] For the library of Alexandria and its history, see M. El Abbadi, *Life and Fate of the Ancient Library of Alexandria* (2nd ed., Paris: UNESCO/UNDP 1992); *The Library of Alexandria: Centre of Learning in the Ancient World* (ed. R. MacLeod, London: I.B. Tauris Publishers 2000).

[56] E. Bickermann, "Zur Datierung des Pseudo-Aristeas," *ZNW* 29 (1930) 280-98; cf. more recently, e.g., R. Sollamo, "The Letter of Aristeas and the Origin of the Septuagint," in *X Congress of the International Organization for Septuagint and Cognate Studies: Oslo, 1998* (ed. B.A. Taylor, SBLSCS 51, Atlanta: SBL 2001) 329-42, 331-36.

[57] See U. Wilcken, Review of "W. Dittenberger, Orientis Graeci Inscriptiones Selectae, Supplementum Sylloges Inscriptionum Graecarum, vol. 1 (Leipzig: Hirzel 1903)," *Archiv für Papyrusforschung* 3 (1906) 313-36, 321; cf. idem, "IV. Bibliographie," *Archiv für Papyrusforschung* 4 (1907) 198-268, 205; N. Peters, *Das Buch Jesus Sirach oder Ecclesiasticus* (EHAT 25, Münster: Aschendorff 1913) XXXII-XXXIII.

Does the *Letter of Aristeas* allude to the Prologue to Ecclesiasticus or is it the other way round? With the possible exception of the phrase ἕξιν περιποιέω in line 11, there are no quotations of and allusions to other texts in the Prologue to Ben Sira, while several allusions and quotations occur in the *Letter of Aristeas*.[58] Hence, the *Letter of Aristeas* alludes to the prologue of Ecclesiasticus in its use of the phrase ἕξιν περιποιέω.

As an apropos it should be noted, that this observation is of great importance for the dating of the *Letter of Aristeas*. The *Letter of Aristeas* must have been written later than the Prologue of Ecclesiasticus. Taking into consideration that its author might not have been familiar with the Prologue to Ecclesiasticus immediately after the grandson finished his translation of Ecclesiasticus, a date for the *Letter of Aristeas* after 100 BCE seems likely.

For the interpretation of the prologue to Ben Sira and its tripartite lists, the *Letter of Aristeas'* allusion to the prologue is crucial. It provides an ancient interpretation of the prologue's tripartite lists. By way of its allusion to the prologue of Ecclesiasticus, the *Letter of Aristeas* compares the education of the Pentateuch-translators in Jewish literature with the learning of Ben Sira.

A closer comparison of *Let. Aris.* 121 with line 11 of the Prologue to Ecclesiasticus helps to better understand how the *Letter of Aristeas* read the phrase "the law, the prophets, and the other books of the fathers" in the prologue to Ecclesiasticus:

τὴν τῶν Ἰουδαϊκῶν γραμμάτων ἕξιν περιεποίησαν αὐτοῖς
they had acquired proficiency in the Jewish writings for themselves (*Let. Aris.* 121).

ἐν τούτοις ἱκανὴν ἕξιν περιποιησάμενος
acquiring considerable proficiency in these (Prologue to Ecclesiasticus 11).

In line 11 of the Prologue to Ecclesiasticus, ἐν τούτοις refers to "the law, the prophets, and the other books of the fathers" mentioned in lines 8-10. When *Let. Aris.* 121 replaces the ἐν τούτοις of Ben Sira with τῶν Ἰουδαϊκῶν γραμμάτων ("the Jewish writings"), the phrase "the law, the prophets, and the other books of the fathers" from the prologue to Ecclesiasticus is interpreted as the entirety of Jewish literature. Hence, as an early interpretation of the Prologue to Ecclesiasticus 8-11, *Let. Aris.* 121 understands the triad "the law, the prophets, and the other books of the fathers" as a tripartite description and categorization of all Jewish literature.

---

[58] For allusions and quotations in the *Letter of Aristeas*, see the list compiled by N. Meisner, *Aristeasbrief* (JSHRZ 2.2; Gütersloh: Gütersloher Verlagshaus 1973) 87.

LISTS OF JEWISH LITERATURE IN CONTEMPORARY OR LATER TEXTS

In a letter written some time in the first half of the 1ˢᵗ century BCE,[59] 2 Macc 2:13-15 states:

> 13 The same things are reported in the records and in the memoirs of Nehemiah, and also that he founded a library and collected the books about the kings and prophets, and the writings of David, and letters of kings about votive offerings. 14 In the same way Judas also collected all the books that had been lost on account of the war which had come upon us, and they are in our possession. 15 So if you have need of them, send people to get them for you.

Various scholars refer to this statement as proof for a closed tripartite canon in Maccabean times.[60] Contrary to this interpretation it needs to be stressed that the types of texts which according to 2 Macc 2:13-15 were collected by Nehemiah and reassembled by Judah Maccabee are typical for ancient Near Eastern temple libraries. That the reassembling of the Jerusalem temple library, as mentioned in 2 Macc 2:14, marks the closing of the Hebrew canon or had a more significant influence on the development of the Hebrew canon as the pre-Maccabean temple library is therefore improbable.[61]

A quadripartite description of Jewish literature can be found in Philo's description of the Therapeutes. According to paragraph 25 of the treatise *On the Contemplative Life*, the individual Therapeutes would not have taken anything into the holy rooms of their houses. The only exception to this rule was literature.

> ἀλλὰ νόμους καὶ λόγια θεσπισθέντα διὰ προφητῶν καὶ ὕμνους καὶ τὰ ἄλλα οἷς
> ἐπιστήμη καὶ εὐσέβεια συναύξονται καὶ τελειοῦνται
> but laws and words which were revealed through prophets and hymns and the
> other [books] by which knowledge and piety are increased and perfected.

---

[59] The dates assigned to 2 Macc 1:10-2:18 vary from 103-102 BCE (Goldstein, *II Maccabees*, 161-67) to before 63 BCE (M. Hengel, *Judentum und Hellenismus: Studien zu ihrer Begegnung unter besonderer Berücksichtigung Palästinas bis zur Mitte des 2.Jh.s v.Chr.* [2nd ed., Tübingen: Mohr Siebeck 1973] 186-87) or around 60 BCE (E. Bickermann, "Ein jüdischer Festbrief vom Jahre 124 v.Chr. [II. Macc. 1, 1-9]," *ZNW* 32 [1933] 233-254, 234-35; cf. idem., "The Colophon of the Greek Book of Esther," *JBL* 63 (1944) 339-62, 357; N. Walter, *Der Thoraausleger Aristobulos: Untersuchungen zu seinen Fragmenten und zu pseudepigraphischen Resten der jüdisch-hellenistischen Literatur* (TU 86, Berlin: Akademie-Verlag 1964) 17-18). For a late date of 2 Macc 1:10-2:18, cf. also C. Habicht, *2. Makkabäerbuch* (JSHRZ 1.3; Gütersloh: Gütersloher Verlagshaus 1976) 199-200.

[60] Leiman, *Canonization*, 51-124; Beckwith, *Old Testament Canon*, 150-52; van der Kooij, "The Canonization of Ancient Books Kept in the Temple of Jerusalem," passim; idem, "Canonization of Ancient Hebrew Books and Hasmonean Politics," passim.

[61] For a more detailed study of 2 Macc 2:13-15, see A. Lange, "2 Maccabees 2:13-15: Library or Canon?," in *The Books of the Maccabees: History, Theology, Ideology: Papers of the Second International Conference on the Deuterocanonical Books, Pápa, Hungary, 9-11 June, 2005* (eds. G.G. Xeravits and J. Zsengellér, JSJSup 118, Leiden: Brill 2007) 155-67.

This text has been interpreted as a quadripartite,[62] tripartite,[63] or bipartite[64] exclusive list of Jewish scriptures. But a careful reading shows that comparable to the prologue to Ecclesiasticus the quadripartite phrase used by Philo strives for comprehensiveness when it describes the books studied by the Therapeutes. Philo constructs the first three groups of texts without articles. He does not speak about *the* laws, *the* words revealed by prophets and *the* hymns but just about laws, words and hymns. The indeterminate state of the words νόμους, λόγια, and ὕμνους as well as their plural forms show that no exclusive collection of laws, words, and hymns is described by Philo. Furthermore, with the last category of "the other books" (τὰ ἀλλά) Philo makes this list as inclusive and comprehensive as possible. That in *Contempl. Life* 25 Philo provides a list of canonical books studied by the Therapeutes, is therefore more than unlikely. Just the opposite! Philo describes the textual genres of laws, prophetic words, and hymns studied by the Therapeutes. And not to forget anything, he adds the all inclusive phrase "the other books" to his list.[65]

It is only in the work of Josephus Flavius, at the end of the 1st cent. CE, that the three categories of Jewish literature observed in the prologue to Ecclesiasticus are combined with the idea of an exclusive canonical list containing 22 sacred books.[66]

> (8)[38] For we have not an innumerable multitude of books among us, disagreeing from and contradicting one another, [as the Greeks have,] but only twenty-two books, which contain the records of all the past times; which are justly believed to be divine; and of them five belong to Moses, which contain his laws and the traditions of the origin of mankind till his death. This interval of time was little short of three thousand years; but as to the time from the death of Moses till the

---

[62] See e.g. H.A. Wolfson, *Philo: Foundations of Religious Philosophy in Judaism, Christianity, and Islam* (Structure and Growth of Philosophic Systems from Plato to Spinoza 2, Cambridge: Harvard University Press 1948) 1: 117; H.B. Swete, *An Introduction to the Old Testament in Greek* (rev. by R.R. Ottley, Cambridge: Cambridge University Press 1914) 217; VanderKam, "Revealed Literature," 22.

[63] See e.g. Leiman, *Canonization*, 31; Beckwith, *Old Testament Canon*, 115-17; idem, "Formation," 54-55 ("the other books" refers to texts of almost canonical authority); Burkhardt, *Inspiration*, 138-40; VanderKam, *Dead Sea Scrolls Today*, 145; Sundberg, "Septuagint," 81-82; Trebolle Barrera, "Origins," 131-32; Flint, "Scriptures," 283-84; van der Kooij, "Canonization of Ancient Hebrew Books and Hasmonean Politics," 32-33.

[64] Campbell, "4QMMT[d]," 188.

[65] Cf. F. Siegert, "Early Jewish Interpretation in a Hellenistic Style," in *Hebrew Bible / Old Testament: The History of Its Interpretation*, vol. 1: *From the Beginnings to the Middle Ages (Until 1300)*, part 1: *Antiquity* (eds. M. Sæbø in cooperation with C. Brekelmanns and M. Haran; Göttingen: Vandenhoeck & Ruprecht 1996) 130-98, 176: "Philo does not deal with the... question of a canon. In this respect he is not different from all the other Jewish Sages and Rabbis."

[66] For an excellent analysis of this passage, see S. Mason, "Josephus and His Twenty-Two Book Canon," in *The Canon Debate*, 110-27; cf. idem with R.A. Kraft, "Josephus on Canon and Scriptures," in *Hebrew Bible / Old Testament*, 1/1: 217-35; cf. also Flint, "Scriptures," 284-86.

reign of Artaxerxes king of Persia, who reigned after Xerxes, the prophets, who were after Moses, wrote down what was done in their times in thirteen books. The remaining four books contain hymns to God, and precepts for the conduct of human life (Josephus, *Ag. Ap.* I 38-40).

In my opinion, it is Josephus' reference to the twenty-two holy books of Judaism which gave rise to the interpretation of the earlier tripartite lists of Jewish literature. Only in light of Josephus' elaboration could they have been understood as canonical lists.

A slightly earlier forerunner to Josephus' ideas of canon can be found in a paratext to 2 Maccabees 3-7[67] which was written between 20 and 54 CE,[68] i.e. *4 Maccabees*.[69]

10 While he was still with you, he taught you the law and the prophets. 11 He read to you about Abel slain by Cain, and Isaac who was offered as a burnt offering, and of Joseph in prison. 12 He told you of the zeal of Phineas, and he taught you about Hananiah, Azariah, and Mishael in the fire. 13 He praised Daniel in the den of the lions and blessed him. 14 He reminded you of the scripture of Isaiah, which says, "Even though you go through the fire, the flame shall not consume you." 15 He sang to you songs of the psalmist David, who said, "Many are the afflictions of the righteous." 16 He recounted to you Solomon's proverb, "There is a tree of life for those who do his will." 17 He confirmed the saying of Ezekiel, "Shall these dry bones live?" 18 For he did not forget to teach you

---

[67] For 4 Maccabees as a paratext to 2 Maccabees 3-7, see H.-J. Klauck, *4. Makkabäerbuch* (JSHRZ 3.8, Gütersloh: Gütersloher Verlagshaus 1989) 654-57 and D.A. deSilva, *4 Maccabees* (Guides to Apocrypha and Pseudepigrapha, Sheffield: Sheffield Academic Press 1998) 28-30.

[68] For the date of *4 Maccabees*, see E. Bickermann, "The Date of Fourth Maccabees," in *Studies in Jewish and Christian History* (AGJU 9, Leiden: Brill 1976) 1: 275-81, 276-77, 279-80; cf. deSilva, *4 Maccabees*, 14-18. Criticism of such an early date of *4 Maccabees* (see e.g. J.W. van Henten, *The Maccabean Martyrs as Saviours of the Jewish People: A Study and 2 and 4 Maccabees* [JSJSup 57, Leiden: Brill 1997] 73-78) is based on the observation that the Jerusalem temple is only mentioned in a historical retrospect (*4 Macc* 3:10-4:26) which is a paratext to 2 Maccabees 3. Hence, *4 Maccabees* must have been written after the destruction of the Herodian temple in 70 CE. But the putative setting of *4 Maccabees* forbids references to later events at the temple. It seems furthermore unlikely that the story about Apollonius' failed raid on the temple treasury would have been an ideal and inspiring paradigm which promises divine help and support to the faithful in a time of persecution. After all, the temple was destroyed in 70 CE without any intervention from god. Hence, the paradigmatic use of the Apollonius story in *4 Macc* 3:26-4:14 points to a date before the destruction of the Herodian temple in the year 70 CE. Although *4 Maccabees* has been variously subjected to literary criticism there are no clear cut indications of later redactions (for a history of research and the arguments in favor of the unity *of 4 Maccabess*, see deSilva, *4 Maccabees*, 30-32).

[69] The commentary of D.A. DeSilva, *4 Maccabees: Introduction and Commentary on the Greek Text in Codex Sinaiticus* (Septuagint Commentary Series, Leiden: Brill 2006) was not yet available to me when I finished this article and can therefore not be considered.

the song that Moses taught, which says, 19 "I kill and I make alive: this is your life
and the length of your days" (*4 Macc* 18:10-19).

Only rarely has this passage been understood as referring to the later
Hebrew canon.[70] Mostly, scholars have emphasized the ambiguity of this
report that the father taught his seven sons Jewish scriptures.[71] R.A. Kraft is
representative:

> We are clearly viewing here a perspective conscious of a wide array of scriptural
> writings, although the evidence is insufficient to demonstrate more than a vague
> nod in the direction of what will become "canon."[72]

In a medley without apparent sequence, various passages are quoted, alluded, and referred to in the father's scriptural curriculum:

Gen 4:8	*4 Macc* 18:11
Genesis 22	*4 Macc* 18:11
Gen 39:7-23	*4 Macc* 18:11
Num 25:7-13	*4 Macc* 18:12
Daniel 3	*4 Macc* 18:12
Daniel 6	*4 Macc* 18:13
Isa 43:2	*4 Macc* 18:14
Ps 34:20	*4 Macc* 18:15
Prov 3:18	*4 Macc* 18:16
Ezek 37:3	*4 Macc* 18:17
Deut 32:39, 47; 30:20	*4 Macc* 18:19

The passages are concerned with death, suffering, and the prospects of the
suffering just. In the style of an inclusion, the list of references opens and
closes with passages taken out of the beginning and the end of the law (i.e.
Gen 4:8 and Deut 32:39, 47). It is as if the beginning and the end of the
Pentateuch would comprise all the other scriptures mentioned. Daniel,

---

[70] See e.g. van der Kooij, "The Canonization of Ancient Books Kept in the Temple
of Jerusalem," 29: "Apparently, the expression 'the Law and the Prophets' was used to
designate the whole collection of biblical books. This does not mean, however, that all
authoritative books outside the Law made up a section of Prophets. It might well be
that all authors of ancient books were regarded as prophets."

[71] Trebolle Barrera ("Origins," 131) notes, "it is not possible to know whether
David's Psalter and the book of Daniel are included among the prophets." Similarly,
Flint ("Scriptures," 283) emphasizes, "It is possible, but by no means certain, that here
the prophets includes David's Psalter, the book of Daniel, and (surprisingly), the book
of Proverbs."

[72] R.A. Kraft, "Scripture and Canon in Jewish Apocrypha and Pseudepigrapha," in
Hebrew Bible / Old Testament, 1: 199-216, 212. Cf. also idem, http://ccat.sas.upenn.edu
/gopher/other/journals/kraftpub/Judaism/Scripture%20and%20Canon%20in%20Jewis
h%20Apocrypha%20and%20Pseudepigrapha.

Psalms, and Proverbs are scattered among the prophetic books quoted, i.e. Isaiah and Ezekiel.

By teaching his children the law and the prophets, the father complies with prescriptions of Deut 4:9 and 10, to teach his sons the covenantal law:

> 9 But take care and watch yourselves closely, so as neither to forget the things that your eyes have seen nor to let them slip from your mind all the days of your life; make them known to your children and your children's children — 10 how you once stood before the Lord your God at Horeb, when the Lord said to me, "Assemble the people for me, and I will let them hear my words, so that they may learn to fear me as long as they live on the earth, and may teach their children to do so."

This means, when the father teaches the books of Genesis, Numbers, Daniel, Isaiah, Psalms, Proverbs, Ezekiel, and Deuteronomy he teaches his sons the law. Are the prophets thus just part of the law and does 4 *Maccabees* regard Daniel, Isaiah, Psalms, Proverbs, Ezekiel as law? This view might be supported by the inclusion observed above. In this case, 4 *Macc* 18:10-19 would be comparable to the other bipartite lists of scriptures. The phrase "the law and the prophets" in 4 *Macc* 18:10 would list two different literary categories of scriptures which are of the same authority. This would also explain why there is no apparent canonical pattern to the sequence of the scriptures mentioned in 4 *Macc* 18:11-19.

A comparison with the texts quoted, referred, and alluded to in 4 Maccabees sheds a different light on what the father teaches his sons though.

4 *Macc* 1:34	Leviticus 11 / Deuteronomy 14
4 *Macc* 2:3	Gen 39:7-12
4 *Macc* 2:5	Exod 20:17 / Deut 5:21
4 *Macc* 2:8	Ex 22:25 / Lev 25:35-38; Deut 15:1-2
4 *Macc* 2:14	Deut 20:19-20; Exod 23:4-5
4 *Macc* 2:17	Numbers 16
4 *Macc* 2:19	Gen 34:25-30; 49:7
4 *Macc* 2:19	Gen 2:7
4 *Macc* 3:6-18	2 Sam 23:13-17 par 1 Chr 11:15-19
4 *Macc* 3:21	Exod 30:12
4 *Macc* 5:26	Leviticus 11 / Deuteronomy 14
4 *Macc* 5:29	Exod 24:3, 7
4 *Macc* 7:11	Num 17:2, 4, 10-15LXX[73]
4 *Macc* 7:14	Genesis 22
4 *Macc* 7:18	Deut 6:5
4 *Macc* 13:9	Dan 3:8-30
4 *Macc* 13:13	Genesis 22

[73] For a similar reading of Num 17, see Wis 18:20-25. Cf. Klauck, *4. Makkabäerbuch*, 720 n. 11b.

4 Macc 13:13	Deut 6:5
4 Macc 15:31	Gen 5:5-8:22
4 Macc 16:3	Dan 6:1-28; 3:8-30
4 Macc 16:20	Genesis 22
4 Macc 16:21	Dan 6:1-28; 3:8-30
4 Macc 17:19	Deut 33:3
4 Macc 18:7	Gen 2:22LXX
4 Macc 18:8	Deut 22:25
4 Macc 18:8	Exod 22:16
4 Macc 18:8	Gen 3:1-7, 13

Next to the passages out of the Pentateuch, 4 Maccabees refers only to Dan 3:8-30; 6:1-28 and 2 Sam 23:13-17. Both the Pentateuch and the book of Daniel are part of the father's curriculum while none of the books of the deuteronomistic history are. This is all the more astonishing as the story of David's thirst in 2 Sam 23:13-17 (cf. 1 Chr 11:15-19) is referred to in 4 Macc 3:6-18 as exemplary behavior. That the books of 1 Samuel-2 Kings do not occur in the fathers curriculum although the author of 4 Maccabees was familiar with them could thus hint to the idea of canonical exclusivity in 4 Maccabees. This is even more probable as the persecution of Elijah which is described in 2 Kgs 19:1-8[74] would have been a fitting role model for the seven martyred sons and could thus have been easily a part of the father's curriculum.

Hence, 4 Maccabees seems to consciously exclude at least the books which were later labelled the former prophets from what it regards worthwhile to be taught.[75] Such exclusivity hints at the concept of a closed canon. This canon is bipartite[76] in its structure and therefore different from the one described by Josephus. The books of Daniel, Proverbs, and Psalms are regarded as much as prophets[77] as the books of Isaiah or Ezekiel.

Further confirmation for the existence of the concept of a closed canon before the destruction of the Herodian temple (70 CE) might be found in early Christian literature. The gospels, the book of Acts, and Paul's letter to the Romans variously refer to the law and the prophets (Matt 5:17; 7:12; 11:13; 22:40; Luke 16:16; 24:27; John 1:45; Acts 13:15; 24:14; 26:22; 28:23; Rom 3:21) or the law of Moses, the prophets and the psalms (Luke 24:44). While in some if not in most cases these early Christian texts do not refer to a closed

---

[74] Elijah even wishes to die in 2 Kgs 19:4.

[75] Another hint at exclusivity could be found in 4 Maccabees' relation to its base text, 2 Maccabees 3-7. Although rewriting it extensively, 4 Maccabees never mentions the work, while other texts are referred to explicitly. But the reason for not mentioning 2 Maccabees could also be found in the putative setting of 4 Maccabees during the Hellenistic Religious Reforms of Antiochus IV Epiphanes—a time when 2 Maccabees' reporting about these events could not have been written yet.

[76] For a bipartite canon in 4 Macc 18:10-19, cf. also Swanson, Closing, 250-53; Fabry, "Qumrantexte," 266.

[77] Cf. Swanson, Closing, 252.

canon but are in line with the ancient Jewish texts discussed above, in some cases a new meaning of the phrase "the law and the prophets" seems to evolve. The most interesting example is Acts 13:15. The verse is part of an earlier itinerary tradition which Luke incorporated into the book of Acts.

> 13 Then Paul and his companions set sail from Paphos and came to Perga in Pamphylia. John, however, left them and returned to Jerusalem; 14 but they went on from Perga and came to Antioch in Pisidia. And on the sabbath day they went into the synagogue and sat down. 15 After the reading of the law and the prophets, the officials of the synagogue sent them a message, saying, "Brothers, if you have any word of exhortation for the people, give it." (Acts 13:13-15)

It describes a public reading out of Law and Prophets in a synagogue. In this pre-Lukan Christian tradition, verse 15 describes the canon of texts read in a synagogue service. Hence, in Acts 13:15, the phrase "the law and the prophets" describes a distinct corpus of literature and does not function as the designation of two literary categories anymore.[78]

CONCLUSION

In ancient Jewish literature before the turn of the eras, neither the bipartite, nor the tri- or quadripartite lists of Jewish authorities refer to canons. The bipartite lists describe Moses and the prophets as a group of halakhic authorities through which God revealed his law to Israel. They imply neither a dual categorization of Jewish literature nor a dual canon.

The tripartite and quadripartite lists are striving to itemize the different categories of Jewish literature in a comprehensive way. Contrary to the common scholarly reading of the prologue to Ecclesiasticus, its tripartite lists do not describe the three parts of the later TaNaKH but three categories of Jewish literature. Far from being an exclusive canonical list, the different parts of the triplet "the law, the prophets, and the other (books [of the fathers])" describe the whole ensemble of ancient Jewish literature. Similarly, the quadripartite lists from MMT C 10-11 and Philo's treatise *On the Contemplative Life* recommend the study of all Jewish literary authorities.

This observation corresponds well with the fact that the literary categories mentioned in the different bi- tri-, and quadripartite lists are not restrictted to the books of the later Hebrew canon. E.g., CD xvi 2-3 demonstrates that the category Moses or law is not restricted to the Pentateuch but encompasses other Jewish literature, too—in this case the book of *Jubilees*.

The scholarly reading of the tripartite and bipartite lists in the prologue to Ecclesiasticus and elsewhere as canonical lists is influenced by Josephus' tripartite description of the 22 sacred books of Judaism in *Ag. Ap.* I 38-40. His writings attest to the earliest preserved list that combines a limited number

---

[78] A more detailed study of the early Christian references would go beyond the limits of this article and must thus be undertaken elsewhere.

of books with the three literary categories mentioned in the prologue to Ecclesiasticus and elsewhere.

Although Josephus' apology *Against Apion* marks hence a turning point in the canonical history of the TaNaKH, Josephus neither invented the idea of canonical exclusivity nor marks its beginning. Already before the destructtion of the Herodian temple in the year 70 CE, both *4 Maccabees* 18:10-19 and the itinerary tradition of Acts 13:15 developed the bi- and tripartite categorizations of Jewish literature into at least two but possibly three parts of an exclusive collection of holy books, i.e. a canon. But most probably the idea of exclusive canonicity was not accepted at once by all of Judaism. That Josephus is able to present the idea of canon as an opinion shared by all Jews to his audience reflects the religious reality of Judaism after the destruction of the Herodian Temple. This means, the idea of canon became dominant in ancient Judaism because of the loss of the Temple as the common Jewish cultural mark and characteristic. What provoked Judaism to develop the idea of canon already before the year 70 CE cannot be discussed in the limited space of this article. It is significant that the idea of canon evolves at the same time as the first efforts towards the textual standardization of Jewish scriptures can be found. Hence, it stands to reason that the idea of canon and the idea of textual standardization go back to the same cause, i.e. the increased influence of Greek culture due to the active Romanization of the territories conquered by the Roman empire.[79]

---

[79] With regard to the canonical history of the Hebrew Bible I will argue this point in more detail elsewhere. For Roman cultural imperialism as the catalyst of the idea of textual standardization in ancient Judaism, see my articles "'Nobody Dared To Add To Them, To Take from Them, Or To Make Changes' (Josephus, *Ag. Ap.* 1.42): The Textual Standardization of Jewish Scriptures in Light of the Dead Sea Scrolls," in *Flores Florentino: Dead Sea Scrolls and Other Early Jewish Studies in Honour of Florentino García Martínez* (eds. A. Hilhorst *et al.*, JSJSup 122, Leiden: Brill 2007) 105-26 and "One Text or Many? The Textual Standardization of Jewish Scriptures," in *From Qumran to Aleppo: A Discussion with Emanuel Tov about the Textual History of Jewish Scriptures in Honor of his 65th Birthday* (eds. J. Zsengellér, A. Lange, and M. Weigold, FRLANT, Göttingen: Vandenhoeck & Ruprecht, forthcoming). For the Romanization of conquered territories during the reign of Augustus, see R. MacMullen, *Romanization in the Time of Augustus* (New Haven: Yale University Press 2000).

"CUT HER AWAY FROM YOUR FLESH"
DIVORCE IN BEN SIRA

Nuria Calduch-Benages
(Pontifical Gregorian University, Rome)

The Book of Ben Sira is known for its decidedly misogynist outlook, a feature that it shares with other Wisdom books (cf. Proverbs) and other Jewish authors of the Greco-Roman era (cf. Flavius Josephus). Whether this hostile attitude to women simply reflects the patriarchal society of the time (Gilbert, Di Lella, Camp),[1] or a personal obsession of the sage (Trenchard),[2] or faithfulness to tradition for pedagogical purposes (Wischmeyer),[3] or an attempt at the construction of an ideal androcentric reality (Schroer)[4] is debated by authors of all tendencies, not exclusively feminist.

These debates are often complicated by the enormous contrast between the figure of Lady Wisdom, always seen in a positive light, and the negative attitude of the sage towards women in general. This contrast certainly is astonishing and provokes very different reactions among readers (cf. e.g. McKinlay, Bergant and Strotmann).[5]

---

[1] M. Gilbert, "Ben Sira et la femme," *RTL* 7 (1976) 426-42; P.W. Skehan and A.A. Di Lella, *The Wisdom of Ben Sira* (AB 39, New York: Doubleday 1987); L. Archer, *Her Price is Beyond Rubies. The Jewish Woman in Graeco-Roman Palestine* (JSOTSup 60, Sheffield: JSOT Press 1990); C.V. Camp, "Understanding a Patriarchy: Women in Second Century Jerusalem Through the Eyes of Ben Sira," in *"Women Like This." New Perspectives on Jewish Women in the Graeco-Roman World* (ed. A.-J. Levine, SBLEJL 1, Atlanta: Scholars Press 1991) 1-39.

[2] W.C. Trenchard, *Ben Sira's View of Women. A Literary Analysis* (BJS 38, Chico: Scholars Press 1982).

[3] O. Wischmeyer, *Die Kultur des Buches Jesus Sirach* (BZNW 77, Berlin: de Gruyter 1995).

[4] S. Shroer, *Die Weisheit hat ihr Haus gebaut. Studien zur Gestalt der Sophia in den biblischen Schriften* (Mainz: Matthias-Grünewald 1996).

[5] J.E. McKinlay, *Gendering Wisdom the Host. Biblical Invitations to Eat and Drink* (JSOTSup 216 and GCT 4, Sheffield: Academic Press 1996) 160-78; D. Bergant, *Israel's Wisdom Literature. A Liberation-Critical Reading* (Minneapolis: Fortress Press 1997); A. Strotmann, "Das Buch Jesus Sirach: über die schwierige Beziehung zwischen göttlicher Weisheit und konkreten Frauen in einer androzentrischen Schrift," in *Kompendium Feministische Bibelauslegung* (eds. L. Schottroff and M.T. Wacker, Gütersloh: Gütersloher Verlagshaus 1998) 428-40.

Women in the Book of Ben Sira

In the Book of Ben Sira much attention is given to women.[6] About 100 verses of his book speak of them, either directly or through expressions like "the mother's womb" (1:14; 40:1; 46:13Hb; 49:7; 50:22) or "born from a woman" (10:18). Some verses are part of a larger literary unit: 3:1-16 (respect for the father and mother); 7:18-28 (family relations, vv. 24-26: daughters and spouse); 9:1-19 (dangerous women); 23:16-27 (sexual passions, vv. 22-27: the adulteress); 25:13-26 (the evil spouse); 26:1-18 (the good and the evil spouse) and 41:14–42:8 (true and false shame, vv. 22-24: the married woman, the prostitute and the maidservant). Some verses are part of a smaller literary unit: 7:27-28 (parents), 22:3-5 (daughters), 36:21-27 (the wife) and 42:9-14 (daughters). To this list can be added a series of verses dispersed throughout the book: 4:10; 7:19; 15:2; 19:2.11; 20:4; 23:14; 25:1.8; 28:15; 30:20; 33:20; 34:5; 35:14; 37:11; 40:19.23; 42:6; 47:6Hb.19, in which mention is also made of widows, virgins, Lady Wisdom, and, of course, women in general.

In the book, mothers, spouses, widows, daughters, virgins, maidservants, popular singers, courtesans and prostitutes always appear in relationship to a man who, in every case, constitutes the only point of reference (son, husband, father, eunuch, master or victim/customer). Moreover, all these women are described from a masculine point of view: that of the Jewish sage, who, faithful to the tradition of the ancients, writes his book thinking only and exclusively of his young disciples in whom he wants to inculcate a rigorous doctrine/discipline regarding women.

Married women receive special attention. The sage divides them in two basic ethical categories: the good spouses and the bad spouses (cf. esp. 25:13–26:18[7] and 36:21-27). This division, made from a completely androcentric perspective, is exclusively concerned with the happiness, the desire, the convenience and the authority of the husband. In other words, with regard to the spouse, goodness or wickedness have always to be understood from the perspective of the husband.

The Syriac Version and Women

The Syriac version of the Book of Ben Sira[8] probably was written by a Jew (3-4th century CE) and revised by a Christian before the 5th century CE. Com-

---

[6] For a general presentation, cf. N. Calduch-Benages, "Ben Sira y las mujeres," *Reseña Bíblica* 41 (2004) 37-44.

[7] Greek II and Syriac contain an addition of 9 verses (26:19-27) missing in Hebrew and Greek I. According to P.W. Skehan, "The presumption is that the verses were composed in Heb, though they are not extant in that language" (Skehan and Di Lella, *The Wisdom of Ben Sira*, 346).

[8] Cf. N. Calduch-Benages, J. Ferrer and J. Liesen, *La Sabiduría del Escriba. Wisdom of the Scribe. Edición diplomática de la versión siríaca del libro de Ben Sira según el Códice Ambrosiano con traducción española e inglesa. Diplomatic Edition of the Syriac Version of the Book*

pared with the Hebrew and Greek text this version is characterized by a series of significant theological changes regarding belief in eternal life, the creation of wisdom, the authority of the Jewish "fathers," the practice of poverty and especially regarding the attitude towards women. With regard to women, the Syriac version is more benevolent, or at least more respectful in some aspects.

On the theme of women, the Syriac version basically coincides with the Hebrew/Greek text, but there are some exceptions to this general rule. There are inexplicable changes (modifications, additions and omissions) that do not fall under the category of linguistic errors due to a mistaken or excessively subjective interpretation of the Hebrew text. Other changes, however, seem to have been inserted deliberately into the text for reasons of a different kind. Moreover, the translator perhaps decided not to translate some verses of the Hebrew text because he did not agree with the content or perhaps they offended his sensibility.

I mention five texts that are significant regarding women: in the first two the translator diverges from the original text, introducing some changes that favour women (37:11 and 40:1);[9] in the other three he prefers to remain silent and not to translate a series of expressions in bad taste, some of which (especially 42:14a: "The wickedness of a man is better than the goodness of a woman") have become classical examples of a misogynist attitude often quoted by authors (41:22-24; 42:6).

BEN SIRA AND DIVORCE

My objective is not to take up the whole theme of Ben Sira and women, which would certainly go beyond the limits of this paper, but rather I would like to focus on one particular aspect of this theme: divorce. Divorce is a topic that touches upon the whole institution of family, primarily upon the two spouses, the husband and the wife.[10] For this topic we take into

---

of Ben Sira according to Codex Ambrosianus, with Translations in Spanish and English (Biblioteca Midrásica 26, Estella: Verbo Divino 2003) 13-58.

[9] Sir 37:11a Greek/Hebrew: "Do not consult with a *woman* concerning her rival;" Syriac: "With a *woman*, do not commit adultery." Sir 40:1 Greek/Hebrew: "A heavy destiny was assigned (Hebrew: 'has been assigned by God') to every person, a heavy yoke is upon *the sons of Adam*, from the day they went forth from their *mother's womb* till the day they return to the *mother* of all (Hebrew: + 'the living');" Syriac: "Great things God has created and many labours for human beings, from when they went forth from *their mother's womb* and till they rest in the land of life."

[10] On divorce in Ben Sira, cf. J.J. Collins, *Jewish Wisdom in the Hellenistic Age* (OTL, Louisville: Westminster John Knox 1997) 65-66. On divorce in second temple Judaism, cf. L. Archer, *Her Price is Beyond Rubies*, 217-20; J.J. Collins, "Marriage, Divorce and Family in Second Temple Judaism," in *Families in Ancient Israel* (eds. L.G. Perdue, *et al.*, Louisville: Westminster John Knox 1997) 104-62, here 115-21; D. Instone-Brewer, *Divorce and Remarriage in the Bible. The Social and Literary Context* (Grand Rapids: Eerdmans 2002) 59-84.

consideration those texts of Ben Sira that mention divorce either explicitly or allude to it indirectly. Aside from Warren Trenchard's monograph (1982) on women in Ben Sira, the texts dealing with divorce have not been the subject of a specific study. This paper will explore Sir 7:26 (cf. 42:9); 25:26 and 28:15.

Your Spouse and Divorce (Sir 7:26)

The second part of Sir 7[11] (vv. 17-36) contains some advice concerning family life (vv. 18-28), divine cult (vv. 29-31) and service to one's neighbour (vv. 32-35) culminating in v. 36: "In all that you do, think of the end and thus you will not commit sins." In 7:18-28, the sage gives the disciple pieces of advice on domestic life (vv. 18-21), then on the possessions of the husband (vv. 22-26), and finally, on one's father and mother (vv. 27-28).[12]

Characteristic of 7:22-26 is the quadruple repetition of the possessive pronoun לך referring to livestock, to sons, to daughters, and, in the last place, to the spouse. The text is in line with the tradition of the Decalogue which groups together in the last commandment house, woman, servants and livestock (Exod 20:17; cf. Deut 5:21 where the woman is mentioned first, followed by house, fields, servants and livestock). The advice of the sage concerning livestock and sons follows the same linguistic pattern (imperative + imperative) and is formulated positively; the same applies to the advice concerning daughters except for v. 24b ("do not show yourself too indulgent with them"). However, when it comes to the spouse (v. 26), Ben Sira not only changes the pattern, introducing an antithetical proposition, but also expresses himself exclusively in the negative mode: אשה לך אל תתעבה ושנואה אל תאמן בה ("If you have a spouse, do not abhor her, but if she is hateful, do not trust her").

a) First stich. In 7:26a, the use of the verb תעב is surprising. It is not frequent in the Old Testament and in the *pi'el* it means: to regard as an abomination, abhor, or cause to be an abomination, make abominable.[13] In Deut 7:26, it refers to idols, and in Deut 23:8; Job 19:19 and 30:10 to persons. In the last two instances, it expresses the repugnance, which the friends of Job feel when confronted with his festering wounds. Apart from 7:26, Ben Sira also uses תעב in 11:2b (Mss A and B): "Do not abhor a man for his looks," which the Greek translates with βδελύσσω (cf. 16:8; 20:8). In 7:26a,

---

[11] On the thematic and literary unity of Sir 7, cf. C. Granados, "La humildad, camino del amor. Análisis estructural y semántico de Eclo 7," *EstBíb* 62 (2004) 155-69.

[12] These verses exist in Greek and Syriac but are missing in Hebrew (Ms A), probably because of homoiarcton. Cf. J. Haspecker, *Gottesfurcht bei Jesus Sirach. Ihre religiöse Struktur und ihre literarische und doktrinäre Bedeutung* (AnBib 30, Rome: PIB 1967) 298, note 39. According to J.H.A. Hart, *Ecclesiasticus. The Greek Text of Codex 248* (Cambridge: University Press 1909) 110-11: "the verses (27-28) complete the scale of duties ascending from cattle to God."

[13] Cf. the two possible translations that A.A. Di Lella proposes in his commentary: "If you have a wife, abhor her not (let her not seem odious to you)."

the sage offers no explanation for אל תתעבה,[14] nor does he add reasons or specify concrete situations, but he only limits himself to saying: Do not abhor your wife. It is therefore understood that one should not abhor her, in no case, in no circumstance. Although the text does not explicitly mention divorce, various authors detect here an allusion to it.[15] Yaron, e.g. considers תעב in this case to be synonymous with שנא (meaning 'to divorce') and thinks that the sage uses it in order to avoid repetition of the expression in the same verse. Hence his translation: "Hast thou a wife divorce her not, and trust not a divorcee".[16] However, the use of תעב instead of גרש, the technical expression for divorce (ἐκβάλλω in the LXX),[17] attested in the Old Testament (cf. Num 30:10; Lev 21:7.14; 22:13; Ezek 44:22) and also in Qumran (4Q159 2-4, 10; CD xiii 17; 11Q19 lix 4) should put us on our guard against Yaron's interpretation.[18]

Let us now turn to the Greek version: γυνή σοί ἐστιν κατὰ ψυχήν μὴ ἐκβάλῃς αὐτήν ("If you have a wife that pleases you, do not cast her out"). With the addition of κατὰ ψυχήν (lit. "according to [your] soul")[19] the translator breaks away from the parallelism which is characteristic of 7:22a (κτήνη σοί ἐστιν), 23a (τέκνα σοί ἐστιν) and 24a (θυγατέρες σοί εἰσιν) and makes a clear concession to the husband, appealing to his personal taste. If the spouse is pleasing to the husband, then Ben Sira advises not to cast her

---

[14] The verb תעב leads us to the noun תועבה (abomination), a strong expression that normally refers to the sins of idolatry (esp. in Deut and the later prophets) and, in some cases, to matters of a sexual nature (Lev 18:22.26.27.29; 20:13; Deut 22:5; 23:18). C. Mopsik, *La Sagesse de Ben Sira. Traduction de l'hébreu, introduction et annotation* (Les dix paroles, Paris: Verdier 2005) 111 quotes these texts in order to justify his translation of אל תתעבה in 7:26a ("qu'elle ne te répugne pas") and his surprising explanation: "Il est donc probable que l'aversion ou la répugnance dont il est question dans ce verset […] se rapporte à la sexualité feminine."

[15] Among others, Ryssel, Smend, Box and Oesterley, Spicq, Snaith, Morla Asensio in their respective commentaries. J.W. Gaspar, *Social Ideas in the Wisdom Literature of the Old Testament* (The Catholic University Studies in Sacred Theology 2/8, Washington: The Catholic University of America Press 1947) 35 and A. Minissale, *Siracide (Ecclesiastico)* (NVB 23, Roma: Paoline 1980) 65 also see an allusion to divorce in 7:19a. Thus, Minissale proposes to translate אל תמאס (do not despise) with "do not send away."

[16] R. Yaron, "On Divorce in Old Testament Times," *RIDA* 4 (1957) 117-28, here 118. See also Collins, *Jewish Wisdom*, 66: "Ben Sira is most probably advising against trusting a divorced woman, probably on the realistic ground that 'hell hath no fury like a woman scorned.'"

[17] Other technical expressions are שלח, הוציא, עזב, and the disputed שנא to which we will return later. Cf. Yaron, "On Divorce," 117-21.

[18] The translation by O. Kaiser is extremely favourable to wives and eliminates all possible allusions to divorce: "Hast du eine Frau, so bleibe ihr zugetan" (*Weisheit für das Leben. Das Buch Jesus Sirach. Übersetzt und eingeleitet* [Stuttgart: Radius 2005] 23).

[19] Latin: *secundum animam tuam* (= Syro-Hexaplaric: ܐܝܟ ܢܦܫܟ, "according to your soul"). A. Minissale, *La versione greca del Siracide. Confronto tra testo ebraico e versione greca alla luce del metodo midrascico-targumico* (AnBib 133, Roma: PIB 1995) 254 understands this as "un'aggiunta esplicativa."

out. With the verb ἐκβάλλω ("repudiate, send away"),[20] the translator passes from cause to effect,[21] leaving open for the husband the possibility of divorce, a possibility that was certainly not foreseen in the Hebrew text. In ancient law, the verb ἐκβάλλω (together with ἀποπέμπω and ἐκπέμπω) was used as the technical expression for a husband taking the initiative to separate from his wife.[22] Thus, for example, Demosthenes 4th century BCE) tells us how Phrastor, an Athenian of Aegilia put away (ἐκβάλλει) his wife after living with her for about a year (Against Neaera 51), and Androcides (5/4th century BCE) tells us of the scandal caused by Callias, son of Hipponicus (I,125). After having married a young woman, Callias took as wife her mother also, i.e. his mother-in-law. The three of them lived together in the same house, until the young woman, on the point of suicide, made her escape. Shortly afterwards Callias grew tired of his mother-in-law also and sent her off (ἐξέβαλε).[23]

b) Second stich. In 7:26b, Hebrew and Greek coincide. Both texts present a man married to a "hateful/hated" wife שנואה (Greek: μισουμένη; Latin: odibili).[24] In this case, the sage advises the husband not to trust her, because, understandably, the "hateful/hated" woman represents a serious danger to the husband. According to Trenchard, "This line is merely a corrective, added to line a [7:26a] to dampen the effect of what could be taken as an unconditional injunction against abhorring one's wife".[25] It is evident that the problem here is the interpretation of שנואה, a feminine passive participle from שנא, which has the same meaning in all West Semitic languages: to hate, to feel aversion toward someone or something.

We will now explore several different connotations of the word שנואה.

(1) First of all, the expression can refer to a woman that a man has to put up with, for whatever reasons, because she makes herself hateful, horrible and detestable to the man. In other words, this woman is at the opposite pole of the woman "that pleases you" of the Greek version. Consequently, it is most probable—although the text does not state it—that the husband ends up by sending her off. This is the case in Prov 30:23a. Among all the things that make the earth tremble, there is the "woman שנואה (Greek: μισητή) who finds a husband." Some think of a spinster of a certain age, unbearable and without any redeeming features. On the basis of the context, we prefer to think that it refers to a hateful, horrible or undesirable wife who in the end is

---

[20] Syriac: ܡܢܫܒܝܗ ܠܐ (do not send her away). Latin: non proicias illam.

[21] Minissale, La versione greca, 190.

[22] A.R.W. Harrison, The Law of Athens, The Family and Property (2nd ed., Bristol Classical Paperbacks, London: Bristol Classical Press 1997) 1: 40.

[23] Charondas, the giver of laws of the Thurians, said: "If a man sends his wife away (ἐκβάλη) he may not marry a woman younger than the wife whom he had sent away (ἐκβληθείσης)" (Diodorus Siculus XII,18; 1st century BCE).

[24] Syriac: ܘܐܢ ܒܝܫܐ ܗܝ (and if she is wicked).

[25] Trenchard, Ben Sira's View of Women, 91.

sent off by the husband. The characters in Prov 30:21-23[26] find themselves in situations which were once sources of envy, humiliation or resentment. This is the case with the servant who becomes king, with the fool who, thanks to a stroke of fortune, fills up with bread, with the maidservant who takes the place of her mistress, and with the wife who, after having been rejected/sent off by her husband, succeeds in getting married again. On this last one, Alonso Schökel comments: "when in the end she finds a husband, her resentment bursts free and she becomes unbearable."[27]

It seems that Ben Sira employs the verb שנא also in 42:9d referring to a married daughter. In spite of the bad condition of Mss B ([…] פן ובבתוליה) and Mas ([…] פן יה[..]וב)[28] and notwithstanding their differences we can, with the help of the versions,[29] attempt to reconstruct the Hebrew text as follows: ובעלה פן תשנא (and when married, lest she be hated). That is to say: the father suffers because of his daughter, who, if married, is hated and then sent away by the husband. If this were the case, the daughter would return to the house of her father, and then he would again have to take care of her, at least until she finds a new husband. And the worst of it is that the honour of the father would suffer a hard blow.[30] Mopsik, on the other hand, basing himself on b.*Sanh.* 100b, understands that the father suffers on account of his married daughter not bearing children,[31] since a barren woman ran the risk of being sent away by the husband (cf. y.*Yebam.* 64a).

(2) The participle שנואה could also be taken as the neglected spouse, the one not loved, the one not preferred, which would presuppose a polygamist marriage, or at least a bigamist marriage.[32] This is the position of Sauer who,

---

[26] On this numerical proverb, cf. R.C. van Leeuwen, "Proverbs 30:21-23," *JBL* 105 (1986) 599-610.

[27] L. Alonso Schökel and J. Vílchez Líndez, *Proverbios* (NBE, Sapienciales I; Madrid: Cristiandad 1984) 519.

[28] P.C. Beentjes, *The Book of Ben Sira in Hebrew. A Text Edition of all Extant Hebrew Manuscripts and a Synopsis of all Parallel Hebrew Ben Sira Texts* (VTSup 68, Leiden: Brill 1997) 167. Cf. the reconstruction by Yadin: ובימיה פן תן[נש]ה ("and in her heyday lest she be [forgotten]") in "The Ben Sira Scroll from Masada," in *Masada VI: Yigael Yadin Excavations 1963-1965. Final Reports* (eds. J. Aviram, *et al.*, Jerusalem: Israel Exploration Society 1999) [182], [218], [219] and the note by E. Qimron in [229].

[29] Greek: καὶ συνῳκηκυῖα, μήποτε μισηθῇ ("and if married, lest she be hated"); Syriac: "and (staying) with her husband, lest she be rejected" (ܬܣܬܢܐ ܕܠܐ).

[30] Camp, "Understanding a Patriarchy," 37: "As his property, he [the father] is honor-bound to prevent encroachment on them [his daughters]."

[31] Mopsik, *La Sagesse de Ben Sira*, 253. Cf. J.C. Greenfield, "Ben Sira 42.9-10 and its Talmudic Paraphrase," in *A Tribute to Geza Vermes. Essays on Jewish and Christian Literature and History* (eds. P.R. Davies and R.T. White, JSOTSup 100, Sheffield: Academic Press 1990) 167-73.

[32] Cf. R. Egger-Wenzel, "Spricht Ben Sira von Polygamie?," in *Jahrbuch der Universität Salzburg 1993-1995* (ed. A. Buschmann, München: Roman Kovar 1996) 57-64. And cf. the situation of Rachel and Leah in Gen 29:31.33 or the legislation of Deut 21:15-17 which deals with the case of a husband with two wives, one preferred and the other hated, שנואה/אהובה.

following Ginzberg and Kuhn, translates שנואה with "Nebenbuhlerin," i.e. rival, intruder, or competitor of the spouse (cf. Sir 25:14 [disputed text]; 26:6; 37:11).[33] Although we do not know much about the practice of polygamy in the time of Ben Sira, most authors think that though polygamy was permitted in the second temple period (it was declared illegal for Jews by emperor Theodosius I in 393 CE), monogamist marriage was the general rule.[34] This commonly-held view has been challenged by the Babatha archive from Nahal Hever near the Dead Sea (early 2nd century CE). A Greek papyrus dated the 9th July 131 CE contains the conflicting claims of the two wives (Babatha and Miriam) of Yehuda. This case shows that polygamy, or at least bigamy, was not such an exceptional practice among the Jews of the Tannaitic period.[35]

3) We also have to take in consideration the use of the verb שנא in the Judeo-Aramaic marital contracts from the colony of Elephantine in Upper Egypt (5th century BCE).[36] While in these juridical documents the verb גרש does not appear, the Aramaic תרך does and in most cases it is accompanied by the noun בית in the expression "drive [him/her] from the house" (AP 15,30; BMAP 7,30; BMAP 6,16).

On the basis of a study of the only three contracts preserved in good condition (AP 15; BMAP 2; BMAP 7), H. Nutkowicz recently has demonstrated that the verb שנא in this specific matrimonial context does not mean "to divorce" — as is usually held — but rather "to break a covenant". The expression under consideration is part of the formalities of separation of spouses, which go through various stages: the declaration of hate, the acquiring of the right to be divorced and the actual leaving of the house. In other words, שנא introduces the separation, and marks the rupture but not the dissolving of the marriage.[37]

Taking into account the fact that the matrimonial contracts from Elephantine employ a juridical language that is not proper to Ben Sira, nevertheless we believe that what has been said about the verb שנא also applies to Sir 7:26b. Here, instead of affirming explicitly the divorce as the Versions do, the participle שנואה rather denotes a strong disagreement

---

[33] G. Sauer, *Jesus Sirach/Ben Sira* (ATDA 1, Göttingen: Vandenhoeck & Ruprecht 2001) 90, note 113. Cf. also N. Peters, *Das Buch Jesus Sirach oder Ecclesiasticus. Übersetzt und erklärt* (EHAT 25, Münster: Aschendorff 1913) 73; H. Duesberg and I. Fransen, *Ecclesiastico*, in *La Sacra Bibbia... a cura di Mons. Salvatore Garofalo. Antico Testamento* (ed. G. Rinaldi; Torino: Marietti 1966) 124; L. Alonso Schökel, *Proverbios y Eclesiástico* (Los Libros Sagrados VIII.1, Madrid: Cristiandad 1968) 168.

[34] Collins, *Jewish Wisdom*, 65; Idem, "Marriage, Divorce and Family," 121-22, 128-30; Instone-Brewer, *Divorce and Remarriage*, 59-65. Polygamy was prohibited in Qumran (cf. CD iv 20-v 2; 11Q19 lvii 15-19).

[35] N. Lewis, *The Documents from the Bar-Kokhba Period in the Cave of the Letters* (Jerusalem: Israel Exploration Society 1989) 113-15. See also 22-24.

[36] Cf. the following expressions: כסף שנאה, "the money of hate" (AP 15,23; BMAP 2,8.9; 7,22.25) and דין שנאה, "the law or judgement of hate" (AP 18,1; BMAP 7,34.39).

[37] Cf. H. Nutkowicz, "A propos du verbe śn' dans les contrats de marriage judéo-araméens d'Éléphantine," *Trans* 28 (2004) 165-73, here 169, 172.

between husband and wife ("but where there is ill feeling")[38] that weakens the affective ties between the spouses and can become the beginning of a definite separation.

It is noteworthy that while in the text of Ben Sira the initiative for the separation/divorce comes from the husband (cf. the Talmudic law), in the Elephantine contracts the wives too have the freedom to decide to separate from their spouse.[39] Thus we read in AP 15,23: "Tomorrow or another day (if) Miphtahiah should stand up in the congregation and say, I hate (שנאת) Azor my husband" and AP 9,8-9: "If tomorrow or another day you lay out this land and then my daughter hates you (תשנאנך), and goes away from you." This juridical practice reflects the free condition of women and at the same time testifies to a mental openness and broadness of vision that do not seem typical of the time.[40]

The papyri of Elephantine are not the only ones to attest the freedom of women to divorce their husbands. Among the documents found by Yigail Yadin in Nahal Se'elim, just south of Nahal Hever, there is a divorce bill sent by a wife to her husband in 135 CE. Shelamzion, daughter of Joseph Qesbshan, says to her husband Eleazar, son of Hananniah: "This is from me to you a bill of divorce and release (גט שבקין ותרבנין)" (P. Se'elim 13).[41]

The Evil Wife and Divorce (Sir 25:26)

In 25:13–26:18 Ben Sira offers four instructions on the married woman, in which the two aforementioned ethical categories alternate: wickedness and goodness. The evil wives of 25:13-26 and 26:5-12 are set in contrast with the good wives of 26:1-4 and 26:13-18. The contrast between both figures is disproportionate, given the fact that the evil wives receive greater attention than the good ones. Moreover, the merits of the good wives are narrowed down to attitudes and actions that are in favour of their husbands.

After the fatal affirmation of 25:24 ("From a woman sin had its beginning and because of her we all die"), the sage concludes his first instruction on the evil wife with two verses (vv. 25-26), which, though missing in Hebrew, have been preserved in the Versions. The Greek text runs like this:

[25]μὴ δῷς ὕδατι διέξοδον.μηδὲ γυναικὶ πονηρᾷ παρρησίαν· [26]εἰ μὴ πορεύεται κατὰ χεῖρά σου ἀπὸ τῶν σαρκῶν σου ἀπότεμε αὐτήν
Do not give water an outlet, nor boldness of speech to an evil wife; if she does not walk by your hand, cut her off from your flesh.

[38] Translation by Di Lella (Skehan and Di Lella, *The Wisdom of Ben Sira*, 23).

[39] Whether this is due to an Egyptian influence or rather the fruit of an ancient West Semitic tradition attested since the 19th century BC is a matter of debate among scholars. Cf. E. Lipiński, "Marriage and Divorce in the Judaism of the Persian Period," *Trans* 4 (1991) 63-71.

[40] Cf. Nutkowicz, "A propos du verbe *sn',*" 173.

[41] Cf. T. Ilan, "Notes and Observations on a Newly Published Divorce Bill from the Judean Desert," *HTR* 89 (1996) 195-202.

Let us analyse in greater detail v. 26, which, in the words of Cohen, contains a 'pithy phrase or sentence' that can be considered as the crystallization of the concept of divorce.[42]

a) First stich. In 25:26a Ben Sira presents the motive[43] (the only one!) that can bring a husband to separate himself from an evil spouse. The expression "if she does not walk by your hand" (reconstructed Hebrew: אם לא תלך על ידך) is so generic as to embrace all possibilities in favour of the husband, and can be understood as a broad interpretation of the legislation on divorce in Deut 24:1-4. Instead of the controversial expression ערות דבר (lit.: "naked-ness of a matter"), "some indecency" (24:1), which seems to restrict the sup-posed fault of the woman to the sexual sphere, in Sir 25:26a the sage uses an image that denotes total submission to the husband. A spouse that "does not walk by the hand" of the husband, is an independent spouse that does not want to be governed, directed or controlled in any circumstance or situation of life.[44] Snaith remarks in a very acute way: "Ben Sira seems remarkably liberal — perhaps because of his prejudice!"[45]

In fact, the advice of the sage is in line with the later legislation according to which any motive alleged by the husband was valid in order to justify divorce. According to the school of Hillel, "[He may divorce his wife] even if she spoiled his dish" and R. Akiba adds "even if he found someone more beautiful than her" (m.Gitt. 9,10).[46] Flavius Josephus is of the same mind when he writes: "At this time I also divorced/sent away my wife [his second wife], being displeased at her behaviour" (Vita, 426) or also: "One who wishes for whatever reason [...] to be divorced from a woman who is living with him..." (Ant.Jud. 4,253; cf. Matt 19:3-9). The same goes for Philo of Alexandria in Spec.Leg. 3,30, where he presents the case from the perspective of the woman.[47]

b) Second stich (25:26b). In the case of an evil and rebellious wife Ben Sira does not hesitate to recommend a divorce. His wording is powerful: "cut her from your flesh" (reconstructed Hebrew: מבשרך גזר/כרת אותה). This original metaphor can be understood as a reply to Gen 2:24 where man and

---

[42] B. Cohen, Jewish and Roman Law. A Comparative Study (New York: The Jewish Theological Seminary of America 1966) 1: 387.

[43] Latin adds: 25,35bet confundet te in conspectu inimicorum (cf. 42:11).

[44] Some translations that have been proposed: if she does not behave according to your wishes/if she does not do what you want/if she does not want to submit to you/ if she does not obey you punctually/if she go not as you would have her/if she refuses to walk by your side/ if she does not accept your control.

[45] J.G. Snaith, Ecclesiasticus or The Wisdom of Jesus, Son of Sirach (CNEB, Cambridge: Cambridge University Press 1974) 131.

[46] Conversely, according to the school of Shammai, "a man should divorce his wife only because he has found grounds for it in unchastity" (m.Gitt. 9,10).

[47] Cf. R. Neudecker, "Das 'Ehescheidungsgesetzt' von Dtn 24,1-4 nach altjüdischer Auslegung. Ein Beitrag zum Verständnis der neutestamentlichen Aussagen zur Ehe-scheidung," Bib 75 (1994) 350-87, esp. 356-60.

woman are said to become "one flesh" (cf. Gen 2:23),[48] or also as a kind of *formula contraria,* that preceded the document of divorce and that indicated the separation of the spouses (cf. Hos 2:4 "She is not my wife and I am not her husband").[49] In this respect, it is worth mentioning a Babylonian marriage contract from ca. 625-623 BCE where we find the same metaphor that is employed in Ben Sira, with a slight variation. Here the metaphor does not refer to divorce but to the commitment to be established between the two future spouses. It is a curious case in which it is the bride who contracts her marriage (the groom's request for the bride was most often addressed to the bride's father, brother or mother). The son of Nadinu says to his fiancée Qunnabatu: "Cut yourself off from any other man. Be a wife," and the text continues: "Qunnabatu consented (to this proposal) and she will cut herself off from any other man."[50]

Ms 248 completes the stich by adding to it δίδου καὶ ἀπόλυσον ("give and send [her]"). Still more explicit is Syriac: ܗܒ ܠܗ ܘܫܪܝܗ ܡܢ ܒܝܬܟ ("give to her[51] and dismiss her from your house").[52] These two texts seem to suppose the presentation by the husband of a document of divorce, the ספר כריתות (Deut 24:1.3; Isa 50:1; Jer 3:8),[53] which literally means, "document of cutting," "deed of cutting asunder." This expression probably harks back to the ceremony that accompanied the divorce. In an Old Assyrian document of divorce (ca. 1400 BCE) the husband says: "I have cut off the fringe of her garment" (*sí-is-sí-ik-ta-ša ab-ta-táq*).[54] It is not surprising, therefore, that from this ancient ritual the document of divorce took its name of "document of cutting."

With the addition "dismiss her from your house," the Syriac version signals the conclusion of the process ending in divorce. The same expression is found in Deut 24:1-2 where the action of the husband (ושלחה מביתו, "he sent her away from his house") corresponds to that of the wife (ויצאה מביתו, and she left his house).[55] Given that cohabitation is the essential element of a

---

[48] Camp, "Understanding a Patriarchy," 29: "But 'one flesh' also implies, specifically, an exclusive sexual relationship. Thus, the particular way in which the wife has not walked by her husband's side is also suggested."

[49] Z.W. Falk, *Hebrew Law in Biblical Times. An Introduction* (2nd ed., Winona Lake: Eisenbrauns 2001) 151. For other interpretations, cf. Trenchard, *Ben Sira's View of Women,* 84.

[50] Cf. M.T. Roth, *Babylonian Marriage Agreements: 7th-3rd Centuries B.C.* (AOAT 222, Neukirchen-Vluyn and Kevelaer: Neukirchener and Butzon & Bercker 1989) 39-40.

[51] It can refer to the divorce document, or, according to Smend, to the dowry or to the material goods in the case of a rich wife, cf. R. Smend, *Die Weisheit des Jesus Sirach* (Berlin: Reimer 1906) 233.

[52] Latin adds: 25:36b*ne semper te abutatur* (cf. 26:10).

[53] Greek: τὸν βιβλίον τοῦ ἀποστασίου; Latin: *libellus repudii.*

[54] For this and other legislative Sumerian texts that contain the same expression, cf. P. Koschaker, *Neue keilschriftliche Rechtsurkunden aus der El-Amarna Zeit* (ASAW 36/5, Leipzig: Hirzel 1928) 24.

[55] The terminology for divorce is very similar in Roman law: *discidium* ("a cutting asunder"), *dimittere* ("to send away"), *domo expellere* ("to drive out of the house"), *baete*

marriage, the wife leaving the house marks the effective dissolution of the matrimonial bond.

c) The Babylonian Talmud contains 31 verses from the Book of Ben Sira, 12 of which deal with women.[56] Not all verses are authentic quotations: there are also close renderings, which we will quote hereafter. In b.*Sanh.* 100b we read:

"An evil woman is a plague to her husband (אשה רעה צרעת לבעלה). What is the solution? (מאי תקנתיה) Let him banish [divorce] her from his house (יגרשנה מביתו) and be healed from his plague (ויתרפא מצרעתו)."

While the first phrase reminds us of Sir 26:7 ("An evil wife is an ox yoke which chafes; taking hold of her is like grasping a scorpion"), the last one certainly is inspired by the extended form of Sir 25:26 as found in Syriac and the Greek Ms 248.[57] Like Ben Sira, the rabbis recommended that the husband divorce an "evil wife," because she is considered as a disease (lit.: leprosy), which if not dealt with in time, could destroy the health of the husband. Metaphors change but the ideas are the same.

The Valiant Wife and Divorce (Sir 28:15)

Sir 28:15 is part of a passage dedicated to the abuses of the tongue (28:13-26), in which the sage warns about gossip, lies and, in a special way, about slander. The first section focuses on the destructive force of slander (28:13-18) and the second praises piety as a remedy for it (28:19-26).

Slander (lit.: the third tongue) causes various disasters: it leads many into exile, destroys strongholds and overturns the house of the nobility (28:14). Even entire families fall victim to its devastating power; it is an irresistible power that destroys peace and sows discord among its members. In 28:15 the sage affirms:

γλῶσσα τρίτη γυναῖκας ἀνδρείας ἐξέβαλεν καὶ ἐστέρεσεν αὐτὰς τῶν πόνων αὐτῶν

---

foras ("go out"). On divorce in both legislations, cf. B. Cohen, *Jewish and Roman Law*, 1: 377-408.

[56] Cf. T. Ilan, *Integrating Jewish Women into Second Temple History* (TSAJ 76, Tübingen: Mohr Siebeck 1999) 155-74: "Ben Sira's Misogyny and its Reception by the Babylonian Talmud." For other perspectives on this theme, D.S. Levene, "Theology and Non-Theology in the Rabbinic Ben Sira," in *Ben Sira's God. Proceedings of the International Ben Sira Conference Durham—Ushaw College 2001* (ed. R. Egger-Wenzel, BZAW 321, Berlin: de Gruyter 2002) 305-20, esp. 309-11.

[57] Cf. B.G. Wright III, "B. Sanhedrin 100b and Rabbinic Knowledge of Ben Sira," in *Treasures of Wisdom. Studies in Ben Sira and the Book of Wisdom. Festschrift M. Gilbert* (eds. N. Calduch-Benages and J. Vermeylen, BETL 143, Leuven: University Press and Peeters 1999) 48.

The third tongue has driven away [from their houses] valiant women and deprived them of the fruit of their work.[58]

Besides the context, the use of the verb ἐκβάλλω (Hebrew: גרש) also indicates that Ben Sira is referring to divorces caused by slander. "The third tongue" became the standard formula in the Rabbinic writings for a slanderer. Thus, in b. 'Arak. 15b: "The third tongue (לישון תליתאי) kills three, viz. the slander, the slandered, and he who believes the slander" (cf. Midr.R. Lev 26; y.Pe'a 16a). In our text, the third tongue refers to a "third person," who interferes maliciously with the life of a couple in order to disrupt the harmony between husband and wife.[59] The instruction is imparted in a general way, and therefore it is difficult to find allusions to concrete situations or persons. Most authors, among whom is Di Lella,[60] understand 28:15 to be about a husband who confiding in false accusations that reached him from a third person, decides to send away his wife. According to Vaccari,[61] the situation described in 28:15 corresponds rather to a bigamist marriage in which the jealousy between the two wives is the cause of the divorce. In support of this reading he quotes as example the case of Abraham with his two spouses, Sarah and Hagar, in Gen 21:10.14.

Breaking up the marriage and causing her to be sent away, slander also deprives the wife of the fruit of her work and toil. Behind the Greek τῶν πόνων αὐτῶν we can suppose the Hebrew יגיע that, like πόνος, can mean the "work" or the "fruit of the work."[62] In his commentary Vella inclines towards a third meaning of the Hebrew word, viz. "offspring," since in his opinion, this is more appropriate in the context.[63] We do not know on what he bases his choice, because we could not find any text at all in which יגיע means offspring.

In 7:26, the sage gave advice about divorcing one's wife (Greek: "the wife who pleases you"), in 25:26, about the divorce of the evil and rebellious wife, and finally, in 28:15 about the divorce of the valiant spouse. In the latter, the Greek text speaks of γυναῖκας ἀνδρείας, i.e. wives who are valiant, coura-

---

[58] In Hebrew the entire passage is missing. Curiously, in 28:15, Syriac does not mention the wives: "An intriguer has brought many into captivity and he has separated them from their riches." Cf. Latin: [28,19]lingua tertia mulieres viritas eiecit et privavit illas laboribus suis.

[59] R.A.F. MacKenzie, Sirach (OTMes 19, Wilmington: Michael Glazier) 113, notes: "Iago, villain of Shakespeare's tragedy Othello, would be a prime example."

[60] Skehan and Di Lella, The Wisdom of Ben Sira, 365.

[61] A. Vaccari, I libri poetici della Bibbia tradotti dai testi originali e annotati (Roma: PIB 1925) 370. Similarly, Trenchard, Ben Sira's View of Women, 262, note 311.

[62] Thus Smend, Die Weisheit, 253 and J. Vella, "Eclesiástico," in La Sagrada Escritura. Antiguo Testamento (eds. Profesores de la Compañía de Jesús, BAC 312, Madrid: BAC 1970) 5: 110. M.Z. Segal prefers חיל (Spr bn-syr' hšlm, [Jerusalem: Bialik Institute 1953, 4th ed. 1997] 175); A. Kahana (Dbry šm'wn bn-syr'. Hsprym hhyṣwnym. Krk šny [Jerusalem: Mayer Lambert 1937, reprint 1970] 56) and E.S. Hartom (Hsprym hhyṣwnym. Bn-syr' [Tel Aviv: Yavneh Publishing House 1963] 101) read מעל.

[63] Vella, Eclesiástico, 110.

geous, strong, capable and excellent. The adjective ἀνδρεία applied to a woman also appears in 26:2a ("a valiant wife rejoices her husband") and in
Prov 31:13a ("a valiant woman, who will find her?") as a translation for חיל.
In Sir 28:15 the cause of the divorce has nothing at all to do with the woman,
but has everything to do with a terrible weapon, the lethal power of which
supersedes that of a sword to such an extent that it is more preferable to die
than to live under its iron yoke (28:20-21).

In conclusion, in 28:15, both husband and wife fall victim to sneaky
slander. She will be sent away unjustly and he, if we understand 28:16 as
referring to the husband, will never have rest nor live in peace. That will be
his punishment for having given credit to the third tongue.

CONCLUSION

The Book of Ben Sira is a wisdom book written with an eminently
pedagogical intention. Its author did not mean to write an account of his
time but to instruct his young disciples in the way of life that leads to true
wisdom. For this reason his interest in social, economic or political themes, is
marked by a decidedly pedagogical orientation. The book contains little
information and few historically documented data. This thwarts any attempt
to reconstruct in an accurate way the society of that time with all its
institutions, customs and tensions. This difficulty has made itself felt in our
study on divorce. The Qumran documents were also not of great help, since
they rarely speak of divorce (11Q19 liv 4-5; 11Q19 lxvi 8-11; CD xiii 15-17)
and some of the references are difficult to understand (CD iv 20–v 2; 11Q19
lvii 15-19).[64]

The second difficulty for the present study is tied up with the
complicated textual evolution of the Book which remains until today a major
challenge for scholars. Of the three texts studied here, only one (7:26) occurs
in the Hebrew Mss A and B, both of which are badly preserved as far as this
particular verse is concerned, and this one text differs considerably from the
Greek, Syriac and Latin Versions. For the other texts we had to make use of
the versions in order to reconstruct a hypothetical Hebrew original.

As far as 7:26 is concerned, the Hebrew text is ambiguous. It does not
speak clearly of divorce, although the use of the verb שנא probably has to be
understood as a breakdown of marriage (cf. the matrimonial contracts from
the Elephantine colony). By contrast, the Greek version (followed by Syriac
and Latin) is more concrete and leaves open the possibility of divorce for the
husband who is displeased with his wife.

In 25:26, with extremely harsh language, Ben Sira recommends divorce
to the husband of an evil and rebellious wife. The content of Greek I is
further elaborated in Greek II and Syriac, where there is an unmistakable
allusion to the document of divorce. Here the thought of the sage is in

---

[64] See Instone-Brewer, *Divorce and Remarriage*, 65-72 and Collins, "Marriage, Divorce and Family," 128-30.

harmony with the later rabbinic tradition as recorded in the Talmud (cf. b.*Sanh.* 100b), according to which only the husband can initiate divorce. One has to wait for the Herodian period to find women (Salome, Herod's sister, and Herodias, Agrippa's daughter) who take the initiative in a divorce from their husbands (cf. *Ant.Jud.* 15,11; 18,17).

Finally, 28:15 justifies concluding that divorce was a relatively frequent practice at the time of Ben Sira. If nothing else, the sage alludes to some cases of divorce of marriages that were destroyed by the third tongue, or slander. His discourse is, however, so general that no further consequences can be gleaned from it. Without going into possible reasons, Flavius Josephus also refers to divorce as a common practice in the society of his day (cf. *Ant.Jud.* 4,253).

In spite of the scarcity of information (there is e.g. no mention of the consequences for the spouses or for the children of divorced parents), all indications seem to confirm that Ben Sira defended divorce, always and whenever the husband took the initiative. The wife appears to be completely dependent on the husband having no choice but to accept his will for her (cf. by contrast, the texts of Elephantine and *Papyrus Se'elim* 13). This position of the sage need not surprise us, for it is in line with his negative attitude towards women in general.

DAS VERHÄLTNIS DER חכמה ZUR תורה IM BUCH BEN SIRA
KRITERIEN ZUR GEGENSEITIGEN BESTIMMUNG

Friedrich V. Reiterer
(Universität Salzburg)

Es gibt wenige Ergebnisse, welche in der wissenschaftlichen Diskussion allem Anschein nach zu einem überzeugenden, allseits anerkannten Ergebnis geführt haben. Die Gleichsetzung von Weisheit und Tora im Werk Ben Siras scheint eines davon zu sein. Für O. Kaiser gibt der Gott der Väter Israels „seinem Volk an seiner verborgenen Weisheit in Gestalt der Tora"[1] Anteil und „die Mose von Gott selbst gegebene Tora (ist) der Inbegriff und die Quelle der Weisheit (Sir 45:5 mit 24:23ff.)."[2] In vergleichbarer Weise hebt E. Zenger hervor,

> die nachexilische Weisheitstheologie betrachtet *die Tora* Israels als die größte und eigentliche Weisheitsgabe Gottes... (Jener begegnet) dem Geheimnis des alles durchwaltenden Gottes..., wer die Tora zur Lebensmaxime macht. Klassisch formuliert findet sich diese Weisheitstheologie... vor allem im Sirachbuch...

Kurz zusammengefasst: Weisheit und Tora sind zu identifizieren.[3] Diese These geht vor allem auf die Ausführungen von Marböck[4] — der sich allerdings differenzierter als die Rezipenten äußerste — und in dessen Gefolge auf jene von Schnabel zurück. Wenn man bei Marböck liest, dass

> die erste ausdrückliche Verbindung von Weisheit und Mosetora (vgl. Dtn 4:6f), die in 17:7-14 geradezu als universale Schöpfungsordnung erscheint, ...Israels

---

[1] O. Kaiser, *Die alttestamentlichen Apokryphen. Eine Einleitung in Grundzügen* (Gütersloh: Chr. Kaiser und Gütersloher Verlagshaus 2000) 87.

[2] Kaiser, *Apokryphen* 88.

[3] Vgl. z.B. M. Witte, *Vom Leiden zur Lehre. Der dritte Redegang (Hiob 21-27) und die Redaktionsgeschichte des Hiobbuches* (BZAW 230, Berlin: de Gruyter 1994) 195: „Obwohl in der Identifikation der חָכְמָה mit der תּוֹרָה gipfelnde Weisheitsschrift des Ben Sira (vgl. 17:11ff; 24:23; 45,5; u.ö) eine den Proverbien vergleichbare optimistische Anthropologie enthält, deren Ethik auf die Erlangung der Gottesfurcht ausgerichtet ist, begegnen doch vereinzelt Aussagen, die das Niedrigkeitsmotiv führen und sich auf der Linie von Ps 143:2 mit der Niedrigkeitsredaktion berühren."

[4] Vgl. z.B. J. Marböck, *Weisheit im Wandel. Untersuchungen zur Weisheitstheologie bei Ben Sira* (BZAW 272, Berlin: de Gruyter 1999) (= BBB 37, Bonn: Hanstein 1971) 90.

Identität angesichts zeitgenössischer Rede von Weisheit und Weltgesetz (vgl. Stoa)[5]

stärkt, dann sieht man, dass der Autor inzwischen die Relation vorsichtig beschreibt. Da nun Schnabel besonderen Wert auf die Identifikation legt und diese These auch ausführlich durchspielt, sei seine Untersuchung vorgestellt.

Schnabel legt eine Definition von dem vor, was er unter Identifikation versteht,[6] und hält fest, dass er sieben Beispiele einer „explicit evidence" für die Identifikation vorfindet. Denn „the law is a sure way to wisdom. To keep the law is to be wise".[7] Zu den sicheren Stellen rechnet er 1:26; 17:11; 19:20; 21:11; 24:23; 34:8 und 45:5c.d. „The implicit evidence" lässt eine weitere Gruppe anführen. „Twelve passages presuppose, imply, or result in the identification of law and wisdom."[8] Darüber hinaus benennt er noch weitere „secondary passages".[9] Er hebt hervor, dass man bei der Analyse unterschiedliche Erscheinungen des Parallelismus genau zu untersuchen habe, wodurch in seinen Augen bisher nicht berücksichtigte Ergebnisse erreicht werden:

> The chiastic structure of the verse suggests that wisdom is also identified with the control of the 'natural' inclination (יצר) and the fear of the Lord with obedience to the Torah. It has not been observed yet that besides this structural parallelism we also find a synonymous parallelism with regard to the content: as obedience to the law leads to inner discipline and a godly life, so does accomplished wisdom which corresponds with commitment to God. In other words: obedience to the law is accomplished wisdom—both are strongly linked with the fear of the Lord, and both are the foundation and the means of attaining a godly life which is in accordance with God's commandments.[10]

Da Schnabel erfreulicherweise ein ausgeprägtes Gespür für literarische Gegebenheiten besitzt, verwundert, dass er den literarischen Kontext von Einheiten nicht berücksichtigt. Er greift seine Beispiele isoliert heraus und

---

[5] J. Marböck, „Das Buch Jesus Sirach," in E. Zenger et al., Einleitung in das Alte Testament (6. aufl., Kohlhammer Studienbücher Theologie 1,1, Stuttgart: Kohlhammer 2006) 408-16, 415 (1. aufl., 1995, 285-92, 363); J. Marböck, „Gesetz und Weisheit. Zum Verständnis des Gesetzes bei Jesus Ben Sira," in idem, Gottes Weisheit unter uns. Zur Theologie des Buches Sirach, (ed. I. Fischer, HBS 6, Freiburg: Herder 1995), 52-72 (= BZ NF 20 [1976] 1-21) passim;

[6] Vgl. E.J., Schnabel, Law and Wisdom from Ben Sira to Paul: A Tradition-Historical Enquiry into the Relation of Law, Wisdom, and Ethics (WUNT 2/16, Tübingen: Mohr Siebeck 1985) 90.

[7] Schnabel, Law 70.

[8] Vgl. Schnabel, Law 73; er führt folgende Belege an: 1:26; 2:15-16; 6:36; 15:15; 19:24; 24:22; 24:32-33; 33:2-3; 38:34c,d/39:8; 44:4c; 51:15c,d und 51:30a,b.

[9] Vgl. Schnabel, Law 77; es sind dies nach seinen Angaben 1:5; 19:19; Prol. 1-3; Prol. 12-14; Prol. 29,35-36.

[10] Schnabel, Law 70f.

beschäftigt sich nicht weiter mit der gesamten Einheit, in der seine Belege stehen.

1. BELEGSTELLEN

Um eine systematische Untersuchung vornehmen zu können, ist es unumgänglich, das Material zu sammeln, zu sichten und dann zu untersuchen, wobei die Kriterien für den Untersuchungsteil noch näher zu bestimmen sind. Vor jedem weiteren Schritt sei daran erinnert, dass das Buch nur zu 64%[11] in hebräischen Versionen erhalten ist. Daher wird man das griechische Material, wo eine gesamte, im ausgehenden 2. Jh. v. Chr. angefertigte Version erhalten ist, als Grundlage nehmen. Wollte man den gesamten Bereich weisheitlicher Thematik, also das einschlägige Wortfeld, erörtern, wären auch die Vorkommen von παιδεία und γνῶσις usw. einzubeziehen, wodurch sich die Anzahl der Belege deutlich erhöhen würde. Entsprechend der gewählten Thematik, werden die Parallelworte aber nicht an sich systematisch umfassend behandelt, sondern so weit es für die Behandlung nötig ist, da es um die Relationen von (ה)חכמ / σοφ* und תורה / νομ* gehen soll. Um die Belege auch visuell eindrücklich vorzustellen, wird eine graphisch übersichtliche Präsentation gewählt:

Obowohl der sirazidische Text in den Handschriften — mit wenigen Ausnahmen bei einzelnen Worten — nicht vokalisiert ist, wird die Punktation gesetzt. Die Wortwurzel ist unvokalisiert, während das Adjektiv חֲכָם und das Nomen חָכְמָ mit Vokalzeichen versehen sind: es soll die Übersichtlichkeit erhöht werden. In der folgenden Liste werden auch die syrischen Belege in den zur Untersuchung anstehenden Versen angeführt. Die kursiv gesetzten griechischen Belege gehören zu G^{II}.

---

[11] Vgl. F.V. Reiterer, „Text und Buch Ben Sira in Tradition und Forschung," in F.V. Reiterer, *„Alle Weisheit stammt vom Herrn…" Gesammelte Studien zu Ben Sira* (ed. R. Egger-Wenzel, BZAW 375, Berlin: de Gruyter 2007) 3-49. 32-34 (= F.R. Reiterer u.a., *Bibliographie zu Ben Sira* [BZAW 266, Berlin: de Gruyter 1998] 1-42); vgl. als Textausgaben: P.C. Beentjes, *The Book of Ben Sira in Hebrew. A Text Edition of All Extant Hebrew Manuscripts and a Synopsis of All Parallel Hebrew Ben Sira Texts* (VTSup 68, Leiden: Brill 1997) (2. aufl. Atlanta: SBL 2006); N. Calduch-Benages, J Ferrer und J. Liesen, *La Sabiduría del Escriba. Wisdom of the Scribe. Edición diplomática de la versiòn siriaca del libro de Ben Sira según el Códice Ambrosiano, con traducción española e inglesa. Diplomatic Edition of the Syriac Version of the Book of Ben Sira according to Codex Ambrosianus, with Translations in Spanish and English* (Biblioteca Midrásica 26, Estella: Verbo Divino 2003); J. Ziegler, *Sapientia Iesu Filii Sirach* (Septuaginta. Vetus Testamentum Graecum auctoritate Societatis Litterarum Gottingensis editum XII.2, Göttingen: Vandenhoeck & Ruprecht 1965).

Kapitel	σοφ*-Vorkommen	νομ*-Vorkommen
Prolog[12]		0:1 νόμος
	0:3 σοφία	
		0:8 νόμος
	0:12 σοφία	
		0:14 ἔννομος
		0:24 νόμος
		0:36 ἐννόμως
1	1:1a σοφία	
	1:3b σοφία	
	1:4a σοφία	
	1:6a σοφία	
	1:8a σοφός	
	1:14a σοφία	
	1:16a σοφία	
	1:18a σοφία	
	1:20a σοφία	
	1:25a σοφία	
	1:26a σοφία	
	1:27a σοφία	
2		2:16b νόμος
	3:25b חָכְמָה	
3	3:29b חָכְמָה ,חָכָם, σοφός	
4	4:11a ܚܟܡܬܐ, σοφία	
	4:23b חָכְמָה, ܚܟܡܬܐ, σοφία	
	4:24a חָכְמָה, ܚܟܡܬܐ, σοφία	
6	6:18b חָכְמָה, ܚܟܡܬܐ, σοφία	
	6:22a σοφία	
	6:32a חכם, ܚܟܡ	
	6:33b ܚܟܡ, σοφός	
	6:34b ܚܟܡܬܐ, σοφία	
	6:37d חכם, σοφία	
7	7:5b σοφίζειν	
	7:19a σοφός	
8	8:8a חָכָם, ܚܟܝܡܐ, σοφός	
9	9:14b חָכָם, ܚܟܝܡܐ, σοφός	
		9:15b νόμος
	9:17b ܚܟܝܡܐ, σοφός	
10	10:1a ܚܟܝܡܐ, σοφός	
	10:25a ܚܟܝܡܐ, σοφός	
	10:26a חכם, σοφίζειν	
11	11:1a חָכְמָה, ܚܟܡܬܐ, σοφία	

[12] Die Zählung folgt F.V. Reiterer, unter Mitarbeit von R. Egger-Wenzel and I. Krammer and P. Ritter-Müller, *Zählsynopse zum Buch Ben Sira* (FoSub 1, Berlin: de Gruyter 2003).

	11:15a חָכְמָה, ܚܟܡܬܐ, σοφία	
14	14:20a חָכְמָה, ܚܟܡܬܐ, σοφία	
		15:1b תּוֹרָה, νόμος
15	15:3b σοφία / 15:3a ܚܟܡܬܐ	
	15:10a חָכָם, ܚܟܝܡܐ, σοφία	
	15:18a חָכְמָה, ܚܟܡܬܐ, σοφία	
17		17:11b νόμος
18	18:27a ܚܟܝܡܐ, σοφός	
	18:28a ܚܟܡܬܐ, σοφία	
	18:29a ܚܟܡ, ܚܟܝܡܐ, σοφίζειν	
19		19:17b νόμος
	19:20a ܚܟܡܬܐ, σοφία	19:20b νόμος
	19:22a ܚܟܝܡܐ, σοφία	
	19:23b σοφία	
		19:24b νόμος
20	20:5a ܚܟܝܡܐ, σοφός	
	20:7 חָכָם, ܚܟܝܡܐ, σοφός	
	20:13a חָכְמָה, חָכָם, σοφός	
	20:27a ܚܟܡܬܐ, σοφός	
	20:29a σοφός	
	20:30a ܚܟܡܬܐ, σοφία	
	20:31b ܚܟܡܬܐ, σοφία	
21	21:11b σοφία	21:11a νόμος
	21:13a ܚܟܝܡܐ, σοφός	
	21:15a ܚܟܝܡܐ, ܚܟܝܡܐ, σοφός	
	21:18a ܚܟܡܬܐ, σοφία	
	21:26b ܚܟܝܡܐ, σοφός	
22	22:6c ܚܟܡܬܐ, σοφία	
23	23:2b σοφία	
		23:23a νόμος
24	24:1a ܚܟܡܬܐ, σοφία	
		24:23b νόμος
	24:25a ܚܟܡܬܐ, σοφία	
25	25:5a ܚܟܡܬܐ, σοφία	
	25:10a σοφία	
27	27:11a ܚܟܡܬܐ, ܚܟܝܡܐ, σοφία	
32	32:4c חכם, ܚܟܡ, σοφίζειν	
		32:15a תּוֹרָה, νόμος
		32:17b תּוֹרָה
	32,16d+ חָכְמָה, ܚܟܡܬܐ	
	32,17a חָכָם	
	32:18a חָכְמָה, חָכָם ܚܟܝܡܐ[13]	32:18d+ תּוֹרָה
		32:24a תּוֹרָה, νόμος
33	33:2a חָכָם, σοφός	33:2a תּוֹרָה, νόμος

[13] So in 7h3; vgl. 7a1: ܒܪܘܝܐ.

		33:3a νόμος
		33:3b תּוֹרָה, νόμος
	33:18a חכמה, ܚܟܡܬܐ	
	33:18c+ חָכָם	32:18d+ תּוֹרָה
34	34:8b חָכְמָה, ܚܟܡܬܐ, σοφία	34:8a νόμος
35		35:1 νόμος
37	37:19a חכם, חָכָם, ܚܟܝܡܐ	
	37:20a חכם, ܚܟܝܡܐ, σοφίζειν	
	37:21b σοφία	
	37:22a חכם, חָכָם, ܚܟܝܡܐ, ܚܟܝܡܐ, σοφός	
	37:23a חכם, חָכָם, ܚܟܝܡܐ,ܚܟܝܡܐ, σοφός	
	37:24a חָכָם, ܚܟܝܡܐ, σοφός, σοφίζειν	
	37:26a חָכָם ܚܟܝܡܐ, σοφός	
38	38:2a חכם, ܚܟܡ	
	38:24a חכם, חָכְמָה, ܚܟܡܬܐ, ܚܟܡܬܐ, σοφία	
	38:25a חכם, ܚܟܡ, σοφίζειν	
	38:31b ܚܟܡ, σοφίζειν	
	,	38:34d νόμος
39	39:1a ܚܟܡܬܐ, σοφία	
	39:6c σοφία / 39:6b ܚܟܡ	
		39:8b νόμος
	39:10a ܚܟܡܬܐ, σοφία	
40	40:19d+ חָכְמָה, ܚܟܡܬܐ	
	40:20b σοφία	
41		41:4b תּוֹרָה
		41:8b תּוֹרָה, νόμος
	41:12b חָכְמָה	
	41:14b חָכְמָה σοφία	
	41:15b חָכְמָה σοφία	
42		42:2a תּוֹרָה, νόμος
	42:6a חָכָם H^B	
	42:21a חָכְמָה, ܚܟܡܬܐ, σοφία	
43	43:33b σοφία	
44	44:4c חָכָם, σοφός / 44:4b ܚܟܡܬܐ, ܚܟܝܡܐ	
	44:15a חָכְמָה, σοφία	
		44:20a νόμος
		45:5c תּוֹרָה, νόμος
		45:17d νόμος
45	45:26a חָכְמָה, ܚܟܡܬܐ, σοφία	
46		46:14a νόμος
47	47:14a חכם, ܚܟܝܡܐ, σοφίζειν	
49		49:4c תּוֹרָה, νόμος
50	50:23a חָכְמָה, ܚܟܡܬܐ	
	50:27d σοφία / 50:27a ܚܟܝܡܐ	

51

50:28b חכם, ܚܟܡ, σοφίζειν
51:13b σοφία
51:15b חָכְמָה
51:17b σοφία

51:19b νόμος

51:25b חָכְמָה, ܚܟܡܬܐ

Auffällig ist, dass über die griechischen σοφ* Belege hinaus relativ häufig
(ה)חכמ vorkommt, ohne dass eine Entsprechung in der griechischen Version
gegeben ist, so in 3:25b+; 4:23b; 6:32a; 11:15a; 32:16d+,17a,18a; 37:19a; 38:2a;
40:19d+; 41:12b; 42:6a; 50:23a; 51:15b; 51:25b. Somit kommen zu den 88 griechischen nochmals 15 Belege, sodass sich insgesamt 103 Verse ergeben.
Die Verwendung von νομ* ist in 35 Versen gegeben: Die Parallelisierung der
griechischen und hebräischen Version ist konsequenter als im weisheitlichen
Bereich gegeben, doch liegen in 32:17b,18d und 41:4b nur hebräische Bezeu-
gungen vor.
   Die Verteilung zwischen Weisheit und Gesetz ist sehr ungleich. Den
mehr als 100 Belegen für *Weisheit/weise sein* stehen (inklusive den Prolog) 35
Belege für *Gesetz* gegenüber. Von diesem Befund aus gesehen wird die Frage
immer interessanter, wie das Verhältnis von „Weisheit" und „Gesetz" zu
bestimmen ist. Im Verhältnis zu diesen zahlreichen Belegen ist es auffallend,
dass חָכְמָה / σοφία und תורָה / νόμος nur in 19:20a,b; 21:11a,b; 33:2a,18c+d+ (nur
H); 34:8a,b im gleichen Vers belegt sind.

2. WEISHEIT UND GESETZ ALS THEMA LITERARISCHER EINHEITEN

Es ist schon festgestellt worden, dass sich in Ben Sira ganze Gedichte
schwerpunktartig mit *Weisheit* beschäftigen.[14] Folgende Passagen werden als
eigenständige Einheiten über Weisheit angegeben: 1:1-10; 4:11-19; 6,18-37;
14:20-15:10; 18:27-29; 19:20-24; 20:27-31; 21:12-28; 24:1-22.23-34; 37:16-26;
38:24-39:14; 51:13-30.[15] Dieser für Sira und sein literarisches Werk besonders
bedeutsame Bereich wird also in vielen literarischen Einheiten umfassend
behandelt und von verschiedenen Seiten her beleuchtet.
   Im Gegensatz dazu unterscheidet sich die Behandlung von Gesetz
grundlegend.

[14] Vgl. die grundlegende Untersuchung O. Rickenbacher, *Weisheitsperikopen bei Ben
Sira* (OBO 1, Freiburg and Göttingen: Universitätsverlag 1973).
[15] Bei manchen dieser Beispiele weichen die Abgrenzungen in den verschiedenen
Werken von einander ab; darauf wird hier nicht weiter Rücksicht genommen, da die
Angaben für den ersten Überblick genügen. Einschlägige Auflistungen finden sich
auch in den Lexikabeiträgen, einleitenden Werken und auch in Einzeluntersuchun-
gen; vgl. u.a. J. Marböck, „Sirach / Sirachbuch," in *TRE* 31: 307-17; idem, *Buch*; F.V.
Reiterer, „Jesus Sirach / Jesus Sirachbuch / Ben Sira / Ecclesiasticus," in *WILAT*, Stuttgart 2007, http://www.wilat.de. [Abschnitt 5.1].

Beachtenswert ist im Gegensatz zur Weisheit und Gottesfurcht, dass das Gesetz, die Torah bei Ben Sira schon rein literarisch nie direkter Gegenstand einer Abhandlung eines Gedichtes oder einer großen Perikope ist, vom Abschnitt 32(35),14-24 abgesehen.[16]

Selbst diese Beobachtung wird man kritisch hinterfragen, da die Einheit 32:14-24 herausstellen will, wie man richtig Gott sucht (אל דורש 32:14a). H[B], einen Stichos mehr als G aufweisend, hebt noch stärker als G hervor, dass dafür Erziehung (מוסר) und Bildung (לקח / ܡܠܦܢ) unerlässlich sind (32:14a.c). Was tut nun jener, der nach Gott strebt? Er kann entweder das Gesetz erforschen (דורש תורה / ὁ ζητῶν νόμον [32:15a]) oder Gott achten (יי ירא / οἱ φοβούμενοι κύριον; [32:16a]) oder als Weiser (איש חכם / ἀνὴρ βουλῆς) seine Bildung (כחמה / διανόημα, [32:18a]) in der Öffentlichkeit anbieten. Belehrung und Ausbildung[17] wird in diesem Abschnitt mit der Treue zum Gesetz[18] bzw. zum Gebot[19] auf die gleiche Ebene gestellt, wobei anzumerken ist, dass wegen der Möglichkeit einer verkorksten Auslegung der תורה (32:17b) und der Parallelisierung mit מצוה (32:23b) תורה u.a. als Gebot oder als eine Sammlung von Einzelvorschriften verstanden wird. Eine Anspielung an die mosaische Tora ist nicht gegeben. Letztlich geht es aber in diesem Gedicht um das Vertrauen auf Gott (בוטח ביי, 32:24b) und nicht um תורה, wobei jedoch das viermalige Vorkommen von תורה als Leitwort auffällig ist. Im Gedicht überwiegen die Worte aus dem „weisheitlichen" Wortfeld. So ergibt sich, dass es zwar sirazidische Abschnitte gibt, die sich mit der „Weisheit", aber keine vergleichsgleichen, die sich mit dem „Gesetz" beschäftigen.

Dass innerhalb der Einheit nur das Adjektiv חָכָם bzw. σοφός in 32,18a und zudem in keiner Parallele zu einem Wort aus dem Wortfeld von „Gesetz" vorkommt, deutet unterschiedliche Bedeutung der Lexeme „Weisheit" und „Gesetz" an.

3. GRUNDELEMENTE DER WEISHEITSVORSTELLUNG IM SIRAZIDISCHEN WERK

Sira verwendet חָכְמָה / σοφία bzw. die Derivate der zugrunde liegenden Wurzeln polysem. Daher geht es darum, die polysemen Aussagefelder von „Weisheit" zu erheben. Als zentraler Ansatz zur Beschreibung der Verwendungsbereiche dient die Beobachtung, dass es Stellen gibt, die sich intensiv mit der Weisheit beschäftigen, ohne dass man beschreiben kann, wie die Weisheit inhaltlich zu erfassen ist. Die Aussagen über die Weisheit sind sehr allgemein und die behandelten Themen kreisen um breitere Zusammenhangsfragen. Zugleich sind das diese Stellen, die besonders nachdrücklich dazu mahnen, sich die Weisheit anzueignen. Eine zweite Gruppe konzent-

---

[16] Marböck, Weisheit, 85.

[17] Vgl. מוסר / παιδεία, 32:14a; לקח / ܡܠܦܢ, 32:14c+; תחבולות / δικαιώματα, 32:16b; חכמות / ܚܟܡܬܐ, 32:16d; תוכחות / ἐλεγμός , 32:17a; חכמה / διανόημα, 32:18a; עצה / βουλή, 32:19a.

[18] Vgl. תורה: 15a,17b,18d,24a.

[19] Vgl. מצוה, 32:23b,23d+.

riert sich auf konkrete Bereiche, wo die Weisheit in Erscheinung tritt und wie sie realisiert wird. Das führt in Analogie zur an den Universitäten üblichen Unterscheidung zwischen Grundlagenforschung und angewandter Forschung zu einer ähnlichen Bezeichnung, nämlich חָכְמָה / σοφία als eine *grundlegende Gegebenheit* (1.) und חָכְמָה / σοφία *als eine angewandte Größe* (2.), sodass im Folgenden die „Grundlagenweisheit" und die „angewandte Weisheit" behandelt werden.

3.1. *Grundlagenweisheit*

Auf der ersten Ebene (Sir 1:1-10; 4:11-19; 6,18-37; 14:20-15:10; 24:1-22; 51:13-30) wird die *Weisheit an sich* als sehr zentral und häufig als aktive, einer Frau vergleichbare Wirklichkeit beschrieben. Die Aktivitäten bzw. Verhaltensweisen der Weisheit sind denen unter Menschen vergleichbar. Es werden viele Verben verwendet, die auch für menschliches Verhalten gebraucht werden. Auffallend ist in diesen Gedichten der Gegensatz einerseits zwischen der Intensität der Beschreibung des Strebens nach Weisheit und andererseits der Allgemeinheit des Wortes „Weisheit".

In diesem Zusammenhang wird die Beziehung der Weisheit zu Gott behandelt. Es wird die Herkunft der Weisheit dargestellt: Als Geschöpf Gottes — an manchen Stellen nahezu Gott gleich beschrieben — spielt sie nach dem Plan Gottes innerhalb der Schöpfung eine herausragende Rolle. Diese Weisheit ist eine Gabe Gottes, die es zu erstreben und zu erwerben gilt. In diesen Einheiten spielt die תורה (15:1b: תורה / ܢܡܘܣܐ / νόμος; 24:23b: ܢܡܘܣܐ / νόμος; 51:19b: νόμος) keine besondere Rolle und wird nie in direkte Parallele zur „Weisheit" gestellt.

3.2. *Angewandte Weisheit*

Auf der zweiten Ebene ist die Weisheit eine menschlich realisierte Gegebenheit, die sich in konkreten Lebensvollzügen, Entscheidungen und Haltungen manifestiert. Diese Weisheit ist nicht angeboren, sondern muss erst erworben werden. Sie befähigt, einmal angeeignet, zu klugen und das Leben erhaltenden Taten. Hierzu sind zu rechnen Sir 18:27-29; 19:20-24; 20:27-31; 21:12-28; 37:16-26; 38:24-39:14. Auf der Ebene der Lebenspraxis gibt es des Öfteren Querbezüge zur Tora.

4. „WEISHEIT" UND STRUKTUR DES SIRAZIDISCHEN WERKES

Da graphische Darstellungen helfen können, die Materialien besser einzuordnen, wird das Buch schematisch in 10-Kapitel-Blöcke gegliedert und in diese dann das Thema Weisheit eingefügt. Auf diese Weise soll ein einfacher Überblick über die Verteilung erfolgen:

Kapiteleinteilung in Zehnergruppen					
1-10	11-20	21-30	31-40	41-50	51
Grundlagenweisheit					
1:1-10; 4:11-19; 6:18-37	14:20-15:10[20]	24:1-22:23-34			51:13-30
Angewandte Weisheit					
	18:27-29; 19:20-24; 20:27-31	21:12-28; 24:23-34	37:16-26; 38:24-39:14[21]		

Der Überblick zeigt eine interessante Verteilung der Einheiten mit dem Thema „Weisheit": Weder die „Grundlagenweisheit", noch die „angewandte Weisheit" sind gleichmäßig über das sirazidische Werk verteilt.

Abschnitte, die sich mit der Grundlagenweisheit beschäftigen, stehen am Anfang (1:1-10), in der Mitte (24:1-22) und am Ende (51:13-30) des Buches und belegen so die tragende Rolle für das gesamte Werk. Daneben finden sich im ersten Viertel des Buches weitere drei Passagen aus der gleichen Gruppe (4:11-19; 6:18-37 und 14:20-15:10). Auffällig ist, dass zwischen diesen *keine Einheiten zur angewandten Weisheit* vorkommen. Nach dem Kapitel 24 stehen ausgenommen am Buchende (51:13-30) *keine Einheiten zur Grundlagenweisheit*.

Nimmt man die angewandte Weisheit in den Blick, stellt sich die Lage anders dar: Gegen Ende ersten Buchblockes — eine Einteilung, die 24:1-22 als eine die Struktur prägende Passage qualifiziert — stehen vier Einheiten (18:27-29; 19:20-24; 20:27-31; 21:12-28), die zur angewandten Weisheit zu rechnen sind. Nach dem Scharniertext 24:1-22 stehen wieder deren drei aus der gleichen Klasse (24:23-34; 37:16-26; 38:24-39:14). Diese Gruppe wird von sieben Einheiten gebildet.

Aufgrund dieser Beobachtungen erkennt man einen Plan des Autors, den er mit den verschiedenen Dimensionen von Weisheit verfolgt: Er bietet einerseits eine grundlegende Beschreibung der Weisheit, andererseits legt er die bedeutungsvolle Rolle der *angewandten Weisheit* als konkrete Erscheinung dar. Wenn man demnach in allgemeiner, wenig differenzierter Weise von „Weisheit" im Buch Ben Sira spricht, vermischt man Inhalte, die der Autor getrennt und in ihrem je eigenen Gewicht gesehen haben möchte.

5. σοφία / חכמה IM KONTEXT DER GRUNDLAGENWEISHEIT

5.1. *Die Weisheit als Geschöpf des Herrn (1:1-10)*

Pauckenschlagartig wird schon im ersten Kolon (1:1a) festgehalten, dass alle Weisheit beim Herrn (παρὰ κυρίου) und seit jeher (ܡܢ ܚܠܡܐ; 1:1b) oder für

---

[20] Vgl. genauer, weil die Einheit über die Kapitelgrenze hinüber geht: 14:20-27; 15:1-10.

[21] Vgl. genauer, weil die Einheit über die Kapitelgrenze hinüber geht: 38:24-34; 39:1-14

immer (εἰς τὸν αἰῶν; 1:1b) bei ihm ist. Daher untersteht sie nicht der menschlichen Verfügungsgewalt. Er, der Herr, kann als einziger mit diesem Wort (εἷς ἐστιν σοφός) bezeichnet werden. „Früher als sie alle (= Schöpfungs-werke) ist erschaffen die Weisheit (ἔκτισται σοφία) // die verständige Einsicht (σύνεσις φρονήσεως) von Ewigkeit her (ܡܢ ܠܥܠܡܐܕܝܢ / ἐξ αἰῶνος)"; (1:4a,b). Sie zeichnet sich durch besonders kluge und umfassende Befähigungen aus (ܣܘܟܠܬܢܘܬܐ / τὰ πανουργεύματα; 1:6b), Eigenschaften, die nur Gott oder Menschen zugeordnet werden. Neben der ausdrücklichen und mehrfachen Hervorhebung, dass die Weisheit geschaffen wurde, wird erwähnt, dass sie *allen Menschen* (μετὰ πάσης σαρκός) als Geschenk (κατὰ τὴν δόσιν; 1:10a) — also nicht als eine angeborene Größe —vermittelt wird, wobei die *Achtung* vor Gott[22] (ܠܡܕ ܬܢܘܠܡܗ) oder die *Liebe* zu Gott (τοῖς ἀγαπῶσιν αὐτόν) das Zuteilungskriterium schlechthin ist. Nicht zu übersehen ist die universale Tendenz: die Weisheit ist eine Gabe Gottes an die Menschen, nicht nur an Israel. Man trifft auf Aussagen über die Weisheits bzw. deren Verhältnis zum Herrn, nicht jedoch auf solche, wie sich die Weisheit in konkreten Realisierungen zeigt. Als Paralleltermini stehen hier σοφία und σύνεσις φρονήσεως, was darauf hinweisen kann, dass die Bedeutungsfülle, welche σοφία eigen ist, nicht durch ein einzelnes Wort adäquat zur Sprache gebracht wird.

5.2. *Die Weisheit kümmert sich um ihre Anhänger (4:11-19)*

Über die Weisheit (חכמות / σοφία) erfährt man in 4:11a, dass sie selbst ihre Kinder (בניה) *belehrt* (למדה) bzw. nach G *erhöht* (ἀνύψωσεν). Der Plural חכמות weist nicht auf verschiedene Weisheiten hin, wie das Verb bzw. das enklitische Possesivpronomen, die im Singular stehen, belegen. Es handelt sich um einen Intensivplural, mit dem die Fülle vorhandener und potentieller Weisheit in ein Wort verdichtet wird. Es ist auf den Unterschied zwischen der hebräischen und syrischen Fassung einerseits und der griechischen und der lateinischen andererseits hinzuweisen: Langsam wechseln die semitischen Versionen in die erste Person und in 4:17a spricht die Weisheit in der ersten Person („ich gehe mit ihm"; אלך עמו / ܐܙܠ ܥܡܗ). Die griechische und die lateinische Version bleiben durchgängig in der dritten Person.

Wer sich um sie bemüht (4:11b) und sie liebt (4:12a,14b), gewinnt Leben (4:12a) und Ansehen (4:13a), gefällt Gott (4:12b) und steht unter seinem Segen (4:13b). Der Dienst an ihr wird dem am Heiligtum gleichgesetzt (4:14a). Obwohl das der Auserwählte, das ist der zukünftige Weisheits-schüler, noch nicht weiß, hat sie ihn für sich ausersehen (4:17a), wendet sich ihm zu (4:18a), prüft und testet ihn (4:17,c), bevor sie ihm ihre Geheimnisse

---

[22] Vgl. R. Egger-Wenzel, "'Faith in God' Rather Than 'Fear of God' in Ben Sira and Job: A Necessary Adjustment in Terminology and Understanding," in *Intertextual Studies in ben Sira and Tobit, FS A.A. Di Lella* (eds. J.J. Corley und V. Skemp, CBQMS 38, Washington: CBA 2004) 211-26. passim.

kundtut (מסתרי ... וגליתי / ἀποκαλύψει ... τὰ κρυπτὰ αὐτῆς; 4:18b). Auffällig ist die Gleichsetzung „des Dienstes an der Weisheit" (משרתיה / ܟ̇ܡܫܡܫܬܐ) und „des Dienstes" (משרתי) am „Heiligtum" oder am „Heiligen" (קדש / ܩܘܕܫܐ in Syr ist eindeutiger: das Heiligtum). Es ist deutlich, dass die Weisheit ganz nahe an den Ort, der nur Gott zusteht und wo er gegenwärtig wird, herangerückt wird. Auffällig ist auch das Verb שרת, das als Fachausdruck der Kultsprache die elitäre Sphäre der Weisheit betont.

Hier steht die dramatische Bemühung der Weisheit um ihre Kinder, die auf diesem Weg Gott gefallen und zur Fülle der Weisheit und des Lebens kommen. Die Weisheit — vielleicht Gott selbst — macht sich auf, um zu den Anhängern zu kommen. Diese können durch ihr Tun zeigen, dass sie sich gewinnen lassen, aber nicht von sich selbst aus aktiv tätig werden: Zudem kommen nur nach vorhergehendem Test Bewährte in die Sphäre der Weisheit, die aber ganz intim enge Verbindungen einschließt. Die Schüler haben Zutritt zur innersten Kammer (בחדרי מבית) der Weisheit (4:15b). Dort halten sich nur Familienmitglieder auf, und im Kontext einer werbenden Frau nur der Liebhaber; vgl. die zweimalige Erwähnung der Liebe in 4:12a (H^A, Syr, G),14b ([Syr], G). Bei der Fülle der Gedanken wird fast übersehen, dass in einem Kolon angegeben wird, wie sich die Weisheit konkret realisiert: „er regiert / richtet gerecht / korrekt / wahrhaftig"; (4:15a). Es wird im ganzen Gedicht kein Parallelausdruck zu חכמה verwendet.

5.3. *Der mühselige Erwerb der Weisheit (6:18-37)*

Die Einheit, in der nachdrücklich und drängend dafür geworben wird, Weisheit zu erwerben beginnt: „Kind, kümmere dich (ἐπίλεξαι[23]) um Bildung (παιδείαν) von Jugend an // und bis du ergraut bist, wirst du Weisheit (σοφίαν) gewinnen"; (6:18a,b). Man spürt in der Übersetzung die Aktualität der Thematik zur Zeit des Übersetzers durch, da in Alexandria die Beschäftigung mit philosophischen Themen gesellschaftsprägend war. Wer seinen Platz im Zentrum damaliger „Intelligentia" erlangen bzw. behaupten wollte, hatte sich auf diesem Felde besonders zu engagieren. Daher wird schon im einleitenden Vers festgehalten, dass man die Weisheit zu erwerben und sich um sie zu bemühen hat: sie ist also keine angeborene Selbstver-ständlichkeit. Deren Aneignung wird ein langer Weg, den man nicht früh genug beginnen kann, wohl wissend, dass der Weisheitserwerb als Frucht der Bildung eine Lebensaufgabe im wahrsten Sinne des Wortes ist.

---

[23] Ziegler, emendiert zu ἐπίδεξαι; vgl. zur Stelle. Die Empfehlung, „*Erziehung anzu-nehmen*", ist möglich und ergibt einen Sinn. Im Kontext des gesamt Gedichtes aber, wo es um die Bemühung um Weisheit geht, passt besser die viel breiter belegte Version ἐπίλεξαι in der Bedeutung von „*auswählen*", medium: „*sich kümmern, bei sich erwägen*". Damit kommt das aktive Mitwirken des Weisheitsschülers gut zum Ausdruck.

5.3.1. Das eigene Engagement des Weisheitsschülers

Den Aspekt der aktiven Mitwirkung greifen im gleichen Gedicht bei Heraushebung durch eine nochmalige, persönlich-fürsorgende Anrede בני / τέκνον 6,32a,b auf und wird im nächsten Stichus (6,33a.b) weiter entwickelt. Die Unterschiede zwischen der (a) hebräischen und (b) griechischen Version sind derart, dass es besser ist, die beiden Versionen unabhängig von einander zu besprechen.

(a) „Wenn du willst, mein Kind, wirst du weise (תחחכם / ܬܚܟܡ) // wenn du sie bedenkst (תש[י]ם לבך), wirst du klug (תערם / ܬܗܘܐ ܚܟܝܡ)." Der reflexiv-passive Doppelungsstamm von חכם kombiniert Vorgang und Ziel: (α) Der Vorgang besteht darin, dass der Eleve selbst aktiv dazu beizutragen hat, sich selbst zu entwickeln. (β) Der reflexive Doppelungsstamm weist darauf hin, dass man sich sehr anstrengen muss und es auch schwer sein wird, das beabsichtigte Ergebnis zu erreichen. (γ) Das Ziel besteht darin, „weise zu werden": daran kann man erkennen, dass die gleiche Wurzel (חכם / ܚܟܡ), mit der man das Ergebnis חָכְמָה formuliert, am besten den Entwicklungsweg beschreibt.

Das Thema wird im nächsten Vers weiter entfaltet: „Wenn du hingehst (אם תובא), um zuzuhören (לשמע), // und dein Ohr hinneigst (והט אזנך), wirst du erzogen/ausgebildet werden (תוסר)"; (6:33a,b). Diese beiden in einen lockeren externen Parallelismus gesetzten Wenn-Sätze (אם – אם [6:32a / 6:33a]) bringen bekräftigend und vorwegnehmend die Information, dass die Bemühung um Weisheit Erfolg haben wird, um weise, gebildet und (aus)gebildet zu sein. Man erinnert sich daran, dass es ein wünschenswertes und in der Öffentlichkeit herzeigbares Entwicklungsziel ist, wenn man durch sein Verhalten seine Bildung zeigt, wie die Worte des Vaters Tobits an seinen Sohn Tobias belegen: „Gib acht auf dich bei all deinen Werken (ἐν πᾶσι τοῖς ἔργοις σου), Kind, und zeig, gut erzogen / (aus)gebildet zu sein (ἴσθι πεπαιδευμένος) durch dein gesamtes Benehmen (ἐν πάσῃ ἀναστροφῇ σου)"; (Tob 4:14).

(b) Der Grieche setzt einen anderen Akzent: „Wenn du willst, Kind (τέκνον), wird du erzogen / (aus)gebildet werden (παιδευθήσῃ) // und wenn du deine Seele (τὴν ψυχήν) darein gibst (ἐπιδῷς), wirst du ein Alleskönner sein (πανοῦργος ἔσῃ)"; (6:32a,b). Die Anrede τέκνον weist auf kein so enges Verhältnis hin wie בני. Wenn Sira schon in der Familie eine gewisse Distanz zwischen den Eltern und den Kindern gewahrt sehen will (vgl. Sir 30:9[24]), dann gilt das umso mehr für den übersetzenden Enkel, der wohl auch die zahlreichen Philosophenschulen in Alexandria vor Augen hat. In die Richtung dieser Schulen weist auch die Akzentuierung, dass es um Erziehung / Bildung geht (παιδευθήσῃ). Im Kolon 6:32b wird der „philosophische" Ausbildungshorizont des Übersetzers unterstrichen (ἐπιδίδωμι τὴν ψυχήν), wie sich aus folgenden

---

[24] „Verzärtele das Kind und es wird dich in Schrecken setzen, / scherze mit ihm und es wird dich betrüben".

Überlegungen ergibt: Die Phrase ἐπιδίδωμι τὴν ψυχήν ist auf den hebräischen Ausgangstext hin zu befragen, wobei שׂים לב von Hᴬ einen ersten Anhaltspunkt bietet:

- Die Verbindung von שׂים und לב zur Beschreibung von „*sich widmen, intensiv nachdenken, sich kümmern*" ist häufig belegt: שׂים (אֶת) לב und häufiger שׂים עַל לב.[25]
- Das Substantiv נֶפֶשׁ bezeichnet in der Phrase שׂים נֶפֶשׁ[26] immer *Leben*, das eingesetzt wird.
- Wenn man die LXX-Übersetzung überprüft, sieht man, dass mehrheitlich das Verb שׂים mit Hilfe von τίθημι und das Nomen לב mittels καρδία, selten mit διάνοια und nur ein Mal mit ψυχή,[27] (ἔθεντο ἐπὶ ψυχήν ; Jes 42:25) übertragen wird.

Insgesamt ist es aufgrund des Befundes sehr wahrscheinlich, dass dem Übersetzer nicht שׂים נֶפֶשׁ, wie ψυχή andeutet, sondern שׂים לב wie in Hᴬ bezeugt vorgelegen ist. Worauf ist dann aber die Wahl von ψυχή anstelle von καρδία zurückzuführen?

Das Herz spielt für den griechisch Denkenden zur Beschreibung geistiger Tätigkeiten nicht die gleiche Rolle wie für hebräisch Sprechende bzw. Denkende[28]. Im Gegensatz dazu fungiert ψυχή in allen philosophischen Richtungen[29] als zentraler Terminus, der je nach dem gemeinten Teil der ψυχή vor allem die rationalen Fähigkeiten einschließt[30]. Interessant ist, dass

---

[25] Vgl. Ex 9:21; 1Sam 9:20; 25:25; 2Sam 13:33; 18:3; 19:20; 1Kön 9:3; Ijob 1:8; 2:3; 34:14; Jes 41:22; 42:25; 47:7; 57:1,11; Jer 12:11; Ez 40:4; 44:5; Dan 1:8; Mal 2:2.

[26] Vgl. וְאֶשִׂימָה נַפְשִׁי בְכַפִּי / „das Leben auf das Spiel setzen", (Ri 12:3); vgl. in dieser Bedeutung auch 1Sam 19:5; 28:21; Ijob 13:14; 1Kön 19:2: das Leben gleich wie das anderer machen, d.h. töten; das Leben erhalten: Ps 66:9.

[27] Um diesen Inhalt zum Ausdruck zu bringen kann man auch נֶפֶשׁ verwenden, aber dann wird als Verb נתן gebraucht, wie man z.B. in der nicht häufig belegten Phrase נתן לבב + נפשׁ sieht; vgl. ... עַתָּה תְּנוּ לְבַבְכֶם וְנַפְשְׁכֶם לִדְרוֹשׁ (1Chr 22:19).

[28] Wenngleich man in der älteren Zeit „das *Herz* des Menschen als Sitz seines seelisch-geistigen Lebens" (J. Behm, "καρδία," in ThWNT 3: 611-16. 611) ansah und dieses Verständnis auch in der Stoa nachwirkte, blieb man im griechischen Kontext „bei der Frage nach dem Sitz des geistigen Lebens (im Hinblick auf das Herz) im Körper stehen und dringt nicht zur eigentlichen Übertragung des Begriffes καρδία ins Geistige vor"; Behm, καρδία 612.

[29] Vgl. z.B. F. Rüsche, *Blut, Leben und Seele. Ihr Verhältnis nach Auffassung der griechischen und hellenistischen Antike, der Bibel und der alten alexandrinischen Theologen. Eine Vorarbeit zur Religionsgeschichte des Opfers* (Studien zur Geschichte und Kultur des Altertums, Ergänzungsband 5, Paderborn: Schöningh 1930); F. Rüsche, *Das Seelenpneuma. Seine Entwicklung von der Hauchseele zur Geistseele. Ein Beitrag zur Geschichte der antiken Pneumalehre* (Studien zur Geschichte und Kultur des Altertums 18,3, Paderborn: Schöningh 1968 [1st ed. 1933]).

[30] Die griechischen Denker beschreiben unterschiedliche Bereiche der ψυχή. „Das λογιστικόν kommuniziert am stärksten mit dem reinen, nur dem Denken zugänglichen Sein, ...Darum muß der Mensch durch lebenslanges Bemühen um rechte Erkenntnis

der Übersetzer das Entwicklungs- und Erziehungsziel benennt und bewertet. Er wird πανοῦργος[31], jemand der πᾶν und ἔργον beherrscht, also ein *Alleskönner*, ein *gut gebildeter und zugleich praktischer Tausendsassa*. Der Übersetzer wählt seine Worte demnach so, dass er der philosophisch geschulten Hörerschaft entgegenkommt, diese aber zugleich in seine biblisch grundgelegte Vorstellung lenkt. Hätte er sich ganz der griechischen Gedankenwelt angeschlossen, wäre er auf der rationalen Ebene verblieben. חכמה / σοφία ist aber ganzheitlich und schließt neben den rationalen auch die praktischen Bereiche ein.

5.3.2. *Das Vorbild der alten Weisen*

Im weiteren erfährt man, dass sich der Weisheitsschüler bemühen sollte, viel Zeit im Kreis der Alten (πρεσβυτέρων; 6,34a) zu verbringen, um dem Verständnisvollen (συνετόν; 6:36a) und dessen Weisheit (τῇ σοφίᾳ / ܚܟܡܬܗ; 6:34b) zu folgen. Deren geradezu göttlichen Ausführungen (διήγησιν θείαν; 6:35a) und gehaltvollen Beispielerzählungen (παροιμίαι συνέσεως; 6:35b) lauscht er. Vor allem soll er Achtung vor Gott pflegen (והתבוננת ביראת עליון; 6:37a; vgl. die legistische Ausrichtung in G: ἐν τοῖς προστάγμασιν κυρίου) und Gottes Anordnungen (ובמצותו[32]; ἐν ταῖς ἐντολαῖς) bedenken. Dann wird der Schüler fähig zur Einsicht (vgl. das Kausativum; יבין לבך; 6:37c), daher das umfassende לב. So wird der Suchende weise (יחכמך; 6:37d).

Anders der Grieche, der die eben beschriebenen Aussagen als Stufen zur Weisheit und nicht schon als Ziel sieht, was heißt, das „das (unbändige) Verlangen nach Weisheit dir gegeben werden wird" (καὶ ἡ ἐπιθυμία τῆς σοφίας δοθήσεταί σοι [6:37d]), wobei man das passivum divinum zu beachten hat.

5.4. *Das leidenschaftliche Streben nach Weisheit (14:20-15:10)*

In der vorherigen Einheit wurde die Empfehlung an den Weisheitshungrigen ausgesprochen, durch den Besuch bei weisen Alten sich Weisheit anzueignen. Nun wechselt der Gesichtspunkt: Glücklich ist der, so steht es im einleitenden Vers, der durch das eigene Nachsinnen zur Weisheit kommt: „Glücklich (אשרי) der Mensch (אנוש), der über die Weisheit (בחכמה) nachsinnt

---

dem λογιστικόν die ihm gebührende Herrschaft über die anderen Seelenteile sichern"; A. Dihle, "ψυχή," in ThWNT 9: 604-14. 609.

[31] Generell ist den LXX-Übersetzern bewusst, dass man *klug sein* (עָרוּם) bzw. *(praktisch) weise sein* (חָכָם) oder *(praktisch) einsichtig sein* (מֵבִין) nicht mit im alexandrinischen Umfeld fast selbstverständlich rational verstandenem σοφός richtig wiedergibt, sondern auch in der Übersetzung darauf hinweist, dass die praktische Seite eine bedeutsame Rolle spielt. Daher wird vor allem עָרוּם (Spr 12:16; 13:16; 14:8,15,18; 15:5; 19:25; 22:3; 27:12), חָכָם חכם (Ijob 5:12; Spr 13:1; 21:11) und מֵבִין (Spr 28:2) mittels πανοῦργος übertragen.

[32] Vgl. Sir 6:37b (ובמצותו והגה תמיד) mit Ps 1:2 (וּבְתוֹרָתוֹ יֶהְגֶּה יוֹמָם וָלָיְלָה).

(יהגה) // der um Einsicht (ובתבונה) sich bemüht"; (14:20a,b)[33]. Mit dem Thema
„Nachsinnen" hat die vorangehende Einheit über den Weisheitserwerb
(6:18-37) aufgehört (6:37b). Was also am Ende der Aneignung von Weisheit
durch Lehrer erreicht wird, steht am Beginn im *individual-persönlichen* Bereich.

Hier wird חכמה der תבונה, wenngleich nachordnend, parallel gesetzt. Man
beobachtet also eine sachte Akzentverlagerung im Bereich der Weisheit:
beim Nachsinnen handelt es sich nicht so sehr um eine praktische Ebene,
sondern um eine rationale, weshalb das Derivat der Wortwurzel בין („ein-
sehen, verstehen") gut gewählt erscheint.

Im Weiteren wird die engagierte und leidenschaftliche Bemühung um
Weisheit unter Benutzung vieler erotischer — welche Sira allerdings auch
schon in der vorigen Einheit einstreute — Aktionen beschrieben: Wie ein
junger Mann sich hinter einer verehrten und ersehnten Frau nachschleicht
und jeden ihrer Wege erkunden und kennen will, so macht es auch der
Weisheitsschüler, der die Wege der Weisheit auszuspionieren sucht. Ben
Sira kommt offensichtlich der Umstand sehr gelegen, dass חכמה ein gramma-
tisches Femininum ist, weswegen sich auf harmlos erscheinenden, „gewollt-
zufälligen" Wege die Anspielung an eine Frau ergibt; vgl. die Possesivpro-
nomina (14:21: דרכיה[34] / ܐܘܪ̈ܚܬܗ - τὰς ὁδοὺς αὐτῆς / ܟܘܠܗܝܢ).

Geradezu aufdringlich versucht sich der Weisheitsschüler — angesta-
chelt durch das frühere Angebot, in die Kammer (4:15b) der Umworbenen
zu gelangen? — an die Weisheit heranzumachen. Ununterbrochen beobachtet er sie, er stellt ihr nach, versucht von ihr einen Blick zu erhaschen und
schlägt vor deren Haus das Lager auf, ja richtet sich bei ihr häuslich ein, wie
die Jungen eines Vogels in deren Nest.

Wie schon bei 6:18-31 und 6:32-37 innerhalb von 6:18-37 gibt es eine
zweiteilige Argumentationskette, deren zweiter Abschnitt in 15:1 einsetzt:
Wer Gott achtet (ירא יי), umwirbt im besprochenen Sinne die Weisheit und
wer die Anleitung (תורה) einhält (תופש), vermag ihr nachzufolgen (ידריכנה[35];
15:1a,b). In diesem Kontext bezeichnet תורה die vorher vom Weisheitslehrer
aufgestellten Regeln zum Weisheitserwerb. Jede andere Interpretation bringt
kontextfremde Zusammenhänge ein. Man kann z.B. keine implizite oder
explizite Anspielung an jene תורה erkennen, die auf Mose zurückgeht. Dies
gilt auch dann, wenn man im neuzeitlichen theologischen Sprachgebraucht
vielfach beim Wort *tôrā* fast unausweichlich an diese denkt. חכמה wird nicht
direkt, sondern nur indirekt im Personalpronomen zur Sprache gebracht.

Nach der Bekräftigung, dass die Bemühung um Weisheit nicht vergeb-
lich ist und mit Erfolg beschieden sein werde, wird deren Reaktion beschrieben: wie eine Mutter für das Kind, ja wie eine junge Frau — noch in der
Begeisterung der frischen Liebe — ihrem Geliebten Speise und Trank

---

[33] Vgl. J. Corley, "Rhyme in the Hebrew Prophets and Wisdom Poetry," *BN* NF
132 (2007) 55-69, 64.

[34] H^A dürfte nicht die ursprünglichere Version bewahrt haben: תבונתיה, da die
Wiederholung des in V 20a im Singular (תבונה) stehenden Wortes nicht gut zum Kontext passt.

[35] Man beachte das Kausativum: „es wird ein Weg der Nachfolge entwickelt".

zubereitet, so macht es auch die Weisheit: sie reicht allerdings *Brot der Klugheit* (לחם שכל [H^{A,B}]; ἄρτον συνέσεως) und *Getränk der Einsicht* (מי תבונה: [H^{B.Am}];[36] ὕδωρ σοφίας). Der Grieche — vermutlich durch den von der griechischen Philosophie geprägten rationalen Aspekt der Weisheit beeinflusst — verwendet für תבונה σοφία.[37]

Die Wirkungen sind faszinierend: Wenn sich der Weisheitsschüler auf sie stützt, kann er ohne Gefährdung leben, er ragt unter seinen Zeitgenossen heraus, erlangt Ruhm und Ehre. Es wird nicht positiv gesagt, in welchen konkreten, praktischen Handlungen und Haltungen die Weisheit in Erscheinung tritt, wohl aber wird das nahe Verhältnis zu Gott hervorgehoben. Es ist des Weisen Privileg, Gott zu loben: „Im Mund des Weisen (חכם) wird das (Gottes-)[38] Lob (תהלה) formuliert (תאמר)"; (15,10)[39]. So wird am Ende des Gedichtes als Klammer das Stichwort חכמה von 14:20 aufgenommen und die Hauptaussage deutlich herausgehoben. Der Weise ist aber nicht weise für sich, vielmehr sollte er die Weisheit weitergeben. Wie geschieht das? Wer mit Weisheit umgehen kann und wer sich ihr zuvor untergeordnet hat und so lernte, ihr gefügig zu sein (6:24,25[40]), erwirbt sich die Qualifikation, selbst Weisheit zu vermitteln, d.h. selbst ein Weisheitslehrer zu sein: „Und wer sie (בה / ܟܡ) beherrscht (משל / ܐܠܘ), lehre sie (ילמדנה / ܢܐܠܦܝܗ)"; (14:20b[41]). Weisheit wird zum Lehrgegenstand, was wohl voraussetzt, dass es auch einen Platz gibt, wo man die Lehrtätigkeit vorgenommen hat; vgl. בית מדרש in 51:23b

Wenn auch schon die letzten Worte des Gedichtes (15:10) behandelt worden sind, sei doch auf jene Personen hingewiesen, die nach 15:7-9 die Weisheit *nicht* erlangen können. Es sind dies: *nichtsnutzige Menschen* (מתי שוא / G interpretiert die Mangelhaftigkeit als *Torheit*: ἄνθρωποι ἀσύνετοι), *hochmütige Menschen* (אנשי זדון / G verallgemeinert zu ἄνδρες ἁμαρτωλοί, also „sündige Menschen"), *Übermütige* bzw. *Zügellose* (מליצים / vgl. in G: ὑπερηφανία), *Lügner* (אנשי כזב / ἄνδρες ψεῦσται) und *Gewaltverbrecher* (רשע / ἁμαρτωλοῦ). Diese Liste, die sehr konkrete Übel aufreiht, hebt diese Einheit von den anderen Gedichten über grundlegende Weisheit ab, wo derartige Aufzählungen nicht vorkommen. Die Auseinandersetzung mit dieser Thematik geschieht in der „angewandten Weisheit"; vgl. 18:27-29; 19:20-24; 20:27-31; 21:12-28. Die Verse

---

[36] Dagegen sprechen H^A und H^{Bm} vom *Ertrag*, was nicht gut zum Kontext passt.

[37] Die σοφία ist nach A. Dihle, *Die Vorstellung vom Willen in der Antike* (Sammlung Vandenhoeck, Göttingen: Vandenhoeck & Ruprecht 1985) 68, die „theoretische… Intelligenz…, (die) auf dem Gebiet der Ethik… zu allgemeingültigen moralischen Phänomenen und Normen leiten, nicht aber im Einzelfall das rechte Ziel des Handeln auswählen" kann.

[38] Dass es sich trotz der allgemeinen Formulierung um Gotteslob handelt, geht aus dem vorhergehenden Vers hervor.

[39] Vgl. Corley, „Rhyme," 64.

[40] Vgl. „Bring deine Füße in ihre Fesseln, deinen Hals unter ihr Joch! Beuge deinen Nacken, und trage sie, werde ihrer Stricke nicht überdrüssig!" (Sir 6:24-25).

[41] Der Grieche setzt einen anderen Akzent, in dem er hervorhebt, dass Gott jenem, der sich um die rechte Weisheit bemüht, wohl tunt: καὶ ὁ κύριος εὐοδώσει αὐτόν.

15:7-9 schlagen eine Brücke zur angewandten Weisheit. Dieser „Überleitung" folgen wir aber jetzt nicht, sondern wenden uns dem mehr oder weniger in der Mitte des ganzen Buches stehenden Weisheitstext zu.

5.5. Der Ort der Weisheit in Schöpfung, Welt- und Volksgeschichte (Sir 24:1-22)

Da Sira ein Meister der Mehr- ja Vieldeutigkeit ist, kann man verschiedene Zugänge zu Sir 24:1-22 wählen, wobei man bei der Entfaltung eines Gedankens — mehr oder weniger ungewollt — andere Aspekte zurücktreten lässt. Dadurch ergibt sich das Risiko, andere Akzente zu setzen, als sie der Autor gesehen haben will. Daher werden mehrere Fragestellungen behandelt:

5.5.1. Die Weisheit spricht über sich selbst

5.5.1.1. Die „personifizierte" Weisheit. Die Weisheit (ܚܟܡܬܐ / σοφία) zeichnet sich durch die Fertigkeit des Sprechens aus. Diese Redefähigkeit, die an sich in der Verfügungsgewalt Gottes liegt (vgl. Ex 4:11; Ez 33:22), unterscheidet Menschen z.B. von Tieren, die nicht sprechen können: Die Weisheit lobt sich (ܬܫܒܚ – ܢܦܫܗ; αἰνέσει – καυχήσεται [24:1a.b]; ܬܫܒܚ; καυχήσεται [24:2b]), ergreift das Wort (ܦܘܡܗ ܬܦܬܚ; στόμα αὐτῆς ἀνοίξει [24:2a]) in ihrem Volke (ܒܓܘ ܥܡܗ / ἐν μέσῳ λαοῦ αὐτῆς) und hält sich dabei inmitten der Versammlung des Höchsten (ἐν ἐκκλησίᾳ), den Scharen (ἔναντι δυνάμεως) des Herrn auf. Offensichtlich ist der himmlische Thronrat gemeint. Das Reden ist also eine Möglichkeit, die Weisheit als „personifizierte" Größe zu beschreiben.

5.5.1.2. Die Herkunft der Weisheit. Sie ging aus dem Mund des Höchsten hervor (ܗܘܬ ܚܠܩܝ ܦܘܡܗ; ἀπὸ στόματος ὑψίστου ἐξῆλθον [24:3a]); vgl. Weish 7:26. Mit mythischen Bildern beschreibt sie ihren Wohnsitz: sie wohnte (ܫܟܢܬ ܚܡܕܬ; κατεσκήνωσα [24:4a]) auf den Höhen (ܒܪܘܡܐ ܥܠܝܐ; ἐν ὑψηλοῖς [24:4a]) und deren Thron ist auf einer Wolkensäule (ܚܡܕܬ ܟܘܪܣܝܗ; ἐν στύλῳ νεφέλης [24:4b]). Ihr Wohnsicht ist also jenem Gottes gleich und sie hat einen Thron (ܟܘܪܣܝܐ; ὁ θρόνος [24:4b]) wie der himmlische Herrscher: Hier haben wir eine Umschreibung der Gegebenheit, dass Sira die Weisheit in die Sphäre Gottes stellt und diese — schillernd formulierend — nahezu Gott gleich setzt.

5.5.1.3. Der Tätigkeitsbereich der Weisheit. Die Weisheit umschreitet allein (ܚܕܪܬ ܒܠܚܘܕ; ἐκύκλωσα μόνη [24:5a]), d.h. aus eigener Kraft, den Himmelskreis und geht bis in die tiefsten Abgründe hinab (ܚܠܟܬ ܐܢܐ; περιεπάτησα [24:5b]): wieder ist der Herrschaftsbereich so beschrieben, wie der Gottes; vgl. Dtn 32:22; 1Sam 2:6 und Ps 139:8ff[42].

---

[42] Vgl. Dtn 32:22: „In meiner Nase ist Feuer entbrannt. Es lodert bis in die unterste Totenwelt, verzehrt die Erde und was auf ihr wächst und schmilzt die Fundamente der Berge"; 1Sam 2:6: „Der Herr macht tot und lebendig, er führt zum Totenreich hinab und führt auch herauf"; Ps 139:8ff: „Steige ich hinauf in den Himmel, so bist du dort; bette ich mich in der Unterwelt, bist du zugegen. 9 Nehme ich die Flügel des

Sie beherrscht (ܐܫܬܠܛܬ; ἡγησάμην [24:6a-b]) die Fluten des Meeres, die Völker und Nationen. Ihr Wirkungsbereich ist universal. Die Weisheit herrscht über die gesamte Schöpfung, die belebte, wie unbelebte, die menschliche und die außermenschliche. Die Formulierung *Fluten des Meeres* ist mehrdeutig, da einerseits das realistische Meer und andererseits dessen mythische Erscheinung gemeint ist, womit also umfassende Herrschaft zum Ausdruck gebracht wird. Ihr eigentlicher Herrschaftsbereich wird (ܫܘܠܛܢܝ ܗܘܐ; ἐν Ιερουσαλημ ἡ ἐξουσία μου [24:11b]) dann Jerusalem. Darauf hinzuweisen ist, dass auch zum Ausdruck kommt, dass umfassend alle Völker von der Weisheit affiziert werden.

Die Weisheit sucht (ܒܥܝܬ; ἐζήτησα [24:7a]) einen Ort, wo sie Ruhe finden — diese konnte sie offensichtlich unter den Völkern nicht antreffen — und wohnen (ܐܫܪܐ; αὐλισθήσομαι [24:7b]) kann. Schließlich findet sie Ruhe auf dem Zion (ܐܢܝܚܬܢܝ; με κατέπαυσεν [24:11a]).

Die Weisheit tut Dienst im heiligen Zelt Gottes, einem Priester gleich (ܫܡܫܬ; ἐλειτούργησα [24:10a]). Oben (4:14) wurde — auch unter Verwendung der Kultsprache; vgl. ܫܡܫ — gesagt, dass jener einen Gottesdienst feiert, der der Weisheit dient.

Die Weisheit lädt alle ein, zur ihr zu kommen (ܣܠܩܘ; προσέλθετε [24:19a]) und sich an ihr zu sättigen (ܬܬܣܒܥܘܢ; ἐμπλήσθητε [24:19b]). Man kann sie verzehren (ܐܟܠܝ; οἱ ἐσθοντές με [24:21a]), man kann sie trinken (ܫܬܝ; οἱ πίνοντές με [24:21b]). Auf sie kann man hören (ܕܫܡܥ ܠܝ; ὁ ὑπακούων [24:22a]) und mit ihr kann man arbeiten (ܦܠܚܘܗܝ; οἱ ἐργαζόμενοι ἐν ἐμοι [24:22b]).

5.5.2. *Gottes Verhältnis zur Weisheit*

Gott liebt die Weisheit (ܪܚܝܡܬܐ ܠܗ ܐܟܘܬܝ; ἠγαπημένῃ ὁμοίως με [24:11a]), die er selbst erschuf (ܕܒܪܢܝ; ὁ κτίσας με [24:8b]; ܐܬܒܪܝܬ; ἔκτισέν [24:9a]). Die Dauer der Weisheit ist ohne Grenzen: vor der materiellen Schöpfung begann sie und wird nicht mehr enden (ܠܐ ܢܫܠܡ ܕܘܟܪܢܝ; οὐ μὴ ἐκλίπω [24:9b]). Gott erteilt der Weisheit den Befehl (ܦܩܕܢܝ; ἐνετείλατό μοι [24:8a]), in Jakob / Israel Wohnung zu beziehen. Sie wird dann auf dem Zion *fest* installiert (ܣܡܟܬ; ἐστηρίχθην [24:10b]).

Morgenrots und lasse mich nieder am äußersten Meer, [10] auch dort wird deine Hand mich ergreifen und deine Rechte mich fassen. [11] Würde ich sagen: «Finsternis soll mich bedecken, / statt Licht soll Nacht mich umgeben», [12] auch die Finsternis wäre für dich nicht finster, die Nacht würde leuchten wie der Tag, die Finsternis wäre wie Licht".

5.5.3. *Das Beschreibungsmaterial der Weisheit*[43]

Schreiber hat in seiner Untersuchung darauf hingewiesen, dass bei Sira der Weisheit Prädikate zugeordnet werden, die im Zusammenhang des Königs vorkommen[44]. Dieser allgemeine Hinweis lässt sich vertiefen:

5.5.3.1. *Die Weisheit hat einen Thron, nimmt also Regierungsgeschäfte wahr;* vgl. 24:4b. Die Phrase "auf dem Thron sitzen" (יֹשֵׁב עַל־[הַ]כִּסֵּא / καθίζω ἐπὶ τοῦ θρόνου[45]) ist mit wenigen Ausnahmen[46] die Umschreibung für *aktuelle und praktizierte* Regentschaft eines Königs, meistens eines Davididen,[47] und unter diesen ist Salomo herauszuheben.[48]

5.5.3.2. *Die Weisheit ist am/im Himmelsrund* (γῦρος), *also universal präsent;* vgl. Sir 24:5. Auch vom König schreibt Ps 72:8: „Er herrsche von Meer zu Meer, vom Strom bis an die Enden der Erde…" Der eigentliche Herr im universalen Sinne ist und bleibt JHWH selbst, und kein (davidischer) König: „Er ist es, der über dem Erdenrund (τὸν γῦρον τῆς γῆς) thront (הַיֹּשֵׁב / ὁ κατέχων) [Jes 40:22]; vgl. Ijob 22:13-14).

5.5.3.3. *Die Völker sind Besitz der Weisheit, über welche sie Macht ausübt;* vgl. Sir 24:6b. Während diese universale Macht nach Sira der Weisheit direkt zukommt, ist der Einflussbereich, allerdings als Gabe Gottes, auch im königlichen Kontext anzutreffen: „Ford're von mir, und ich gebe dir die Völker zum Erbe, die Enden der Erde zum Eigentum"; Ps 2:8; vgl. 72:8-10.

5.5.3.4. *Die Weisheit wird von Gott am Zion eingesetzt und regiert von dort aus;* vgl. Sir 24:10b. Auch von König David liest man Ähnliches: „Dort [V. 13: am Zion] lasse ich Davids Macht erstarken und stelle für meinen Gesalbten ein Licht auf"; (Ps 132/131[LXX],17).

5.5.3.5. *Jerusalem ist der Machtbereich:* vgl. Sir 24:8c,d,11b. Mehrfach wird festgehalten, dass David in Jerusalem und dann von dort aus regierte; vgl.

---

[43] Vgl. F.V. Reiterer, „Aspekte der Messianologie der Septuaginta. Der Weisheit Beitrag zur Entwicklung messianischer Vorstellungen," in *Im Brennpunkt: Die Septuaginta III. Studien zur Theologie, Anthropologie, Ekklesiologie, Eschatologie und Liturgie der Griechischen Bibel* (eds. H.-J. Fabry and D. Böhler, BWANT 174, Stuttgart: Kohlhammer 2007) 226-244. 229-231.

[44] S. Schreiber, *Gesalbter und König. Titel und Konzeptionen der königlichen Gesalbtenerwartung in frühjüdischen und urchristlichen Schriften* (BZNW 105, Berlin: de Gruyter 2000) 197: „Diese eher sekundären Anklänge genügen nicht, um die Weisheit als königliche Gestalt zu charakterisieren".

[45] In der LXX gibt es eine Variante, vgl. 1Sam 1:9: ἐπὶ τοῦ δίφρου.

[46] Vgl. JHWH (1Kön 22:19; 2Chr 18:18; Ps 9:5,8; 47:9; Jes 6:1; Klgl 5:19); Eli (1Sam 1:9; 4:13), der Hohepriester Jeschua (Sach 6:13) und einmal die Torheit (Spr 9:14).

[47] Adonija (1Kön 1:24); Joschafat (1Kön 22:10; 2Chr 18:9) und allgemein (Dtn 17:18; 1Kön 1:27; Ps 122:5; 132:12; Jer 13:13; 17:25; 22:2,4,30; 29:16; 33:17; 36:30).

[48] 1Kön 1:13,17,20,30,35,46,48; 2:12,19,24; 3:6; 8:20,25; 1Chr 28:5; 29:23; 2Chr 6:10,16.

u.a. „... in Jerusalem war (David) dreiunddreißig Jahre König...;" 2Sam 5:5; auch bei späteren Königen bildet Jerusalem das selbstverständliche Machtzentrum, vgl. 2Kön 20:13.

5.5.3.6. *Die Weisheit findet in Jerusalem Ruhe;* vgl. Sir 24:8b,11a. In einem Gebiet wie Kanaan, das strategisch und wirtschaftlich für die Großmächte zur Machterhaltung eine außergewöhnlich wichtige Rolle spielte, waren Kriege zu befürchten. Aus diesem Grunde wird die Zusage von (einfacher) *Ruhe* zu einem hohen Ideal, häufig ausdrücklich verbunden mit dem Ende von militärischen Feindseligkeiten; vgl. u.a. im Kontext Davids 2Sam 7:11; 1Chr 23:25. Ruhe ist eine Gabe Gottes. Auf dieser Linie notiert Sira bei Salomo: „Salomo war König (ἐβασίλευσεν) in friedlichen Tagen, Gott verschaffte ihm Ruhe (κατέπαυσεν) ringsum"; Sir 47:13.

5.5.3.7. *Die Präexistenz der Weisheit.* Präexistenz kann nur in Relation zu etwas Existierendem formuliert werden. Die Präexistenz ist nicht wirklich mit dem Blick in die Vergangenheit (vgl. u.a. Jer 6:16; Ps 78:2f), und sei sie noch so weit entfernt, gleichzusetzen. Ausdrücklich legt Sira darauf Gewicht, dass die Weisheit vor der Schöpfung (vgl. Sir 1:4.8) — und nach dieser ist: „Vor der Zeit, am Anfang, hat er mich erschaffen, und bis in Ewigkeit vergehe ich nicht / πρὸ τοῦ αἰῶνος ἀπ' ἀρχῆς ἔκτισέν με καὶ ἕως αἰῶνος οὐ μὴ ἐκλίπω;" (Sir 24:9a,b). Diese Dimension, die die Weisheit als vor- und immaterielle Schöpfungsgegebenheit[49] erscheinen lässt und sie so einerseits der „gewöhnlichen" Schöpfung enthebt, sie andererseits als konkrete Realisation in diese integriert, hat den Verfasser von Spr 8:22-31 beeinflusst.

Wie soll man aber die unübersehbare Annäherung an den königlichen Bereich verstehen? Eine zu enge Zusammenschau ist nicht gerechtfertigt. Dort, wo Sira sich mit David und Salomo beschäftigt, gibt es keine gleichen Formulierungen. Daher ist jenen zuzustimmen, die betonen, dass Sira die Weisheit nicht als eine königliche Erscheinung darstellen will. Vielmehr formuliert er die Bedeutung der Weisheit mit damals wertvollen und allgemein verständlichen sprachlichen Mitteln. Wenn man Herrschaftsthemen zur Sprache bringen wollte, konnte man nur Anleihen aus dem für das (davidische) Königshaus entwickelten Wortarsenal nehmen, da jenes auf diesem Felde konkurrenzlos war. Vergleichen möchte man diesen Vorgang mit einem Künstler, der wertvolle Erze oder Edelsteine usw. verwendet, um ein Kunstwerk zu schaffen, wobei dann das Dargestellte und nicht das Material an sich die Idee des Künstlers realisiert und vermittelt. Doch deutet die Materialauswahl an, dass der Meister etwas Großes gestalten möchte.

---

[49] Vgl. F.V. Reiterer, „Die immateriellen Ebenen der Schöpfung bei Ben Sira," in F.V. Reiterer, *"Alle Weisheit stammt vom Herrn ...". Gesammelte Studien zu Ben Sira,* (ed. R. Egger-Wenzel, BZAW 375, Berlin: de Gruyter 2007) 185-227 (= in *Treasures of Wisdom. Studies in Ben Sira and the Book of Wisdom* [eds. N. Calduch-Benages und J. Vermeylen, BETL 143, Leuven: Peeters 1999] 91-127).

Hinter dieser an Herrscher„terminologie" angelehnten Beschreibung verbirgt sich eine neue Konzeption Siras, die weit über die (abstrakte) Beschreibung und Analyse der Weisheit hinausgeht. Da Sira kein weltfremder, sich fern ab von den damals wichtigen gesellschaftlichen Themen im stillen Kämmerlein nur mit schönen Gedanken beschäftigender „Stubengelehrter", sondern ein politisch engagierter Mann war, zeigt sich hier — mehr tastend als konzeptionell ausgereift — seine Vorstellung vom Weisen. Die Weisheit als eine Art der Gottesgegenwart bzw. des konkreten Gotteswirkens in Schöpfung und Geschichte befähigte den von ihr Durchdrungenen in der aktuellen Krisenzeit Perspektiven für die Zukunft zu entwickeln. Voraussetzung dafür war, dass ein angehender Weisheitslehrer eine Ausbildung erhielt und sich selbst weiterbildete. Er selbst wurde politisch einflussreich. Dieser Typ eines „Weisheitslehrers" entfernte sich vom Tora-Gelehrten, wie ihn Esra dargestellt hatte, wobei Siras Weiser die mosaische Tora in seine Konzeption mit hinein nahm. Obwohl auf Israel, d.h. auf die an den Herrn Glaubenden konzentriert, ist die weisheitliche Lehre zugleich grundsätzlich universal. Die Weisheit in Sir 24 bereitet demnach die theologisch-politische Entwicklung des Weisen bzw. des (schriftgelehrten) Weisheitslehrers[50] vor. Die Weisheitslehrer waren später jene, die als bestens und breit Ausgebildete die diplomatischen Agenda in den Händen haben werden, wie man z.B. in den Makkabäerbüchern sieht. Die hier angestossene, auf der Erkenntnis der Gottesgegenwart in der Weisheit basierende Entwicklung hat nicht nur in der Schechina-Vorstellung[51] einen entscheidenden Schritt gesetzt, sondern erweist Sira auch als gesellschaftspolitisch weitblickenden und wirkungsvollen Konzeptionisten.[52]

5.6. Sir 51:13-30

Während am Beginn des Buches (a) das Verhältnis zwischen Gott und der Weisheit, in Kap 24 (b) das Verhältnis der Weisheit zu Gott, zur gesamten Schöpfung und zu Israel im Zentrum stand, beschäftigt sich (c) die abschließende Einheit mit dem Verhältnis Siras zur Weisheit. Es ist der Abschluss des gesamten Buches, in welchem der Weisheitslehrer zeigen kann, wie fruchtbar er sich mit der Weisheit beschäftigt hat. Damit ist er ein

---

[50] Vgl. Reiterer, „Aspekte," 231-34.

[51] Vgl. B. Janowski, „'In Jakob nimm Wohnung!' Sirach 24 und die alttestamentliche Schekina-Theologie," in *Figures in Biblical and Cognate Literature. The Reception and Function of Biblical Figures in Deuterocanonical and Other Early Jewish Literature* (eds. H. Lichtenberger and U. Mittmann-Richert, DCLY 2008, Berlin: de Gruyter 2008) (forthcoming).

[52] Der weisheitliche Ansatz fungiert als bedeutsame Triebfeder bei Neuntwicklungen. Sowohl die Konzeption „messianischer" Erwartungen (vgl. Reiterer, „Aspekte," 231-40) wie die über den religiösen Bereich hinaus wirkende Rolle der Weisheitslehrer, vgl. die in den Makkabäerbüchern beschriebene Tätigkeit, hätte sich wohl ohne den sirazidischen Beitrag kaum so entwickelt, wie man ihn vorfindet.

anschauliches Beispiel dafür, wie die Weisheit zu einem vorbildlichen Abschluss gekommen ist.

5.6.1. Die Beziehung zwischen Sira und der Weisheit

Sira sucht (חפצתי בה ובקשתיה; ἐζήτησα [51:13b]) schon seit seiner Jugend die Weisheit, denn Siras Lebensziel ist es, nach Weisheit zu streben (אדורשנה; ἐκζητήσω [51:14b]), vgl. das geflügelte Wort vom „lebenslangen Lernen". Sira verlangte mit Leidenschaft, geradezu vor Begierde brennend nach ihr (חריתי נפשי; διαμεμάχισται [51:19a]; נפשי נחתי ; κατεύθυνα [51:20a]) und wandte nie seinen Blick (פני לא אהפך; ܘܩ ܠܐ ܐ; διηκριβασάμην [51:19b]) von ihr ab. Er war ihretwegen erregt (מעי יהמו; ܡܥܝ ܡܥܘ; ἡ κοιλία μου ἐταράχθη [51:21aα]), womit wieder das Bild der Begegnung mit einer sehnsüchtig erwarteten Frau aufgenommen wird. Er suchte (בה לחביט; ܟ ܗܡܟ; τοῦ ἐκζητῆσαι [51:21aβ]) sie verzweifelt.

Sira beschreibt die Weisheit so drastisch und unvermittelt direkt, dass er sie geradezu *umgreifen / anfassen* kann (ܘܢ ܐܘܝ [51:19faα]; der nicht gut erhaltende H^Q-Text spielt auf *Klugheit* an [ערמימ], G versteht dieses Kolon als beklagenswerten Unwissenheitszustand über sie: τὰ ἀγνοήματα αὐτῆς) und sie zeigt sich ihm dann als Vermittlerin von *Einsicht* (ܟ ܐܘܝ ; H^Q: אתבונן; ἐπενόησα [51:19faβ]. Interessant ist, dass der gestörte H^B-Beleg eine sichtbare Gegebenheit andeutet [ואביט]).

5.6.2. Die Beziehung zwischen der Weisheit und Sira

Die Weisheit ging auf ihn zu (H^Q באה לי / תפלה אתפלל H^B = ܡܗܠܝ ܝܢ; ἔναντι ναοῦ ἠξίουν![53] [51:14a]). Die Weisheit ist Sira zur Amme, d.h. zur Ersatzmuter, geworden (עלה היתה; ܐܘܝ!; προκοπὴ ἐγένετό [51:17a]), hat ihm also das Leben erst ermöglicht. Ohne sie würde er nicht leben. Sie gab ihm zu essen und zu trinken, hat ihn gehen und alle nötigen Handgriffe und Fertigkeiten gelehrt, die man zum erfüllten Leben braucht. Sie ist so umfassend und vielseitig, dass Sira darin das einzig Erstrebenswerte sieht.

5.6.3. Sira animiert zur Aneignung von Weisheit

Für die Beschäftigung mit der Weisheit wirbt 51:23a-26c und stellt sich selbst als „Anschauungssubjekt" dafür hin, was man gewinnt, wenn man sich um sie so intensiv wie er selbst müht.

5.6.4. Voraussetzung zur Gabe der Weisheit

Die Weisheit ist nicht durch die Geburt vermittelt. Man muss sich um sie mühen, und die Mühen werden herausfordernd und belastend sein. Aber das ist noch zu wenig, um zur Weisheit zu gelangen. Weisheit setzt Integrität und Reinheit voraus (51:20b). Auch hier ist Sira ein Vorbild: er hat sich zuvor gereinigt (בטהרה; ܟܗܘܝ; ἐν καθαρισμῷ [51:20c]).

---

[53] „Am Tore des Heiligtums lernte ich sie schätzen".

Im abschließenden Abschnitt (51:13-30) nimmt Sira Themen von früher auf, bleibt bezüglich des Inhaltes, was Weisheit eigentlich bedeute, genauso allgemein wie in den früheren Belegen zur „Grundlagenweisheit". Seine Absicht ist eine andere: Er will den Wert und den Weg des Weisheitserwerbes darlegen. Der Wert zeigt sich vor allem im Erfolg. „Durch sie werdet ihr viel Silber und Gold erwerben"; (51:28b). Daneben steht das oben beschworene Ziel der Ruhe im umfassenden Sinne: „Viel Ruhe habe ich gefunden;" (51:27a). Besonders ist herauszuheben, dass Sira nach Manier der Philosophenschulen selbst eine gegründet hat („Verweilt in meinem Lehrhaus": בבית מדרשי; ܒܝܬ ܐܘܠܦܢܐ; ἐν οἴκῳ παιδείας; [51:23b]) und dort die „Lehrkanzel" („mein Lehrstuhl": בישיבתי; ܒܡܬܝܒܬܗ [51:29a]) selbst betreut.

5.7. *Zwischenzusammenfassung*

Wer auf der Basis der eben behandelten Abschnitte zur Weisheit die Frage beantwortet sehen will, in welchen konkreten Gegebenheiten die Weisheit realisiert wird, bekommt keine Antwort. Es geht nämlich um die grundsätzlichen Rahmenbedingungen zum Verständnis der Weisheit.

- Sie ist vom Herrn geschaffen, geht der anderen Schöpfung voraus, endet nicht und ist den Menschen von Gott zugewiesen (1:1-10).
- Die Weisheit, in ihr wird ja Gott selbst aktiv bzw. in ihr wirkt er direkt, bemüht sich um ihre Anhänger (4:11-19).
- Der Erwerb der Weisheit bereitet große Mühen, wenngleich der zu erwartende Ertrag einst alles in den Schatten stellen wird. Man kann nicht früh genug mit der Aneignung beginnen und es wird bis zum Lebensende kein Aufhören geben. Bei gereiften Vorbildern kann man gelebte „Schaubilder" finden (Sir 6:18-37).
- Das Streben nach Weisheit soll so leidenschaftliche Züge haben, wie das Werben um eine Geliebte. Sie ihrerseits wird in gleicher Weise reagieren: Leidenschaft und lebenserfüllender Sinn sind demnach unabdingbar. Der Ertrag wird sich in der Lebensfreude und Anerkennung in der Öffentlichkeit zeigen (14:20-15:10).
- Wo ist denn diese Weisheit einzuordnen? Sie, die Gott liebt, wurde vor der Schöpfung vom Herrn geschaffen: sie ist auf die ganze Welt, auf die Völker und vor allem auf Israel hingerichtet. Sie ihrerseits erwartet angenommen zu werden, damit sie ihre Wirkungen entfalten kann (Sir 24:1-22).
- Die Weisheit ist den Menschen nicht angeboren. Aber man kann sie erwerben: Voraussetzung dafür ist die leidenschaftliche Begeisterung, sich auf dieses schwierige Unterfangen einzulassen. Dass es sich lohnt, dafür kann Sira auf sich selbst verweisen. Er hat ein Lehrhaus, in dem man eine Ausbildung mitmachen kann, denn dort unterhält er einen Lehrstuhl (Sir 51:13-30).

Das, was man unter diesem Gesichtspunkt unter „Weisheit" versteht, lässt sich demnach nicht in einfache Worte kleiden und ist auch ohne Erläuterung nicht mit *einem* terminus zu beschreiben — ausgenommen durch „Weisheit" selbst.

6. σοφία / חכמה IM KONTEXT DER ANGEWANDTEN WEISHEIT

Die Beschreibung, worin die Weisheit konkret besteht und was durch sie und von ihr ausgeschlossen wird, wird in den folgenden Einheiten behandelt.

6.1. *Säulen der Weisheitslehre (18:27-29)*

Das erste längere Gedicht über die konkrete Weisheit hebt hervor, dass ein Weiser ein vorsichtiger (ܙܗܝܪ; ἐν παντὶ εὐλαβηθήσεται [18:27a]) und achtsamer (παροιμίας ἀκριβεῖς [18:29b]) Mensch ist. Besonders dann, wenn es leicht ist, sich zu vergehen, hält er sich von Schlechtem und Übel fern (ܡܢ ܒܝܫ; ἀπὸ πλημμελείας [18:27b]). Seine Weisheit vermittelt er durch einschlägige Reden und Sprüche. Wie man bei Sira sieht, ist die kluge Rede eine der bedeutendsten Aufgaben eines Weisen. Er wird von der Weisheit schwärmen und so deren Lob (δώσει ἐξομολόγησιν [18:28b]) öffentlich (ܒܫܘܒܚܐ [18:28b]) weitersagen, wohl um möglichst viele in deren Nachfolge zu locken. Die zweimalige Anspielung auf die Weitergabe der Weisheit (18:28a,29a), die den Hörer zu Botschaftern der Weisheit, zu Weisheitslehrern machen will, zeigt, dass es eine der zentralen Aufgaben ist, die Weisheit, nachdem man sie sich angeeignet hat, auch weiterzugeben. Ohne ausdrücklich darauf Bezug zu nehmen, nimmt Sira das Thema der Weitergabe des „Überkommenen" an die nächsten Generationen auf, wie man z.B. in Ps 78:3-8 und Dtn 6:20f liest. Innerhalb des sirazidischen Werkes wird das Thema der Weisheitsschule, vgl. oben 5.6., vorbereitet. Die mehrfache Hervorhebung führt nicht nur dazu, dass man sich der Thematik bewusst wird, sondern gibt Antwort auf ein konkretes Bedürfnis, das nach verschiedenen Anspielungen vor allem in der Herausforderung durch den Hellenismus zu suchen ist: Der Einfluss der griechischen Geistigkeit wird demnach nicht nur durch wirtschaftliche Lockmittel verbreitet, sondern überzeugt auch aufgrund der Argumente und Lehren. Dagegen will nun Sira eine „autochthone" Lehre, fussend auf der eigenen Tradition, setzen.

6.2. *Achtung vor Gott versus Schlechtigkeit (19:20-24)*

In 19:20a werden Weisheit (σοφία) und Achtung vor Gott / Gottesfurcht (φόβος κυρίου) gleichgesetzt, worauf dann auch 19:24a wieder zurückkommt. Dass die Grundlagenweisheit mit der Achtung vor Gott zu tun hat, wurde schon in 1:10a; 6:37a gesagt, aber sie wurden nicht identifiziert: Die in einer konkret praktizierten Einstellung greifbare Gottesfurcht war die Voraussetzung, damit die von Gott ausgehende Weisheit erlangt werden kann. Man kann daher zurück schließen, dass die hier gemeinte Weisheit auch eine aktuell-konkrete Größe ist. Für eine konkrete Dimension von Weisheit spricht auch 19:20b. Da es in der Grundlagenweisheit keine partielle Differenzierung gegeben hat, fällt auf, dass man in 19:20b liest, *„in jeder Weisheit"*. Das setzt doch wohl voraus, dass es unterschiedliche Realisationen von Weisheit gibt. Diesen verschiedenen Erscheinungsformen von konkreten Weisheitsbeispielen ist aber gemeinsam, dass sie sich im *„Machen/Vollbringen* einer Anleitung (ποίησις νόμου)" realisieren. Was meint nun νόμος? Weder vom Kontext her, noch innerhalb dieses Verses gibt es einen Hinweis auf die mosaische תורה. νόμος ist neben der Anleitung des Weisheitslehrers jede Weisung Gottes. Mit ihrer Hilfe meistert man das konkrete Leben am besten. Diesen νόμος kann man trotz hoher Intelligenz (σύνεσις) auch bewusst und absichtlich ignorieren (19:24a). Damit erweist man sich weder als klug noch als Gott gegenüber ehrfürchtig. Wer sich auf Schlechtigkeiten und Verfehlungen (πονηρία, βουλὴ ἁμαρτωλῶν; [19:22a.b]; ܪܫܥܐ [19:23b]) spezialisiert hat (πονηρίας ἐπιστήμη), sich durch Gerissenheit hervortut (πανουργία; [19:23a]), wird trotz seiner Intelligenz keine σοφία besitzen (19:22a). Deutlich wird, dass die abgelehnten Bereiche nicht abstrakt sind, sondern in konkreten Handlungen begegnen. Ebenso konkret ist die Weisheit.

6.3. *Der Wert qualifizierter Weisheitsrede (20:27-31)*

Der Wert der Weisheit zeigt sich auf verschiedenen Ebenen, doch ist besonders wichtig, dass vorhandene Weisheit in der Öffentlichkeit sichtbar gemacht wird: „Besser einer, der seine Torheit (μωρία) verbirgt, als einer, der seine Weisheit (σοφία) verbirgt" (20:30), ein gelungener Spruch, den Sira in 41:15 nochmals zitiert.

Man erkennt einen *Weisen* (σοφός) an seinem qualifizierten, guten und daher wertvollen Sprechen (ἐν λόγοις). Er ist kein Schwätzer. Ein solcher ist bei den politisch Mächtigen (20:17b,28b) angesehen und als Mitarbeiter erwünscht. Dieser kann aufgrund seiner gehobenen Position auch Vieles zum Positiven wenden (20:28b). Das zeigt schon, dass dieser Weise in der Öffentlichkeit eine gewichtige Rolle erhalten wird. Er — so würde man modern formulieren — geht verantwortlich mit den natürlichen Ressourcen um und hat erkennbar guten Erfolg: „Wer das Land bebaut, schichtet hohe Garbenstöße auf ..." (20:28a). Wer sich dagegen bestechen lässt, wird geblendet und kann sich nicht zu den Weisen rechnen. Generell gilt, dass Dummheit und Vernünftigkeit keine angeborenen, sondern erworbene Fertigkeiten sind.

6.4. *Anstand, Klugheit und Öffentlichkeit (21:12-28)*

Eben wurde notiert, dass man sich die Weisheit erst durch Erziehung und (Aus)bildung (παιδευθεύειν [21:12a]) erwerben muß. Das thematisiert die vorliegende Einheit mit vielen Beispielen, die den Vorrang des Weisen gegenüber dem Unklugen und Ungebildeten illustrieren sollen. Hierbei sind die Vergleiche, wonach die mentale Befähigung des Weisen (γνῶσις σοφοῦ; [21:13a]) wie ein Sturzbach (κατακλυσμός) — der allerdings nicht vernichtet, dem sich aber auch nichts in den Weg stellen kann — anschwillt und dessen Rat (βουλὴ αὐτοῦ; [21:13b]) wie Leben erhaltendes (πηγὴ ζωῆς; [21:13b]) Quellwasser wirkt, besonders anschaulich. Das Gegenteil trifft für einen Toren zu: Seine Fähigkeiten (ܠܒܗ; ἔγκατα; [21:14a]) mag man mit einem undichten Brunnen vergleichen, der kein Wasser zu halten vermag. Dessen Verhalten führt zum Tod.

Wo sind nun herausragende Realisationsfelder, in denen sich die positiven und die negativen Verhaltensweisen besonders deutlich zeigen: in der bedächtigen, oder nicht bedächtigen Redeweise (21:15-17,20.24-26):

Im Munde (ἐν στόματι) der Toren (μωρῶν) liegt deren Herz (ἡ καρδία αὐτῶν), im Herzen (ἐν δὲ καρδία) der Weisen (σοφῶν) ruht dessen Mund (στόμα αὐτῶν) (21:26).

Die Antipoden erweisen sich in der Fähigkeit, die Weisheit und die weisheitliche (Aus)bildung als zentralen Wert zu erfassen (21:18-19:21). Kein Verleumder ist weise (21:28). Besonders zu erwähnen ist nun wieder die Rolle des Weisen für die Gesellschaft, da man das, was er zu sagen hat, sehr ernsthaft bedenken wird: „Die Rede des Weisen (στόμα φρονίμου) begehrt man in der Versammlung (ἐν ἐκκλησίᾳ), und seine Worte (τοὺς λόγους) überdenkt man im Herzen (ἐν καρδίᾳ)"; (21:17a).

6.5. Die Weisheit in der mosaischen Tora (24:23-34)

Mit einer nachdrücklichen Betonung setzt V 23a ein: ταῦτα πάντα. Was jetzt kommt ist die bindende Zusage Gottes, die in der Offenbarung des Mose greifbar ist, wobei die Formulierungen verständlich und zugleich verschleiernd mehrdeutig sind: „Dies alles ist das Bundesbuch (βίβλος διαθήκης) des höchsten Gottes, das Gesetz (νόμος), das Mose uns vorschrieb"; (24:23a.b). Für griechische Ohren verständlich handelt — anders als an vielen anderen Stellen, wo vom Herrn die Rede ist — das Kommende vom θεός ὕψιστος. Der größte aller großen Götter, monotheistisch wie polytheistisch von der je eigenen Position aus zu verstehen, ist jener, der sich in dem von Mose überkommenen Schrifttum kundtut.

In diesem Werk ist Weisheit (σοφία [24:25a]) und Wissen (σύνεσις [24:26a]) im Überfluss vorhanden und bildet wie die lebensspenden großen Gewässer Pischon, Tigris, Euphrat, Jordan, Nil und Gihon, also alle wichtigen Flüsse, Grundlage für das Leben und erhalten das Leben. Der Weisheit geht es um Leben und Lebenserhaltung; vgl. oben 4:12a; 21:13b. Das Werk des Mose ist übervoll an Weisheit und man kommt an kein Ende, wollte man diese umfassend zu erforschen trachten (vgl. 24:28,29).

Sira sieht sich selbst wie eine „Wasserleitung", durch welche Schulung (διδασκαλία [24:33a]) und Belehrung wie Bildung (παιδεία [24:32]) geleitet und transportiert werden. Seiner Gegenwart, aber auch allen kommenden

Generationen soll sie weitergegeben werden („Und ich hinterlasse sie [die Schulung = διδασκαλία aus 24:33a] den fernsten Generationen" [εἰς γενεὰς αἰώνων; 24:33b]). Mit welcher Autorität sich Sira ausgestattet sieht, erkennt man daran, dass er seine Lehre und Belehrung wie Prophetie (ὡς προφητεία [24:33a]), also direkt von Gott bestätigt empfindet. Eigenartigerweise meidet Sira, obwohl schon in 24:25a genannt, jetzt den terminus technicus σοφία. Sira kommt es offensichtlich darauf an, dass seine eigene Lehre als Ausbildungsgut in den Mittelpunkt gestellt wird. Seine Lehre, welche auf der mosaischen Offenbarung aufruht, bildet jetzt das Zentrum der Bildung und Ausbildung. Die Sprüche des Weisheitslehrers soll man jetzt hören und befolgen, weil er ja die unumgängliche Quelle darstellt. Und andernorts sieht er ja im Weisheitslehrer den in der Weisheit gegenwärtigen Herrn wirksam, vielleicht sogar gegenwärtig.

6.6. Weisheit für sich und für die Gesellschaft (37:16-26)

Die Einheit 37:16-26 beginnt mit der unvergleichlichen Bedeutung des *Wortes*: dieses steht am Anfang jeglichen *Werkes*; (37:16a). Die Parallelführung von Wort und Werk, welche griechische Vorstellungen voraussetzt, knüpft am λόγος an. Für die Griechen ist der λόγος das allumfassende Grundprinzip, berührt sich zugleich mit der im Hebräischen belegten bedeutungsvollen Rolle von דבר, wenn auch in einem anderen Sinne. Zugleich impliziert λόγος / דבר eine Anspielung an den göttlichen bzw. universalen Ausgangspunkt. Dieser wiederum lässt die grundlegenden Dimensionen der Herkunft und des „Wesens" der σοφία anklingen. Dem entspricht, dass מחשבת (H^{B.Bm.D}) / βουλή in 37:16b zum דבר / λόγος (37:16a) parallel gestellt wird. Pläne / Rat, wofür verschiedene Auzdrücke verwendet werden (βουλή [21:13b]; מחשבת / βουλή [37:16b; vgl. 24:29b]; תחבולות / מחשבת [37:17]) beschreiben die Hervorbringungen bzw. Leistungen der Weisheit und sind auf ihre Art deren direkte, konkrete Verwirklichung.

Das Organ, die „Mechanik", wo diese Umsetzung bzw. Realisierung im Menschen geschieht, ist das Herz (vgl. καρδία in 21:26; 37:17), weswegen es als Ausgangspunkt dafür (ἴχνος) bezeichnet wird (37:17). Die nächste Stufe der Aktualisation ist dann die Rede bzw. die Zunge: Sie kann sogar als Kontrollorgan (ἡ κυριεύουσα … γλῶσσά; 37:18c) angesehen werden.

Wie bedeutsam sind nun diese Erträge der im Wort erscheinenden, durch das Herz erstellten Konkretionen der Weisheit? Sie treffen das Innerste der Werte und das Zentrum der Existenz, nämlich „Gutes und Böses, Leben und Tod"; (Sir 37:18b). Die menschliche Realisation dieser zentralen Erscheinungen ist der Weise. An seiner Gestalt und seinem Wirken für die Gesellschaft kann man erkennen, wie Weisheit „funktioniert" und welches Gewicht sie hat:

19 Es gibt Weise (חכם; G „Multitalente," πανοῦργος), die sich für viele als weise erweisen (חכם),
für sich selber aber sind sie Toren.

20 Es gibt Weise (חכם), dessen Wort (בדברו) zurückgewiesen wird,
von allen Genüssen sind sie ausgeschlossen.
  21 Denn vom Herrn (παρὰ κυρίου) wurde ihm keine Huld (χάρις) zuteil,
weil ihm alle Weisheit (πάσης σοφίας) fehlt.

22 Es gibt Weise (חכם / σοφὸς), die sich selbst gegenüber (לנפשו / τῇ ἰδίᾳ ψυχῇ) weise
(חכמ) sind;
  die Frucht ihres Wissens (פרי דעתו / οἱ καρποὶ τῆς συνέσεως) zeigt sich an ihrem
Leib.
23 Es gibt Weise (חכם), die für ihr Volk weise sind (יכמה; *der das Volk erzieht*: τὸν ... λαὸν
παιδεύσει);
  die Frucht ihres Wissens (פרי דעתו / οἱ καρποὶ τῆς συνέσεως) ist von Dauer.
24 Wer weise (חכם) ist für sich selbst, sättigt sich an Genüssen,
alle, die ihn sehen, preisen ihn glücklich.
    25 Des Menschen Leben (חיי איש / ζωὴ ἀνδρός) währt zählbare Tage (מספר ימים),
das Leben des Volkes Israel unzählbare Tage (ימי אין מספר / ἀναρίθμητοι).
26 Wer weise (חכם עם) ist für das Volk, erlangt Ehre,
sein Ruhm wird dauernd weiterleben (עומד בחיי עולם); (37:19-26).

Sira unterscheidet analog der Differenz zwischen der Grundlagenweisheit
und der angewandten Weisheit auch innerhalb der angewandten Weisheit
mehrere Ebenen. Es gibt Menschen, die sich mit der „Weisheit" auseinander-
setzen, sich diese aneignen, ohne dass sich die Ergebnisse einstellen,
welche von der Weisheit zu erwarten sind: sie haben weder Erfolg noch
Nutzen und sind auch nicht angesehen. Die misslungenen Beispiele lassen
keine Zweifel an der Weisheit als Weisheit aufkommen, vielmehr gibt Sira
zwei Gründe für den Fehlschlag an:

- Der erste Grund ist darin zu sehen, dass man sich zu wenig um sich
selbst kümmerte. Die positive Einstellung zu sich ist unverzichtbar!
Schon bei der Nächsten- und Fremdenliebe (Lev 19:18,34) war als
Meßlatte die *Liebe zu sich* genannt worden. Wer sich trotz der
Ermangelung der gesunden Selbstachtung mit der Weisheit beschäftigt, kann zwar angelerntes Schulwissen sammeln, ist aber für sich
selbst auf der Strecke geblieben: er ist für sich selbst eben ein Tor (נואל
[H^B,Bm,D]; der Grieche sagt gleich: „nutzlos" / ἄχρηστος [37:19b]).
- Der zweite Grund kann der sein, dass der Herr ihm die χάρις nicht
gegeben hat (οὐ γὰρ ἐδόθη [37:21a]). Wie man aus anderen Belegen
weiß, geschieht dies dann, wenn man sich ohne Achtung vor Gott oder
ohne anständig zu sein, der Weisheit genähert hatte (vgl. 1:10a; 6:37a;
19:20a). Eine derartige Aussage über die Weisheitsaneignung setzt
voraus, dass man „Weisheit" erwerben und sie sich durch Ausbildung
aneignen kann. Diese inkriminierte Weisheit ist also „Lernergebnis" —
wohl einer Weisheitschule —, welches man sich nur äußerlich und
nicht auch zugleich innerlich angeeignet hatte. Diesem Produkt ver-
weigert Gott die Zustimmung.

Wenn Sira auf diese Weise von „Weisheit" spricht, führt sie nicht zur oben geforderten, guten Persönlichkeitsentwicklung. Was ist dann nötig?

Kennzeichnend für den Weisen sind sein kultiviertes Auftreten und seine tiefsinnigen und aufbauenden Worte: Lehre und Lebensanleitung sind die Wirkungsfelder des Weisen. Worte setzen nun Hörer voraus. Solche können einen elitären Kreis, einen Geheimzirkel bilden. Solche meint Sira dezidiert nicht. Die Wirkung der Worte eines echten Weisen zeigt sich in der Öffentlichkeit, im sozialen Umfeld und im politischen Einfluss: „Es gibt Weise, die für ihr Volk weise sind; die Frucht ihres Wissens ist von Dauer" (37:23a,b). Darin zeigt sich auch eine wesentliche Aufgabe, der sich Sira verpflichtet sieht: Der Weisheitslehrer ist für die gedeihliche Entwicklung des gesamten Volkes mit-, vielleicht sogar hauptverantwortlich; vgl. unten 38:33. Neben diesem Aspekt ist es ein Anliegen Siras, in der heraufdämmernden und schon spürbaren Krisenzeit Zukunftsperspektiven anzudenken.[54] Es geht nicht nur, vielleicht nicht einmal besonders um den Einzelnen, sondern um das Volk, welches als Volk überdauern werde, denn „das Leben des Volkes Israel währt unzählbare Tage"; 37:25b.

6.7. Das öffentliche Wirken des schriftgelehrten Weisen (38:24-39:14)

Der häufig untersuchte und längste Abschnitt, der sich mit dem Weisen bzw. seiner Weisheit beschäftigt beginnt: „Die Weisheit (חכמה / ܚܟܡܬܐ / σοφία) des Schriftgelehrten (סופר / ܣܦܪܐ / γραμματέως) vermehrt (תרבה / ܬܘܣܦ) die Weisheit (חכמה / ܚܟܡܬܐ / [nicht in G]). Wer frei ist von Arbeit, kann sich als weise erweisen (יתחכם / ܢܬܚܟܡ / σοφισθήσεται)"; (38:24). Nachdrücklich und direkt geht es um „Weisheit konkret und aktuell". Zudem spricht Sira von zwei Ebenen von Weisheit:

–   Die Weisheit, die sich als ganze entfaltet und wozu der schriftgelehrte Weisheitslehrer einen wesentlichen Beitrag leistet, und

–   jene Weisheit, die den Weisheitslehrer überhaupt befähigt, zu dieser Weiterentwicklung beizutragen: die Weisheit, von der aus der Weisheitslehrer agiert, wurde aus der mosaischen Schrift gewonnen. Sira reiht sich in die seit Esra nachweisbare Linie der „Schriftgelehrten" ein (vgl. Esra 7:6[55],11 Neh 8:1,4,5,9,13; 12:26,36), und hat sich, wie der Enkel im Prolog festhält, intensivem Schriftstudium gewidmet:

---

[54] Vgl. F.V. Reiterer, „Der Pentateuch in der spätbiblischen Weisheit Ben Siras," in *A critical study of the Pentateuch. An Encounter between Africa and Europe* (ed. E. Otto, Altes Testament und Moderne, Münster: LIT 2005) 160-83, wo gezeigt wurde, dass die Geschichtspräsentation wesentlich dem Nachweis diente, dem Volk zu zeigen, dass es in allen Phasen der Geschichte wesentlich um den Aufweis ging, dass Gott in bedrohter Lage einen guten Ausweg auftut. Aus dieser Erfahrung kann man Hoffnung für die Gegenwart schöpfen.

[55] Vgl. „Dieser Esra kam also von Babel herauf. Er war ein Schriftgelehrter (סֹפֵר), bewandert (מָהִיר) im Gesetz des Mose (בְּתוֹרַת מֹשֶׁה), das der Herr, der Gott Israels, gegeben hatte (נָתַן)" (Esra 7:6).

Mein Großvater Jesus befasste sich sorgfältig mit dem Gesetz, mit den Propheten und mit den anderen von den Vätern überkommenen Schriften. Er verschaffte sich eine gründliche Kenntnis von ihnen und fühlte sich dann gedrängt, auch selbst etwas zu schreiben, um dadurch Bildung und Weisheit zu fördern. Wer es sich mit Liebe aneignet, wird es in einem gesetzestreuen Leben noch vermehren (Sir 0:7-14).

Nach dieser grundsätzlichen Stellungnahme wird die Frage gestellt, wie sich jemand als weise erweisen (יתחכם / ܢܚܟܡ / σοφισθήσεται) könne, der schwerer Arbeit nachgehen muss (38:25). Wie oben schon gesehen, vgl. z.B. 24:23-34, versteht Sira in der praktischen Weisheit eine Gegebenheit, die man einerseits erwerben und erlernen kann und muss und andererseits Ruhe benötigt, um auf schwierige Fragen gute neue Lösungsvorschläge zu entwickeln. Dafür benötigt man Zeit.

Sira zählt wichtige und die Gesellschaft erhaltende, von ihm sehr geschätzte Berufe auf wie den Landwirt, Handwerker, Künstler, Schmied und Töpfer. Er schließt:

Ohne sie wird keine Stadt besiedelt, und wo sie sich niederlassen, hungern sie nicht. Aber zur Volksversammlung (ܟܢܫܐ ܕܥܡܐ / εἰς βουλὴν λαοῦ) werden sie nicht hinzugezogen, in der Gemeinde (ܒܩܗܠܐ / ἐν ἐκκλησίᾳ) ragen sie nicht hervor. Sie sitzen auf keinem Richterstuhl (δίφρον δικαστοῦ) und das Kompendium des Gesetzes (διαθήκην κρίματος) kennen sie nicht (38:32,33).

Hier geht es wohl um die Rechtsgrundlagen, die man sowohl innerhalb des eigenen Volkes wie auch den Griechen gegenüber begründen und verteidigen kann.

Wo liegt nun der Schlüssel zu dieser Fertigkeit? Von zwei Säulen wird sie getragen: Einerseits die Achtung vor Gott (ܕܚܠܬ ܐܠܗܐ [38:34d]), die in 19:20 mit der Weisheit gleich gesetzt wird, und andererseits das Gesetz des Lebens (ܢܡܘܣܐ ܕܚܝܐ [38:34e][56]; G spricht vom νόμος ὑψίστου), das in 24:23a,b,25a,b als eine Quelle der Weisheit dargestellt wird: Beide werden in Syr parallelisiert. Wem diese Quelle nicht zugänglich ist, der bringt es nicht zu weiser Ausbildung (ܘܡܣܟܠܘܬܐ; G: Bildung und Rechtskunde — παιδείαν καὶ κρίμα) und zu weisen Merksätzen (ܒܚܟܡܬܐ; G: παραβολαί [38:33d,e]). Diese Fertigkeiten hat sich aber der weise Schriftgelehrte angeeignet, da man folgendes von ihm sagen kann:

Die Weisheit (σοφία) aller Vorfahren ergründet er und beschäftigt sich mit den Weissagungen (ܢܒܝܐ / προφητείαι);
er achtet auf die Reden (ܬܫܥܝܬܐ / διήγησις) berühmter Männer, und in die Tiefen der Sinnsprüche (παραβολαί) dringt er ein.

---

[56] Vgl. F.V. Reiterer, „Neue Akzente in der Gesetzesvorstellung: תורת חיים bei Ben Sira," in Gott und Mensch im Dialog, FS O. Kaiser (ed. M. Witte, BZAW 345/II, Berlin: de Gruyter 2004) 851-71, 852-56.

Er erforscht die Weisheit der Sinnsprüche (ܪܕܗܝܗ ܪܕܝܝܘ) / den verborgenen Sinn der Gleichnisse (ἀπόκρυφα παροιμιῶν) und verweilt über den Rätseln der Sinnsprüche (ܪܕܝܝܕܗ ܠܝܘ / ἐν αἰνίγμασιν παραβολῶν) (39:1-3).

„Der Herr, der Große" (κύριος ὁ μέγας) kann ihn mit „verständigem Geist" (ܪܕܗܝܕܠܝܝ ܪܘܝ / πνεύματι συνέσεως [39:6a]) ausstatten, ihm „weise Merksätze" bzw. „Rat und Einsicht" (ܪܝܝܝܝ ܪܕܗ / βουλὴ καὶ ἐπιστήμη [39:7a]) verleihen, sodass er auf der Basis des „Gesetzes des Lebens" bzw. „des Herrn" (ܪܘܝ ܪܝܘܝ / νόμος διαθήκης κυρίου [39:8b]) seine „gelehrte Ausbildung" (ܪܕܝܝܝ ܪܘܠܘ / παιδείαν διδασκαλίας [39:8a]) vertreten und verbreiten kann. Er wird mit Gewicht vor Gott beten können und selbst fähig sein, Weisheitssprüche zu prägen (ܪܕܗ / ῥήματα σοφίας [39:6d]). Das sind die richtigen Voraussetzungen für einen Weisen. Dieser kann der in 38:33 geforderten Aufgabe entsprechen: Er tritt in der Volksversammlung auf, entwickelt Lösungen für die anstehenden Fragen und kann das Regenten-/Richteramt ausüben; vgl. 4:15a.

Der in 38:24-39:14 beschriebene Weise ist zugleich ein Schriftkundiger, der in der Gesellschaft eine bedeutende Rolle spielt. Auf der Basis der Offenbarung des Herrn und des Studiums von altüberkommenen Sinnsprüchen, welche nicht in der Offenbarung gestanden sein müssen, entwickelt der eine doppelte Fähigkeiten: Er kann selbst neue Sprüche formulieren, welche er dann auch lehrt, und für die Gesellschaft anstehende Fragen, auch solche rechtlicher Natur, lösen. Er selbst steht mit Gott in Gebetskontakt, denn Gott ist der Urgrund seiner Qualifikation.

6.8. Zwischenzusammenfassung

Im Bereich der angewandten Weisheit bringt Sira eine Serie von Beispielen, an denen man sehen kann, wie sich die Weisheit konkret umsetzen lässt bzw. was sie ausschließt:

- Der Weise ist immer vorsichtig, meidet Übel und wirkt selbst als Lehrer der Weisheit (18:27-29).
- Weisheit und Achtung vor Gott zeigen sich in der Lebenspraxis nach den vielfältigen Regeln des Weisheitslehrers und schließen Liebäugeln mit Schlechtigkeit und Gerissenheit aus (19:20-24).
- Die zentrale Leistung des Weisen besteht in hilfreicher und guter *Rede*, welche anderen zugute kommt. Grundsätzlich gilt, dass der Weise auch von seiner Weisheit profitiert, die Weisheit aber wesentlich für die gesellschaftliche Öffentlichkeit bestimmt ist (20:27-31).
- Geradezu überströmend und zugleich Leben erhaltend wie eine Quelle ist die Weisheit, die sich besonders in kluger Rede kundtut. Unter anderem erkennt man einen Weisen daran, dass er sich zu benehmen weiß und z.B. nicht ohne Vorankündigung in ein Nachbarhaus stürzt (21:12-28).

- Eine besondere Realisation der Weisheit ist die mosaische Lehre mit den zahlreichen Anleitungen und dem daraus erfließenden Leben (24:23-34).
- Der Weise hat für sein Volk zu wirken und auf sich selbst zu schauen. Dann wird er zu einem Beispiel, das auf sich selbst als Lehrmodell für seine Schüler verweisen kann (37:16-26);
- Der schriftgelehrte Weise studiert die Offenbarung. Er ist wichtiger als die wertvollsten Berufe, denn er gewährleistet das Funktionieren der Gesellschaft. Er ist fähig, anstehende Fälle zu klären, nützliche Sinnsprüche zu entwickeln und auch andere zu lehren.

7. PARALLELTERMINI

In der hebräischen Poesie[57] ist der Parallelismus — meistens innerhalb eines aus zwei Kola bestehenden Stichus — eine, wenn nicht die bedeutendste und prägendste stilisitische Erscheinung, die dazu dient, durch Doppelausdrücke die Inhalte unter verschiedenen Gesichtspunkten zu betrachten. Falls σοφία / חכמה und νόμος / תורה Worte gleichen Inhalts sind, ist davon auszugehen, dass sie auch parallel gesetzt werden. Daher legt es sich nahe, die positiven Parallel- bzw. die antithetischen Oppositionstermini zu σοφία / חכמה und νόμος / תורה zu erheben.

Es ist noch eine Notiz darüber anzubringen, warum auch in der griechischen Übersetzung die aus dem Hebräischen stammende stilistische Eigenart zu untersuchen ist: Der Enkel hebt die Großartigkeit der Israel in der Offenbarung geschenkten Gabe im Gegenüber zu den verschiedenen Kulturgütern in Alexandria hervor. Er bemüht sich um eine hochwertige Übersetzung und beherrscht die Stilmittel sowohl der hebräischen wie der griechischen Dichtkunst. Daher können an die griechische Übersetzung die gleichen Anfragen wie an die hebräischen Textzeugen gerichtet werden.

Der oben vorgenommenen Unterscheidung folgend, werden die Zeugnisse für die Grundlagenweisheit (1), für die angewandte Weisheit (2) getrennt vorgestellt. Da die untersuchten Termini auch darüber hinaus verwendet werden, werden diese Belege zu einer eigenen Gruppe zusammengefasst (3). Es wird sich herausstellen, ob es hier Entsprechungen oder Differenzen gibt.

---

[57] Vgl. E.D. Reymond, *Innovations in Hebrew Poetry. Parallelism and the Poems of Sirach* (Studies in Biblical Literature 9, Atlanta: SBL 2004) 114f und Fn 4 (114-115); F.V. Reiterer, „Gott und Opfer," in *Ben Sira's God. Proceedings of the International Ben Sira Conference Durham – Ushaw College 2001* (ed. R. Egger-Wenzel, BZAW 321, Berlin: de Gruyter 2002) 136-79, 137.

7.1. *Die Parallelen zu* σοφία / חכמה

7.1.1. *Die synonymen Paralleltermini*

(1) Folgende Parallelen finden sich in den Passagen zur grundlegenden Weisheit:

1:4	σοφία	//	σύνεσις φρονήσεως
6:18	παιδείαν	//	σοφίαν
6:32	תערם – παιδευθήσῃ	//	תתחכם – πανοῦργος ἔσῃ
14:20	בחכמה – ἐν σοφίᾳ	//	ובתבונה – ἐν συνέσει
15:3	ἄρτον συνέσεως	//	ὕδωρ σοφίας

Als Parallelen sind ausschließlich Worte verwendet worden, die aus dem gleichen Wortfeld stammen. Hier nun lässt sich keine typische Erscheinung verfolgen. Es mag verwundern, dass σοφία mehrheitlich nicht an erster Position steht.

(2) Folgende Parallelen stehen in den Passagen zur angewandten Weisheit:

19:22	σοφία	//	βουλή
20:27	ὁ σοφός	//	ἄνθρωπος φρόνιμος
21:18	σοφία	//	γνῶσις
39:6	πνεύματι συνέσεως	//	ῥήματα σοφίας

Wiederum bewegt sich die Wortwahl im Bereich des gleichen Wortfeldes, wobei jetzt doch auffällt, dass σοφία / σοφός deutlich häufiger an erster Position steht.

(3) Über die angegebenen Einheiten hinaus, trifft man in Ben Sira auf folgende Parallelbelege:

1:27	σοφία γὰρ καὶ //		πίστις καὶ πραότης
	παιδεία		
4:24	תבונה – σοφία	//	חכמה – παιδεία
10:1	κριτὴς σοφός	//	ἡγεμονία συνετοῦ
10:25	οἰκέτῃ σοφῷ	//	ἀνὴρ ἐπιστήμων

Bei diesen Beispielen, die nicht in umfangreicheren Weisheitsgedichten stehen, ist die Verteilung unter Zugrundelegung des hebräisch-griechischen Befundes mit der vorherigen Gruppe vergleichbar. In den griechischen Belegen ist σοφία / σοφός nur an erster Position belegt.

Für unser Generalthema ist festzuhalten, dass kein Beleg für eine Parallele mit תורה, νόμος anzuführen ist.

7.1.2. *Die Antonyme zu* חכמה / σοφία

Es wird die gleiche Untergliederung wie im vorherigen Abschnitt beibehalten.

(1) In den Passagen zur grundlegenden Weisheit stehen *keine* Gegenbegriffe zu חכמה / σοφία.

(2) Folgende Gegenbegriffe stehen in den Passagen zur angewandten Weisheit:

20:31   τὴν μωρίαν   //   τὴν σοφίαν
21:26   μωρῶν   //   σοφῶν
37:19   חכם – ἀνὴρ πανοῦργος   //   נואל - ἄχρηστος

Die Worte werden ausschließlich aus dem zu *weise* oppositionellen Wortfeld genommen.

(3) Über die angegebenen Einheiten hinaus trifft man auf folgende Oppositionsbelege:

20:7   חכם – ἄνθρωπος σοφός   //   כסיל – ἄφρων
20:13   חכם – ὁ σοφός   //   כסילים – μωρῶν
10:23   דל משכיל – πτωχὸν   //   איש חמם – ἄνδρα ἁμαρτωλόν
         συνετόν
32:18   איש חכם – ἀνὴρ βουλῆς   //   לץ – ὑπερήφανος
41:15   אולתו – τὴν μωρίαν   //   חכמתו – τὴν σοφίαν

Deutlich übersteigt die Zahl dieser Belege jene vom vorhergehenden Beispiel. Eine leicht mehrheitliche, nicht wirklich markante Anzahl der Belege führt *weise* an der ersten Position im Parallelismus.

Es ist notierenswert, dass kein Beleg für einen Oppositionsausdruck im Kontext der Grundlagenweisheit gegeben ist. Für unser Generalthema ist festzuhalten, dass kein Beleg mit תורה, νόμος anzuführen ist.

7.2. *Die Parallelen zu* תורה / νόμος

In diesem Schritt werden die Paralleltermini zu תורה / νόμος erhoben.

7.2.1. *Die synonymen Paralleltermini*

(1) Eine Gruppe von zu Gesetz parallelen Worten wird aus der Gesetzessprache genommen.

45:5c   מצוה – ἐντολάς   //   תורת חיים ותבונה – νόμον ζωῆς καὶ
                                             ἐπιστήμης
45:17a,d מצותיו – ἐν ἐντολαῖς   //   חק ומשפט – ἐν νόμῳ
44:20   מצות עליון – νόμον   //   בא בברית – ἐν διαθήκῃ μετ' αὐτοῦ
         ὑψίστου

Die „Vorlagen" für das griechische νόμος sind unterschiedlich. In den Beispielen ist nur einmal das hebräische Wort erhalten, und zwar in תורת חיים, der phraseologischen Eigenprägung Siras[58].

(2) Zwei weitere Beispiele sind zum Bereich geistiger Fähigkeiten zu rechnen.

17:11   ἐπιστήμην   //   νόμον ζωῆς
39:8   ἐκφανεῖ παιδείαν διδασκαλίας //   ἐν νόμῳ διαθήκης κυρίου

---

[58] Vgl. „Es konnte keine direkte Parallele zur Phrase : תורת חיים gefunden werden. Wir treffen demnach auf eine von Sira stammende Eigenprägung"; Reiterer, Akzente 869.

(3) Die größte Anzahl der Belege hat theologische Zusammenhänge zum Inhalt

15:1b	ὁ φοβούμενος κύριον	//	ὁ ἐγκρατὴς τοῦ νόμου
19:20	φόβος κυρίου	//	ποίησις νόμου
19:24	ἔμφοβος	//	παραβαίνων νόμον
21:11	ὁ φυλάσσων νόμον	//	συντέλεια τοῦ φόβου κυρίου
2:16b	ζητήσουσιν εὐδοκίαν	//	ἐμπλησθήσονται τοῦ νόμου

Die Achtung vor Gott ist eine der Haltungen eines Menschen, der das Gesetz einhält. Dadurch findet der Mensch Anerkennung und Wohlwollen bei Gott. Wer weise ist, hält eo ipso das Gesetz; vgl. 33,2a.

7.2.2. Der Oppositionsausdruck zu תורה */ νόμος*

41:8b	ἄνδρες ἀσεβεῖς	//	ἐγκατελίπετε νόμον θεοῦ ὑψίστου

8. ZUSAMMENFASSUNG

Mit den vorgelegten Überlegungen wurde eine weit verbreitete These überprüft, da die Argumente, die für die Identifikation von Gesetz und Weisheit angegeben werden, nicht sehr präzise sind. Nach den vorausgehenden Untersuchungen ist das Ergebnis, das recht kurz gehalten werden kann, folgendes:

Man kann kein einzelnes Gedicht, das sich mit Weisheit beschäftigt, für die „Definition" von Weisheit als zentral und andere als weniger bedeutsam qualifizieren. Wenn man von Weisheit im Buch Ben Sira spricht, hat man die Spannungsbögen, die zugleich eine Art Strukturierung darstellen, und zusammengehörende Textblöcke zu berücksichtigen. Interessant ist, dass Sira kein Gedicht dem „Gesetz" widmet.

Es erscheint nicht nur sinnvoll, sondern notwendig, dass man zwischen den Bedeutungsnuancen von „Weisheit" unterscheidet: Die wichtigste Schwerpunktsetzung liegt darin, dass Sira zwischen grundlegenden Aussagen über die Weisheit (Grundlagenweisheit) und den konkreten Realisationen (angewandte Weisheit) unterscheidet. Zu der Grundlagenweisheit zählen 1:1-10; 4:11-19; 6,18-37; 14:20-15:10; 24:1-22; 51:13-30 und zur angewandten Weisheit gehören 18:27-29; 19:20-24; 20:27-31; 21:12-28; 37:16-26; 38:24-39:14.

Innerhalb dieser Textgruppen akzentuiert Sira Weisheit markant: Weisheit ist eine vorgeschöpfliche Setzung des Schöpfers sein. Sie ist Geschenk der Herrn an die Menschen, insbesondere an Israel. Weisheit kann die Triebfeder weisen Verhaltens des, weil von der Weisheit geprägt, Weisen sein. Weisheit kann auch gelehrt und auf diesem Wege angeeignet werden. Voraussetzung dafür ist aber die persönliche Qualifikation, sodass der Weisheitserwerb an sich nicht schon zu positiven Ergebnissen führt.

Die Differenz zwischen „Grundlagenweisheit" und „angewandter Weisheit" hält sich bis in die Parallelenbildung durch. Auf dieser Basis gibt es

Differenzierungen, die einen neuen Durchblick durch die sirazidische Intention ermöglichen.

Will man so wie Sira über Weisheit sprechen, sind die Blöcke „Grundlagenweisheit" und „angewandte Weisheit" als ganze zusammen zu sehen. Das Herauslösen einzelner, wenn auch für besonders bedeutsam angesehener Passagen birgt die Gefahr in sich, dass man einseitige Ergebnisse erzielt.

Das Gesetz ist bei Sira nie eine vorgeschöpfliche Gegebenheit.

Auch beim „Gesetz" ist zwischen verschiedenen Bedeutungs- und Anwendungsbereichen zu unterscheiden[59]: Gesetz kann die Innenstruktur des Geschaffenen sein, Gesetz kann die Offenbarung als Ganze bzw. die einzelne darin enthaltene Vorschrift sein, Gesetz des Mose bezeichnet Teile der zur Zeit Siras zumindest weitgehend schriftlichen Offenbarung, in den Augen des Enkels handelt es sich um den „Pentateuch". Gesetz kann aber auch den verbindlichen Weisheitsspruch eines Weisheitslehrers bezeichnen.

Auf der Ebene der Realisation treffen sich angewandte Weisheit und konkretiesierte תורה. Doch sind die inneren Implikationen zu unterscheiden: Wer einen Weisheitsspruch nicht erfüllt, der gilt als unklug, ja als dumm. Wer ein Gesetz nicht einhält wird schuldig und ist unter die Sünder zu rechnen.

Es gibt keine direkte Parallelsetzung[60] von σοφία / חכמה und νόμος / תורה im Buch Ben Sira.

Aufgrund des Befundes ist es nicht möglich, ohne genaue Differenzierung über das Verhältnis von σοφία / חכמה und νόμος / תורה zu sprechen: die *Grundlagenweisheit* hat keinen Bezug zum „Gesetz"; das Verhalten aufgrund der *angewandten Weisheit* hat allenthalben Berührungspunkte im Ergebnis mit der Gesetzeserfüllung. Für eine Identifikation von חכמה / σοφία und תורה / νόμος konnte kein Beleg gefunden werden.

---

[59] Vgl. Reiterer, „Akzente," 856; zum Ganzen F.V. Reiterer, „The Interpretation of the Wisdom Tradition of the Torah within Ben Sira," in *The Wisdom of Ben Sira. Studies on Tradition, Redaction, and Theology* (ed. A. Passaro, Deuterocanonical and Cognate Literature Studies 1, Berlin: de Gruyter 2007) (forthcoming).

[60] Das gilt trotz der Feststellung von Schnabel, Law 70f, wo er „Gesetz" und „Weisheit" sich in 17:11 (προσέθηκεν αὐτοῖς ἐπιστήμην // καὶ νόμον ζωῆς ἐκληροδότησεν αὐτοῖς) und 21:11 (ὁ φυλάσσων νόμον κατακρατεῖ τοῦ ἐννοήματος αὐτοῦ // καὶ συντέλεια τοῦ φόβου κυρίου σοφία) poetisch entprechend angibt.

DOES WISDOM COME FROM THE TEMPLE?
BEN SIRA'S ATTITUDE TO THE TEMPLE OF JERUSALEM

József Zsengellér
(Reformed Theological Academy, Pápa)

INTRODUCTION

Working on the phenomenon of *monotemplism*, which is a theological reality in the canonical literature of the Old Testament and a historical non-reality in the life of the communities of the Israelite people,[1] I was faced with the fact that there is no hint of the temple in the early[2] wisdom literature. The only mention of a temple is Qohelet 4:17

> Guard your steps when you go to the house of God (בית אלהים), to draw near to listen is better than the sacrifice offered by fools: for they do not know how to keep from doing evil.

Even in this short reference, which is part of the larger passage of 4:17-5:6, Qohelet does not deal with the temple as an institution but warns "against thoughtless rushing to the temple."[3] He here compares making a conscious oath with making one that is not-well considered. In 5:1 the same situation is put concretely, and God's dwelling place is defined as not being the temple but heaven, in contrast to the earthly dwelling of a human being.

Consequently early wisdom in general wrestles with the moral dimension of sacrifice, but does not discuss the theological relevance of

---

[1] I introduced this term, which refers to the phenomenon when a religious community accepts only one sacred site (or temple) for the worship of their deity. See my discussion of this whole problem in J. Zsengellér, "Monotemplism. The exclusivity of the place of worship in Israel's theology and religious praxis. (A theory never realized in praxis)," in *Elmélet és gyakorlat a zsidó-keresztény gondolkodás történetében* ([*Theory and Praxis in the Jewish-Christian History of Thinking*] eds. B. Ódor and G.G. Xeravits, Pápa: PRTA and Budapest: L'Harmattan 2005) 12-75. (Hungarian, forthcoming in *ZAW* in German).

[2] According to our discussions in this conference I utilize this expression here to refer those wisdom books called traditionally canonical.

[3] J.L. Crenshaw, "Ben Sira," in *NIB* 5: 601-867; cf. T. Krüger, *Kohelet (Prediger)* (BK 19, Neukirchen: Neukirchener Verlag 2000) 207.

temple or sacrifice. Walter Zimmerli defined the nature of the movement as "tempel- und opferfreien Pietismus."[4] The Wisdom of Solomon continues this line. But in Ben Sira we encounter a different feeling. Although writing of wisdom he is interested in offerings, temple officials and the temple itself. In this paper I try to detect the nature and reason of this unique temple oriented wisdom of Ben Sira: Does it derive from the period in which it was written? Is it connected to the profession of Ben Sira? Has it any relation to other views on the temple of YHWH?

In previous scholarly studies the problem of Ben Sira's attitude to the cult was extensively discussed, but did not result in a consensus. However, his positive approach was noted even by those who held the opinion that the cult had no major part in the theological ideas of Ben Sira.[5] His attitude to priesthood and liturgy was also studied. According to J.G. Snaith both topics are discussed by Ben Sira because they are entailed by the obedience to the Law, and Snaith did not attach great importance to the positive discussion of offerings and temple ceremonies.[6] In the last two decades new attention has been paid to Ben Sira's outlook on priesthood, mainly because these data are the only concrete connections to historical realities of the writer's time.[7] By probing this connection his partners in conversation can be detected.[8]

In spite of this increased interest in the priesthood in Ben Sira, the perception of the temple itself stayed in the shadows. For example Boccaccini devoted just a 12 line paragraph to the temple, Wright only the half of this,[9] only listing the content of verses referring to the temple without further discussion.

---

[4] W. Zimmerli, "Das Buch Kohelet: Traktat oder Sentenzensammlung?," VT 24 (1974) 221-30 discussed Qoh 9:2 and referred to Ps 40:7-9; 50:7-15; 51:18ff and Jes 66:3. Cf. also the negative evaluation of cult in wisdom literature by G. von Rad, Weisheit in Israel (Neukirchen: Neukirchener Verlag 1970) 240-44.

[5] R. Smend, Die Weisheit des Jesus Sirach erklärt (Berlin: Reimer 1906) 24 and R. Pfeiffer, History of New Testament Times (New York: Harper 1949) 374-75.

[6] J.G. Snaith, "Ben Sira's Supposed Love of Liturgy," VT 25 (1975) 167-74.

[7] This feature was studied closely first by S. Olyan, "Ben Sira's Relationship to the Priesthood," HTR 80 (1987) 261-86. More recently by B.G. Wright, "Fear the Lord and Honour the Priest: Ben Sira as Defender of the Jerusalem Priesthood" in The Book of Ben Sira in Modern Research (ed. P.C. Beentjes, BZAW 255, Berlin: de Gruyter 1997) 189-222. G. Boccaccini, Roots of Rabbinic Judaism. An Intellectual History from Ezekiel to Daniel (Grand Rapids: Eerdmans 2002) 134-50. B.G. Wright, "Ben Sira and the Book of the Watchers on the Legitimate Priesthood," in Intertextual Studies in Ben Sira and Tobit (eds. J. Corley and V. Skemp, CBQMS 38, Washington: Catholic Biblical Association 2005) 241-54.

[8] Cf. also G. Boccaccini, Middle Judaism: Jewish Thought, 300 B.C.E. to 200 C.E., (Minneapolis: Fortress 1991) chapter 2; Wright, "Fear the Lord;" M.W. Duggan, "Ezra, Scribe and Priest, and the Concerns of Ben Sira," in Intertextual Studies in Ben Sira and Tobit, 201-10.

[9] Boccaccini, Roots of Rabbinic Judaism, 134; Wright, "Fear the Lord," 195. In the commentary of P.W. Skehan and A.A. DiLella, The Wisdom of Ben Sira (AB 39, New York: Doubleday 1987), in the chapter concerning the teaching of Ben Sira, only

Of course, in the development of postexilic Jewish theology Torah seems to replace the previous theological importance of the temple.[10] As a further step, wisdom is closely identified with Torah or Torah with wisdom.[11] This is expressed also by Ben Sira several times (e.g. 1:26-27; 15:1; 21:11; 24:23; 34:8). It should be noted, however, that in the Book of Ben Sira this close association does not mean an exclusive expression of wisdom. In the words of Jessie Rogers: "Law thus is a conduit for Wisdom, but Wisdom is not summed up without remainder in the Law."[12] Wisdom/Torah became the centre of religion. Torah is taught in the בית מדרש, in the synagogue and not only in the temple. On the other hand, Ben Sira makes a twist in this whole system or idea of development. He identifies Torah and wisdom but at the same time he is speaking about the house of wisdom and the House of God. He does not separate wisdom/Torah from the temple. In his book he mentions temple, temple worship, i.e. liturgy, priests and offerings several times in different contexts but seemingly along a consistent line of theology. To answer our questions we discuss first the dwellings of God, then cult as practice and personnel, and than the theological ideas concerning the temple.

CHARACTERIZATION OF THE DWELLING OF GOD

Temple played a prominent role in the life of Israel in the post-exilic, pre-Hellenistic period. It was not only the centre of the religious, but also of the national life. It was not only an edifice but an institution as well. The religious personnel were responsible for the correct cultic activity and for the regular conduct of community life. Collecting taxes and judging "personal problems" were included in the everyday activities. In the Hellenistic period, the definition of the Jerusalem temple as a religious place was in transition because the Hellenistic reforms transformed it into the political centre of the people of Israel too. The Council of Elders, led by the High

---

temple worship is mentioned briefly: 87-88. J.J. Collins, *Jewish Wisdom in the Hellenistic Age* (OTL, Louisville: Westminster John Knox Press 1997) 51-52 pointed out that the exceptional character of Ben Sira's Wisdom found expression in the cult of the Jerusalem temple.

[10] The theological importance of making a covenant on the basis of the Torah is the main concern of Neh 8-10. This passage seems to be the latest phase of the editorial work of the book of Nehemiah. J.L. Wright, *Rebuilding Identity. The Nehemiah-Memoir and its Earliest Readers* (BZAW 348, Berlin: de Gruyter 2004) presents how the temple oriented worldview served by priests changed to a Torah oriented one served by the *sopherim*.

[11] Deut 4:6; Jer 8:8; Ezra 7:14.

[12] J. Rogers, "'It Overflows Like the Euphrates with Understanding:' Another Look at the Relationship between Law and Wisdom in Sirach," in *Of Scribes and Sages. Early Jewish Interpretation and Transmission of Scripture* (ed. C.A. Evans, JSPSup 50, SSEJC 9, London: T&T Clark 2004) 114-21, esp. 116. See also the discussion of this topic in Collins, *Jewish Wisdom in the Hellenistic Age*, 45; 54-56.

Priest as the uppermost head of Israel, sat in the temple complex.[13] The Jerusalem temple, the place of meeting between God and man became a place of meeting of the people and its leaders as well. This situation combined with other radical Hellenistic reforms in cult and cultural life caused a struggle for power among the (priestly) aristocracy on the one hand and rivalry among wise/scribal circles on the other.[14] In this context the position of Ben Sira concerning the temple should be discussed.

1) Wisdom literature discusses the nature of God as being in heaven and men on earth (Job 1; Qoh 5:2). In Ben Sira 1:6-8 God is sitting on his throne, but the location of this throne is not defined. The depiction of God sitting on his throne is not used any more in his book. In the previous Jewish literature (biblical books) well known to Ben Sira, the throne is in the heavenly temple of God.[15] Although this context and that of 24:4, where the throne of wisdom is mentioned, can be determined as a heavenly dimension, other references in the book describe God's dwelling in the earthly temple in Jerusalem.[16] God is omnipotent, but close to human beings. He gives his wisdom so that he and the world can be understood.

2) In the book, this closeness of God to humanity is set mostly according to Deuteronomical and Deuteronomistic theological formulations. This appears first at the beginning of the second part of the book. The praise of wisdom in chapter 24 describes the presence of wisdom in a congregational situation. The introduction formula (v.1.) has three definitions of his attendance:

(a)   among her own people
(b)   in the assembly (ἐκκλησία) of the most High

---

[13] See e.g. 6:34; 30:24 [33:19], and the decree of Antiochus III in Josephus, *AJ* 12.138-144. Cf. K. Bringmann, *Hellenistische Reform und Religionsvervolgung in Judäa: Eine Untersuchung zur jüdisch-hellenistischen Geschichte* (175-163 v. Chr.) (Göttingen: Vandenhoeck & Ruprecht 1983) 69-73; R. Horsley and P. Tiller, "Ben Sira and the Sociology of the Second Temple," in *Second Temple Studies III: Studies in Politics, Class and Material Culture* (eds. P.R. Davies and J.M. Halligan; JSOTSup 340, Sheffield: Academic Press 2002) 74-107; E. Haag, *Das hellenistische Zeitalter. Israel und die Bibel in 4. bis 1. Jahrhundert v. Chr.* (Biblische Enzyklopädie 9, Stuttgart: Kohlhammer 2003) 56-62. On the political leadership of the high priest in this period see J.C. VanderKam, *From Joshua to Caiaphas. High Priests after the Exile* (Minneapolis: Fortress Press and Assen: Van Gorcum 2004) 122-24.

[14] Cf. R. Horsley, "The Politics of Cultural Production in Second Temple Judea: Historical Context and Political-Religious Relations of the Scribes Who Produced *1 Enoch, Sirach* and *Daniel*," in *Conflicted Boundaries in Wisdom and Apocalypticism* (eds. B.G. Wright and L.M. Wills, SBLSS 35, Leiden: Brill 2006) 123-45; esp. 132-33.

[15] Ps 11:4 mentions God being in his temple in Jerusalem, although his throne is in the heaven.

[16] 36:12 (36:18) states that Jerusalem is the foundation of God's throne. But see the next note. Collins, *Jewish Wisdom in the Hellenistic Age*, 49 says: "it is possible that 'her people' in v. 1 refers to this heavenly assembly, but it is more likely to refer to Israel, among whom Wisdom settles in vv. 8-12."

(c)   in the presence of his power (δυνάμις)

According to Smend's previous suggestion, DiLella interprets this as a celestial scene.[17] But δυνάμις can not be taken as a translation of צבאות in this case, since the latter word is not used in the Hebrew texts of the Book of Ben Sira, nor in the biblical wisdom literature. Another reason is that the Greek translation (LXX) has not utilized one word to express the epithet צבאות, and used δυνάμις on its own. Furthermore δυνάμις is in the singular and צבאות is plural. Consequently 24:1-2 is not a celestial, but a liturgical situation which can occur only in the temple.

The first person singular "Song of Wisdom" explains wisdom's origin from God (v. 3), living with him in heaven (v. 4a), taking part in his work as part of his presence in the form of a pillar of cloud during the wandering of Israel in the wilderness (v. 4b), and finally finding her place in Jacob and Israel. (v. 8).[18] Thus wisdom comes from heaven to earth to stay among Israel, the people of God. This earthly place is defined in detail in the following verses:

> 10. In the holy tent I ministered before him,
>   and then in Zion I took up my post.
> 11. In the city he loves as he does me, he gave me rest.
>   In Jerusalem is my domain.
> 12. I have struck root among the glorious people.
>   In the portion of the Lord is my inheritance.

The whole image is a summary of the Deuteronomistic vision of the Jerusalem temple, which takes over the place of the holy tent. It is in Jerusalem the beloved city (Ps 50:2), which is in Israel the portion of the Lord (Deut 32:9).

In the next sections of this praise the work of wisdom is depicted in poetical forms. It is connected to the temple in two ways. First, the smell of wisdom is identical with that of the incense used in the Tent of Meeting, (24:15) or better to say wisdom is acting as the incense of the service. This image is borrowed from Exodus.[19] Since the use of the listed perfumes is restricted to the liturgical service (Exod 30:38) and authorised personnel, wisdom became a tool of intermediation between man and God. It is a priestly function in the temple.[20] The effect of this action is God's conciliation and man's well being. The second connection of wisdom to the temple is the

---

[17] R. Smend, *Die Weisheit des Jesus Sirach erklärt*, 216. J. Marböck, *Weisheit im Wandel* (BBB 37, Bonn: Peter Hanstein 1971) 58-60: "…in V.4. vom Wohnsitz der Weisheit in der Höhe und von ihrem Thron auf der Wolkensäule die Rede ist;" Skehan and DiLella, *The Wisdom of Ben Sira*, 331.

[18] Cf. the discussion of this description by Marböck, *Weisheit im Wandel*, 63-68. More recently by Collins, *Jewish Wisdom in the Hellenistic Age*, 50-51.

[19] Cf. Marböck, *Weisheit im Wandel*, 74.

[20] Skehan and DiLella, *The Wisdom of Ben Sira*, 335.

imagery of living water (24:25-31) coming from the temple and giving life to the earth presented in the vision of Ezekiel about the new temple of Jerusalem (Ez 47:1-12).[21] Ben Sira envisions wisdom as originating from the Law and the Jerusalem temple like a rivulet that becomes a river and then a sea to teach more and more people, not only in Israel, but all over the world including the Diaspora.

Chapter 24 presents the temple as the dwelling of God and his wisdom. A place from where wisdom as Torah and teaching can flow out and make land and people prosper, in and outside of Israel.

3) Chapter 36 has the next section about the temple. Ms B 36:13-14 corresponds to the Greek text 36:12-13 and reads:[22]

13. Take pity on your holy city, Jerusalem, the foundation for your throne.
14. Fill Zion with your majesty, your temple with your glory.

Although verse 14 has different readings (λαός) in some Greek manuscripts, היכל in the Hebrew MS B reinforces the "temple" reading and takes this passage as a point of reference. Therefore, if the foundation of God's throne—which itself is in heaven—is in Jerusalem, then it seems to be an eternal position. Ben Sira makes clear in 47:13 that Solomon "established a lasting sanctuary" for God.[23] Zion is an everlasting dwelling place of God, it will be filled with his majesty and glory forever. Consequently, if God has his dwelling place in the Jerusalem temple forever, so has wisdom. Chapter 36 reinforces the introductory and metaphoric definition given by chapter 24 and states that the earthly dwelling of wisdom is in the temple.

4) In the Praise of the Fathers Ben Sira concerns himself five times with the edifice or the institution of the temple.

First, in the praise of Phineas (45:24), the covenant is given to him "to sustain the sanctuary" (לכלכל מקדש, Greek has: προστατεῖν ἁγίων, to rule the holy ones/the holy places). Of course in that time there was no temple but a tent shrine, on the other hand, the continuity of wisdom's presence from the "holy tent in the desert" to the temple on Zion (24:10) makes God's dwelling

---

[21] The primordial allusion of the section is evident, but not exclusive. Cf. the comments of Skehan and DiLella, *The Wisdom of Ben Sira*, 336-37. Although DiLella refers to Ezekiel, he does not mention the origin of the water, i.e. the temple. Rogers, "It Overflows Like the Euphrates," 115-17 emphasizes the prophetic colour of this image, but does not refer to Ezekiel. Similar prophecies can be red in Joel 3:18; Zech 14:8.

[22] This passage is at the end of the major dislocation in the Greek manuscripts. The Old Latin version preserved the earliest sequence of the verses, and our numbering here follows it, according to the presentation of Skehan and DiLella. The numbering of MS B even differs from that of the Greek MSS. On the general problem of the textual witnesses see Skehan and DiLella, *The Wisdom of Ben Sira*, 50-62.

[23] ויצב לעד מקדש recalls Ps 78:69.

in these two dissimilar edifices equal. Consequently the two edifices are made equal.[24] Furthermore, as we can see, to be the leader of the temple personnel in the time of Ben Sira was the task of the high priest, received as a covenantal privilege by Phineas and his descendants.[25]

The second case in this line is the praise of David (47:9-10). The chosen king of Israel introduced liturgical actions, festivals in the Sanctuary (מקדש/ἁγίασμα). Ben Sira had to find some positive motives in David's relation to the Sanctuary and tried to forget his failure to build a lasting construction, a house for God. 1 Chron 23-24 is the scriptural source for the festival(s) Ben Sira connected to David, but the whole idea has a Deuteronomistic overtone. The praise of not God but his "holy Name" is the main concept of the exilic- and post-exilic Deuteronomistic "name-theology."[26]

Solomon is the third person mentioned (47:13). His situation is described as if he had received peace from God in order to be able to build a house for God's name. Here again we meet with the Deuteronomistic "name theology" now combined with the idea of the temple being "eternal" (לעד/εἰς τὸν αἰῶνα). This expression was taken probably from Ps 78:69 and forms an interesting parallel with the eternal glory of David's house mentioned at the end of the previous section. In Solomon's case a man made an edifice for the eternal glory of God; in the case of David God gave eternal glory to a man. Instead of calling the temple היכל/ναὸς, Ben Sira used מקדש/ἁγίασμα, perhaps to make a word-play with the previous sentence,. In this he remained consistent in using the word sanctuary for the temple before the exile.

Concerning the fourth person, Ben Sira does not mention that Zerubbabel led the people back to Jerusalem. According to him, Zerubbabel's main task was to build up God's house again (49:12). This edifice was already a "holy temple" (היכל קדש/ναὸς ἅγιος). To distinguish Zerubbabel from the priesthood, Jeshua son of Jozadak is also listed without further identification, but both of them are connected to the temple building activity. The temple is dedicated to the everlasting glory of God.[27]

At the beginning of Simon's praise (50:1-3) the first deed mentioned of this eminent high priest was to renovate and enlarge the temple of Jerusalem. His priestly duty, or perhaps a special celebration, is described as having taken place in this temple.[28] Verse 5. in MS B mentions אהל as a

---

[24] C.R. Koester, *The Dwelling of God. The Tabernacle in the Old Testament, Intertestamental Jewish Literature and the New Testament* (CBQMS 22, Washington DC: Catholic Biblical Association 1989) 24-25 discusses Ben Sira, but does not mention either 45:24, or 47:9-10 which would underline his argument.

[25] Interestingly, Aaron as the first high priest serving in the holy tent is not connected to the Sanctuary at all.

[26] The most recent discussion of this topic is S.R. Richter, *The Deuteronomistic History and the Name Theology* (BZAW 318, Berlin: de Gruyter 2002).

[27] See the discussion of the different temple theologies below.

[28] A recent discussion of this passage see in O. Mulder, *Simon the High Priest in Sirach 50: An Exegetical Study of the Significance of Simon the High Priest As Climax to the*

parallel of בית כפרת and both refers to the temple or a part of it enforcing the identification of the tent shrine with the temple building.[29] The whole passage reveals the temple as the home of a festival dedicated to the glory of God.[30] In this text temple, priest and deity met and joined in a unique situation.

The key figures of the ancestral history of Israel (two priests and three "politicians") are connected to the temple, which is the house of God, the house of His name and the house of His glory. In chapter 50 as a summary the glory of God and the ancestors is celebrated in this temple.

5) As an autobiographical poem, 51:13-30 forms an epilogue at the end of the book and mentions the temple where Ben Sira prayed for wisdom. This passage of chapter 51 has two Hebrew versions. 11QPs[a] was found in Qumran[31] and MS B in the Cairo Genizah.[32] The two Hebrew texts differ significantly. The Greek version G differs from both of them. In our context verses 13-14 are interesting:

G	MS B	11QPs[a]
Ἔτι ὢν νεώτερος πρὶν ἢ πλανηθῆναί με	אני נער הייתי	אני נער בטרם תעיתי
ἐζήτησα σοφίαν προφανῶς ἐν προσευχῇ μου	וחפצתי בה ובקשתיה	ובקשתיה
ἔναντι ναοῦ ἠξίουν περὶ αὐτῆς	|	באה לי בתרה
καὶ ἕως ἐσχάτων ἐκζητήσω αὐτήν	|	ועד סופה אדורשנה

11QPs[a] presents an acrostic poem, but neither MS B nor the Greek text follows this poetic characteristic. Verse 13 has more or less the same meaning in the Greek as in the Hebrew version, but the first colon of verse 14 in G differs remarkably from 11QPs[a]. MS B does not contain this verse.

	11QPs[a]	Greek
13a	When I was young and innocent,	When I was young and before I was led astray
b	I kept seeking wisdom.	I sought wisdom openly in my prayers.

Praise of the Fathers in Ben Sira's Concept of the History of Israel (JSJSup 78, Leiden: Brill 2003) and VanderKam, *From Joshua to Caiaphas*, 149-50.

[29] Snaith, "Ben Sira's Supposed Love of Liturgy," 173 claims the terms to refer to the Holy of Holies in the temple. According to F. O'Fearghail, "Sir 50:5-21: Yom Kippur or the Daily Whole Offering?," *Bib* 59 (1987) 301-06 it is the outer court or rather the Temple building itself. This later supposition is supported also by Skehan and DiLella, *The Wisdom of Ben Sira*, 552.

[30] Cf. O'Fearghail, "Sir 50:5-21;" and J. Corley's article in the present volume.

[31] J.A. Sanders, *The Psalms Scroll of Qumrân Cave 11 (11QPsᵃ)* (DJD 4, Oxford: Clarendon 1965) 79-85.

[32] P.C. Beentjes, *The Book of Ben Sira in Hebrew* (VTSup 68, Leiden: Brill 2003) 93.

14a She came to me in her beauty	In front of the temple I asked for it,
b until the end I will cultivate her.[33]	and to the very last I will seek it.

The first (13a) and last (14b) lines form a time frame of the bicolon. From the time he became self-conscious until the time he can think, he seeks wisdom. On the other hand the two verses form a chiastic parallelism: 13a-14b; 13b-14a. This is a typical Hebrew form of poetry here and reinforces a supposed Hebrew original of the Greek text. Formally there is this chiastic parallelism, but 13a-b is parallel to 14b. 14a represents the new information in the sequence of the parallelism. This new information is totally different in the two texts. The Hebrew text of 14a is difficult and makes place for conjectures. בתרה can be interpreted as the defective reading of התאר[34] and presents some erotic overtone of the poem.[35] As an other unusual defective reading it even could be תורה (She came to me in the Torah). Another possibility is if the root of the word was בתר (She came to me partially = I received her to some extent). None of these solutions reproduces the Hebrew original of G, which mentions the temple.

In our context the Greek text makes more sense. God's wisdom comes from the temple. To receive it man has to pray for it, not only alone, but in the community, in the temple itself. Temple is the starting point. This version reinforces the interpretation of the book's opening passage about God as the origin of wisdom and creates a frame for the whole book of Ben Sira.[36] In 1:8 God is sitting on his throne which is in his heavenly temple, and Ben Sira started seeking wisdom in God's temple.

Concluding this topic we can state that for Ben Sira God came near to human beings in his temple, and caused wisdom to dwell there as well. And this is not a temporary situation but an everlasting position. This means that being a scribe and perhaps a priest, Ben Sira locates the primary place for getting contact with wisdom in the temple. And this temple is the only one in Jerusalem. Accordingly his בית מדרש (51:23) could have been in the temple too.[37] Unlike Ben Sira's opponents and other intellectual groups, Ben

---

[33] Skehan and DiLella, *The Wisdom of Ben Sira*, 572. The translation of García Martínez is more poetic: "Although still young, before going astray. I searched for her./Beautiful she came to me and when at last I found her." Cf. F. García Martínez, *The Dead Sea Scrolls Translated. The Qumran Texts in English* (Leiden: Brill 1994) 306.

[34] Skehan and DiLella, *The Wisdom of Ben Sira*, 574 present the cases of defective readings of התאר in Qumran and Masada to support this word as the source of בתרה.

[35] Sanders, *The Psalms Scroll*, supposed first this erotic meaning of the whole poem. Against this view see T. Muraoka, "Sir 51:13-20: An Erotic Hymn to Wisdom?," *JSJ* 10 (1979) 166-78.

[36] Cf. also the order of the book presented by Collins, *Jewish Wisdom in the Hellenistic Age*, 46 where Part I and Part II end with 24:1-34 and 51:30 respectively. Both passages have a key role in our discussion.

[37] On the scribal activity of Ben Sira in the temple see Duggan, "Ezra, Scribe and Priest," 206-09. According to L.L. Grabbe, *Judaic Religion in the Second Temple Period:*

Sira is not critical of the place, because of its personnel, a subject to which we turn now.

DEFINING CULT: LITURGY AND PERSONNEL

The main topic of criticism among emerging rival religious groups within Jewish society of Persian-Hellenistic time was the proper liturgy and personnel. Hasidim, Qumran community, Enochites, Essenes, Pharisees, Sadducees, Samaritans, groups in voluntary or forced exile in Egypt or in Trans-Jordan had different views of these questions. I don't want to discuss this topic too extensively here, just to make some remarks regarding Ben Sira.

As a general statement we can say that Ben Sira is not critical concerning cultic topics. He neither condemns cultic practice nor the cultic personnel.[38] What he says seems to be some type of confirmation of a status quo. Consequently Ben Sira must have had close personal contact with the Jerusalem temple.

Liturgy has two aspects in Ben Sira: offerings and ceremonies. He mentions several types of offerings in different passages (7:29-31; 24:15; 35:1-13; 45:14-16; 50:12-19) identifying them as fulfilment of the Law on the one hand, but—and this is equally important—on the other hand emphasizing their spiritual significance in gaining God's forgiveness. Describing the musical worship in the time of David (47:9-11), the garments of Aaron (45:8-13), and the service of Simeon (50:5-21) Ben Sira attributes to liturgy also spiritual meaning. In the case of David it is the forgiveness of sins (47:11); in the case of Aaron it is the joy of the eyes and heart (45:8-13); in the case of Simon it is blessing. This spiritualization of liturgy leads to the better understanding of ceremonies and sacrifices, therefore to a more accurate fulfilling of the Law of God, and consequently to a more conscious, wise living of life. All religious activities displayed by Ben Sira are restricted to the sole holy place, to the temple of Jerusalem.[39]

Ben Sira does not formulate any direct criticism against the mainstream Jerusalem priesthood, or against any of the priestly groups. Indeed he praises the priests of past and present.[40] In 7:29-31 he connects part of the

---

Belief and Practice from the Exile to Yavneh (London and New York: Routledge 2000) 57-58, Ben Sira was the inaugurator of the tradition of "scribalism."

[38] Arguing for this, Snaith, "Ben Sira's Supposed Love of Liturgy," 172 says, especially concerning the praise of the fathers, that "we need to distinguish between nostalgic honour of the past, expressed in biblical reminiscences, and genuine knowledge of contemporary practice in the Temple." Whether we distinguish or not, in both cases the depictions are positive.

[39] As presented above Ben Sira equates the tent shrine with the temple of Jerusalem.

[40] Olyan, "Ben Sira's Relationship to the Priesthood" 276, discusses the positive evaluations of Ben Sira, but refers to the anti-Zadokite tone of the description of Simon in chapter 50. Similarly Horsley and Tiller, "Ben Sira and the Sociology of the Second Temple," 99-104 stress his positive relationship to the Jerusalemite priesthood. On the

Shema (Deut 6:5) to the priests, giving them more honour, since they are mentioned parallel to God. By this positive evaluation of the Jerusalem priesthood Ben Sira reinforces their position in the society, and stresses the legitimacy of the Aaronide priesthood in a period of competition between the different groups of priesthood in Jerusalem.[41] Interestingly Zadok was mentioned only in MS B 50:24 and 51:12a-o and not together with the other priests in the praise of the fathers.[42]

In his interpretation of cult Ben Sira invented temple-piety in wisdom and supports the ruling priestly group of the temple closely connected to this wisdom.

Compilation of Previous Temple Theologies

After the catastrophe of the captivity of Jerusalem and the destruction of the temple on Zion, the previous temple theology, which identified God's presence with the temple on Zion had to be revised. Two such attempts were made. The first was the so-called priestly theology of glory invented by the prophet Ezekiel.[43] He implied that God's glory lives in the temple and in case of his disfavour it departs from the temple and stays with those who still deserve it. Of course his glory can return when God's anger has passed. The second attempt was made by the Deuteronomistic school(s): a name theology. God is living in heaven and put his name into the temple (Deut

---

other hand, Wright, "Fear the Lord and Honour the Priest" points out that by making anti-mystery and anti-visionary remarks (e.g. 3:21-24, 34:1-8), Ben Sira formulates an indirect criticism against priestly groups connected to the *Astronomical Book*, the *Book of the Watchers* and *Aramaic Levi*. These groups could have formed a marginal part of the official priestly staff. Cf. Wright, "Ben Sira and the Book of the Watchers," 241-54. See also his summarizing article Wright, "Putting the Puzzle Together: Some Suggestions concerning the Social Location of the Wisdom of Ben Sira," in *Conflicted Boundaries in Wisdom and Apocalypticism*, 89-112.

[41] The groups we can identify are the Levites, Aaronides, Zadokites. Cf. Wright, "Putting the Puzzle Together," and VanderKam, *From Joshua to Caiaphas*. Olyan and Wright argue for an Aaronide commitment of Ben Sira, though Boccaccini argues for a Zadokite one. Cf. Olyan, "Ben Sira's Relationship to the Priesthood," 275-81; Wright, "Ben Sira and the Book of the Watchers," 242-46; Boccaccini, *The Roots of Rabbinic Judaism*, 135.

[42] A.A. DiLella, *The Hebrew Text of Sirach: A Textcritical and Historical Study* (Studies in Classical Literature 1, The Hague: Mouton 1966) 101-05 examined this passage and concluded that it was a later addition. See below.

[43] Cf. A. Ruwe, "Die Veränderung tempeltheologischer Konzepte in Ezechiel 8-11," in *Gemeinde ohne Tempel. Community without Temple* (eds. B. Ego, *et al.*, WUNT 118, Tübingen: Mohr Siebeck 1999) 3-18. W. Brueggemann, *Theology of the Old Testament. Testimony, Dispute, Advocacy* (Minneapolis: Fortress Press 1997) 671-72.

12:5; 1 Kings 8:27-30). His name represents him there instead of his actual presence.[44]

Like the Scripture itself, Ben Sira utilizes both of these crisis theologies. At least 13 times he mentions the word "name" instead of God.[45] In 36:11-14 he connects God's name in Israel with Jerusalem. 47:13 relates that Solomon erected a house for God's holy Name. Zerubbabel and Joshua rebuilt the temple "destined for everlasting glory" (49:12). According to 36:13 the glory of the Lord fills the temple. But not only are these two ideas connected, but also the idea of Zion as well (36:18-19; 48:18.24). Having the two theologies (these theologies would have made an eventual second destruction of the temple theologically understandable), Ben Sira could refer to Zion without any problem of making it a real earthly abode of God.[46] Instead he made it the home of wisdom, a new representative of God.

The theological principle of Ben Sira was based on the conviction that the Jerusalem temple—which is Zion—is the sole legitimate temple with the sole legitimate cult performed by the sole legitimate priesthood. This monotemplistic attitude of the book found support in an interesting addition in 51:12.

The beautiful psalm in MS B 51:12a-o has no other textual witness. Its origin is still open to question, but the majority of scholars seems to support its authenticity as a poem created sometime before the rise of the Hasmonean priesthood.[47] Yet, one has to consider that this psalm was not included in the Greek translation made by the grandson of Ben Sira.

The main issue this psalm presents is the return of Israel to Zion. There are two lines of reasoning coming to this result: first is the section verses e-i. Here God redeemed Israel and gathered them from dispersal, rebuilt his city (Jerusalem) and its sanctuary (the temple) where the eternal house of David and the sons of Zadok have the leadership. This is a current historical

---

[44] S.D. McBride, "The Deuteronomic Name Theology" (PhD thesis, Harvard University, Cambridge, 1969) and Richter, *The Deuteronomistic History and the Name Theology*. Cf. also my article: Zsengellér, *Monotemplism*. 25-26.

[45] These instances are as follows:

17:10	to praise his holy name
23:9	name of the Holy
36:11-14	Gods name in Israel, an in Jerusalem
39:9	the name of wisdom
39:14	to glorify the name of Lord
39:35	praise the name of the Lord
47:10	praised his holy name
47:13	Solomon erected a house for his holy Name
50:20	to pronounce his holy name
51:1	Praise the name of the Lord
51:3	glory of your name
51:10	I will praise your name
51:12	the praise of his name

[46] The pre-exilic Zion-theology is reinforced by the theological crisis of the Exile and became an element of post-exilic prophetic visions as well. Cf. Zech 8:3, 9:9.

[47] Cf. the discussion of DiLella, *The Hebrew Text of Sirach*, 101-05.

overview and theological credo. Next to this line of reasoning there is another one, genealogical in nature, in section verses j-m. In these verses through the patriarchs Abraham, Isaac and Jacob we come to Zion, the chosen place of God. This is in parallel with the main concern of the Deuteronomic and Deuteronomistic theology.

If we contemplate a dialogue between Ben Sira and the writers of 1 Enoch and the Aramaic Testament of Levi in other cases,[48] here we also have to take into account a dialogue, but in this case the partners of discussion are different. As noted already by DiLella,[49] verse m states that "God has chosen Zion," that is Jerusalem for his dwelling. And this theological statement is in opposition to the statement of the Samaritans who had a rival temple on Mount Gerizim.[50] I would not base my statement only on this sole expression. Rather I suggest that the two lines of reasoning mentioned above explain that Ben Sira's dialogue partners in this case are the Samaritans. On the one hand the theological phenomenon of return as the remainder of Israel excludes others from the religious community living in the former land of Israel. This is expressed in the book of Ezra-Nehemiah, and even in Deuteronomy 7. On the other hand the genealogical line of the ancestors from Abraham to Jacob represents the common roots of Jews and Samaritans, but Zion at the end of this line excludes the Samaritans from this pedigree. There is a third reason, but it is not so direct as these previous ones: The sons of Zadok as the chosen high priests oppose the true Aaronid line maintained by the Samaritans.[51]

Consequently this poem is a parallel of the short numerical proverb of 50:25-26, where the inhabitants of Shechem are called the foolish people (גוי נבל).[52] The same expression can be found in the so-called 4QApocryphon of Joseph (4Q372).[53] This later text describes how the tribe of Joseph was lost and corrupted, and they, the foolish people built a high place for themselves on a very high mountain, and blasphemed against the tent of Zion and took into possession the territory and the bones of Joseph (lines 11-15). This last reference connects the description directly to Shechem where according to the Torah Joseph was buried. Testament of Levi 7:2 also describes the people

---

[48] See the articles of Wright, cf. note 39. above.

[49] Skehan and DiLella, The Wisdom of Ben Sira, 571.

[50] On the existence of the Gerizim temple see Y. Magen, "Mt Gerizim—A Temple City," Qadmoniot 33/2 (2000) 77-118 (Hebrew). According to the coins found in the ruins under the Mary Theotokos temple, Magen dates the building of this Samaritan temple to the Persian period. See Y. Magen, et al., Mount Gerizim Excavation I. The Aramaic, Hebrew and Samaritan Inscriptions (Judea and Samaria Publications 2, Jerusalem: Israel Antiquities Authority 2004).

[51] According to the Samaritan tradition, the line of the Aaronide priesthood is corrupted by Eli from the line of Ithamar. The true line continued by Uzzi from Eleazar's family among the true Israelites (Samaritans).

[52] See J. Purvis, "Ben Sira and the Foolish People of Shechem," JNES 24 (1965) 88-94.

[53] It was published by E.M. Schuller, "4Q372 1. A Text about Joseph," RevQ 14 (1990) 349-76.

living in the city of Shechem as foolish.[54] גוי נבל is the first designation of the Samaritans, and the Book of Ben Sira is the earliest text preserving this expression. Verses 50:25-26 together with the psalm of 51:12a-o brings the book of Ben Sira into dialogue with another group in Judaism in an apologetic way.

There is a good reason why the Greek text has not preserved 51:12a-o from the pre-Hasmonean version of the book. Ben Sira's grandson living in the time of John Hyrcanus could not give a text supporting temple and priesthood to the Diaspora Jews in Egypt if he declared that the chosen priesthood belongs to the Zadokites who were no longer in authority.[55] He left this passage out and does not refer even to that priesthood which has its pedigree in the family that liberated, cleaned and rededicated the temple.

CONCLUSION

Wisdom seems not to be a genre with narrow thematic concerns. It can discuss all the elements of faith even if it pays more attention to the moral dimensions. Ben Sira opened a new way of writing wisdom. He describes Torah/wisdom as coming out of the temple, as the central meeting point of men and God, and in this sense as the source of teaching. In doing so Ben Sira follows the previous idea of monotemplism and perpetuates the importance of the temple in Jerusalem. Unlike other wisdom teachers he supports a temple oriented scribal practice closely connected to the Aaronid priestly line.

Originally Ben Sira wrote his book for Jews in Palestine, but his grandson made it available to the Greek speaking Diaspora as well. In this context the temple theology of the Greek Ben Sira became more apologetic in nature. The temple of Leontopolis was built between the writing of the book by Ben Sira and the translation by his grandson. The temple of Mount Gerizim was still in use by the Samaritans. As a result the monotemplistic commitment of Ben Sira became a type of temple propaganda like the one presented in the books of the Maccabees.[56]

At the same time, Ben Sira fought against independent religious cultural lifestyles in Judaism and considered the temple of Jerusalem as the only

---

[54] Cf. my discussion in J. Zsengellér, *Gerizim as Israel. Northern Tradition of the Old Testament and the Early History of the Samaritans*, (Utrechtse Theologische Reeks 38, Utrecht: Utrecht University 1998) 159-63 and "Kutim or Samarites. A History of the Designation of the Samaritans," in *Proceedings of the Fifth International Congress of the Société d'Études Samaritaines. Helsinki, August 1-4, 2000* (eds. H. Shehadeh, *et al.*, Paris: Geuthner 2005) 87-104.

[55] The Hasmonean Simon was made high priest in 140 BC, and this function was given to this family "forever, until the rise of the true prophet" (1 Macc 14:41).

[56] See J. Zsengellér, "Maccabees and Temple Propaganda," in *The Books of the Maccabees. History, Theology, Ideology. Papers of the Second International Conference on the Deuterocanonical Books, Pápa, Hungary, 9-11 June, 2005* (eds. G.G. Xeravits and J. Zsengellér, JSJSup 118, Leiden: Brill 2007) 181-95.

institution to keep the people of Israel together in a situation of religious, cultural and moral pluralism. His struggle was not successful, since this cultural diversity was gaining more and more ground supported by the foreign political power. On the other hand, his definition of temple as the source of wisdom, Torah and holiness enforced or provided the theological basis for the later idea of the temple as the *genizah* of the holy books, the Holy Scriptures.[57] Oddly enough his book was one of those which in spite of being collected in the temple and frequently used for teaching was nevertheless not taken into the canonical corpus.[58]

---

[57] On the temple as mediator of the canonical process see J. Zsengellér, "Temple and Sacred Text—Jewish and Samaritan Perspectives," in *Rudolf Macuch Festchrift* (ed. R. Voigt, Berlin: forthcoming).

[58] I would like to thank Jack Pastor and John J. Collins for revising the English of this paper.

SIRACH 44:1-15
AS INTRODUCTION TO THE PRAISE OF THE ANCESTORS

Jeremy Corley
(Ushaw College, Durham)

A major component of our human identity consists in belonging to a people or nation. For instance, a British person may not always act like Winston Churchill or Queen Victoria, but these figures are important in British history, in some sense defining aspects of the national character. In a similar way, Ben Sira's list of famous ancestors serves in some sense to shape the perception of Israelite national character. By selecting personages deemed to be "men of loyalty," Ben Sira seeks to describe the essence of Israelite national character in terms of loyalty to Israel's God. In a comparable manner, but in a Christian context, the author of Hebrews 11 presents biblical figures, from Abel to the prophets, as examples of faith.[1]

Ben Sira's love for his people appears most clearly in his full appreciation of the recently deceased high priest Simeon II, whom he doubtless knew. The sage honours a significant departed friend by remembering him at the conclusion of the Praise of the Ancestors. If (as is likely) the sage had an important role in educating scribes at the temple, he would often have witnessed the kind of liturgy described in Sir 50:5-21.[2] By lovingly recording Simeon's central place in the temple worship, Ben Sira is able to present his deceased friend as the latest in the long line of Israelite heroes. With many scholars, I assume that the Praise of the Ancestors comprises 44:1-50:24 and thus culminates in the praise of Simeon II.[3]

Like most of the psalms, the preceding poem (Sir 42:15-43:33) offers praise to God. By contrast, the Praise of the Ancestors is unusual among

---

[1] P.M. Eisenbaum, *The Jewish Heroes of Christian History: Hebrews 11 in Literary Context* (SBLDS 156, Atlanta: Scholars Press 1997) 35-41.

[2] P.W. Skehan and A.A. Di Lella, *The Wisdom of Ben Sira* (AB 39, New York: Doubleday 1987) 550. For the suggestion that Ben Sira was one of the "scribes of the temple," see M. Hengel, *Judaism and Hellenism* (2 vols., London: SCM 1974) 1: 133; J. Marböck, *Weisheit im Wandel* (BBB 37, Bonn: Hanstein 1971, reprint: BZAW 272, Berlin: de Gruyter 1999) 96.

[3] M.Z. Segal, *Spr bn-syr' hšlm* (3rd ed., Jerusalem: Bialik Institute 1972) 303; B.L. Mack, *Wisdom and the Hebrew Epic: Ben Sira's Hymn in Praise of the Fathers* (CSHJ, Chicago: University of Chicago Press 1985) 195-98; T.R. Lee, *Studies in the Form of Sirach 44-50* (SBLDS 75, Atlanta: Scholars Press 1986) 10-21; P.C. Beentjes, "The 'Praise of the Famous' and Its Prologue," *Bijdragen* 45 (1984) 374-83, esp. 379-80.

Second Temple Jewish literature, because it praises human beings rather than God. Interestingly, the opening of both long poems is similar: while 42:15a H^M declares: "I will now recall (אזכרה נא) the works of God," 44:1a H^B declares: "I will now praise (אהללה נא) men of loyalty."[4] The linkage between the two poems seems deliberate, as Ben Sira has reversed the expected introductory verbs, since we might have expected God to be praised for his works (with verb הלל, as in 47:10), and then the devout to be recalled (with verb זכר).[5]

Whereas earlier biblical writers had acknowledged God's action through figures like Abraham and Moses (e.g., Psalm 105; Neh 9:6-37), Ben Sira actually praises the illustrious figures themselves. Such praise of human figures occurs occasionally in the Hebrew Bible; for instance, Prov 31:10-31 celebrates the capable woman, who is thrice the object of the verb הלל ("praise") in Prov 31:28-31, while a royal prince receives praise in his wedding song in Psalm 45.[6] Nevertheless, it is widely believed that Ben Sira here betrays the influence of Hellenism, where renowned figures from the past or present were acclaimed, using the Greek rhetorical form of the encomium. Indeed, Thomas Lee has observed that Sir 44:1-50:24 reflects many features of the Greek encomium.[7] As a learned scribe who had travelled in foreign lands (34:12; 39:4), Ben Sira was surely aware of the cultural phenomenon of the encomium. Similar hero lists occur in other biblical books preserved in Greek (1 Macc 2:51-60: Heb 11:4-38). Hence this study will note points of contact with some Greek encomiastic texts, even if the Hebrew sage may not have known any of the specific Greek examples quoted in this article.

---

[4] Lee, *Studies in the Form*, 3-4; Beentjes, "The 'Praise of the Famous,'" 375. In this article all biblical translations are mine, unless otherwise indicated. In this article H^B = Genizah MS B, H^{Bm} = the margin of Genizah MS B, and H^M = the Masada scroll; G = Greek and S = Syriac.

[5] The sage also connects 43:33 (if we accept Segal's reconstruction) and 44:1 by means of a link word (the root חסד, "loyalty"), as well as the accusative marker את.

[6] Vocabulary shared between Sir 44:1-15 and Prov 31:10-31 includes four key words: הלל ("praise": Sir 44:1; Prov 31:28, 30, 31); חסד ("loyalty": Sir 44:1, 10; Prov 31:26); חיל ("valour, wealth, capability": Sir 44:6; Prov 31:10, 29); חכמה ("wisdom": Sir 44:15; Prov 31:26).

[7] For Lee's survey of various proposals regarding the genre of 44:1-50:24, see his *Studies in the Form*, 21-82; for his reasons for viewing the passage as a kind of extended encomium of the high priest Simeon see p. 81. Lee's view does not command universal acceptance. C.A. Rollston has noted the non-encomiastic features of the poem in his M.A. thesis, "The Non-Encomiastic Features of Ben Sira 44-50" (Emmanuel School of Religion, Johnson City, TN, 1992), and Burton Mack has called the work a Hebrew epic (*Wisdom and the Hebrew Epic*, 136), while Ralph Hildesheim regards the composition as a midrash (*Bis daß ein Prophet aufstand wie Feuer* [Trierer theologische Studien 58, Trier: Paulinus 1996] 52-53). For outlines of the historical development of the Greek encomium, see Lee, *Studies in the Form*, 103-206; A. Schmitt, "Enkomien in griechischer Literatur," in *Auf den Spuren der schriftgelehrten Weisen* (eds. I. Fischer, *et al.*; FS Johannes Marböck, BZAW 331, Berlin: de Gruyter 2003) 359-81.

One of the most common uses for the Greek encomium was to praise those who had died, and this is also the purpose of Sir 44:1-50:24. Ben Sira's commemoration of heroes from Israel's remote and recent history does not offer consolation by referring to a glorious afterlife for these individuals (although it notes that Enoch and Elijah were taken up alive to heaven). In fact, according to the earliest manuscripts, Ben Sira has no belief in the afterlife, since in his view the underworld offers no possibility either of enjoyment or of praising God.[8] Thus, 14:16b H^A declares: "In Sheol there is no possibility to seek pleasure." Moreover, 17:27-28 G says: "Who will praise the Most High in Hades, in place of those living and offering thanksgiving? From someone dead, as from someone non-existent, thanksgiving has perished; someone living and healthy will praise the Lord." Hence 38:21 H^B advises the bereaved to let go of the memory of a deceased person: "Do not remember him, for there is no hope for him. What will you benefit? But you will harm yourself." Instead, 41:3-4 H^M(B) urges a calm acceptance that death is final: "Do not be afraid of death, the decree for you; remember, anyone before or after is in company with you. This is the end of all flesh from God, and how can you refuse the Law of the Most High? For ten or a hundred or a thousand years—there are no life-giving reproofs in Sheol."[9]

However, Ben Sira does consider that (in some way) a person can survive death through having descendants (44:11-13a). The notion of survival through one's progeny appears in the sage's declaration about the good son: "The father died, and it is as if he did not die, for after him he left someone like him" (30:4 G). Similarly, Ben Sira states: "A child and a city will cause a name to endure" (40:19a H^B).[10] This thought of survival through

---

[8] So A.A. Di Lella, "Conservative and Progressive Theology: Sirach and Wisdom," *CBQ* 28 (1966) 139-54, esp. 143-46; J.J. Collins, *Jewish Wisdom in the Hellenistic Age* (Louisville: Westminster John Knox 1997) 92; M. Gilbert, "Siracide," *DBSup* fasc. 71, cols. 1389-437, esp. 1436; G. Boccaccini, *Middle Judaism: Jewish Thought 300 B.C.E. to 200 C.E.* (Minneapolis: Fortress 1991) 120.

[9] On 41:1-4 see F.V. Reiterer, "Deutung und Wertung des Todes durch Ben Sira," in *Die alttestamentliche Botschaft als Wegweisung* (ed. J. Zmijewski, Stuttgart: Katholisches Bibelwerk 1990) 203-36; E. Reymond, *Innovations in Hebrew Poetry: Parallelism and the Poems of Sirach* (SBL Studies in Biblical Literature 9, Atlanta: SBL 2004) 39-43. Ben Sira's grandson and also later copyists inserted references to the afterlife; cf. Gilbert, "Siracide," *DBSup* fasc. 71, cols. 1410-12; Collins, *Jewish Wisdom in the Hellenistic Age*, 95. While the Hebrew form of 7:17 does not imply the afterlife, the Greek form does; cf. Skehan and Di Lella, *The Wisdom of Ben Sira*, 201-2. Moreover, when it encounters passages contrary to belief in an afterlife, the Syriac text often omits them (e.g., 41:4cd) or modifies them (e.g., 17:27); cf. M.D. Nelson, *The Syriac Version of the Wisdom of Ben Sira Compared to the Greek and Hebrew Materials* (SBLDS 107, Atlanta: Scholars Press 1988) 113-14.

[10] A person may be remembered through having children to continue the family name (40:19) or through becoming the ancestor of a city's inhabitants (16:4). Moreover, his memory may also be kept alive through having a city named after him, as David is remembered from the "city of David" (2 Sam 5:7, 9) and Alexander is remembered from the city of Alexandria.

one's descendants underlies the mention of offspring in the introduction to the Praise of the Ancestors: "With their offspring their prosperity was assured, and their inheritance was for their children's children" (44:11 H[B]/Segal). Moreover, the conclusion to the Praise of the Ancestors expresses the hope that the covenant with Phinehas may continue for Simeon's descendants (50:24 H[B])

In addition, Ben Sira also believes that (in some sense) a person can survive death through being remembered well (44:13b-15). Survival through one's name or reputation is an important theme in Ben Sira's writing: "Ephemeral is a human being in his corpse, yet a reputation of loyalty will not be cut off. Be fearful over a reputation, since it will accompany you better than thousands of desirable treasures. The benefit of a living person is for a number of days, but the benefit of a reputation is for unnumbered days" (41:11-13 H[B/Bm/M]). While a person's life lasts only so many years, a good reputation can survive death. A related idea appears in the words about the men of loyalty in the introduction to the Praise of the Ancestors: "Whereas their corpse was buried in peace, their reputation lives from generation to generation" (44:14 H[M]). Elsewhere, Ben Sira applies this thought to the activity of the wise person: "A people's sage will inherit glory, and his reputation continues in the life of eternity" (37:26 H[D]; cf. 39:9-11 G).

In the Praise of the Ancestors (one of the longest Hebrew poems from the Second Temple period), Ben Sira aims to ensure the glorious memory of Israel's heroes of faith. Since the great poem culminates in a commemoration of the high priest Simeon II (50:1-24), perhaps the whole seven chapters may have been used at some kind of ceremony remembering the past national leaders. This suggestion draws support from the similarities detected with the Greek encomium, which probably originated as a spoken piece of epideictic oratory, rather than simply a written text. Accordingly, I would envisage the whole poem perhaps being used at some national commemoration for great deceased Israelites, most likely a ceremony held in the temple precincts.

Such a context at a ceremony close to the temple is suggested by the two doxologies, where the sage expresses his wish for his audience. Sirach 45:26 and 50:23, which both follow the praise of priestly figures (Phinehas and Simeon), contain the same prayer to God: "May he give you wisdom of heart." The concluding verse of the whole poem (50:24 H[B]) then says: "May his loyalty with Simeon be assured, and may he establish for him the covenant with Phinehas, which will not be cut off for him, or for his offspring, like the days of heaven." The most obvious setting for these sentiments would be a gathering including the leaders of the priesthood, probably somewhere near the Jerusalem temple.

Can we be more specific about a possible occasion? The Praise of the Ancestors makes no strong allusions to the major feasts of Passover, Weeks and Tabernacles, while the celebratory style hardly fits the Day of Atonement.[11] However, one possible occasion is the autumn feast of Rosh Hashanah (ten days before the Day of Atonement), for two reasons. First, Rosh Hashanah is strongly associated with the theme of remembrance, which is also Ben Sira's theme here.[12] In Qumran calendrical documents (e.g., 4Q320 4 iii 6) "the day of remembrance" (יום הזכרון), presumably Rosh Hashanah, is mentioned as a festival occurring between the Feast of Weeks and the Day of Atonement.[13] This title derives from Lev 23:24 (cf. 11QT xxv 3), which describes the day as זכרון תרועה (RSV: "a memorial proclaimed with blast of trumpets"). Second, according to Otto Mulder, Sir 50:5-21 depicts the liturgy of Rosh Hashanah (cf. Lev 23:23-25; Num 29:1-6).[14] Of particular significance is the Genizah Hebrew text of 50:16 [whose glosses I have marked]: "Then the sons of Aaron [the priests] sounded a blast, on the trumpets of beaten metal, [and they sounded a blast] and they let a majestic voice be heard, to make memorial before the Most High." Mulder identifies this action with the ritual for Rosh Hashanah, especially because of the prominent use of trumpets and the importance of the motif of remembrance (cf. Num 10:10). It is also interesting that on "the first day of the seventh month" (Neh 8:2) Ezra proclaimed the Torah at a comparable public assembly in Jerusalem. If my theory is correct, Ben Sira's long public speech near the temple would have occurred on exactly the same calendar date when Ezra stood near the temple to proclaim the "book of the law of Moses" (Neh 8:1).[15]

Accordingly, my tentative suggestion is that the Praise of the Ancestors could perhaps have been proclaimed at a public assembly held near the Jerusalem temple on Rosh Hashanah, when Ben Sira echoed the festival's Hebrew theme of memorial (though using techniques influenced by the Greek encomium). In that case, the praise of God for the marvels of creation

---

[11] F. Ó Fearghail, "Sir 50,5-21: Yom Kippur or The Daily Whole-Offering?," *Bib* 59 (1978) 301-16; C.T.R. Hayward, *The Jewish Temple: A Non-biblical Sourcebook* (London: Routledge 1996) 50.

[12] Note the poem's recurring use of the root זכר (noun "memory": 44:9; 45:1; 46:11, 23; 49:1, 13; cf. causative forms of verb "remember" in 49:9 and 50:16), as well as the related nouns זכרון ("memorial": 45:9, 11) and אזכרה ("memorial": 45:16).

[13] See also 4Q320 4 iv 2, 4 v 5; 4Q321 2 ii 2, 2 ii 6; 4Q409 1 I 5; cf. F. García Martínez and E.J.C. Tigchelaar, *The Dead Sea Scrolls Study Edition* (2 vols., Leiden: Brill 1997, 1998) 2: 681, 683, 689, 839. On the concept of memorial in Second Temple Judaism, see Boccaccini, *Middle Judaism*, 233-39.

[14] O. Mulder, *Simon the High Priest in Sirach 50* (JSJSup 78, Leiden: Brill 2003) 169-73. This day was not so significant in pre-exilic times, but seemingly became more important after the exile, and especially in post-biblical Jewish tradition.

[15] However, Neh 8:1-3 may not actually be connected with the New Year festival; cf. M.W. Duggan, *The Covenant Renewal in Ezra-Nehemiah (Neh 7:72B-10:40)* (SBLDS 164, Atlanta: SBL 2001) 99-101. Furthermore, it is noteworthy that Ben Sira's Praise of the Ancestors does not mention Ezra; on possible reasons see M.W. Duggan, "Ezra, Scribe and Priest, and the Concerns of Ben Sira," in *Intertextual Studies in Ben Sira and Tobit* (eds. J. Corley and V. Skemp, CBQMS 38, Washington: Catholic Biblical Association of America 2005) 201-10, esp. 201-2.

(42:15-43:33) could have served as a liturgical prelude to the Praise of the Ancestors, especially since the theme of "remembering" appears at the opening (42:15a Hᴹ): "I will now recall (אזכרה נא) the works of God." While my tentative proposal is hard to prove, I regard a public speech in the vicinity of the temple (whatever the exact calendar date) as the most likely setting for the Praise of the Ancestors. In my view, a merely literary context in terms of a retelling of Israelite history (perhaps in midrashic style) does not do adequate justice to the rhetorical aspects of the chapters.

According to a common eight-part division of Ben Sira's book, 44:1-15 serves as the introduction to Part VIII (44:1-50:24).[16] Like others of the eight parts of the book, this part is framed by inclusions:

> 44:1a Hᴮᴹ: חסד ("loyalty"); 44:2b Hᴹ: וגדלה ("and greatness");
> 44:2b Hᴮ: מימות עולם ("from the days of eternity").
> 50:24a Hᴮ: חסדו ("his loyalty"); 50:22c Hᴮ: המגדל ("him who makes great");
> 50:24d Hᴮ: כימי שמים ("like the days of heaven").

By way of comparison, we find a similar use of *inclusio* to delimit Part II of Ben Sira's book (4:11-6:17):

> 4:12 Hᴬ: אהביה אהבו חיים ("her friends love life");
> 6:16 Hᴬ: צרור חיים אוהב אמונה ("a faithful friend is a bundle of the living").

Another structural pattern is the use of a refrain. Thus, an almost identical refrain occurs near the conclusion of the sapiential poem opening Part VII (38:24-39:11) and at the end of the introduction to Part VIII (44:1-15):[17]

> 39:10 G: τὴν σοφίαν αὐτοῦ διηγήσονται ἔθνη
> καί τὸν ἔπαινον αὐτου ἐξαγγελεῖ ἐκκλησία.
> Nations will narrate his wisdom, and the assembly will proclaim his praise.
> 44:15 G: σοφίαν αὐτῶν διήγησονται λαοί,
> καί τὸν ἔπαινον ἐξαγγελεῖ ἐκκλησία.
> Peoples will narrate their wisdom, and the assembly will proclaim [their] praise.

A triple *inclusio* also exists between the opening of Sir 44:1-15 and the conclusion of the Torah section (44:17-45:26), since the very last colon (45:26d) echoes the final word of each of the first three bicola (44:1-3b Hᴮ):[18]

---

[16] For the division of Ben Sira's book into eight parts see Segal, *Spr bn-syr' hšlm*, 16 (introduction); Skehan and Di Lella, *The Wisdom of Ben Sira*, xiii-xvi.

[17] Sirach 31:11b (concluding 31:1-11) also contains a refrain similar to 39:10b and 44:15b.

[18] Beentjes, "The 'Praise of the Famous,'" 379. In addition, mention of "honour" (כבוד) in 45:25f recalls its occurrence in 44:2a Hᴮᴹ. The first word in 45:26d (וגבורתכם = "and your might") is textually uncertain but supported by the Syriac; cf. Segal, *Spr bn-syr' hšlm*, 317.

44:1b: בדורותם / 44:2b: עולם 44:3b: בגבורתם

In their generations/ eternity/ for their might.

45:26d Hᴮ (Segal): וגבורתכם לדורות עולם

And your might for eternal generations.

Moreover, 44:1-15 is itself skilfully delimited by a fourfold chiastic *inclusio*:[19]

44:1-2: עולם/כבוד/בדורותם/אהללה

I will praise/in their generations/honour/eternity;

44:13-15: ותהלתם/לדור ודור/וכבודם/עד עולם

To eternity/ and their honour/ from generation to generation/ and their praise.

In addition, a fifth *inclusio* is provided by the word שם ("reputation") in 44:3b and ושמם ("and their reputation") in 44:14b.[20]

A further aspect of the poetry of 44:1-15 is the use of "alphabetic thinking." In a posthumous article, Anthony Ceresko pointed out the "alphabetic thinking" that he found in Psalms 106 and 150, whereby the poem progressively moves through many of the letters of the Hebrew alphabet in order.[21] A similar incomplete phenomenon is visible in Sir 44:1-15. Although we do not find the complete alphabet, we do encounter the following alphabetic sequence of words (discounting initial *waw* in places), whereby nine out of the thirty-six cola begin with a word in an alphabetic pattern: תהלתם/שמם/עד/נחלתם/להשתעות/כל/חכמי/גדלה/אהללה. Furthermore, 44:1b includes the progression *aleph-beth* in אבותינו ("our ancestors"), while 44:2b has the next alphabetic series *gimel-daleth* in גדלה ("greatness"), and 44:7a begins with the common progression *kaph-lamed* in כל ("all").

The length of 44:1-15 (eighteen bicola) is also characteristic of some of Ben Sira's poetry.[22] Just as this passage of eighteen bicola introduces the Torah Section (44:17-45:26), so the Prophets Section of the poem (46:1-49:16) begins with a passage of eighteen bicola on Joshua and Caleb (46:1-10),[23]

---

[19] A threefold *inclusio* is observed by Beentjes, "The 'Praise of the Famous,'" 375; cf. A. Minissale, *La versione greca del Siracide* (AnBib 133, Rome: Pontifical Biblical Institute 1995) 127.

[20] Another example of a Ben Sira pericope delimited by means of *inclusio* is the passage on social duties in 7:18-36 Hᴬ, since 7:18 has the participle אוהב ("friend") and 7:35 Hᴬ has the niphal verb תאהב ("you will be loved"). A further case is 13:1-23 Hᴬ (a passage on caution in dealing with the rich), where 13:1 has the participle נוגע ("one who touches") while 13:23 has the hiphil form יגיעו ("they make... reach").

[21] A.R. Ceresko, "Endings and Beginnings: Alphabetic Thinking and the Shaping of Psalms 106 and 150," *CBQ* 68 (2006) 32-46. A simple example of an alphabetic pattern is Psalm 1, where the first word begins with *aleph* and the last word with *taw*.

[22] Although the Greek text has 17½ bicola (omitting 44:4d), the length of eighteen bicola is generally accepted; cf. Skehan and Di Lella, *The Wisdom of Ben Sira*, 497-98. On arithmetical patterns in the Praise of the Ancestors, see J. Corley, "A Numerical Structure in Sirach 44:1-50:24," *CBQ* 69 (2007) 43-63.

[23] On the contrast between the Torah Section and the Prophets Section in the Praise of the Ancestors, see A. Goshen-Gottstein, "Ben Sira's Praise of the Fathers: A Canon-Conscious Reading," in *Ben Sira's God: Proceedings of the International Ben Sira*

while the concluding section on the high priest Simeon (50:1-24) is twice that length (thirty-six bicola). Moreover, the prologue of eighteen bicola (44:1-15), introducing Part VIII of Ben Sira's book, is the same length as the sapiential poem of 14:20-15:10, introducing Part IV of the book.

To aid the study of 44:1-15, it will be discussed in three sections, dealing in turn with ancestors deserving honour (44:1-6); the contrast between remembered and forgotten ancestors (44:7-9); and the blessings bequeathed by honourable ancestors (44:10-15). In each section, I will present the Hebrew text attested in the Masada scroll and/or the great Genizah manuscript B, generally giving preference to the Masada text.[24] In the case of two Hebrew words (and five parts of words) lacking Hebrew manuscript attestation, the text is reconstructed, usually on the basis of Segal's work. At times I refer to the Greek, which mostly renders the Hebrew faithfully, and occasionally to the Syriac, which sometimes seems to adapt or paraphrase the text rather than translating exactly.[25]

ANCESTORS DESERVING HONOUR (44:1-6)

אהללה נא אנשי חסד את אבותינו בדורותם
רב כבוד חלק עליון וגדלה מימות עולם
רודי ארץ במלכותם ואנשי שם בגבורתם
יועצים בתבונתם וחזי כל בנבואתם
שרי גוי במזמתם ורזנים במחקקתם
חכמי שיח בספרתם ומשלים במשמרותם
חקרי מזמור על קו ונשאי משל במכתם
אנשי חיל וסמכי כח ושקטים על מכונתם

¹I will now praise men of loyalty,
    our ancestors in their generations—

Conference, Durham—Ushaw College 2001 (ed. R. Egger-Wenzel, BZAW 321, Berlin: de Gruyter 2002) 235-67, esp. 241. Note that I regard 44:16 as a gloss, since it is absent from the Masada manuscript; cf. Skehan and Di Lella, *The Wisdom of Ben Sira*, 499.

[24] Editions and studies of the Hebrew text of 44:1-15 include: Y. Yadin, *The Ben Sira Scroll from Masada* (Jerusalem: Israel Exploration Society 1965) 34-38; Z. Ben-Hayyim, *The Book of Ben Sira: Text, Concordance, and an Analysis of the Vocabulary* (Jerusalem: Academy of the Hebrew Language and Shrine of the Book 1973) 53-54; P.C. Beentjes, *The Book of Ben Sira in Hebrew* (VTSup 68, Leiden: Brill 1997) 174-76; Segal, *Spr bn-syr' hšlm*, 302-6; Minissale, *La versione greca del Siracide*, 126-36; E. Reymond, "Prelude to the Praise of the Ancestors, Sirach 44:1-15," *HUCA* 72 (2001) 1-14; idem, *Innovations in Hebrew Poetry*, 78-84.

[25] For the Greek text of 44:1-15 see J. Ziegler, *Sapientia Iesu Filii Sirach* (Septuaginta 12/2, Göttingen: Vandenhoeck & Ruprecht 1980) 331-33. For an analysis of the changes to the Hebrew made in the Greek translation of the passage, see Minissale, *La versione greca del Siracide*, 132-36. For the Syriac text of 44:1-15 see N. Calduch-Benages, *et al.*, *Wisdom of the Scribe: Diplomatic Edition of the Syriac Version of the Book of Ben Sira according to Codex Ambrosianus* (Estella: Editorial Verbo Divino 2003) 240-42. On the Syriac changes to the passage, see Nelson, *The Syriac Version*, 121-23.

²The Most High apportioned an abundance of honour,
 and greatness from the days of eternity—
³ᵃcontrollers of the land for their kingship,
 and men of reputation for their might;
³ᶜadvisers for their understanding,
 and seers of everything for their prophecy;
⁴ᵃprinces of the nation for their planning,
 and leaders for their legislation;
⁴ᶜwise speakers for their literature,
 and rulers for their liturgical duties;
⁵composers of melody according to rhythm,
 and reciters of proverbs in a psalm;
⁶men of power and forceful supporters,
 and those in quietness in their residence.

Because of differences between the various text forms of the passage, discussion of 44:1-6 will have to begin briefly with textual questions. The Masada manuscript omits 44:3ab through homoioarchton or homoioteleuton, while the Greek omits 44:4d. More seriously, the Syriac misses out two bicola (44:3ab, 4ab), perhaps because of a reluctance to celebrate Israelite heroes.²⁶

The interpretation of 44:2a is uncertain. Patrick Skehan takes the word חלק as a noun ("portion"), alluding to Deut 32:9a: "For the portion of YHWH is his people"; on this view, Sir 44:2a could mean: "The portion of the Most High is abundant in honour."²⁷ However, I follow the versions and most commentators in taking חלק as a verb ("he apportioned").²⁸ Note that the phrase "an abundance of glory" (רוב כבוד) occurs in two Qumran texts (4QInstruction and the Apostrophe to Zion in the great Psalms Scroll from Cave 11).²⁹

The interpretation of 44:2b is also uncertain. With Eric Reymond I accept the Masada reading וגדלה, which I understand to mean "and greatness,"

---

²⁶ Nelson, *The Syriac Version*, 121-22.

²⁷ Skehan and Di Lella, *The Wisdom of Ben Sira*, 497-98; cf. P.W. Skehan, "Staves, and Nails, and Scribal Slips (Ben Sira 44:2-5)," *BASOR* 200 (1970) 66-71. Skehan's proposal could receive support from 24:12, which may be retroverted:

ואשריש בעם נכבד   בחלק יי נחלתו

("And I took root in an honoured people, in the portion of YHWH, his inheritance"), according to Segal, *Spr bn-syr' hšlm*, 145.

²⁸ If we ignore the problematic case of חלק in 33:13 Hᴱ, the noun appears eight times elsewhere in the Ben Sira manuscripts, and the verb nine times, though some cases are textually suspect.

²⁹ While 4Q418 126 ii 9 (122 ii 12) employs the phrase: "through the strength of God and his abundant glory (ורוב כבודו) with his goodness," 11Q5 xxii 4 has the phrase: "and who rejoice in the abundance of your glory" (ברוב כבודך); cf. García Martínez and Tigchelaar, *The Dead Sea Scrolls Study Edition*, 2: 875, 2: 1177.

using the feminine noun form.[30] It would also be possible to understand the form as an anomalous suffixed masculine segholate noun, since with the normal spelling וגדלו ("and his/its greatness") it appears in H[B] and it is thus attested in the Greek.[31] The Genizah reading וגדלו could also be interpreted as a qal perfect verb ("and they became great"), with "our ancestors" (44:1a) understood as the plural subject.[32]

In the eight cases where the preposition ב (usually: "in") occurs in 44:3-4, I translate "for," because of the idiom הלל ב, "praise [someone] for [something]" (as in Ps 150:2 and Sir 11:2). At the beginning of 44:3c, I follow the margin of the Genizah manuscript, reading יועצים ("advisers") without a preceding waw ("and").[33] In 44:4a the singular form גוי ("nation," applied to Israel) is confirmed by the Masada scroll and the Greek. In 44:5b, the Genizah manuscript has the reading בכתב ("in writing," as in 39:32; 42:7; 45:11). However, following Skehan, I emend the text to read במכתם ("in a psalm"), so as to fit the rhyme scheme of 44:1-6.[34]

The most significant poetic feature of 44:1-6 is the repeated use of end-rhyme with -tām.[35] Elsewhere Ben Sira often begins pericopes with the use of rhyme, as in the cases of 7:18 (beginning 7:18-36) and 13:1 (beginning 13:1-23):

7:18a H[A]: במחיר ("for a price"); 7:18b H[A]: אופיר ("Ophir").
13:1a H[A]: ידו ("his hand"); 13:1b H[A]: דרכו ("his way").

Here, however, a much more prolonged rhyme serves to indicate the opening of the lengthy Praise of the Ancestors. All eight bicola of 44:1-6 end in -tām (if we assume Skehan's emendation in the last word of 44:5b), apart from 44:2 which ends in -lām. Moreover, the middle four of the bicola (44:3-4) also have the same internal rhyme with -tām. In addition, the first two bicola of the next stanza, namely 44:7-8, also continue the rhymed ending with -tām.

Other features also indicate that the poetry is accomplished. Note that four out of the seven words in 44:1 begin with the first letter of the Hebrew alphabet (aleph) as a sign that a new poem is opening. Alliteration exists between רב (= רוב, "abundance") at the opening of 44:2 and רודי ("control-lers") at the beginning of 44:3. We may observe a word play between משלים

---

[30] Reymond, Innovations in Hebrew Poetry, 78. This feminine Hebrew noun appears in 1 Chr 29:11 and Esth 1:4, as well as in a textual corruption in Sir 3:18 H[A].

[31] We may compare in 6:22 H[A] the form כשמה, understood as kišmōh ("like its name," with a masculine suffix); so Segal, Spr bn-syr' hšlm, 39; cf. E. Kautzsch, Gesenius' Hebrew Grammar (Oxford: Oxford University Press 1910) §§7c, 58g, 91e. For the form גדלו ("his greatness") see Ps 150:2.

[32] Minissale, La versione greca del Siracide, 130; Segal, Spr bn-syr' hšlm, 304.

[33] Minissale, La versione greca del Siracide, 130.

[34] Skehan and Di Lella, The Wisdom of Ben Sira, 499; note that in Isa 38:9 many scholars conjecture מכתם ("psalm") where the Masoretic Text has מכתב ("writing").

[35] Skehan, "Staves, and Nails, and Scribal Slips," 69-70; cf. Beentjes, "The 'Praise of the Famous,'" 376.

("rulers") in 44:4d and משל (collective: "proverbs") in 44:5b,[36] and there is also assonance with במשמרותם ("for their liturgical duties") in 44:4d. Moreover, this stanza is delimited by the word אנשי ("men") in 44:1a and 44:6a.

The sage's statement in 44:1-2 echoes the opening of the encomium on King Ptolemy Philadelphus, composed by the Greek author Theocritus around 273 BC. Thus, Ben Sira's initial declaration, "I will now praise men of loyalty" (44:1a), is akin to the words of Theocritus in his encomium of the Ptolemaic king: "I who know how to praise must sing of Ptolemy" (*Idyll* 17.7-8).[37] Thereafter, Ben Sira's assertion, "The Most High apportioned an abundance of honour" (44:2a) is akin to Theocritus' declaration in praise of Ptolemy: "Countless to tell are the blessings wherewith heaven has honoured the best of kings" (*Idyll* 17.11-12). However, though the Hebrew sage imitates a Greek literary form, his theology reflects Jewish tradition.

Accordingly, the characters celebrated by Ben Sira are called אנשי חסד ("men of loyalty" or "men of piety": 44:1a).[38] The phrase is a significant allusion to Isa 57:1-2, which deals with a related theological issue concerning the death of the devout:

> The righteous person perishes, and there is no one who takes it to heart; and men of loyalty (אנשי חסד) are gathered in, while no one understands, though the righteous person is gathered in from the face of calamity; he enters into peace. They rest upon their couches, one who walks uprightly.[39]

Whereas Third Isaiah is concerned about the unappreciated death of the devout, Ben Sira aims to give public honour to such persons.

The key word חסד ("loyalty" or "piety") is particularly connected with the idea of covenant in the Hebrew Bible (Deut 7:9; 1 Kgs 8:23). This term is appropriate here, since the seven characters listed in the Torah Section (44:17-45:26) are all persons with whom God made or renewed a covenant

---

[36] Similarly, 12:13-14 makes a word play between two senses of חובר ("snake charmer," and "one who associates"); cf. Skehan and Di Lella, *The Wisdom of Ben Sira*, 248.

[37] For both quotations in this paragraph, see A.S.F. Gow, *Theocritus, vol. 1* (Cambridge: Cambridge University Press 1965) 131; cf. Lee, *Studies in the Form*, 159.

[38] Here I translate "men of loyalty" because the Praise of the Ancestors names only male characters. The omission of named female characters from 44:1-50:24 (a distasteful aspect for modern readers) derives from the patriarchal social context. From the literary viewpoint, the Praise of the Ancestors is influenced by the Greek encomium of male characters, where female characters are not common. By way of comparison, note also that Mattathias' encouragement of his sons in 1 Macc 2:52-60 lists only male characters from Israel's history, while Hebrews 11 names only Sarah and Rahab among a long list of male personages.

[39] This Isaiah passage has had an influence on Ben Sira's Praise of the Ancestors (as well as on Wis 4:14-15). Thus, the niphal form נאסף ("gathered in, taken away"), which Isa 57:1 uses once in the singular and once in the plural, appears in the feminine in Sir 44:14a, while Ben Sira mentions Samuel's "resting upon his couch" in 46:19 (cf. 40:5).

(Noah, Abraham, Isaac, Jacob, Moses, Aaron, Phinehas), while the eighth recipient of a covenant (David) is also mentioned seemingly out of sequence in 45:25.[40] The covenant with Phinehas reappears in 50:24, at the end of the praise of Simeon.

The same term חסד ("loyalty") recurs at key points in the poem, to describe the faithful devotion shown by Joshua and Josiah (46:7; 49:3).[41] Ben Sira intentionally employs the term near the opening and near the closing of the Prophets Section (46:1-49:16). In 46:7 he uses the term to describe Joshua (the leader who brought the Israelites into the Promised Land), while in 49:3 the sage again applies the same term to Josiah (the last righteous king before the people were exiled from their land):

46:7a HB: ובימי משה עשה חסד
And in the days of Moses he [= Joshua] performed loyalty.
49:3b HB: ובימי חמס עשה חסד
And in the days of lawlessness he [= Josiah] performed loyalty.

The term also appears in reference to the divine promise to the Davidic line in 47:22a, where the mention of חסד ("loyalty") alludes to God's promise to David in 2 Sam 7:15 and 1 Chr 7:13 (cf. Ps 89:29).[42] While evidence from Qumran and the New Testament (cf. 4Q174; Luke 1:32-33; Heb 1:5) shows that Nathan's oracle was later regarded as messianic, the question of the extent of messianic expectation in Ben Sira is much disputed. On the one hand, Kenneth Pomykala asserts: "Sirach has pointedly assigned the role once played by the Davidic kings to the high priest; hence, for him there is no place for a Davidic messiah."[43] On the opposite side, however, James

---

[40] Cf. J. Marböck, "Die 'Geschichte Israels' als 'Bundesgeschichte' nach dem Sirachbuch," in *Gottes Weisheit unter uns* (ed. I. Fischer, HBS 6, Freiburg: Herder 1995) 103-23, here 123. Rather than eight recipients of a covenant, Marböck lists only seven, omitting Moses (pp. 112-13), since the Hebrew of 45:1-5 does not contain the word ברית ("covenant"). On the Hebrew and Greek terms for covenant in the book, see B.G. Wright, *No Small Difference: Sirach's Relationship to Its Hebrew Parent Text* (SBLSCS 26, Atlanta: Scholars 1989) 178-81.

[41] The Greek of 44:23f also says in reference to Moses that God brought forth "a man of mercy/loyalty" (ἄνδρα ἐλέους).

[42] I reconstruct the Hebrew of Sir 47:22: "[However, Go]d will not forsake steadfast love, and he will not let any of his words fall to the ground. He will not [let be cut off from his chosen one]s offspring, and the posterity [of his frie]nds he will not destroy. And he gave to [Jacob a remnant], and to the h[ouse of David a roo]t." In my view, Ben Sira did not exclude eventual restoration of the Davidic line; cf. J. Corley, "Seeds of Messianism in Hebrew Ben Sira and Greek Sirach," in *The Septuagint and Messianism* (ed. M.A. Knibb, BETL 195, Leuven: Peeters 2006) 301-12. For another perspective see B.G. Wright, "Eschatology without a Messiah in the Wisdom of Ben Sira" (*ibid.*, 313-19).

[43] K. Pomykala, *The Davidic Dynasty Tradition in Early Judaism* (SBLEJL 7, Atlanta: Scholars Press 1995) 152; cf. J.J. Collins, *The Scepter and the Star: The Messiahs of the Dead Sea Scrolls and Other Ancient Literature* (New York: Doubleday 1995) 33-34; G.G.

Martin maintains: "Ideas about Messianism, though never formulated by him into any kind of 'doctrine,' are nevertheless present in his work and especially in parts of the Hymn to the Fathers."[44]

It is noteworthy that the term חסד ("loyalty") also appears in relation to God's loyalty to the descendants of Simeon (50:24, as a final *inclusio* with 44:1): "May his loyalty (חסדו) with Simeon be assured, and may he establish for him the covenant with Phinehas." Here the sage refers to the loyalty deriving from the covenant of high priesthood made with Phinehas (Num 25:12-13), as mentioned in the passage on Phinehas: "Therefore even for him He established a statute, a covenant of peace to maintain the sanctuary, which will be for him and his offspring, the high priesthood for eternity" (45:24).

The noun כבוד ("honour" or "glory," 44:2a, 13b) not only echoes Greek encomia (which often praised dead leaders for their honour), but also introduces a key term in the Praise of the Ancestors.[45] Of Abraham Ben Sira says: "He did not put a stain on his honour" (בכבודו: 44:19), whereas the sage finds fault with Solomon: "But you put a stain on your honour" (בכבודך: 47:20). The noun (now with the nuance of "glory") also appears repeatedly in the description of Aaron (45:7, 8, 12, 20) and of Simeon (50:11, 13), while in the doxology after the praise of Phinehas Ben Sira urges his hearers to bless God "who crowns you with glory" (45:25f).[46] The description of David's liturgical activity mentions his thanksgiving to the Most High through the utterance of כבוד ("glory": 47:8), while Zerubbabel and Jeshua rebuilt the temple for God's eternal honour (49:12). By contrast, 49:5 mentions the people's "glory" or "honour" as being handed over to aliens.

When Sir 44:2b speaks of "greatness (גדלה) from the days of eternity/ antiquity" (גדלה מימות עולם), it anticipates the words of 45:24 regarding the high priesthood given to Phinehas and his descendants: "Therefore even for him He established a statute ... the great [= high] priesthood for eternity (כהונה גדולה עד עולם)" (45:24). Significantly, 50:1a H[B] introduces Simeon as "great among his brothers" or "greatest of his brethren" (גדול אחיו).

While Israel Lévi once proposed that the persons listed in 44:3-6 are famous pagans, textual and literary considerations suggest that these

---

Xeravits, "The Figure of David in the Book of Ben Sira," *Henoch* 23 (2001) 27-38, esp. 34-35.

[44] J.D. Martin, "Ben Sira's Hymn to the Fathers: A Messianic Perspective," in *Crises and Perspectives* (ed. A.S. van der Woude, OTS 24, Leiden: Brill 1986) 107-123, esp. 119; cf. Skehan and Di Lella, *The Wisdom of Ben Sira*, 526 (on 47:11), 528 (on 47:22).

[45] Cf. D.A. deSilva, "The Wisdom of Ben Sira: Honor, Shame, and the Maintenance of the Values of a Minority Culture," *CBQ* 58 (1996) 433-55. According to deSilva, "Ben Sira seeks to promote an evaluation of honor in which the first and definitive criterion is loyalty to God and the covenant" (p. 454).

[46] The term כבודו ("his honour") appears in 45:25c H[B], but the reading and interpretation are much disputed; cf. Skehan and Di Lella, *The Wisdom of Ben Sira*, 510.

persons are in fact Israelites.[47] In particular, although the medieval Genizah text of 44:4a might suggest Gentile rulers where it has "princes of the nations (שרי גוים)," here the more ancient Masada scroll matches the Greek in reading "princes of the nation (שרי גוי)," presumably with reference to Israel. While גוי ("nation") is less common than עם ("people") to denote Israel, it appears in some important biblical passages (e.g., Gen 12:2; Exod 19:6; Deut 26:5).[48] Moreover, if 44:1-15 serves to introduce the Praise of the Ancestors, it is appropriate that 44:3-6 refers briefly to the kinds of persons that will be celebrated in the following text.[49] It may also not be accidental that the listing of twelve categories of persons in 44:3-6 matches the number of the tribes of Israel.[50]

Scholars have attempted to identify these twelve categories with characters that appear later in the Praise of the Ancestors, particularly on the basis of vocabulary found in other biblical texts or in 44:17-50:24.[51] For instance, the reference to characters famed for their kingship or prophecy (44:3) clearly anticipates monarchs like David and Solomon, as well as prophets like Samuel and Elijah. Although some of the twelve categories of person mentioned in 44:3-6 do not correspond exactly to the subsequent characters, much of the vocabulary recurs later in the long poem. Accordingly, we will here examine each of the twelve categories in turn.

In 44:3a the praise of "controllers of the land for their kingship (רודי ארץ במלכותם)" probably includes Solomon, since the verb רדה ("subdue, control, dominate") is used of him in 1 Kgs 5:4 [NRSV: 4:24], and Ben Sira's poem about him includes the noun ארץ ("earth, land": 47:15) and the verb מלך ("reigned": 47:13).[52] Thereafter, 44:3b celebrates "men of

---

[47] So Beentjes, "The 'Praise of the Famous,'" 376-78; *contra* I. Lévi, *L'Ecclésiastique* (2 vols., Paris: Leroux 1898, 1901) 1: 82.

[48] The Greek translation of 44:4a may have wished to offer a more universalistic perspective. A similar change from a national to a more universalistic perspective appears in 44:15a, where the Hebrew term עדה ("congregation") becomes in Greek λαοί ("peoples"); cf. Yadin, *The Ben Sira Scroll from Masada*, 37; Minissale, *La versione greca del Siracide*, 135.

[49] Lee, *Studies in the Form*, 225-26. According to Minissale (*La versione greca del Siracide*, 126-27), 44:3a-4b concerns political functions, whereas 44:4c-5b concerns cultural and spiritual functions.

[50] Beentjes, "The 'Praise of the Famous,'" 377. A superscription appears in the Genizah manuscript (cf. Greek), שבח אבות עולם ("praise of the ancestors of antiquity"), but its originality is doubtful because it is absent from the Masada scroll. Even if it is deemed authentic, the context shows that it must (as admitted by Lévi, *L'Ecclésiastique*, 1: 80) refer to the "ancestors of antiquity," using עולם in the sense "antiquity" as in 44:2b, rather than the "ancestors of the world" (as advocated by Segal, *Spr bn-syr' hšlm*, 303; Hayward, *The Jewish Temple*, 41). Although the term עולם occurs in the sense "world" in 3:18 Hᴬ, that reading is suspicious because it differs from Hᶜ and G.

[51] R. Smend, *Die Weisheit des Jesus Sirach erklärt* (Berlin: Reimer 1906) 417; Skehan and Di Lella, *The Wisdom of Ben Sira*, 500-501; Lee, *Studies in the Form*, 226.

[52] We may compare a passage about the Solomonic king (Ps 72:8): "And may he dominate (וירד) from sea to sea, and from the rivers to the ends of the earth (ארץ)." A

reputation for their might (אנשי שם בגבורתם)," just as Joshua is introduced as a "mighty man" or warrior (גבור: 46:1), while the passage on the Judges mentions "their reputation (שמם)" (46:12b), often gained for acts of valour. In a negative sense, however, the phrase used in 44:3b, אנשי שם ("men of reputation"), forms an ironic echo of Gen 6:4, where the term is applied to the Nephilim: "These are the warriors (הגברים) who were in antiquity, the men of reputation (אנשי שם)."[53] The phrase אנשי שם ("men of reputation") also serves an ironic echo of Num 16:2, where the term refers to those involved in Korah's rebellion.

Just as 44:3c praises "advisers for their understanding (יועצים בתבונתם),"
so the Bible employs the verb "advise" (יעץ) for the activity of the prophets Nathan and Jeremiah (1 Kgs 1:12; Jer 38:15), both of whom appear in Ben Sira's poem (47:1; 49:6). In addition, the related noun "advice, policy" (עצה) is significant in the prophecy of Isaiah, who is also mentioned later (Isa 8:10; 30:1; cf. Sir 48:20-25). By way of contrast, 47:23cd H[B] refers to Rehoboam as one who rejected advice containing understanding: "Broad in folly and lacking in understanding (בינה), Rehoboam made the people rebel by his advice (בעצתו)."[54] Thereafter, 44:3d celebrates "seers of everything for their prophecy (חזי כל בנבואתם)," while the noun "seer" (חזה: 46:15) and the expression "in prophecy" (בנבואה: 46:13, 20) are later applied to Samuel. Moreover, the cognate verb "see" (חזה) is subsequently used for the activity of Isaiah (48:24), with the synonym "see" (ראה) being used of Ezekiel (49:8).[55]

When 44:4a praises "princes of the nation for their planning (שרי גוי במזמתם)," the reference probably includes Moses (Exod 2:14), as well as other important Israelites (Exod 18:25; contrast Ezek 11:1). Then 44:4b celebrates "leaders for their legislation (רוזנים במחקקתם)," perhaps alluding to David, who received "the statute (חק) of kingship" (47:11).[56] There may also be a reference to Moses, whose God-given task was "to teach to Jacob his statutes (חקיו)" (45:5), as well as to Aaron, of whom 45:17 says: "And he

---

reference to Adam may also be implied (cf. Sir 49:16), since in Gen 1:28 God commands humanity: "Be fruitful and multiply and fill the earth (הארץ) and conquer it, and have dominion (רדו) over the fish of the sea and over the birds of the sky and over every living thing creeping on the earth."

[53] Perhaps Ben Sira here makes a deliberate contrast to the Book of the Watchers (1 Enoch 6-7), since for him the true "men of reputation" are not the Nephilim but the characters he will enumerate later in the Praise of the Ancestors.

[54] Rehoboam rejected the advice of the elders and followed the counsel of the younger men (1 Kgs 12:13-14). In Sir 47:23cd the name "Rehoboam" may have added by scribes; cf. Skehan and Di Lella, The Wisdom of Ben Sira, 530.

[55] The unusual phrase in 44:3d, "seers of everything (חזי כל)" (cf. Isa 48:6), echoes the description of God in Sir 15:18 H[B] as "seer of everything (חוזה כל)." The noun "prophet" (נביא) will later be used of Elijah, Elisha, Jeremiah, and the Twelve Prophets (48:1, 8; 49:7, 10).

[56] The term "their legislation (מחקקתם)" calls to mind the word "sceptre (מחקק)" in Jacob's blessing (Gen 49:10), a verse that is often understood to refer to David.

taught his people the statute (חק)."[57] Ben Sira's language in 44:4b echoes the discourse on wisdom in Prov 8:15: "Kings reign through me, and leaders legislate (רוזנים יחקקו) justice." Then Sir 44:4c praises "wise speakers for their literature (חכמי שיח בספרתם)," using vocabulary that recalls Solomon, since 47:14a acclaims him, saying: "You were wise (חכמת)." Thereafter, 47:17 H[B] refers to the literature attributed to Solomon: "With song, proverb, riddle and epigram, you astonished peoples," where "song" refers to the Song of Songs (1:1) while the phrase "proverb, riddle and epigram" alludes to the Book of Proverbs (Prov 1:6).[58]

Although 44:4d has been interpreted in various ways, here I understand it as a reference to temple personnel, especially the priesthood. It is sometimes asserted that the list of categories in 44:3-6 makes no specific mention of priestly figures.[59] There are three major reasons for such an assertion. First, 44:4d is omitted by the Greek text (possibly because of its favourable mention of the priesthood).[60] Second, in 44:4d Yadin read the Genizah Hebrew word as במשמחותם (bĕmiśmĕḥôtām, "in their celebrations"),[61] whereas most scholars read the fifth Hebrew letter as a *resh* rather than a *heth*. Third, there are two possible readings of במשמרותם, which, depending on the vocalization, can be understood as either "in their pointed maxims" (bĕmaśmĕrôtām) or "for their liturgical duties" (bĕmišmĕrôtām). On the basis of the epilogue to Qoheleth (Qoh 12:11), Skehan interpreted במשמרותם as "in their pointed maxims," which is possible, particularly if the word משלים is understood as a participle ("framers of proverbs").[62] However, this interpretation has the weakness of making 44:4d roughly equivalent to 44:5b. More significantly, by far the most common usage of משמרות in the Hebrew Bible (e.g., Num 4:28; 1 Chr 26:6, 12) is to denote "watches" or "guard duties" or "liturgical offices" (even priestly duties of service) in the sanctuary, while the משלים would then refer to the leaders of these liturgical duties. I have adopted this interpretation of 44:4d, already proposed by some scholars,[63] because it nicely fits the context of 44:1-50:24, where the two characters receiving the longest treatment are the priestly figures of Aaron (45:6-22) and Simeon (50:1-24).

Accordingly, the praise of "rulers for their liturgical duties (משלים במשמרותם)" in 44:4d is best understood as referring to those in charge of the sanctuary. Indeed, the verb "rule" (משל) appears in the description of Aaron in 45:17: "And he made him rule (וימשילהו) with statute and judgement," while 1 Chr 26:6 uses a cognate noun for a group of temple gatekeepers:

---

[57] Ezra 7:10b employs a similar phrase for Ezra's role, though Ben Sira ignores him; cf. Duggan, "Ezra, Scribe and Priest," 207.

[58] J. Corley, "An Intertextual Study of Proverbs and Ben Sira," in *Intertextual Studies in Ben Sira and Tobit*, 155-82, here 156.

[59] Collins, *Jewish Wisdom in the Hellenistic Age*, 100; Lévi, *L'Ecclésiastique*, 1.82.

[60] Minissale, *La versione greca del Siracide*, 127, 134.

[61] Yadin, *The Ben Sira Scroll from Masada*, 36.

[62] Skehan, "Staves, and Nails, and Scribal Slips," 69.

[63] Segal, *Spr bn-syr' hšlm* 305; Minissale, *La versione greca del Siracide*, 130.

"And to his son Shemaiah were born sons, the rulers (הממשלים) for their father's house." In the Torah, Aaron's son Eleazar was given oversight of "the guards on duty at the sanctuary (שמרי משמרת הקדש)" (Num 3:32).[64]

Sirach 44:5a praises "composers of melody according to rhythm (חקרי מזמור על קו)," probably with an allusion to David. Indeed, 47:9b H^Bm refers to David's activity providing "the sound of melody (קול מזמור)" for the worship of God, while Amos 6:5 speaks of the rich leisured classes: "Like David they invent instruments of music for themselves." Interestingly, one of the Qumran *Hodayot* employs the noun קו (probably in the sense of "rhythm") when speaking of the composition of hymns: "You placed words to the rhythm (על קו), and the puff of breath from the lips to the beat; you make rhythms (קוים) emerge according to their mysteries and the puffs of breath by their measures" (1QH ix 28-29 [i 28-29]).[65] Then, Sir 44:5b mentions "reciters of proverbs in a psalm (נשאי משל במכתם)," perhaps with an allusion to Solomon. Just as 44:5b mentions "reciters of proverbs (נשאי משל)," 47:17a H^B (as completed by Segal) refers to Solomon's utterance of several literary forms of speech, including the "proverb (משל)."[66]

The expression אנשי חיל ("men of power:" 44:6a) reflects an idiom that can often refer to military might (e.g., Judg 3:29; 2 Kgs 24:16) or professional ability (e.g., Exod 18:21; 1 Chr 26:8), though the noun חיל can also refer to "wealth" or financial strength (e.g., Isa 60:5; Sir 14:15; 40:13). While 44:6a celebrates "men of power (אנשי חיל)," 46:1 calls Joshua "a powerful warrior (גבור בן חיל)," and Josh 11:23 employs the same verb as Sir 44:6b when it concludes the account of the conquest: "And the land had quietness (שקטה) from war."[67] Then 44:6a praises "forceful supporters (סמכי כח)." The participle סומך ("supporter") appears as a divine epithet in parallel with עוזר ("helper") in Isa 63:5 and Sir 51:7 (cf. Ps 54:6). Finally, 44:6b recalls שקטים על מכונתם ("those in quietness in their residence"). Sirach 41:1 H^BM uses a similar phrase when remarking on the tragedy of death coming to someone living in quiet retirement: "Alas for death! How bitter is the memory of you, for a man in quietness in his residence (לאיש שקט על מכונתו)." Minissale also sees a contrast between the heroes from times of war in 44:6a ("men of power and forceful supporters"), and the heroes from peaceful periods in 44:6b ("those in quietness in their residence").[68] However, instead of antithetical parallelism, it could be a case of synonymous parallelism, if

---

[64] Moreover, the reference to ruling is appropriate, since in Ben Sira's day the high priest had *de facto* civil power over Jerusalem as well as religious authority; cf. Hengel, *Judaism and Hellenism*, 1: 271.

[65] García Martínez and Tigchelaar, *The Dead Sea Scrolls Study Edition*, 1: 161. According to the Qumran Cave 11 Psalms Scroll, David wrote psalms (11Q5 xxvii 4).

[66] The expression "reciters of proverbs (נשאי משל)," means literally "those taking up a proverb [or: saying]." There could be a reference to Job (cf. Sir 49:9), since this idiom is used of Job opening some of his speeches (Job 27:1; 29:1).

[67] The phrase "and the land had quietness" appears in connection with the activity of the Judges Othniel, Ehud, Deborah, Barak, and Gideon (Judg 3:11, 30; 5:31; 8:28).

[68] Minissale, *La versione greca del Siracide*, 127.

the phrase חיל אנשי is understood as "men of wealth" (as in G) and סמכי כח as "rich supporters," since in 40:26a וכה חיל may mean "wealth and riches."

Although the reference to characters famed for their kingship or prophecy (44:3) clearly anticipates monarchs like David and Solomon or prophets like Samuel and Elijah, not all the twelve categories of person mentioned in 44:3-6 feature exactly in the subsequent characters, and so Ben Sira may partly be addressing the kinds of persons in his audience. For instance, the sage's purpose in mentioning advisers (44:3c) and musical composers (44:5a) may be not so much to introduce future characters in the poem, but rather to acknowledge such persons among the hearers of his public oration. Moreover, the phrase in 44:4c, "wise speakers (שיח חכמי)," literally "the wise in conversation," could easily be applied to people in Ben Sira's audience, since the phrase reverses the wording of 8:8 H^A: "Do not forsake the conversation of the wise (חכמים שיחת)."

It is interesting to compare Sir 44:4-5 with the four categories of person mentioned in the decree of King Antiochus III (around 198 BC), those recorded as exempted from certain taxes after the Seleucid conquest of Jerusalem. The decree, quoted by Josephus (A.J. 12.3.3 §142), mentions "the senate, the priests, the scribes of the temple, and the temple-singers" (ἡ γερουσία καὶ οἱ ἱερεῖς καὶ οἱ γραμματεῖς καὶ οἱ ἱεροψάλται).[69] The "princes of the nation" and the "leaders" in 44:4ab may correspond to members of the Jerusalem senate, while the "rulers" mentioned in connection with their "liturgical duties" (44:4d) probably refer to the priests. The "wise speakers" commended for their literature (44:4c) and the "reciters of proverbs" (44:5b) may encompass the temple scribes, while the "composers of melody" (44:5a) probably denote the temple singers and musicians. Thus, all the four categories of leaders of society, mentioned in the decree of Antiochus III, seem to be reflected in 44:4-5. To be sure, priests like Aaron and Simeon are instances of "rulers" who fulfilled their "liturgical duties" (44:4d), while King David would be regarded as an example of the "composers of melody" (44:5a; cf. Amos 6:5). However, it makes sense to see Ben Sira hinting at his audience of distinguished members of Jerusalemite society, rather than simply commemorating famous figures from Israel's past. While the kinds of persons mentioned in 44:3-6 often match the kings and prophets celebrated in 46:1–49:16, there is also a nod to the Jerusalem aristocracy and temple personnel doubtless in the audience to hear the poem declaimed by Ben Sira.

CONTRAST BETWEEN REMEMBERED AND FORGOTTEN ANCESTORS (44:7-9)

כל אלה בדרם נכבדו ומימיהם תפארתם
יש מהם הניחו שם להשתעות בנחלתם
ויש מהם שאין לו זכר וישבתו כאשר שבתו
כאשר לא היו היו ובניהם מאחריהם

---

[69] R. Marcus, *Josephus, vol. 7* (LCL, London: Heinemann 1933) 73. For a comparable list see Josephus, A.J. 11.5.1 §128; cf. 1 Esdras 8:22.

⁷All these in their generation were honoured,
    and their splendour was in their days.
⁸Among them were those who left a reputation,
    to be spoken of in their inheritance;
⁹ᵃᵇbut among them were those of whom there is no remembrance,
    and they perished whenever they perished.
⁹ᶜThey have become as if they had never existed,
    they and their children after them.

In regard to textual questions, at the beginning of 44:8b I read לֱהִשְׁתָּעוּת ("to narrate/ be spoken of"), with the margin of the Genizah manuscript. At the end of 44:8b I follow the Genizah manuscript to read בנחלתם ("in their inheritance"), whereas the Greek and Syriac (followed by Minissale) presuppose בתהלותם ("in their praises").[70] The Syriac misses out 44:9cd, perhaps because it seems to oppose belief in the afterlife.[71]

As for poetic devices, Ben Sira marks the end of this stanza by a doubled rhyme: היו היו ("they existed, they have become") in 44:9c, and ובניהם מאחריהם ("and their children after them") in 44:9d. Moreover, the phrase כל אלה ("all these"), opening this stanza, serves to delimit poetic sections elsewhere in Ben Sira (32:13, concluding 31:12—32:13; 37:15, concluding 36:23—37:15). There is assonance in 44:7-8 between ומימיהם ("and from/ in their days," 44:7b) and מהם ("among them," 44:8a, 9a), and also in 44:8 between הניחו ("they left," 44:8a) and בנחלתם ("in their inheritance," 44:8b).

Just as Sir 44:7-9 observes that the dead are easily forgotten, so ancient Egyptian texts often note that many figures have fallen into oblivion despite their past importance. Thus, an Egyptian writing from the Ramesside period, dubbed *The Immortality of Writers*, remarks that famous scribes survive after death through their literary works:

> As to those learned scribes,/ Of the time that came after the gods,/ They who foretold the future,/ Their names have become everlasting,/ While they departed, having finished their lives,/ And all their kin are forgotten.[72]

The author explains how they reached literary immortality: "Man decays, his corpse is dust, / All his kin have perished; / But a book makes him remembered/ Through the mouth of its reciter." The author then lists eight famous Egyptian scribes, before concluding: "Death made their names forgotten/ But books made them remembered!" In an analogous way, Ben

[70] Minissale, *La versione greca del Siracide*, 131. In 44:9a the singular form לו ("to him/it") agrees with the grammatically singular subject יש ("existence/ there is").

[71] Nelson, *The Syriac Version*, 114.

[72] The text appears in M. Lichtheim, *Ancient Egyptian Literature*, vol. 2 (Berkeley: University of California Press 1976) 176-77; this quotation is from p. 176, and the next two are from p. 177. The text also appears in J.B. Pritchard, *Ancient Near Eastern Texts* (Princeton: Princeton University Press 1950) 431-32.

Sira's task in the Praise of the Ancestors is to record the achievements of Israel's past heroes, so that their name does not perish.[73]

Similarly, ancient Greek literature is also aware that important figures from the past are easily forgotten unless they are specifically commemorated. Thus, in his oration *Antidosis* (136-37), Isocrates (436-338 BC) declares:

> I wonder if you realize... how many in the generations that are past have left no name, although they were far better and worthier men than those who are celebrated in song and on the tragic stage. But the latter, you see, found their poets and historians, while the others secured no one to hymn their praises.[74]

In his discourse on *Evagoras* (4), Isocrates expresses his aim in composing his encomium: "The spoken words which should adequately recount the deeds of Evagoras would make his virtues never to be forgotten among all mankind." On a more general level, the first *Pythian Ode* (1.92-93) composed by Pindar (518-438 BC) declares: "When men are dead and gone, it is only the loud acclaim of praise that surviveth mortals." Furthermore, addressing his sixteenth *Idyll* (16.29-30) to King Hiero II of Syracuse around 275 BC, Theocritus asserts that it is the duty of rulers to offer financial support to the arts and "to honour the holy interpreters of the Muses, that even when thou art hidden in Hades thou mayest be well spoken of." In an analogous way, the aim of Ben Sira's poem is to ensure that Israel's virtuous figures will be remembered.

In 44:7b Ben Sira asserts about these persons listed in 44:3-6 that "their splendour (תפארתם) was in/from their days." Ben Sira later uses the noun "splendour" (תפארת) in his descriptions of Aaron and Simeon. Sirach 45:8 H^B says of Aaron: "And He clothed him with a crown of splendour (תפארת), and made him splendid in glory and might," while 50:11b H^B speaks of Simeon being clothed in "garments of splendour (תפארת)." When in 50:1 H^B the sage calls Simeon "the splendour of his people (תפארת עמו)," it seems that Simeon is being portrayed as a new Adam, since the previous verse (49:16b H^B) says: "Above everyone living is the splendour of Adam (תפארת אדם)."[75]

Although 44:7 asserts that "all these" categories of persons listed above (44:3-6) were honoured in their own time, verses 8-9 make a distinction

---

[73] Ben Sira himself seeks a kind of immortality through his writings, since he declares: "Still I shall pour out teaching like prophecy, and I shall bequeath it to eternal generations" (24:33 G). By contrast with his predecessors, Ben Sira is the first known Jewish wisdom writer to sign his book with his name (50:27); cf. Hengel, *Judaism and Hellenism*, 1: 131.

[74] For the four classical quotations in this paragraph, see G. Norlin, *Isocrates, vol. 2* (LCL, London: Heinemann 1929) 263; L. Van Hook, *Isocrates, vol. 3* (LCL, London: Heinemann 1945) 7; J. Sandys, *The Odes of Pindar* (LCL, rev. ed., London: Heinemann 1937) 165; Gow, *Theocritus, vol. 1*, 125. All four of them are mentioned by Lee, *Studies in the Form*, 197, 227, 160-61.

[75] On this phrase in 49:16b see Hayward, *The Jewish Temple*, 44-47.

between those remembered afterwards and those subsequently forgotten. Some left behind a name or reputation, particularly in the biblical narratives and the memory of the people, whereas others have left no memorial.[76] Even though the forgotten ones in a sense may have lived on through their children (44:9d), and thus had some kind of genetic survival, they did not survive in the people's memory (44:9a).

When Ben Sira mentions "those of whom there is no remembrance (זכר)" (44:9a), he is employing another key word in the Praise of the Ancestors. In his reference to Moses in 45:1, Ben Sira adds a parenthesis: "his memory is for good (זכרו לטובה)," while the sage says of the faithful Judges in 46:11: "Let remembrance of them be for a blessing (יהי זכרם לברכה)," in an echo of Prov 10:7: "The memory of a righteous person is for a blessing (זכר צדיק לברכה)." Later in the Praise of the Ancestors, Ben Sira says of Josiah: "May his memory (זכרו) be sweet like honey on the palate" (49:1), while the sage says of Nehemiah: "May his memory (זכרו) be exalted" (49:13).[77]

It is likely that the persons of whom there is no remembrance are the unrighteous who (according to Ben Sira's theology) do not deserve to be recalled to mind. Elsewhere (10:17 H^A) the sage speaks of God's treatment of the arrogant: "And he causes the remembrance of them to cease from the earth (וישבת מארץ זכרם)" (cf. 40:15-16; 41:6-10). It is noteworthy that Ben Sira has omitted from his poem any naming of sinful leaders such as Samson, Saul, and Ahab.[78] So, for instance, in 46:11-12 we are meant to understand that the only judges deserving to be remembered are the Minor Judges (Judg

---

[76] The contrast between the remembered ancestors and those who are forgotten (44:8-9) may be a case of *synkrisis* (comparison), as in Greek encomia; cf. Lee, *Studies in the Form*, 179-81. A similar contrast appears in 48:16 using the same expression יש מהם ויש מהם ("there were some of them … and there were others of them"). In 44:7-9, Ben Sira borrows an idiom from Ezra 10:44: "All these (כל אלה) had taken foreign wives, and among them were some wives (ויש מהם נשים) who had produced children." The phrase הניחו שם ("They left a reputation/ name") is an ironic echo of Isa 65:15, which says of those who abandon God: "And you shall leave your name (והנחתם שמכם) as a curse for my chosen ones, and the Lord YHWH will slay you, but to his servants he will give a different name (שם)."

[77] By contrast, although the idolatrous king Jeroboam is named in 47:23 H^B and G, the line seems overloaded, and the phrase "let there be no memory (זכר) of him" suggests that the original text did not name him because Ben Sira considered that he deserved to be forgotten; cf. Skehan and Di Lella, *The Wisdom of Ben Sira*, 530-31. Elsewhere, Ben Sira says of the devout scribe: "Remembrance of him will not disappear" (39:9 G), whereas the unfaithful wife "will leave her memory as a curse" (23:26 G).

[78] We may also compare the Roman practice of blotting out names of disgraced persons (*damnatio memoriae*), while in Egypt removal of one's name from monuments was even thought to endanger one's existence in the afterlife. Admittedly, Ben Sira includes Solomon as temple-builder and patron of wisdom, despite his mixed record, so that half of the description of Solomon is positive (47:12-18b) and half negative (47:18c-22).

10:1-5; 12:8-15), who "did not turn away from God" (46:11c) and also left descendants after them, so that "their name" continues in their children (46:12b), whereas three Major Judges (Gideon, Jephthah and Samson) do not deserve to be mentioned because of their ties to idol worship or their lack of surviving descendants.[79]

The verb in 44:9b, "they perished, went to their rest, kept Sabbath" (שבתו) is an unusual way of saying "they died." However, a double usage of this verb appears in 38:23 H[Bm]: כשבות מת ישבות זכרו ("When a dead person perishes, his remembrance will perish"), with its allusion to the Hebrew of Deut 32:26. The vocabulary here may be a case of euphemism, since throughout 44:1-15 Ben Sira avoids the verbal root מות ("die"), though it does appear later (46:20; 48:5, 11, 20).[80] The repetitive idiom, "and they perished whenever they perished (וישבתו כאשר שבתו)," expresses indeterminacy of time, just as similar expressions with באשר ("wherever") can express indeterminacy of place (e.g., 1 Sam 23:13; 2 Kgs 8:1).[81]

When Ben Sira asserts: "They have become as if they had never existed" (44:9c), he is echoing Job 10:19: כאשר לא הייתי אהיה ("I shall become as though I had never existed"; cf. Obad 16). The Damascus Document employs a comparable phrase to describe the death of the Watchers: ויהיו כלא היו (CD ii 20; cf. 4Q266 2 ii 20): "And they became as if they had never been."[82] Moreover, 1 Enoch 102:11 reports the sinners' comment on the death of the virtuous, with a similar idiom: "And they perished and became as those who are not."[83] A comparable depiction of the effect of death appears in Wis 2:2: "Hereafter we shall be as though we had never been" (NRSV).

BLESSINGS BEQUEATHED BY HONOURABLE ANCESTORS (44:10-15)

אולם אלה אנשי חסד וצדקתם לא תכרת
עם זרעם נאמן טובם ונחלתם לבני בניהם
בבריתם עמד זרעם ובעבורם צאצאיהם
עד עולם יעמד זרעם וכבודם לא ימחה

---

[79] T.R. Brown, "God and Men in Israel's History: God and Idol Worship in Praise of the Fathers (Sir 44-50)," in Ben Sira's God, 214-20, esp. 218-19. If we compare 44:7-9 with Ben Sira's brief comments on the judges in 46:11-12, we find shared vocabulary including "name/ reputation" (שם: 44:8a; 46:12b); "remembrance" (זכר: 44:9a; 46:11d); "their children" (בניהם: 44:9d; 46:12b).

[80] Possible overtones of the verb may be the sense of rest after the completion of earthly life (like God's rest in Gen 2:1-3 after his creative activity), or the implication that God had caused their life to cease (since the causative hiphil form of the verb appears in this sense in Hos 1:4 and Jer 36:29).

[81] P. Joüon and T. Muraoka, A Grammar of Biblical Hebrew (2 vols., Subsidia biblica 14/1-2, Rome: Pontifical Biblical Institute 1991) §158o.

[82] García Martínez and Tigchelaar, The Dead Sea Scrolls Study Edition, 1.555.

[83] G.W.E. Nickelsburg and J.C. VanderKam, 1 Enoch: A New Translation (Minneapolis: Fortress 2004) 158.

וגויתם בשלום נאספה ושמם חי לדור ודור
חכמתם תשנה עדה ותהלתם יספר קהל

[10] These, however, were men of loyalty,
   and their righteousness will not be cut off.
[11] With their offspring their prosperity was assured,
   and their inheritance was for their children's children.
[12] In their covenant their offspring has continued,
   and so have their descendants because of them.
[13] To eternity their offspring will continue,
   and their honour will not be blotted out.
[14] Whereas their corpse was buried in peace,
   their reputation lives from generation to generation.
[15] The congregation will repeat their wisdom,
   and the assembly will recount their praise.

As for the text, the line ends in 44:10-12 have suffered damage in both Hebrew manuscripts, so that it is necessary to supply two whole words and parts of four more words here (plus the middle of a word in 44:14a). Where the Hebrew of 44:10b has suffered damage, the general meaning is clear, even though the reconstruction of the verb varies among scholars. The reading given here: "and their righteousness will not be cut off" (וצדקתם לא תכרת) follows Yadin and Minissale, whereas Segal supplies the verb "cease" (תשבת), while Skehan and Reymond prefer the verb "be forgotten" (תשכח).[84] In 44:10b I follow the Masada manuscript reading [וצ]דקתם ("and their righteousness"), with the support of the Greek and the Syriac, whereas the Genizah manuscript may imply some belief in the afterlife in its reading ותקותם ("and their hope"). The end of 44:11b is also damaged, but following Segal and Minissale (cf. Syriac) I supply לבני בניהם ("for their children's children").[85] The great Genizah manuscript misses out 44:12ab, either by haplography from the similarity of 44:12a and 44:13a, or by homoioteleuton with 44:11b. In 44:12b following Yadin and Skehan (cf. Greek) I supply the word בעבורם ("because of them").[86] But whereas the Masada scroll begins 44:12b with the word וצאצאיהם ("and their descendants"), because of the rhyme scheme I insert the word בעבורם ("because of them") immediately after the waw ("and"), but without any manuscript attestation for this word order. In 44:13a I also follow the Masada scroll reading זרעם ("their offspring"), with the support of the Greek, whereas the Genizah manuscript (matching the Syriac) has זכרם

[84] Yadin, *The Ben Sira Scroll from Masada*, 37; Minissale, *La versione greca del Siracide*, 131; Segal, *Spr bn-syr' hšlm*, 302; Skehan and Di Lella, *The Wisdom of Ben Sira*, 499; Reymond, *Innovations in Hebrew Poetry*, 80.

[85] Segal, *Spr bn-syr' hšlm*, 302; Minissale, *La versione greca del Siracide*, 132.

[86] Yadin, *The Ben Sira Scroll from Masada*, 37; Skehan and Di Lella, *The Wisdom of Ben Sira*, 499; Segal, *Spr bn-syr' hšlm*, 302.

("their memory").[87] In 44:13b I again follow the Masada text reading וכבודם ("and their honour"), with the support of the Greek and the Syriac, whereas the Genizah manuscript has וצדקתם ("and their righteousness"), perhaps borrowed from 44:10b.

Regarding poetic devices, it is noteworthy that the first three words in 44:10 begin with the first Hebrew letter, *aleph*, as an indication that a new stanza is starting. Moreover, in 44:10a Ben Sira indicates the opening of a new section by repeating from 44:1a the phrase אנשי חסד ("men of loyalty," = third and fourth words in both Stanza I and Stanza III), as well as repeating from 44:7a אלה ("these," = second word in both Stanza II and Stanza III).

The concluding phrase in 44:15 is a kind of refrain, since it roughly echoes 39:10, while 44:15b approximately matches 31:11b. Elsewhere in Ben Sira, refrains can frequently serve to indicate the conclusion of a passage. Two other instances of refrains are the following: 20:30-31 G = 41:14-15 G (concluding 19:20-20:31 and 41:5-15); and 24:34 G = 33:18 G (ending 24:1-34 and 32:14-33:18).[88] Moreover, as in the lament psalms (Pss 79:13; 106:47), the refrain in 44:15 (echoing 31:11; 39:10) demonstrates that one of Ben Sira's favourite terminative themes is "praise," as also in 15:9-10 (ending 14:20-15:10) and 51:11-12 (concluding 51:1-12).[89]

The most striking feature of this stanza is the use of first-word rhyme, whereby the first word (or phrase) in each of the twelve cola of 44:10-15 (from עולם to ותהלתם) ends with the rhyming sound *-ām*, usually formed by the Hebrew third person plural suffix ("their").[90] This rhyme forms a skilful counterpart to the use of end rhyme with *-tām* in 44:1-8. Such first-word rhyme is less common than rhyme at the end of bicola, but it does occur occasionally in Hebrew poetic books:[91]

Prov 11:23: תאות צדיקים אך טוב תקות רשעים עברה
The desire of righteous persons is only goodness;
      the expectation of wicked persons is wrath.
Sir 44:17cd H^B: בעבורו היה שארית ובבריתו חדל מבול
Because of him [= Noah] there was a remnant,
      and with his covenant the flood ceased.

The stanza (44:10-15) asserts that the virtuous deserve to be remembered, by contrast with the forgotten persons of 44:9 (presumably the unrighteous).

---

[87] The Genizah reading (perhaps influenced by Ps 112:6) is favoured by Minissale, *La versione greca del Siracide*, 132.

[88] J. Corley, *Ben Sira's Teaching on Friendship* (BJS 316, Providence: Brown University 2002) 25.

[89] C. Westermann, *Praise and Lament in the Psalms* (Atlanta: John Knox Press 1981) 59, 75. Sometimes Ben Sira directs the praise towards humans (e.g., 31:11; 39:10; 44:15) and sometimes towards God (15:9-10; 51:11-12).

[90] See Reymond, "Prelude to the Praise of the Ancestors," 12. In addition, 44:11a, 12a, 13a also end with the same sound *-ām*.

[91] Other examples of first-word rhyme (also called head rhyme) include Prov 12:15; 14:24; 17:6; Sir 6:11, 13; 42:19; 45:7-9.

Hence the phrase in 44:10a ("These, however, were men of loyalty"),[92] refers not to the previously mentioned forgotten characters (44:9) but rather to those that will be mentioned afterwards (44:17-50:24), most of whom were model Israelites.[93] Indeed, 44:10b H^M asserts of the devout: "their righteousness (צדקתם) will not be cut off." At the beginning of the Torah Section the first recipient of a covenant with God (Noah, 44:17) is described as "righteous" (צדיק), as in Gen 6:9. Later the sage calls Job "the one maintaining all the ways of righteousness (צדק)" (completing 49:9 H^B).

Sirach 44:10b H^M is in line with 40:17 H^M: "Loyalty (חסד) for ever will not be cut off, and righteousness (צדקה) for ever will be established" (cf. Wis 1:15). In Ben Sira's thought, what survives into eternity is not the individual person but rather the devout person's reputation among the people.[94] This helps to explain another saying: "A people's sage will inherit glory, and his reputation continues in the life of eternity" (37:26 H^D). Whereas modern western readers tend to think of eternal life from an individualistic perspective as personal survival after death, for Ben Sira eternal life is the everlasting future of the people of Israel (cf. Sir 37:25; Jer 31:36), rather than individual survival.

The declaration in 44:11a is ambiguous: "With their offspring their prosperity (טובם) was assured." Depending on the covenant promise of life and prosperity (הטוב) in Deut 30:15, my translation understands טובם (literally, "their good") to refer to the blessing conferred on them by God for their loyalty to the covenant. Alternatively, טובם could refer to "their [own] goodness" or "their good action," in parallel with "their righteousness" in 44:10b.[95] Sirach 44:11 alludes to Prov 13:21b-22a, where we find both senses of טוב ("prosperity" and "good"):

את צדיקים ישלם טוב : טוב ינחיל בני בנים

Prosperity will reward the righteous.
The good person will cause children's children to inherit.

Moreover, the thought of Sir 44:10-11 has affinities with the sentiment of Isocrates in his encomium of Evagoras: "To be blessed with many children, who are at the same time good—not even this was denied him" (Evagoras 71).[96]

The statement in 44:12a is also ambiguous. I interpret the phrase to refer to the fidelity of those Israelites: "In their covenant their offspring has

---

[92] The adverbial conjunction אולם, "however," is disjunctive (anarthrous in Sir 44:10a H^M, as in Job 2:5; 5:8; 13:3), and the waw in H^B is unnecessary.

[93] Admittedly, Solomon did not entirely preserve his virtue, but though his sinfulness brought retribution on his descendants (47:20), God's promise in Nathan's oracle (2 Sam 7:14-15) meant that his line was not totally destroyed.

[94] Minissale, La versione greca del Siracide, 131-32.

[95] Ibid., 135.

[96] Van Hook, Isocrates, vol. 3, 45; cf. Lee, Studies in the Form, 132.

continued."[97] However, the opening word בבריתם could be also understood
to mean "on account of [God's] covenant with them,"[98] thereby shifting the
emphasis onto God's fidelity as the reason for the survival of the people of
Israel (cf. Ps 103:17-18). The theme of the continuance of the people in
connection with the covenant is developed in Ben Sira's subsequent words
on Noah (44:17cd):

בבריתם עמד זרעם ובעבורם צאצאיהם 44:12:
In their covenant their offspring has continued,
    and so have their descendants because of them.
בעבורו היה שארית ובבריתו חדל מבול 44:17cd H[B]:
Because of him there was a remnant,
    and with his covenant the flood ceased.

In his introduction, therefore, Ben Sira wishes to highlight the sense of
continuity and survival (44:12), which will be expressed most dramatically
in the story of Noah's flood (44:17).[99]

The threefold repetition of זרעם ("their offspring") in 44:11-13 H[M]
suggests allusions to earlier biblical texts about descendants. In particular,
the Genizah text of 44:21b refers to the promise of descendants made to
Abraham, "to bless nations through his offspring (בזרעו)" (cf. Gen 22:18),
while the Greek text of 44:21d alludes to the promise "to exalt his offspring
(σπέρμα) like the stars" (cf. Gen 15:5).[100] In the subsequent passage about
Joshua and Caleb, Ben Sira refers to Caleb's descendants receiving their promised heritage: "And also his offspring took possession of an inheritance, so
that all the offspring of Jacob might know that it is good to follow YHWH
fully" (46:9d-10b H[B]; cf. Num 14:24).

Perhaps the most important "offspring" in the Praise of the Ancestors,
however, is the offspring of the priestly line. Immediately after describing
Moses' anointing of Aaron as a priest, Sir 45:15d speaks of the priestly covenant echoing Davidic language from Ps 89:30, and the same phraseology

---

[97] In Sir 44:12-13 the repetition of זרעם ("their offspring") with a form of the verb
עמד ("continue") is deliberate, since 44:12a refers to past activity, whereas 44:13a
speaks of future activity.

[98] Minissale, La versione greca del Siracide, 113, 132.

[99] On Sir 44:17-18 see Matthias Weigold's article in the present volume.

[100] Besides this shared reference to "offspring," 44:11-13 also anticipates what the
sage will say about Abraham in 44:19-21 by mentioning three other important themes:
"inheritance" (root נחל: 44:11b, 21e); "covenant" (ברית: 44:12a, 20b); and "honour"
(כבוד: 44:13b, 19b). In addition, while the participial adjective נאמן in 44:11 defines
how the prosperity of the devout is "assured," the same adjective in 44:20 describes
how Abraham was "faithful" when he was tested (cf. Gen 22:1; Neh 9:8; 1 Macc 2:52);
cf. Corley, Ben Sira's Teaching on Friendship, 50. On Sir 44:19-23 see Pancratius Beentjes'
article in the present volume; cf. C.T.R. Hayward, "El Elyon and the Divine Names in
Ben Sira," in Ben Sira's God, 180-98, esp. 187-89.

recurs in a reference to the "covenant with Phinehas" at the close of the passage on Simeon in 50:24d.[101]

45:15d = 50:24d: ‏ולזרעו בימי שמים‏
And for his offspring, like the days of heaven.
Ps 89:30: ‏ושמתי לעד זרעו וכסאו כימי שמים‏
And I will appoint his offspring for ever,
   and his throne like the days of heaven.

Moreover, the "covenant of peace" with Phinehas, consisting of the high priesthood, was "for him and for his offspring" (‏לו ולזרעו‏)" (45:24c H[B]; cf. Num 25:13). Indeed, unlike the Davidic covenant, "Aaron's inheritance is for all his offspring (‏לכל זרעו‏)" (45:25d H[B]), since there are many priests even if only one king is possible.

Sirach 44:14a mentions the burial of devout Israelites: "Their corpse was buried (literally: gathered in, ‏נאספה‏) in peace." This phrase is another echo of Isa 57:1-2, a passage concerned with the death of the "men of loyalty" (‏אנשי חסד‏): "The righteous person is gathered in (‏נאסף‏ = taken away) from the face of calamity; he enters into peace (‏שלום‏)." The wording of Sir 44:14a also alludes particularly to the promise of burial for Josiah, the last king to be praised by Ben Sira (49:1-3), as described in 2 Kgs 22:20 // 2 Chr 34:28: "Therefore I am gathering you to your ancestors, and you will be gathered to [= buried in] your graves in peace (‏ונאספת אל קברתיך בשלום‏)."[102]

Ben Sira several times uses the verb ‏אסף‏ ("gather") in the sense of "bury" or even (in the passive) to mean "die". Interestingly, the qal (active) form of the verb appears in 38:16 H[B], also in the sense of "bury."[103] The use of the niphal (passive) form of the verb ‏אסף‏ ("gather") may allude to the Genesis idiom applied to the patriarchs Abraham and Ishmael: "he was gathered to his people" (Gen 25:8, 17). Elsewhere, Ben Sira employs the niphal form of the verb ‏אסף‏ ("gather") in the sense "die." Thus, in 8:7 H[A] Ben Sira reminds us: "Remember, we are all being gathered in (‏נאספים‏)," while 16:10 H[A] refers to the six hundred thousand Israelites who perished in the desert as punishment for their constant complaining: "the ones gathered in (‏הנאספים‏) for the insolence of their heart."[104] The emphasis on death and burial, repeated periodically throughout the Praise of the Ancestors (46:12, 20; 47:23; 48:5, 11, 13-14; 49:10, 15), suggests that the whole poem was written for some kind of commemoration of the dead. Nevertheless, the use here of

---

[101] Because of the use of Davidic vocabulary for Simeon as well as for Aaron, Robert Hayward asserts (*The Jewish Temple*, 51): "Ben Sira has in some measure transferred to Simon and the Zadokite dynasty royal attributes which were once characteristic of the House of David."

[102] Minissale, *La versione greca del Siracide*, 132.

[103] P.C. Beentjes, "Tränen, Trauer, Totenklage: Eine kleine Studie über Ben Sira 38,16-23," in *Auf den Spuren der schriftgelehrten Weisen* (eds. I. Fischer, *et al.*; FS Johannes Marböck, BZAW 331, Berlin: de Gruyter 2003) 233-40, here 234.

[104] Also in 40:28 H[BM] the term ‏נאסף‏ means "one gathered [to the tomb]," in other words, a dead person.

the verb אסף ("gather, bury") rather than the more common verb קבר ("bury") is possibly a case of euphemism, unless it is just a case of poetic variation.

Sirach 44:14-15 speaks of the value of an honourable reputation, just as in 39:9cd-10ab G Ben Sira commends the honourable reputation of the wise scribe. Moreover, Sir 44:14a echoes the thought of 41:11b H^B: "Ephemeral is a human being in his corpse, yet a reputation of loyalty (שם חסד) will not be cut off."[105] This theme reappears in Ben Sira's brief treatment of the judges who remained faithful to God, so that "their name" (שמם) continues in their children (46:12b). In addition, 47:16a G says of Solomon: "To distant islands your name (ὄνομα) reached," while 49:1 H^B declares: "The reputation (שם) of Josiah is like the incense of spices."

Ben Sira's concern for an enduring posthumous reputation, as a way of transcending death (cf. 1 Macc 6:44), matches the outlook of influential Greek authors. Thus, in his *Symposium* (208D) Plato (427-347 BC) refers to persons who were willing to undergo any hardship (even death) because they "expected to win 'a deathless memory for valour.'"[106] Similarly, in his encomium *Evagoras* (3), Isocrates speaks of those who choose a glorious death, "doing all that lies in their power to leave behind a memory of themselves that shall never die," and then Isocrates goes on to praise Evagoras: "Though a mortal by birth, he left behind a memory of himself that is immortal" (*Evagoras* 71). So too, in his *Histories* (2.43.1) Thucydides commends those who gave up their lives in military combat: "Their glory survives in everlasting remembrance, celebrated on every occasion which gives rise to word of eulogy or deed of emulation."[107]

Sirach 44:15 acclaims the achievements of the devout by referring to "their wisdom" (חכמתם). Since the cognate Hebrew verb is specifically applied in the Genizah manuscript only to Solomon (47:14), Ben Sira is here perhaps thinking of practical rather than theoretical wisdom, to use the categories of Alexander Di Lella.[108] Thus, in the two doxologies, the sage prays for "wisdom of heart" for the successors of Phinehas and Simeon (45:26; 50:23). Esteem for such practical wisdom is evident in the Greek epitaph of a Jewish magistrate named Abramos from the Egyptian city of Leontopolis (perhaps the first century BCE or CE): "For he was not without

[105] On the importance of one's name (שם) in Ben Sira's thought, see J.T. Sanders, *Ben Sira and Demotic Wisdom* (SBLMS 28, Chico: Scholars Press 1983) 17-18.

[106] W.R.M. Lamb, *Plato, vol. 3: Lysis, Symposium, Gorgias* (LCL, London: Heinemann 1925) 197-99. For the next two quotations see Van Hook, *Isocrates, vol. 3*, 5, 45. These Greek parallels are noted by Lee, *Studies in the Form*, 227, 132.

[107] C.F. Smith, *Thucydides, vol. 1* (LCL, revised ed., London: Heinemann 1928) 335; cf. deSilva, "The Wisdom of Ben Sira," 451. According to deSilva, Sir 44:1-50:24 has the purpose of "motivating the hearers to imitate the ancestors' faithfulness and commitment to God through obedience to Torah" (p. 453).

[108] On the distinction between practical ("recipe") wisdom and theoretical ("existential") wisdom see Skehan and Di Lella, *The Wisdom of Ben Sira*, 32-33.

honour in the city, but was crowned in his wisdom with a communal magistracy over all the people" (*CPJ* 1530a lines 5-6).[109]

Finally, the doxology concluding the praise of Phinehas (45:25e-26) contains six echoes of 44:10-15.

44:10b H^M: וצדקתם ("and their righteousness");
    45:26b Segal: בצדק ("in righteousness").
44:11a H^BM: טובם ("their prosperity/good");
    45:26c H^B: טובבם ("your prosperity/good").
44:13a H^BM: עד עולם ("to eternity");
    45:26d H^B: לדורות עולם ("to generations of eternity").
44:13b H^M: וכבודם ("and their honour");
    45:25f H^B: כבוד ("honour/ glory").
44:14b H^M: לדור ודור ("from generation to generation");
    45:26d H^B: לדורות עולם ("to generations of eternity").
44:15a H^B: חכמתם ("their wisdom");
    45:26a H^B: חכמת לב ("wisdom of heart").

In this way, Ben Sira emphasizes some major themes in the Praise of the Ancestors (righteousness, good, eternity, honour, generations, and wisdom).[110]

Moreover, the doxology concluding the praise of Simeon (50:22-24) also contains six echoes of 44:10-15.

44:10a H^BM: אנשי חסד ("men of loyalty");
    50:24a H^B: חסדו ("his loyalty").
44:11a, 12a, 13a H^M: זרעם ("their offspring");
    50:24d H^B: ולזרעו ("and for his offspring").
44:11a H^BM: נאמן ("assured");
    50:24a H^B: יאמן ("may it be assured").
44:12a H^M: בבריתם ("in their covenant");
    50:24b H^B: ברית פינחס ("the covenant with Phinehas").
44:14a H^M: בשלום ("in peace");
    50:23b H^B: בשלום ("in peace").
44:15a H^B: חכמתם ("their wisdom");
    50:23a H^B: חכמת לבב ("wisdom of heart").

---

[109] W. Horbury and D. Noy, *Jewish Inscriptions of Graeco-Roman Egypt* (Cambridge: Cambridge University Press 1992) 95; cf. W. Horbury, "Jewish Inscriptions and Jewish Literature in Egypt, with Special Reference to Ecclesiasticus," in *Studies in Early Jewish Epigraphy* (eds. J.W. van Henten and P.W. van der Horst, AGAJU 21, Leiden: Brill 1994) 9-43, esp. 23-25.

[110] Two further connections are textually uncertain. The noun טובם ("their good") in 44:11a matches the adjective טוב ("good," qualifying YHWH) in 45:25e H^B (where it may however be a gloss), while the phrase לא תשכח ("it will not be forgotten") reconstructed by Skehan in 44:10b matches the similar phrase לא ישכח ("it will not be forgotten") in 45:26c.

In this way, Ben Sira emphasizes his major themes (loyalty, offspring, assurance, covenant, peace, and wisdom), connecting the past achievements of the Israelite heroes with his future hopes for his audience, particularly the Aaronic priesthood.

CONCLUSION

In my view, the Praise of the Ancestors was composed not simply as a history lesson, but rather as the speech uttered at some kind of commemoration for the great figures of Israelite history. The poem memorialized a range of characters, from remote ancestors up to the recently deceased high priest Simeon II. The likely place for this oration would be the vicinity of the Jerusalem temple. Some of the categories of person mentioned in 44:4-5 perhaps refer less to the forthcoming characters from Israelite history and more to the distinguished guests in the audience gathered to hear the speech, perhaps at Rosh Hashanah.

As a "conservative" theologian, Ben Sira lacks the hope of an afterlife for his deceased predecessors. Here he follows traditional Israelite wisdom, as found in the earlier sapiential books (Job 14:7-12; Prov 16:4-5; Qoh 3:19-21). When we go back to the earliest available form of Ben Sira's text (14:16; 17:27-28; 38:21; 41:4), we find similar utterances denying belief in an afterlife. For him, a person survives in his descendants (30:4; 40:19) and in his remembered reputation after death (40:17; 41:11). Accordingly, here Ben Sira celebrates the survival of virtuous ancestors in their descendants who continue to observe the demands of the covenant (44:11-13a), as well as in the honourable memory of them preserved among the people (44:13b-15).

However, Ralph Hildesheim has pointed out that a closer look at the Praise of the Ancestors shows that the sage is not absolutely closed to some specific cases of survival after death.[111] Ben Sira mentions two persons who while still alive were "taken," namely Enoch and Elijah ([44:16]; 48:9; 49:14), even though (by contrast with Enochic literature) what Ben Sira says about the Genesis patriarch is limited—particularly if with Skehan we regard 44:16 as a gloss.[112] More substantially, interpreting the Book of Malachi, Ben Sira has an expectation of Elijah's return (48:10-11), so the implication is that this prophet escaped death and will return to earth in the future. Moreover, 48:14 H[B] reports of Elijah's successor Elisha: "In his life he performed marvels, and in his death portentous deeds." Presumably 48:14b refers to the resuscitation of a corpse thrown into his grave (2 Kgs 13:21), which might conceivably suggest some kind of post-mortem existence.[113]

---

[111] Hildesheim, Bis daß ein Prophet, 261-62.

[112] Skehan and Di Lella, The Wisdom of Ben Sira, 499.

[113] Similarly, 46:20ab H[B] reports of the prophet Samuel: "And even after his death he was sought, and he declared to the king his ways." Presumably this statement refers to the story of King Saul's consultation of the deceased Samuel through the witch of Endor (1 Sam 28), which might suggest the continued existence of the prophet after his death. Unclear is the meaning of the twice-occurring phrase: "May

Thus, we see that although Ben Sira denied belief in an afterlife in the main body of his teaching, his reflection on the biblical narratives led him to a kind of limited openness for it in the cases of Enoch and Elijah (and perhaps Elisha). From a historical perspective, it seems that only a generation later, the tragic conflict between King Antiochus Epiphanes and the devout Jews led to a particular hope in the resurrection (Dan 12:1-3; 2 Macc 7), while the Book of Wisdom subsequently expressed the hope of an afterlife in more philosophical language (Wis 3-4). Hence, in light of this theological development, Ben Sira's grandson and later scribes inserted references to the afterlife in the manuscripts of the book.[114]

There is evidence of the use of Sir 44:1-49:16 less than a century after its composition, since parts of Sirach 44-49 (including 44:1-15) are echoed in the farewell speech of the Maccabean leader Mattathias in 1 Macc 2:51-58. In particular, Sir 44:1-2 finds an echo in 1 Macc 2:51: "Remember the deeds of our ancestors, which they did in their generations, and receive great glory and an eternal name," while the following series of seven characters mentioned in 1 Macc 2:52-58 (Abraham, Joseph, Phinehas, Joshua, Caleb, David, Elijah) selects personages mentioned in Sirach 44-49.[115] Ultimately, the examples of earlier heroes of faith are presented as an encouragement to follow their example. Indeed, Ben Sira would have affirmed the words of Mattathias to his sons: "Children, show courage and be strong in the law, because by it you will gain honour" (1 Macc 2:64).[116]

---

their bones flourish in their place" (46:12 G; 49:10), which may just be a poetic reference to bodily descendants (rather than an allusion to an afterlife).

[114] For instance, the Genizah manuscript implies hope of an afterlife in 44:10b by replacing וצדקתם ("and their righteousness": H^M G S) with ותקותם ("and their hope").

[115] F.M. Abel, *Les Livres des Maccabées* (EtBib, 2 vols., Paris: Gabalda 1949) 1: 46-49. As in the case of Greek encomia, Ben Sira's presentation of dead heroes was designed to encourage their emulation by the living.

[116] I am grateful to Dr Géza Xeravits and Dr József Zsengellér (with their assistants) for organizing the Ben Sira conference at Pápa. For comments on this article, my thanks are due to Bernard Robinson, Patrick Welsh, and the participants at the conference.

THE USE AND INTERPRETATION OF BIBLICAL TRADITION IN BEN SIRA'S PRAISE OF THE ANCESTORS*

Benjamin G. Wright III
(Lehigh University)

In his recent book on scribal education in antiquity, *Writing on the Tablet of the Heart*, David Carr presents the thesis that while ancient scribes did indeed memorize texts, what we might call "pure" memorization was not the ultimate, certainly not the only goal of the educational process. Committing important texts to memory secured cultural continuity across generations, and the scribe's ability to transmit these central texts was highly valued. But as Carr writes,

> The fundamental idea is the following: as we look at how key texts like the Bible and other classic literature functioned in ancient cultures, what was primary was not how such texts were inscribed on clay, parchment, or papyri. Rather what was truly crucial was how those written media were part of a cultural project of incising key cultural-religious traditions—word for word—*on people's minds...* Scribal recollection of early traditions was assured partly through teaching students to read and reproduce written copies of the key traditions. Nevertheless the aim of the educational process was ultimately the scribe's memorization of the cultural tradition and cultivation of his (or occasionally her) ability to perform it.[1]

As part of his discussion of "Hellenistic Judaism," Carr spends considerable time on Ben Sira, for several reasons of which I want only to highlight a few here. First, Ben Sira straddles the border between what Carr calls "pre-Hellenistic Israelite education-textuality," but he also anticipates "changes that are more widely attested elsewhere."[2] Second, Ben Sira represents a "textuality based in the priesthood, or at least closely connected with it."[3]

---

* This paper is a revised version of the paper that I gave at the "Third International Conference on the Deuterocanonical Books: The Book of Ben Sira" in Pápa, Hungary, May 20, 2006. I presented it at the Seminar on Ancient Judaisms and Christianities at the University of Toronto on June 26, 2006. I am grateful for the questions and comments of the conference attendees and the members of SAJC, many of which have shaped its present form of.
[1] D. Carr, *Writing on the Tablet of the Heart: Origins of Scripture and Literature* (New York: Oxford University Press 2005) 8-9.
[2] Carr, *Writing*, 207.
[3] Carr, *Writing*, 207.

Third, Ben Sira, clearly values and employs oral techniques for learning. Indeed the evidence from his book indicates that Ben Sira, as a learned scribe, embodied the oral-textual interplay for which Carr is arguing. Ben Sira admonishes the aspiring student to "Listen to me your father, O child" (3:1), and he proclaims, "Wisdom becomes known through speech and education, through words of the tongue" (4:24). Yet, Ben Sira can still say, "Instruction in understanding and knowledge I have written in this book... Happy are those who concern themselves with these things, and those who lay them to heart will become wise" (50:27-28). Finally, the sources for Ben Sira's knowledge are themselves varied. We see three primary repositories from which Ben Sira drew his learning: (1) the "Torah"; (2) the wisdom of the sages; (3) the way the natural world works.

While the traditional scribal wisdom that Ben Sira learned and then taught undoubtedly has a significant oral component, a few places in his book suggest that at least what he calls "Torah" is not always some body of oral teaching, but it actually involves some written/textual preservation of the law of God. Perhaps the clearest passage is in the famous chapter 24 in which Ben Sira has Woman Wisdom, that desirable female that all his students should court, praise herself. It has become almost a commonplace to say that Ben Sira takes Wisdom, whom God has sent to dwell among his people and to minister in the temple, and relates her closely to Torah. Two things stand out in this relationship, however. First, Wisdom's residence in the Jerusalem temple pushes further the connection between the priesthood—and I would say a particular group of priests—and the teaching of God's law, a task assigned both to Moses and to Aaron in the Praise of the Ancestors.[4] Second, Ben Sira makes an important claim in 24:23:

> All this [i.e. Wisdom's activity] is the book of the covenant of the Most High God, the law that Moses commanded us as an inheritance for the congregations of Jacob.

Although Ben Sira's Hebrew does not survive for this verse and we only have his grandson's translation on which to rely, there is no reason to doubt that Ben Sira himself theorized that heavenly wisdom had become embodied in text. And indeed, when one looks at the Hebrew of Ben Sira, traces of textuality are everywhere. I want to explore some of those traces in this paper.

Scholars have also frequently noted that Sirach does not contain explicit quotes from the Hebrew Bible.[5] Yet the frequency of themes and language

---

[4] On the issue of Ben Sira and his support of particular priests, see S. Olyan, "Ben Sira's Relationship to the Priesthood," *HTR* 80 (1987) 261-86 and B.G. Wright, "'Fear the Lord and Honor the Priest:' Ben Sira as Defender of the Jerusalem Priesthood," in *The Book of Ben Sira in Modern Research* (ed. P.C. Beentjes, BZAW 255, Berlin: de Gruyter 1997) 189-222.

[5] Some see the use of הכתוב in 48:10 as an explicit and formal quotation of Malachi, but I have argued that this participle better fits into the larger series of participles in the passage on Elijah and should not be viewed as a citation formula.

found in works that later came to make up the Hebrew Bible makes it clear that Ben Sira did have access to and had most likely memorized textual sources. Questions about the identity of those sources, their processes of transmission and their authority for Ben Sira often get tied up with the difficult problem of the development of the biblical canon in the Second Temple period. These are questions that I do not intend to address here.[6] I am much more interested in Carr's model of scribal education and textual transmission and how we see it working out in Sirach. Essentially as I understand Carr, even though the memorization of texts was a fundamental aspect of the educational process and one of the scribe's important functions was to preserve these texts across generations, the end of the educational program was intended to give the scribe a proficiency with and mastery of the texts that enabled him to employ them creatively in performances.

Yet, ultimately the performance is what counts, and what gets done with the texts in performance matters most. Thus, in a way, Carr does not go far enough. Two recent books, however, highlight the cultural performance of texts. The first, Hindy Najman's *Seconding Sinai*, focuses on the meaning of pseudepigraphy and the rewriting/interpretation of the Torah of Moses.[7] She asks the question, employing the insights of Michel Foucault, of whether we can really distinguish sharply "between the *transmission* and the *interpretation* of biblical traditions."[8] She identifies what she calls a "discourse tied to a founder," which

> provides… a helpful way to think about the developing conceptions of the Mosaic Law and figure of Moses. On this understanding of a discourse tied to a founder, to rework an earlier text is to update, interpret and develop the content of that text in a way that one claims to be an authentic expression of the law already accepted as authoritatively Mosaic.[9]

For Najman, such discourse, then, offers the possibility of interpretive creativity without claims to innovation, since, as she observes,

---

See B.G. Wright, *No Small Difference: Sirach's Relationship to its Hebrew Parent Text* (SBLSCS 26, Atlanta: Scholars Press 1989) 210.

[6] For a recent attempt to connect the Praise of the Fathers with canonical questions, see A. Goshen-Gottstein, "Ben Sira's Praise of the Fathers: A Canon-Conscious Reading," in *Ben Sira's God: Proceedings of the International Ben Sira Conference Durham—Ushaw College 2001* (ed. Renate Egger-Wenzel, BZAW 321, Berlin: de Gruyter 2002) 235-67.

[7] *Seconding Sinai: The Development of Mosaic Discourse in Second Temple Judaism* (JSJSup 77, Leiden: Brill 2003).

[8] Najman, *Seconding Sinai*, 8.

[9] Najman, *Seconding Sinai*, 13.

> To take personal responsibility for a new interpretation would have been contrary to the Second Temple conception of authority, which always demanded roots in the pre-exilic past.[10]

On the face of it, Ben Sira would seem to present a somewhat unique exception to this claim, since both he and his grandson attach his name to his book, tying it inextricably to his own authority as a scribe/sage.[11] Yet, even Ben Sira, in at least two ways, reveals his desire to connect his teaching and ideology to an even more ancient past. First, in his Praise of the Ancestors (chaps. 44-50) he singles out selected figures from Israel's past and then ties his ideal priest-ruler, Simon II, to them. He thus grounds Simon's actions— and more importantly he positions his assessment of Simon's social, religious and political activities—within the framework of the actions and offices of these ancient figures. Second, by embodying wisdom in Torah, Ben Sira subtly frames all of his wisdom teaching as essentially the Torah of Moses. In this way, one might even argue that Ben Sira participates in Najman's Mosaic discourse.[12] Thus, even though he attaches his name to the book, Ben Sira has not escaped from the perceived necessity of having his own teaching rooted in the pre-exilic past.

The second book, Carol Newsom's *The Self as Symbolic Space*, examines the Serekh Ha-Yahad and the Hodayot from Qumran in an attempt to understand how these texts contributed to the formation of a sectarian identity among the members of the Qumran community.[13] Relying more thoroughly on Foucault than does Najman, Newsom offers

> a way of reading the sectarian texts that draws attention to how the discourse of the community creates an alternative figured world and self-identity, thereby critically engaging other forms of contemporary Judaism.[14]

In order to examine Second Temple Judaism as "a community of discourse," she appeals to the metaphor of culture as conversation. Yet, as she notes, this metaphor can be a troubled one as well, especially when "the language of a culture can no longer be used with automatic ease and unselfconsciousness."[15] Judaism exhibited some "indirect" instances of "a troubled relationship with language." So, for example, its nature as a multi-lingual religion

---

[10] Najman, *Seconding Sinai*, 14.

[11] For the term "scribe/sage," see R.A. Horsley and P. Tiller, "Ben Sira and the Sociology of the Second Temple," in *Second Temple Studies III: Studies in Politics, Class and Material Culture* (eds. P.R. Davies and J.M. Halligan, JSOTSup 340, Sheffield: Sheffield Academic Press 2002) 74-107.

[12] For the criteria of Mosaic discourse, see Najman, *Seconding Sinai*, 16-18.

[13] *The Self as Symbolic Space: Constructing Identity and Community at Qumran* (STDJ 52, Leiden: Brill 2004).

[14] Newsom, *Symbolic Space*, 21.

[15] Newsom, *Symbolic Space*, 5.

raises the issue as does the frequency with which the problem of false speech appears in the literature of this period. But, Newsom writes,

> The major index of an anxious relation to language, however, is simply the ubiquity of biblicizing language and genres in Second Temple literature. Echoes of the biblical text haunt virtually all of the new compositions of this period. It is the "super-adequacy" of the biblical idiom that authors of this period have to confront, a traditional language that both facilitates and authorizes their speech but at the same time dominates it. This is not to say that the literary production of Second Temple Judaism was not creative but to note that authors were always glancing over their shoulders at the speech of scripture. Although seldom made explicit, there is an element of the agonistic in the relation of new texts (rewritten Bible, pseudonymous compositions, commentaries, etc.) to scripture. The new compositions seek both to share in the cultural authority of scripture but also in some measure to co-opt it.[16]

Although Newsom employs this analysis in order to look at Qumran texts, we might see some of the same forces at work in Ben Sira. Whether it is a haunting or not, biblical idiom and the "biblical" text infuse much of Ben Sira's thought and language, and he employs both language and texts in order to authorize his own teaching, to shape it and to construct a world of meaning for his students. Although I am not pursuing in this paper the same ends that Newsom is for Qumran (a task that undoubtedly would require a book-length treatment), certainly Ben Sira's discourse creates a figured world for his disciples as they hear and absorb his teaching. But I have no doubt that however much the biblical texts and idiom might be seen to reflect a Jewish anxiety about language, Ben Sira clearly tried to co-opt them as we can see in the way he employs them throughout his book.

In Ben Sira's praise of important figures in Israel's history, all the way from Adam to Simon II, he would have had numerous opportunities to display his mastery of the textual traditions about them that he had inherited. Indeed, throughout this section he demonstrates just how much of a master of the texts he was. In this paper, however, while trying to take into account some of the issues that Carr, Najman and Newsom raise, I will not be analyzing Ben Sira's discourse per se. At this stage I am more interested in what might be called his intertextual relations, all the while acknowledging that discourse and intertextuality differ from one another.[17] I want to recognize at this juncture that we cannot read Ben Sira's book, *as a text*, as an independent and autonomous work, but that we have to read it in relation to other texts. Those "other" texts exerted pressure on Ben Sira's construction of each figure in the Praise of the Ancestors, and he did not, indeed could not, have created these vignettes outside of the influence of those texts. He constructed his pictures of these figures at least in part by manipulating, shaping,

---

[16] Newsom, *Symbolic Space*, 6.

[17] For the relationship between intertextuality and discourse, see Najman, *Seconding Sinai*, 15 and Newsom, *Symbolic Space*, particularly 85-87, 213-14, 246-49.

framing and interpreting the Israelite texts that transmitted their stories. I
also recognize that intertextual influences might come from within the book
itself. In general I have not looked too far beyond the figures I have chosen
for this paper, but the more one looks at the Praise of the Ancestors, the
more one can see how various aspects of Ben Sira's descriptions of them often stretch out into a network of intertextual relations with other parts of the
book. For reasons of space, analysis of these networks will have to wait until
another time. In order to outline some of the ways that Ben Sira executes all
these tasks, I have selected four examples of ancient Israelite heroes for
whose descriptions Ben Sira takes different tacks: Noah, Moses, Aaron and
David. Ben Sira's treatment of these men amply demonstrates that

1. there is a large web of intertextual relations that shapes Ben Sira's
    descriptions of his heroes and
2. his concern is not to reproduce the texts, but to carry out his own agen-
    das and ideological commitments using these textual traditions as his
    raw material.

I should make some comment about my use of the terms "text" and
"biblical" before moving on. When I use the word "text" in this paper, I do
not have in mind a picture of Ben Sira reading from a scroll; I am referring to
a particular content that has come to Ben Sira in some packaged form that
we could identify as, say, Genesis or Exodus. I do not have any certainty
about the particular form that Ben Sira would have encountered them. I
recognize that these texts had not achieved any final form in this period, but
the manuscripts discovered at Qumran do show an emerging consistency in
them, even if their textual forms have not yet stabilized. So, although I refer
to Genesis or Exodus, for example, and use chapter and verse numbers, this
is for our scholarly convenience and does not assume that Ben Sira posses-
sed anything like a "book" as we would know it. The term "biblical" is also a
term of convenience and denotes only a text that ended up in the Hebrew
Bible. I do not think that Ben Sira had a Bible in any modern sense of the
term. He certainly regarded certain works as authoritative, but I am not concerned here to compile some list of books that Ben Sira regarded as sacred or
canonical. I want to see if in the Praise of the Ancestors I can find evidence to
suggest that Ben Sira knew specific texts and that they provided a resource
for him as he constructed his Praise. I want to look for traces of the "considerable proficiency" that his grandson claims for him in the introduction to
his Greek translation and to see a bit of how this proficiency creates the
foundation for his own performance of the traditions about these pivotal
"historical" figures.

  By looking at how he used biblical sources, I am not implying that Ben
Sira only drew on biblical texts. He almost certainly was acquainted with a
much wider corpus than what we now call the Bible, and they also would
have been part of his network of intertextual connections. Randal Argall, for
example, has argued that Ben Sira knew non-biblical sources about the

patriarch Enoch, and I have tried to show that some of Sirach was intended to counteract claims made in some Enochic books.[18] Unfortunately, there are many cases where we simply do not know if Ben Sira used sources for the Praise of the Ancestors that were not accepted into the Jewish Bible, whereas we can potentially identify texts that later became part of the Hebrew biblical canon (whether or not Ben Sira considered them canonical), and we can ask questions about how those specific texts exerted pressure on what he eventually produced.

One of the difficult issues, however, when treating the book of Ben Sira is how to use the Hebrew texts that have survived. Except for the initial part of the section on Noah, which is the last verse preserved in the Masada manuscript, the Hebrew for the examples I have chosen survives in MS B from the Cairo Geniza and its marginal corrections. As all scholars who work on Sirach know, the Geniza manuscripts, while essentially transmitting Ben Sira's Hebrew, contain numerous corruptions and problems. The Greek translation of Ben Sira's grandson often reflects his grandfather's Hebrew, but it just as often does not provide access to that Hebrew terribly well.[19] Since the Geniza manuscripts are medieval copies of earlier exemplars, as a methodological point we probably should be suspicious of whether the scribes copying the text have harmonized Ben Sira's Hebrew to reflect biblical sources. After all, they most likely knew the biblical text very well themselves, and they might have recognized, and made clearer what they took to be allusions to it. They might even have created biblical allusions where there were none. This, of course, is a conundrum that we scholars cannot adequately solve. I would say, however, that, as we shall see, many of Ben Sira's uses of the text are quite subtle and clever, and I am not convinced that a medieval scribe copying what was by then a non-biblical text would worry much about biblical references. At any rate, I have worked from the methodological assumption that unless I have good reason to doubt it the extant Hebrew of MS B or its marginal corrections is most likely Ben Sira's. This is particularly true if the Greek translation supports the extant Hebrew. I will note textual problems and decisions as they bear on the interpretation of Ben Sira's text.

NOAH (44:17-18)[20]

The Hebrew of these two verses is relatively unproblematic. The Greek appears to have misread ובברּיחתו in v. 17d as ובעבורו (which appears in 17c).

[18] R.A. Argall, *1 Enoch and Sirach: A Comparative Literary and Conceptual Analysis of the Themes of Revelation, Creation and Judgment* (SBLEJL 8, Atlanta: Scholars Press 1995); B.G. Wright, "Putting the Puzzle Together: Some Suggestions Concerning the Social Location of the Wisdom of Ben Sira," in *Conflicted Boundaries in Wisdom and Apocalypticism* (ed. B.G. Wright III and L.M. Wills, SBLSS 35, Atlanta: SBL 2005) 89-112.

[19] Wright, *No Small Difference*.

[20] For much more detail on Ben Sira's treatment of Noah, see Matthias Weigold's contribution to this volume.

Ben Sira highlights Noah's righteousness, his preservation of the human race and the covenant that God made with him.[21] Both adjectives in 17a, צדיק and תמים, derive directly from Gen 6:9 and establish Noah's standing before God. Verse 17b appears to be Ben Sira's interpretive summary of the Flood story: "In a time of destruction, he was the continuator" (תחליף). The idea that because of Noah "there was a remnant" (היה שארית) could have originated in the Genesis narrative.[22] In 7.23 after the flood had destroyed all living things, "Only Noah was left (ישאר) and those with him in the ark." To invoke the idea of the remnant here develops Ben Sira's main point in 17b that Noah was the one who continued the human race.[23] In addition, it might recall prophetic notions that a remnant, which continues to be faithful to God, will be preserved in the midst of a faithless Israel. In this connection, notably Noah's righteousness qualifies him as a תחליף.

Verses 17d and 18 tell the result of the Flood story. Not surprisingly, Ben Sira uses מבול, the same term for flood found in Genesis throughout the Flood narrative. He relates that by a covenant, God made the flood cease. In the Genesis story, God actually makes two covenants with Noah. The first, in 6:18, gives Noah assurance that he, his family and the animals he takes with him will survive the impending destruction. With the second, in 9:8-17, God promises never again to send a flood to destroy the earth. In recalling this covenant, Ben Sira employs a number of terms drawn from the Genesis narrative. The covenant that Ben Sira mentions in 17d, using the expected ברית, almost certainly refers to the second biblical one, since he notes the "eternal sign" that God "established."[24] Although Ben Sira does not mention the rainbow explicitly, his phrase אות עולם probably intends it. In the Genesis narrative, however, the covenant is called "everlasting," but the sign is not. Ben Sira has exactly the reverse. He also uses the verb נכרת (reading with the margin of MS B), the technical term for making a covenant, further reinforcing that the sign/rainbow is the continuing sign of God's covenant. Thus, whereas Genesis has God establishing an eternal covenant with Noah whose sign is the rainbow, Ben Sira has the flood cease through a covenant, which is assured because God established an everlasting sign with Noah—a slight but significant rearrangement of the biblical text. Finally, v. 18b is almost identical to Gen 9:15. In the biblical verse, God promises that the waters "shall never again become a flood to destroy all flesh" (לשחת כל בשר).

---

[21] Noah appears as the first in a series of people with whom God instituted covenants.

[22] The Greek adds here "on the land," but there is no warrant for it in the Hebrew.

[23] Devorah Dimant observes that "Ben Sira ascribes to the motif of Noah as remnant an importance not found in the Genesis account" ("Noah in Early Jewish Literature," in *Biblical Figures Outside the Bible* [eds. M.E. Stone and T.A. Bergren, Harrisburg: Trinity Press International 1998] 126).

[24] The idea of covenant is very important to Ben Sira in the early portions of the Praise. See, for example, B. Mack, *Wisdom and the Hebrew Epic: Ben Sira's Hymn in Praise of the Fathers* (Chicago: University of Chicago Press 1985) 76-77.

Ben Sira reports that God made the covenant with Noah "in order never again to destroy all flesh" (לבלתי השחית כל בשר).

In a very short scope—less than two verses—Ben Sira summarizes the major elements of the biblical story about Noah. The biblical narrative is, of course, much longer than Ben Sira relates, but he alerts his reader to the precise features of the narrative that interest him by employing in his summary the important vocabulary of those scenes within the Noah story. In all but one colon, he uses vocabulary drawn from Genesis. Yet even that one colon, 17b, which I suggest represents Ben Sira's major interpretive understanding of Noah and a significant reason why he includes Noah in the Praise, gets qualified immediately after with biblical language that perhaps represents Ben Sira's explanation for his view of Noah. Noah as remnant constitutes Noah as continuator. So, the survival of the human race after the flood through Noah segues to God's selection of Abraham, whose legacy is covenant and blessing. Ben Sira both summarizes and retells the biblical story of Noah while maintaining points of contact with it. In that retelling, the story both authorizes and grounds Ben Sira's picture of Noah.

MOSES (44:23-45.5)

Moses is, of course, one of the central figures in Israelite history, and he appears in many Pentateuchal narratives. So, unlike the Noah story, which is fairly limited in scope compared to narratives featuring Moses, Ben Sira could not effectively summarize the entire story; he had to select which episodes he wanted to include in his praise. As one might guess, most of Ben Sira's praise of Moses focuses on the Exodus events and the giving of the Law, although he shapes them to fit his own agenda and themes.

Sirach 44:23-45:1 focuses on Moses' stature—of all the descendents of Jacob, he found favor with "all the living," and, as a result, both God and human beings loved him. The phrase מצא חן בעיני, a common Hebrew idiom for finding favor, occurs several times in the Exodus narrative, particularly in Exod 33:12-17 where it comprises a central theme. The passage culminates with God's affirmation to Moses, "I will do the very thing you have asked; for you have found favor in my sight (כי מצאת חן בעיני), and I know you by name."[25] Whether Ben Sira's claim that Moses found favor before all the living reflects any specific biblical passage or an independent use of the biblical idiom for his assessment of Moses' significance is not clear since the phrase is so common. At the end of 45:1, Ben Sira emphasizes that Moses' memory is blessed. While not a statement from biblical sources, having a blessed memory is a central theme in Sirach generally and in the Praise

---

[25] Earlier in Exod 11:3, we find that Moses was "very important in the land of Egypt, in the sight of Pharaoh's officials and in the sight of the people." The phrase here, גדול מאד עיני, parallels מצא חן בעיני, which characterizes the Hebrews' stature with the Egyptians.

specifically (cf. 44:8-10), and the verse brings the person of Moses into the orbit of Ben Sira's larger concerns.

Verse 2 transitions from Moses' stature to his deeds. Most commentators agree that the Greek along with MS B suggest a Hebrew of ויכבדהו כאלהים, "and he made him in glory like the angels/holy ones/God." While not an exact biblical phrase, Ben Sira almost certainly draws on Exod 7:1 where God says to Moses, "I will make you like God to Pharaoh" (ראה נתתיך אלהים לפרעה).[26] At least as far as Ben Sira is concerned, the qualities that endeared him to God also prompted God to grant him such an elevated status.

The last phrase in the verse, ויאמצהו במוראים "and he strengthened him with/in fearful things," probably points to the so-called plagues.[27] Although "fear" is a minor theme in the Exodus story, "fear of God" dominates Sirach. The plagues themselves are not called "fearful" in Exodus, but in Exodus 9 two verses might have prompted Ben Sira to connect these "fearful" acts with the fear of God. In 9:20, when hail is about to come to kill all the livestock, "[t]hose officials of Pharaoh who feared the word of the Lord hurried their slaves and livestock off to a secure place." Fear of God on the part of even the Egyptians resulted in safety from the disaster. Later in 9:30 Moses notes that Pharaoh does not yet "fear the Lord God." The plague of locusts follows as a result. Later at the Reed Sea, when the Pharaoh's charioteers drown in the returning waters, the people of Israel "feared the Lord and believed in the Lord and in his servant Moses." This passage, then, shows how Ben Sira the scribe could use his knowledge of the biblical text to evoke the story, but at the same time he could exploit Exodus in order to reinforce one of his major thematic interests.

Verse 3 follows up v. 2 by noting, "he wrought swift signs/miracles by his word." MS B is defective at this place, but the Greek σημεῖα almost certainly renders אותות, a translation equivalent found elsewhere in Sirach, and the word used of the plagues in Exodus, about which Moses warns Pharaoh in each case. The clause, ויחזקהו לפני מלך "and he strengthened him in the presence of Pharaoh," looks to be a very clever word play based on the Exodus story. The verb חזק is conspicuous in the Exodus narrative, since this is what God does to Pharaoh's heart—he "hardens" it (cf. Exod 9:12, 35; 10:20, 27). In a turnabout, Ben Sira claims that God "hardened" Moses before Pharaoh, probably referring to Moses' steadfast demand that the Hebrews go free. For Ben Sira, Moses is just as unyielding to Pharaoh as Pharaoh is to Israel's God.

---

[26] Some commentators also invoke Ps 8.6, and while that verse might be alluded to, the Exodus 7 passage is more directly relevant. If the Greek translation "angels" or "holy ones" is warranted, it would represent an early interpretation of this phrase. The phrase perhaps also alludes to Moses' shining face that resulted from his reception of the tablets of the Law in Exod 34:29, which later Jewish interpretation took to be the reflection of the divine Shekinah.

[27] The Greek adds "enemies" here probably misunderstanding the reference in the Hebrew.

Ben Sira moves immediately to the Sinai experience in 3c, which notes generally that God gave Moses commandments (ויצוהו) for the people. The sentence probably alludes to the giving of the Decalogue. If so, Ben Sira's language recalls Deuteronomy rather than Exodus. Three times in Deuteronomy's version of the Decalogue (5:12, 15, 16) the verb "to command" (צוה) appears within an injunction, and Deut 5:32, 33 lay heavy emphasis on the exact fulfillment of what God commanded. Verse 3d is defective in Hebrew, but it can be reconstructed with some certainty from the Greek. The revelation of God's glory (probably כבוד, Gk. δόξα) could derive from more than one place in the Exodus story. A likely episode is Exod 24:15-17 in which a cloud covered Mt. Sinai and "the glory (כבוד) of the Lord settled on the mountain." Moses subsequently entered the cloud and encountered God directly.[28] Also possible is a reference to Deut 5:22, the verse that immediately follows the giving of the Decalogue and to which Ben Sira probably alludes later in v. 5, which speaks of "the fire, the cloud and the thick darkness."

Verse 4 recalls 44:23. There Moses "found favor with God and humans"; in this passage, Ben Sira emphasizes Moses' direct access to God, a relationship that no ordinary human being can have. Moses is indeed remarkable, since God selected him out of "all flesh" because of this humility (ענוה) and faithfulness (אמונה). The same qualities get applied to Moses in the incident related in Numbers 12 when Miriam and Aaron speak out against him for marrying a Cushite woman. They ask, "Has the Lord spoken only through Moses?" God answers Moses' siblings apparently because, as the narrator tells us, "Moses was very humble (ענו), more so than any one else on earth" (12:3). In God's response to Miriam and Aaron, we hear that God speaks to prophets through visions and dreams, but not so with Moses. "He is entrusted (נאמן) with all my house. With him I speak face to face" (12:7). The connection is all the more striking since not only does Ben Sira use the same Hebrew roots to describe Moses, his claim of Moses' uniqueness—he was selected out of "all flesh"—reflects the claim in Numbers that Moses was more humble than any other human being "on the face of the earth."

Because of these qualities, Ben Sira tells us in v. 5 that Moses heard God's voice (קול) and went into the thick darkness (ערפל). He then notes that God gave into Moses' hand the commandments (מצוה), "the torah of life and understanding."[29] God's voice, Moses' entry into the cloud and the giving of commandments all come together in Deut 5:22, "These words the Lord spoke with a loud voice (קול) to your whole assembly at the mountain, out

---

[28] The idea that God's glory is in the cloud might also be transferred back in the story to the first moments at Sinai when the mountain is covered in clouds (Exodus 19). Ben Sira might also be alluding to Moses' descent and his shining face, the second time that this event could possibly be in the background.

[29] The Hebrew has the singular מצוה, while the Greek has a plural. The appositive, "torah of life and understanding" might suggest that the plural of the Greek fits better here.

of the fire, the cloud, the thick darkness (עֲרָפֶל), and he added no more. He wrote them on two stone tablets and gave them to me." Exodus 20:21 also notes specifically that Moses enters the darkness to speak with God, and later he descends with the tablets of the law.

From v. 3c through 5d we see a kind of chiastic structure over these bi-cola of a-b-c-b′-a′ (although it is not exact in the number of cola on either side). 3c (=a) refers to the giving of commandments followed in 3d (=b) by Moses' direct contact with God's "glory." Ben Sira's use of Numbers 12 in verse 4 (=c) sits in a rhetorically strategic position in that it provides the reasons why Moses can meet face to face with God. Verse 5a, b (=b′) then has Moses in direct contact with God through his voice and presence in the cloud. This encounter ends in 5c, d (=a′) with Moses receiving commandments "into his hand."

Even though Ben Sira's version of the events surrounding the giving of the tablets of the law in v. 5 shows similarities to both Exodus and Deuteronomy, his language about the law reflects Deuteronomy much more than Exodus. So, for example, the Hebrew term מצוה is more characteristic of Deuteronomy than of Exodus. Ben Sira calls the commandments תורת חיים ותבונה, a phrase that clearly echoes Deut 30:15–16 and 32:46–47, both of which connect the law and its fulfillment with life. Furthermore, the last two clauses of v. 5 reinforce Moses' teaching function: "to teach to Jacob his statutes, and his decrees and ordinances to Israel."[30] The three Hebrew terms חק, עדות and משפט in Sirach match exactly the prescriptions that Moses sets before the Israelites in Deut 4:44-45. Furthermore, the verb למד occurs in connection with Moses only in Deuteronomy (see in particular 4:1, 5).

For his section on Moses, then, Ben Sira drew on Exodus, Numbers and Deuteronomy. Moses stands out as a completely unique individual in the history of Israel because, on the one hand, God made Moses "like God." Ben Sira seems to understand this act as almost a quasi-divine transformation for the lawgiver, since unlike the biblical text where Moses' "god-like" status is relational—he is as God *to Pharaoh*—Ben Sira makes it existential, removing the relational aspects—in fact, "the king" is not mentioned for another three cola.[31] Yet, on the other hand, Moses has special access to the divine presence because he had the personal qualities or charisma to warrant such access. Moses finds favor "with all the living" because of the characteristics of humility and trustworthiness. He was responsible for communicating and teaching that fundamental element of Israel's relationship with God, the Torah. The clear agreement of Ben Sira's language with parallels in these three biblical books suggests that he is working with texts that he has thoroughly mastered. In making his claims about Moses, Ben Sira constantly provides touchstones to his textual sources, however much he has shaped them to fit his own purposes.

[30] In 36:16-17, Ben Sira also puts Israel and Jacob in parallel.
[31] On Exod 7:1 and the implications for Moses' status as "God" in Philo of Alexandria, see the discussion and secondary literature in P. Borgen, *Philo of Alexandria: An Exegete for His Time* (NovTSup 86, Leiden: Brill 1997) 201-05.

AARON (45:6-22)

In this section Ben Sira treats both Aaron specifically and the priesthood in general, and his description of Aaron sets up his later praise of Simon II (chap. 50), which has a close intertextual relationship with the praise of Aaron.[32] Ben Sira divides this section into two major parts, one on the priestly vestments and the other on the priesthood's cultic functions.

With v. 6 we are immediately faced with a difficult textual problem. The Greek adds ὅμοιον αὐτῷ ἀδελφὸν αὐτοῦ after Aaron's name. If the Greek accurately reflects Ben Sira's Hebrew and MS B is a corruption, then the verse should read, "He raised up a holy person like him, Aaron his brother out of the tribe of Levi." Simply following MS B we have, "He raised up a holy one, Aaron out of the tribe of Levi."[33] Whichever text we use, though, we are presented with two basic claims that are important for Ben Sira: (1) Aaron is holy and (2) he comes from the tribe of Levi. Aaron's Levite origins derive from Exodus, where he and Moses are said to be brothers from parents who are Levites (2:1; 4:14). The claim that Aaron is holy might originate in Ps 106:16, where he is called "the holy one of the Lord" (קדוש יהוה).

Ben Sira immediately identifies the basis upon which Aaron receives the priesthood. God established with him a חק עולם, an "eternal statute."[34] Exod 29:9 and 40:15 both call the priesthood "eternal." In 29:9 it is a חקת עולם that confers the priesthood, a phrase very close to Ben Sira's; in 40:15 it is simply כהנת עולם. Ben Sira's exact phrase occurs in two passages in Exodus, 29:28 and 30:21, where it refers to certain priestly prerogatives accorded to Aaron and his sons. In his use of the phrase, Ben Sira transfers the idea of a חק עולם from the prerogatives to the priesthood itself. The prerogatives accompany the priesthood, which Ben Sira takes as the proper subject of this statute.

Due to this eternal statute, God gave Aaron הוד, "splendor," and blessed him with glory (כבוד; reading the verb as ויאשרהו for MS B's וישרתהו). The noun הוד is not applied to Aaron in the biblical accounts, but the idea that Aaron receives glory might derive from Exod 28:2 and 40 where the vestments of the priesthood, to which Ben Sira will move in short order, are for "glorious adornment" (לכבוד ולתפארת). Ben Sira, then, subtly takes the notion of glory that is applied to the priestly vestments in Exodus and transfers it directly to Aaron. So, just as the priesthood is the "eternal

---

[32] For the treatment of Simon II and an assessment of his place in the Praise of the Ancestors, see O. Mulder, *Simon the High Priest in Sirach 50* (JSJSup 78, Leiden: Brill 2003). For a very detailed look at the textual relations of the section of Aaron, see P.C. Beentjes, *Jesus Sirach en Tenach* (Ph.D. dissertation; Katholieke Theologische Hogeschool Amsterdam 1981) esp. 175-99.

[33] See P.W. Skehan and A.A. Di Lella (*The Wisdom of Ben Sira* [AB 39, New York: Doubleday 1987] 509), who argue for the longer verse based on the Greek. M. Segal (*Spr bn-syr' hšlm* [Jerusalem: Bialik Foundation, 1958] 313) thinks the Syriac actually has the closest thing to the original, but its text is still longer than the Hebrew of MS B.

[34] The Greek is actually interpretive here referring to an "eternal covenant."

statute" and not the prerogatives that go along with it, Ben Sira claims that glory resides in Aaron not in his clothes.

Verse 7d is difficult to interpret. MS B(txt) contains the strange epithet בתועפות ראם, "with the horns of a wild ox," a phrase that occurs in Num 23:22 and 24:8. Perhaps, however, we should read with MS B(mg), which has תואר instead of ראם.[35] The verb יאזרהו, "he girded him," although it does not occur in biblical passages about Aaron, serves as the segue from 7c to the actual description of the priestly vestments.[36] Verse 8a, כליל תפארת וילבישהו, "and he clothed him in complete magnificence," continues the theme of the last two clauses. The verb לבש occurs several times in connection with Aaron's vestments in Exodus (29:5, 8; 40:13, 14), and the noun תפארת explicitly recalls Exodus 28:2 and 40.

Verse 8b presents another textual dilemma. The Greek σκεύεσιν probably presupposes the Hebrew בכלי, as Patrick Skehan and Alexander Di Lella and Moshe Segal note.[37] Whether that Hebrew originated from בגדי and has been further corrupted to בכבוד, which stands in the text now, as Skehan and Di Lella argue, or whether the present text ought to be accepted as Segal proposes is not entirely clear. What is certain is that neither the verb פאר nor the noun עוז are applied to Aaron or to his clothes in the biblical texts, but the terms reinforce Aaron's glory and magnificence, ideas that Ben Sira will apply later to his contemporary Simon II (cf. especially 50:5, 11). The list that follows, on the contrary, corresponds precisely with the biblical terms for articles of priestly clothing: מעיל, כתנות, מכנסים.

Now that his readers are no longer in doubt of Aaron's (and by extension his descendents') exceeding glory and thus his claim to the priesthood, Ben Sira moves in v. 9 to descriptions of the clothes themselves. As in Exod 28:31-33, Aaron's robe (מעיל) has bells and pomegranates around its hem, and just as in Exod 28:35, Ben Sira relates that the sound of the bells will be heard when Aaron ministers. Where Ben Sira and Exodus differ, however, is about the function of the bells and about where Aaron exactly serves. In Exod 28:35, the bells apparently let God know that Aaron is coming into or going out of the "holy place" (הקדש) so that he will not die. For Ben Sira, Aaron is heard more specifically in the "sanctuary" (דביר) "as a memorial for the sons of his people." The idea of a memorial (זכרון) is actually connected with the ephod in Exod 28:12, 29, specifically that Aaron bears the names of the "sons of Israel" on the ephod when he comes before God. For some reason that is still unclear to me, Ben Sira seems to be transferring that notion here, even though he does not discuss the ephod until v. 10c.

In the beginning of v. 10, the phrase בגדי קודש comes directly from Exod 28:2, 4, and the three materials that he lists—זהב, תכלת and ארגמן—derive

---

[35] The Greek translator does not really know what to do with this, and taking his cue from the verb he translates, "he clothed him with a robe of glory." See my discussion in *No Small Difference* (171-72) where I tentatively argue for the possible originality of MS B(txt).

[36] The last phrase in MS B is a duplicate and was not part of Ben Sira's text.

[37] Skehan and Di Lella, *Wisdom of Ben Sira*, 509; Segal, *Spr bn-syr'*, 313.

from Exod 28:5 as does the remark that they are skillfully worked (מעשה חשב).[38] Verse 10c gives three additional pieces of priestly clothing: the breastpiece of judgment (חשן משפט), the ephod (אפוד) and the robe?/girdle? (אזור). The first two items appear among the priestly vestments described in Exodus 28. The last is not part of the biblical list of Aaron's clothing. Skehan and Di Lella apparently assume that this is a reference to the sash (אבנט in Exod 28:2, 40), but that is by no means clear to me.[39]

Verse 11 continues from the preceding verse with the materials that were used to make these garments. The first is שני תולעת, "crimson thread," the same material found all over in the Exodus descriptions, both in the prescriptions given to Moses and in the execution of them, except that Ben Sira reverses the terms. This thread is made by a weaver (מעשה אורג), a phrase identical to Exod 39:22, 27. The next two clauses describe the stones that are set in the ephod. While the phrase "precious stones" (אבני חפץ) is not found with respect to the ephod, the engraved signets (פתוחי חותם) are. The Hebrew of MS B and the Greek of v. 11c are completely different and too difficult to reconstruct in such a way as to be useful for my purposes here. V. 11d, however, specifically mentions the function of the stones as a memorial "for the number of the tribes of Israel" (cf. above v. 8; see Exod 28:21 for the term שבט). Ben Sira's description of the stones abbreviates the longer account found in Exodus 28 and 39, and consequently, as we have already seen, he plants biblical vocabulary in the midst of his own summarizing comments, in this case terms like, "tribes," "remembrance," "stones."

In verse 12, Ben Sira reprises his picture of the glorious high priest. He begins with the golden crown, עטרת פז, a term not used at all of Aaron's vestments in the biblical text, but one that might betray Ben Sira's support for the ideal of a high priestly ruler of Israel.[40] Ben Sira envisions this crown as being upon the מצנפת, and there is a plate (ציץ) on which is engraved, according to Exod 28:36, "Holy to the Lord," although Ben Sira does not report the words of the inscription. The end of v. 12 returns to a list of adjectives meant to emphasize the amazing sight created by the high priest as he officiates. This vision relates to Ben Sira's later description of Simon II as he officiates in the Temple, and it reinforces Ben Sira's support of the

---

[38] Does the reference to Aaron as holy in v. 6 have any connection with applying an adjective used of his clothes to Aaron himself as we saw above?

[39] Skehan and Di Lella, *Wisdom of Ben Sira*, 512.

[40] For an argument on this point, see my paper "Ben Sira on Kings and Kingship" (paper delivered at the conference "Representations of Hellenistic Monarchy in Hellenistic Culture," Somerville College, Oxford University, March 24-26, 2003). See also M. Himmelfarb, "The Wisdom of the Scribe, the Wisdom of the Priest, and the Wisdom of the King According to Ben Sira," in *For a Later Generation: The Transformation of Tradition in Israel, Early Judaism and Early Christianity* (eds. R.A. Argall, et al., Harrisburg: Trinity Press International 2000) 89-99.

Aaronid priesthood and the high priest's position as the one who rules
Israel.[41]

In v. 13, Ben Sira makes the transition from the high priest's vestments to
his cultic service via a sweeping statement about the high priestly office
using the vehicle of these vestments to do it. The Hebrew of the verse is
fragmentary but seems to represent Ben Sira's ideology of the priesthood in
his own time. He probably relies, however, on a statement like that in Exod
29:29–34, which explicitly limits the high priestly garments to Aaron and his
sons. Interestingly, in the Exodus version of the regulations for the
ordination sacrifice, we find that no "outsider" (זר) can eat of it. Ben Sira has
adopted this term in order to indicate that no one but Aaron's descendents
may wear the priestly vestments, thereby clarifying who can legitimately
hold the high priestly office. At the same time he transports the ancient
tradition of the priesthood into his own time, in a sense skipping the generations from Aaron to his own day. "Before him no one had these, and no outsider (זר) has ever worn them, except his sons alone and his descendents for
all generations."

We now turn to the high priest's cultic functions. Verse 14 outlines the
מנחה or daily cereal offering in which half is burnt in the morning and the
other half in the evening (described in Lev 6:19–23). According to Leviticus,
which Ben Sira seems to follow, the offering is to be "regular" (תמיד). In
agreement with the language of Leviticus, Ben Sira prescribes that the sacrifice is to be completely burned (כליל תקטר).

Even though for Ben Sira an Aaronid priesthood is the only legitimate
one, he further grounds it in Mosaic authority. He has already employed
Mosaic texts to authorize his description of the glorious stature of Aaron and
his descendents, and now he appeals not to textual authority, but to the
"historical" Moses who ordained Aaron. Of course, here as well, Ben Sira
adapts the textual tradition he has inherited. In v. 15, he notes that Moses
ordained (ימלא את ידו), using the technical phrase found in Exodus 29. The
description of Moses' actual ordination of Aaron comes from Leviticus 8 in
which he invests Aaron with the priestly clothing and anoints him with oil.
Ben Sira's version has Moses anointing Aaron with oil, qualifying it with the
adjective "holy" (הקדש). Ben Sira then goes beyond what we read in the
Pentateuch when he says that God made an "eternal covenant" (ברית עולם)
with Aaron and his descendents "for the days of heaven."[42] Never does God
make an eternal "covenant" with Aaron, although in several places, as we
have seen, the priesthood and its prerogatives constitute a חק עולם. Of
course, God does make such a covenant with Phinehas, to which Ben Sira

---

[41] On Ben Sira's views of the priesthood, see Olyan, "Ben Sira's Relationship,"
Wright, "Fear the Lord" and "Ben Sira and the Book of the Watchers on the Legitimate
Priesthood," in *Intertextual Studies in Ben Sira and Tobit* (eds. J. Corley and V. Skemp,
CBQMS 38, Washington: Catholic University of America 2005) 241-54.

[42] The phrase is found in Deut 11:21 and Ps 89:30, but I am not sure if Ben Sira
would have taken the phrase from there or not. Himmelfarb, "Wisdom of the Scribe,"
95 argues that it originates in Psalm 89.

refers in 45:24. Here he retrojects the covenantal connection backwards in time, and thus he equates the "statute" with the "covenant." This rewriting strikes me as part of Ben Sira's ideological program to create the foundation for an Aaronid priesthood whose right it is to serve at God's altar and to hold the high priesthood.[43] As priest, Ben Sira says that Aaron and his descendents will serve (לשרת) God and "bless his people with his name." With respect to the last clause, Ben Sira might well be drawing on his personal experience (as we perhaps see in chapter 50), but just as likely he has two biblical passages in mind. In Lev 9:22-23 Aaron blesses the people as he does in v. 15, but perhaps more significantly in Num 6:23–27 Aaron *and his sons* invoke God's name (cf. 50:20)—"So shall *they* put my name upon the people of Israel, and I will bless them"—which brings the focus back to the importance of the priesthood belonging to Aaron's descendents down to Ben Sira's time.

Sirach 45:16 begins with a similar claim to one we saw above with Moses—God chose Aaron from all the living, and as with Moses, only God's election permits him to draw near (להגיש) to God to offer sacrifices. The verb נגש is clearly a technical term for the priest approaching the altar, and it occurs frequently in Exodus, Leviticus, Numbers and Deuteronomy. The words that Ben Sira employs for the sacrifices offered by Aaron are also technical: עלה ("burnt offering"; see Leviticus 1); חלבים ("fat offerings"; see Leviticus 3);[44] להקטיר ריח ניחח ואזכרה ("to burn sweet smelling incense as a memorial"; almost an exact replica of Lev 2:9); לכפר ("to atone"; see Lev 16:34 on the day of atonement).[45]

The language of v. 17, in which God gives Aaron מצות, as he did Moses, also confers authority on Aaron over statutes (חוק) and judgment (משפט), and subsequently he is charged to "teach his people statues (חק), and ordinances (משפט) to the children of Israel." Teaching language is familiar from Deuteronomy and resembles Ben Sira's statement that Moses was to teach Israel חקיו ועדותיו ומשפטיו—in both cases utilizing the verb למד. Deuteronomy also charges priests to teach, specifically in 33:10 where Levi is commanded to "teach Jacob thy ordinances (משפטיך) and Israel thy law (תורתך)." Oddly enough, while this and other places in Deuteronomy establish a teaching and decision-making function for the levitical priests, Ben Sira never mentions the levitical priesthood while favoring an Aaronid one. Yet, by explicitly pointing out in v. 6 that Aaron was of the tribe of Levi, he can exploit the language of Deuteronomy by attaching the priestly teaching function to Aaron in order to further his own priestly ideology.

Verses 18-19 relate the rebellion of Korah found in Numbers 16-17. Ben Sira narrates an abbreviated version of the story that is full of interesting interpretations. He begins by saying, "Strangers (זרים) burned with anger

---

[43] On Ben Sira and an Aaronid priesthood, see Olyan, "Ben Sira's Relationship."

[44] The Greek misreads this word as אלהים.

[45] The idea of atoning for Israel might be broader than any specific ritual, however. See, for example, Ben Sira's comments on Phinehas who "atoned for the people of Israel" (45:23).

(וַיָּחֵרוּ) against him (i.e. Aaron)." This clause sets up Ben Sira's entire reading of the story. First, in Numbers Korah, Dathan and Abiram rise up against both Moses and Aaron; in Sirach only Aaron is the object of their opposition. Ben Sira attributes their rebellion to jealousy, a motivation he supplies. The phrase עֲדַת קֹרַח in 18b derives from Num 16:40 (17:5 in MT) toward the end of the narrative.

Second, the verb "to burn with anger" is actually used of Moses in the biblical story (Num 16:15) and not of the rebellious group. Ben Sira creates an interesting parallel in his text when he says that the rebellious three were angry with "wrath and anger" (אַף). When he speaks of their destruction (v. 19), it happens because God "saw it and became angry" (וַיִּתְאַנַּף). God then destroys them in his "burning anger" (בַּחֲרוֹן אַפּוֹ). The language of burning sets the stage for Ben Sira's recounting of the punishment. In Num 16:35 fire went out from the Lord and consumed the rebels who were offering incense. Ben Sira explicitly notes this punishment by fire as God's response. In what is perhaps an allusion to the opening of the earth, which swallowed up Korah and his entourage, Ben Sira says that God wrought a "sign" (אוֹת).

Third, the noun זֵר parallels Ben Sira's previous use of this term in v. 13 with respect to the Aaronid priestly garments. In this case it probably derives from Num 16:40 (17:5 in MT), where at the end of the Korah episode, Eleazar fashions a bronze covering for the altar as a "reminder to the people of Israel that no stranger (זָר), who is not a descendent of Aaron, should draw near to burn incense before the Lord lest he become like Korah and his company." So, no "stranger/outsider" may wear the priestly vestments, and strangers who presume to usurp the cultic prerogative of the Aaronid priests risk God's anger. By recalling the punishment suffered by Korah, we might speculate that, given the narrowed focus on Aaron in this passage, Ben Sira might be issuing a warning to any potential contemporary "usurper" of the priesthood (at least from his perspective).

As a result of this episode, according to Ben Sira, God gave Aaron glory (v. 20). This verse comes between Ben Sira's version of the rebellion of Korah and his report of Aaron's inheritance. Interposed between these two episodes in the text of Numbers is the story of Aaron's staff that blooms. Perhaps Ben Sira means to allude to that story via the idea of Aaron receiving glory, but this is by no means assured. Verses 20b-22 almost certainly rely on Numbers 18, which delineate the inheritance of Aaron and his descendents, even to the point that, except for his mention of the bread of the presence (cf. Lev 24:5-9), Ben Sira follows the order of the biblical text in which the list of the offerings that are due Aaron precedes the denial of any land to him. So, Ben Sira relates that the "holy offerings" (תְּ[רוּמֹת] קֹדֶשׁ; cf. Num 18:19) belong to Aaron. He notes that the offerings from the fire (אִשֶּׁי, cf. Num. 18:9) will be Aaron's food. Indeed, Ben Sira calls these things a "gift" (מַתָּנָה), the same word used in Num 18:7 to characterize the Aaronid priesthood. Aaron does not inherit land, however. In denying Aaron this legacy, Ben Sira agrees with Num 18:20, a verse he echoes closely, if we can reconstruct the missing elements in the Hebrew text with some degree of probability.

Num 18:20:

בארצם לא תנחל וחלק לא יהיה לך בתוכם
אני חלקך ונחלתך בתוך בני ישראל

Sir 45:22:

אך [בארצם or perhaps ארץ העם] לא ינחל ובתוכם לא יחלק נחלה
אשי יי⁴⁶ ח[ל]קו נח[ל]תו בתוך בנ[י] ישראל

To review briefly the section on Aaron, Ben Sira draws on quite a range of biblical texts in order to create his ideology of an Aaronid priesthood as the only legitimate Israelite priesthood. He repeatedly reiterates that Aaron was glorious, both in his vestments and as a result of the Korah rebellion, a passage that makes a clear distinction between Aaron and his sons and "outsiders" who are illegitimate. Ben Sira probably even takes passages linked to the Levites and applies them to Aaron. Throughout this section, Ben Sira carefully lays the groundwork for his praise of Simon II in chapter 50. I am also relatively convinced that these statements reflect contemporary issues concerning the priesthood that Ben Sira thought he had to address, but even though his ideological commitments seem pretty clear, the specific circumstances to which he was responding are less certain.

DAVID (47:2–11)

The importance of the priesthood to Ben Sira conditioned my choice of Aaron for this paper, and so Ben Sira's view of kingship motivated my choice of David. Ben Sira's assessment of the monarchy bears directly on his representation of Simon II, whom he constructs as ideal priest and ruler. In that light David would be a potentially illuminating figure, even though Ben Sira is generally ambivalent about the institution of the monarchy.[47] Moreover, looking at Ben Sira's praise of David allows us to examine a figure whose biblical traditions fall outside of the Pentateuch.

After his brief note in v. 1 that Nathan prophesied during the time of David, Ben Sira begins his discussion of the king in v. 2 by employing sacrificial imagery, which frames the section in cultic language, which is more at home in a priestly context than a royal one:[48] "Like the choice fat lifted up from the sacred offerings, so was David from Israel." The phrase

---

[46] Here we encounter a textual difficulty. The Greek has αὐτὸς γάρ, which makes God the portion of Israel as in the Numbers text. The Hebrew of MS B continues with the theme of the verse that the offerings are Aaron's inheritance. Either the Hebrew is corrupt, and it originally resembled Num 18:20 where God is Aaron's portion, or the Greek ignores the emphasis of the Hebrew on the offerings and aligns the text with the verse in Numbers. The reconstructions here are those of Segal, who recognizes the similarity with Numbers.

[47] See Wright, "Ben Sira on Kings" and Himmelfarb, "The Wisdom of the Scribe."

[48] See G.G. Xeravits, "The Figure of David in the Book of Ben Sira," *Henoch* 23 (2001) 29.

"to lift up the fat" (רום חלב) from an offering occurs in Leviticus 4:8, 19 and represents separating out the best portion of the sacrifice. Thus is David the best of all of Israel. Additionally, the verb is actually used of David in Ps 89:20.[49] What strengthens the possibility that Ben Sira relied on this Psalm in this place is that the end of the section on David in v. 11 seems to be drawn both from Psalm 89 and from 2 Samuel 7 (see below).

Ben Sira's report of David's confrontations with lions and bears forms the transition to his retelling of the Goliath episode; as such it probably alludes to the justification that David gives Saul in 1 Sam 17:34-36 for his willingness to fight the giant.[50] He relates that whenever a lion or a bear threatened his father's sheep, he would "catch it by the jaw, strike it down and kill it." David's response to Saul in 1 Samuel, however, gives no indication of any playfulness on David's part. For Ben Sira, not only did David overcome these ferocious beasts, he made sport of them, and thus he magnifies David's stature (an intent we see elsewhere in the Praise, cf. Moses and Aaron above).

Verses 4-5 relate David's encounter with the Gittite giant. Ben Sira calls Goliath גבור, as does 1 Sam 17:51, and he says that David was "in his youth" (בנעוריו). The Samuel narrative throughout identifies David as a נער (see, for example, 2 Sam 17:33). Ben Sira's summary of the Goliath story features similar language to the biblical text, but it comes in explanations of the consequences of actions that in the Bible are intended or about to happen. So, in 1 Sam 17:46, David says to Goliath, "This very day the Lord will deliver you into my hand, and I will strike you down (והכיתך)." In Ben Sira's retelling, he gives the result, while utilizing the same verb: "In his youth he struck down (הכה) a giant." In 1 Sam 17:26, David asks, "What shall be done for the man who kills this Philistine and takes away the reproach (חרפה והסיר) from Israel?" Ben Sira in 4b reports the result: "And he took away the reproach (ויסר חרפת) of the people." Although Ben Sira uses the same term for slingshot, קלע, as the biblical story, the entirety of 4c, d looks to be his moral indictment of Goliath's hubris: "When his hand let fly the sling and he shattered the pride of Goliath." This condemnation of Goliath also reflects Ben Sira's clear distaste for the Philistines, which he exhibits elsewhere (cf. 47:7; 50:25-26)

Verse 5 veers away from the story as it is preserved in the MT and looks like Ben Sira's own summarizing interpretation of the longer narrative. 1 Samuel describes Goliath as a "man of war" (איש מלחמה), whereas Ben Sira calls him איש יודע מחלמות. Ben Sira says that David "called upon God Most

---

[49] See Skehan and Di Lella, *Wisdom of Ben Sira*, 525. See also T.R. Lee, *Studies in the Form of Sirach 44-50* (SBLDS 75, Atlanta: Scholars Press 1986) 214.

[50] I recognize that the MT of 1 and 2 Samuel have many textual problems of the their own and that Ben Sira might well have known a very different version of these stories. In his summary of the story, however, it seems to me that Ben Sira uses language that could have been found in others versions as well. On this passage, see Xeravits ("Figure of David," 30), who calls it the "lion-bear affair" and notes the occurrence of the text in the Syriac Apocryphal Psalms.

High," but he actually never prays in the narrative; he simply claims in his speech to Goliath that God will enable him to defeat the giant. As a result of his trust in God, David was able to overcome this man and "lift up the horn of his people." While none of this vocabulary occurs in the biblical story, the idea of raising or breaking one's "horn" is clearly an important motif in this section.

The Greek and Hebrew of Sirach differ at the beginning of v. 6. The Greek has the generic "they sang of him," whereas the Hebrew gives a specific group, "daughters" (בנות), who did the singing. The Hebrew of MS B is close to the MT, which has "women" (נשים) singers.[51] Whoever Ben Sira imagined singing, he employed the same verb, ענה, as the Samuel narrative, and he also supplies the same number of David's vanquished foes, "tens of thousands" (רבבה). The last clause of v. 6 summarizes David's numerous military campaigns. The claim that David "wiped out the enemy on every side" (הכניע צר מסביב)[52] does not occur of him in the biblical texts, but one wonders with Skehan and Di Lella if this might not be a reference to 1 Sam 14:47: "He fought against his enemies on every side (וילחם סביב בכל איביו) —against Moab, against the Ammonites, against Edom, against the kings of Zobah and against the Philistines."[53] While the actual wording differs between Sirach and 1 Samuel, it is similar enough. One other matter inclines me to think this connection possible here. The last member of the enemies' list in 1 Samuel is the Philistines, and Ben Sira singles them out in the very next clause. Furthermore, the same coalition of enemies is found in 1 Chron 18:1, which employs the same verb as Ben Sira, כנע "to subdue," to describe David's victorious campaigns against the Philistines. After defeating the Philistines in Chronicles he takes on Moab, king Hadadezer of Zobah and in chapter 19 the Ammonites.

Ben Sira's remarks about the Philistines in 7b and c find no biblical parallels. He notes that David waged war against these enemies of Israel and "broke (שבר) their horn until today." This last phrase creates two intertextual parallels within Ben Sira's text. First, it recalls the statement in v. 4 that David "shattered (שבר) the pride of Goliath." Second, it forms a matching opposite with Ben Sira's assessment of v. 5 that David's killing of Goliath "raised the horn of his people."

In v. 8 Ben Sira segues from David the military man toward David the liturgical reformer. He says of the king: "In everything he did he gave praises to God Most High giving glory. With his whole heart he loved his Maker." David as a man of prayer is much more the picture of the Chronicler than of the Deuteronomist, and Ben Sira may have taken this view of David from Chronicles, if he knew these books. Skehan and Di Lella

---

[51] I would be more inclined in favor of the Greek here if the Hebrew had matched the biblical account. That it does not suggests a more complicated relationship between Hebrew and Greek than simple textual corruption.

[52] Ben Sira also refers to "enemies on every side" in 46:5 about Joshua. Unfortunately, the Hebrew is not extant in that place,

[53] Skehan and Di Lella, *Wisdom of Ben Sira*, 526.

suggest that the phrase "he loved his Maker with his whole heart" is a reference to Deut 6:5.[54]

Verses 9–10 are fragmentary in MS B and in a different order from the Greek. Ben Sira's remark in v. 9, that David established "stringed music" (נגינות) before the altar and "sweet melody" (מזמור), might well depend on the traditional superscriptions to the Psalms, many of which contain these terms. The Hebrew is not extant in v. 10a, b, but the Greek makes clear that Ben Sira at least was familiar with the tradition found in 1 Chronicles 23 that David organized the priestly services in the Temple, a task he could accomplish because of the peace his military campaigns had achieved. These verses resume the emphasis on Temple worship that Ben Sira established at the beginning of the section (v. 2).[55]

Ben Sira ends his praise of David with what appears to be an allusion to the Bathsheba incident: "The Lord forgave his sin." V. 11b, "He raised up his horn forever," probably goes with 11c and d, which refers to the promise of dynastic rule that Nathan gave to David in 2 Samuel 7. In fact, 11c, d combine a number of elements from 2 Samuel 7 and Psalm 89, both of which treat the divine establishment of a Davidic dynasty. For the phrase "lifted up his horn" with respect to David, see Ps 89:18, 25 as well as v. 5. According to Ben Sira, God gave to David a חק ממלכת, "statute of kingship," a phrase that does not occur in either biblical passage and appears to be Ben Sira's own articulation of what God promised to David. For the phrase "established (הכין) his throne" in v.11d, see 2 Samuel 7.[56]

Although not a covenant in 2 Sam 7, God's promise to David does take the form of a covenant (ברית) in a number of other places. On his deathbed in 2 Sam 23:5, God's promise becomes a covenant in David's mouth, and Ps 89:3 and 28 refer to a covenant between God and David. Of course, Ben Sira only mentions a covenant with David in 45:25 at the end of the section on Phinehas, where he employs it as a contrast to the priestly covenant made with Aaron, in effect downplaying the Davidic covenant in favor of the priestly one.[57] Géza Xeravits has also argued that despite the reference to a covenant with David in 45:25, by not mentioning the covenant in 47:1-11, by qualifying David's "horn" as eternal in v. 11, and by leaving unqualified the "statute of kingship," Ben Sira actually does not extend God's promise of a throne to any succeeding dynasty.[58]

---

[54] Skehan and Di Lella, *Wisdom of Ben Sira*, 526.

[55] Xeravits, "Figure of David," 32. He (36-38) argues against those who see messianic references in the section on David. I agree with him that arguments in support of messianism here are weak.

[56] Psalm 89:4 has the verb "establish," but it refers to David's descendents: "I will establish (אכין) your descendents forever, and I will build (בניתי) your throne." For a history of interpretation of the promise in 2 Samuel 7, see W.M. Schniedewind, *Society and the Promise to David: The Reception History of 2 Samuel 7:1-17* (New York: Oxford University Press 1999).

[57] Himmelfarb, "Wisdom of the Scribe," 96.

[58] Xeravits, "Figure of David," 35.

Furthermore, by invoking the promise to David in this last verse, Ben Sira creates a sort of inclusio for the entirety of 47:1-11. In 47:1 the prophet Nathan, who was active in David's time, introduces the section, and v. 11 highlights Nathan's two most conspicuous prophetic pronouncements: (1) his confrontation with David about the sin with Bathsheba and his announcement that God had forgiven that sin and (2) his revelation of the promise of monarchical rule in 2 Samuel 7.

In his praise of David, Ben Sira most likely drew from a variety of places in his textual repertoire. He focuses on several central themes: David's military prowess, his love of God, especially as expressed through his composition of psalms, his impact on the Temple service and his kingship. Yet, by mentioning his kingship only once in these eleven verses, Ben Sira essentially relegates the monarchy to a subsidiary position. David was a beloved figure and the first king, and Ben Sira really cannot get around that. The monarchy, however, presents a bit more of a problem, since there was no king in Ben Sira's time. Interestingly Ben Sira mentions David twice more (48:15 and 49:4) in connection with his righteous behavior (apparently despite his tryst with Bathsheba), but he does not express any nostalgia for a Davidic monarch. In fact, he seems perfectly content with a high priest who fulfills the role of king.[59] Indeed, in 49:4 where Ben Sira notes that of all the kings only David, Hezekiah and Josiah were righteous, he also observes, "all of them [i.e. the Davidic kings] were great sinners." As a result of their abandonment of the Law, God "gave their power (קרנם) to another and their glory to a foreign nation," a transparent reference to the Babylonians who ended the Davidic dynasty. The passage also draws the reader back to the section on David by the use of קרן. David's "horn" might be raised forever, but that of his descendents was forfeit due to their wickedness.

CONCLUSIONS

As I began to work on the Praise of the Ancestors for this paper, I was not entirely certain of the direction I would take. Because of the three studies that I discussed above, I have thought a lot more about texts, what forms they took and how they functioned and were employed in antiquity. All too often, I know that my modern conceptions of a text have exerted too much influence on how I think about ancient texts. As a result I have often swung the pendulum too far in the direction of being extremely, maybe even overly, suspicious of modern claims that ancient authors had in mind any specific texts. This suspicion was reinforced in my Ph.D. dissertation, however, when I looked at what relation if any the translation of Ben Sira's grandson had with the Septuagint. In that study I was reacting to Rudolph Smend's imaginative construction of a translator sitting with text in hand

---

[59] For more argumentation, see Wright, "Ben Sira on Kings" and Himmelfarb, "The Wisdom of the Scribe."

consulting individual passages as they came up, and I found in my work that this picture made no sense for Ben Sira's grandson.[60]

The Praise of the Ancestors, and particularly the examples that I have examined in this paper, however, show that Ben Sira certainly knew the Israelite textual tradition extraordinarily well. The specific details of the language and contexts in the Praise I think demonstrate that much at least. We cannot, though, attribute every place where our Hebrew texts reflect biblical passages to some later harmonization or corruption. That effort would strain credulity. The passages I have examined here lend credence to a model of ancient learning that suggests that ancient scribes had mastered their textual inheritance, that indeed they were "inscribed on their minds." In his own performance, Ben Sira shows himself to be a gifted oral communicator. Although his teaching became enshrined in a "book" very early (perhaps/probably by Ben Sira himself) since his grandson certainly translated a written version into Greek, the language and forms of his teaching indicate that he most likely delivered it orally. He built his Praise of the Ancestors on the foundation of the Israelite textual tradition that he had learned. Yet, he had his own interests, agendas and ideological commit-ments, and he used those texts that he had mastered as resources for pur-suing them. They provided the raw material for his work. However "ago-nistic" (to use Newsom's term) Ben Sira's relationship was to the "biblical" texts, they dominated his own work at the same time that he strove to co-opt them for his own purposes. And yet, I think with Najman that Ben Sira, were we able to ask, would have seen his book as an "authentic expression" of those texts. His grandson perhaps said it best in the Prologue to his Greek translation when he says that when his grandfather "had acquired consi-derable proficiency in them [i. e. the Law, the Prophets and the other books], he was himself also led to write something pertaining to instruction and wisdom, so that by becoming familiar also with his book those who love learning might make even greater progress in living according to the law."

Ben Sira certainly participated in a whole range of conversations in his contemporary world, and he taught young men who would go out and be part of that world. Through various devices Ben Sira tried to ensure that his students would accept his values and ideas as their own.[61] Identifying the possible texts he knew constitutes only a preliminary step in any attempt to discover how he performed the texts, and even more importantly to work out how he constructed his own discourse(s) that created the figured world in which he and his students lived and that left a legacy through both his words and his students' lives. How does his use of texts reveal his interests? How does the way he manipulates the language of his texts provide clues to

---

[60] R. Smend, *Die Weisheit der Jesus Sirach erklärt* (Berlin: Georg Reimer 1906) LXIII cited in Wright, *No Small Difference*, 120.

[61] For one analysis of how he does this, see B.G. Wright, "From Generation to Ge-neration: The Sage as Father in Early Jewish Literature," in *Biblical Traditions in Trans-mission: Essays in Honour of Michael A. Knibb* (eds. C. Hempel and J.M. Lieu, JSJSup 111, Leiden: Brill 2006) 309-32.

his ideological commitments and concerns? In this paper I have only touched on this fascinating issue, since not only does Ben Sira take interpretive approaches to individual figures, but his understanding of these ancient worthies fits into several larger themes in the Praise of the Ancestors and indeed in the book as a whole. Ben Sira was situated at a very significant moment in Judean history, and if we pay close attention to the larger discourse of his book, we find that his use of texts opens one window not only into his own views, but also into the broader concerns of Jews, or at least a particular segment of elite Jews, in the early second century BCE.

BEN SIRA 44:19-23—THE PATRIARCHS
TEXT, TRADITION, THEOLOGY

Pancratius C. Beentjes
(Faculty of Catholic Theology, Utrecht)

INTRODUCTION

Compared to other portrayals of biblical heroes by Ben Sira, the presentation of the Patriarchs is quite remarkable. For within the "Praise of the Famous" (Sir 44-50), Abraham, Isaac, and Jacob are given only a dozen lines (Sir 44:19-23). As far as I am aware, till now this passage has either been investigated from a mere *text critical* point of view[1] or with attention only to Abraham.[2] A full investigation into this small passage, however, will reveal that Ben Sira's portrayal of the Patriarchs contains quite a lot of important and intriguing aspects.

TEXT

The Hebrew text of this passage is found only in MS B.[3] It belonged to a rather extensive section of MS B (Sir 40:9-49:11) that at the time of its discovery consisted of nine leaves and had been acquired for the Bodleian Library, Oxford, by professor Archibald H. Sayce.[4] The Hebrew text of these

---

[1] Especially by F.V. Reiterer, *"Urtext und Übersetzungen" Sprachstudie über Sir 44,16-45,26 als Beitrag zur Sirachforschung* (ATSAT 12, St. Ottilien: EOS Verlag 1980) 94-120. The article by H.V. Kieweler, "Abraham und der Preis der Väter bei Ben Sira," *Amt und Gemeinde* 37 (1986) 70-72 to a high degree is a *meditation* upon Sir 44:19-23.

[2] G. Sauer, "Der Abraham-Gestalt im 'Lob der Väter.' Auswahl und Intention," *Wiener Jahrbuch für Theologie* 1 (1996) 387-412.

[3] Unfortunately, the text of the Masada Scroll ends with Sir 44:17c. See Y. Yadin, *The Ben Sira Scroll from Masada* (Jerusalem: The Israel Exploration Society and The Shrine of the Book 1965) [= *Masada VI. Yigal Yadin Excavations 1963-1965, Final Reports* (Jerusalem: Israel Exploration Society and The Hebrew University of Jerusalem 1999) 151-225].

[4] The nine leaves were given the signature: "Ms.Heb.e.62." A.H. Sayce acquired for the Bodleian Library some of the Elephantine papyri as well. See B. Porten, "Elephantine Papyri," *ABD* 2 (1992) 445-55 (esp. 446).

nine leaves was published for the first time in January 1897,[5] together with
two leaves which already in 1896 had been identified by Solomon Schechter
as being the Hebrew text of Sir 39:15b-40:8.[6]

In MS B—just as in MSS E, F, and the Masada Scroll—the Hebrew text is
arranged in a stichometrical way: each verse or half of a verse is written in
two distinct columns, which are clearly marked off by a rather wide blank
space.[7]

As far as the Hebrew text of Sir 44:19-23 is concerned, there are some
particularities to be mentioned:

1. The Hebrew text of the passage under discussion has two small lacunae, about the reconstruction of which there can be no doubt:

Sir 44:21a   בש[בו]עה

Sir 44:21e   [מ]ים

2.The passage dealing with the Patriarchs has three *marginal readings* (Bm.)
which will be discussed in due course:

Sir 44:19b (MS B)	מום	(Bm.)	דופי
Sir 44:22a (MS B)	בן	(Bm.)	כן
Sir 44:23a (MS B)	ויכננהו בברכה	(Bm.)	ויכנהו בבכרה

3. Studying the Book of Ben Sira, the reader is constantly confronted with the
annoying question of *verse numbering*. As to the verse numbering of Sir
44:19-23, there are two main differences to be found. The first one is due to
the Greek, the Syriac, and the Latin translations, since they have two more
lines than the Hebrew of MS B. The other variation in numbering is produced
by the question of where to start vs. 23.

In order to dispel the confusion caused by differing numbers, F. Reiterer
and his collaborators in 2003 published a synopsis[8] which integrates the
numbering of Greek text editions (Ziegler; Swete; Rahlfs), Hebrew text
editions (The Academy of the Hebrew Language; Beentjes), Syriac editions
(De Lagarde; Mossul; Ambrosianus; Peshitta Institute), Latin editions (Biblia
Sacra/Rom; Stuttgart), and some modern translations of the Book of Ben Sira

---

[5] A.E. Cowley and Ad. Neubauer, *The Original Hebrew of a Portion of Ecclesiasticus
(XXXIX.15 to XLIX.11) together with the Early Versions and an English Translation, followed by the Quotations from Ben Sira in Rabbinical Literature* (Oxford: Clarendon Press
1897).

[6] S. Schechter, "A Fragment of the Original Text of Ecclesiasticus," *Expositor* (5th
series) 4 (1896) 1-15.

[7] See *Facsimiles of the Fragments hitherto recovered of the Book of Ecclesiasticus in
Hebrew* (Oxford and Cambridge: University Press 1891).

[8] F.V. Reiterer, *Zählsynopse zum Buch Ben Sira* (FoSub 1, Berlin: W. De Gruyter
2003).

(NRSV; EÜ; Revised Luther Bible; JSHRZ).[9] In the following chart all current verse numberings of Sir 44:19-23 have been listed according to Reiterer's synopsis:

Reiterer	Hebrew	Greek	Syriac	Latin
44:19a	44:19a	44:19a	44:19a	44:20a
44:19b	44:19b	44:19b	44:19b	44:20b
44:20a	44:20a	44:20a	44:20a	44:20c
44:20b	44:20b	44:20b	44:20b	44:20d
44:20c	44:20c	44:20c	44:20c	44:21a
44:20d	44:20d	44:20d	44:20d	44:21b
44:21a	44:21a	44:21a	44:21a	44:22a
44:21b	44:21b	44:21b	44:21b	44:22b
44:21c	-------	44:21c	44:21c	44:22c
44:21d	-------	44:21d	44:21d	44:23a
44:21e	44:21c	44:21e	44:21e	44:23b
44:21f	44:21d	44:21f	44:21f	44:23c
44:22a	44:22a	44:22a	44:22a	44:24a
44:22b	44:22b	44:22b	44:22b	44:24b
44:22c	44:22c	44:23a	44:23a	44:25a
44:23a	44:23a / 22d[10]	44:23a	44:23b	44:25b
44:23b	44:23c / 23a	44:23b	44:23c	44:26a
44:23c	44:23d / 23b	44:23c	44:23d	44:26b

[9] *Hebrew* text editions: *Spr bn-syr'. The Book of Ben Sira. Text, Concordance and an Analysis of the Vocabulary* (The Historical Dictionary of the Hebrew Language, Jerusalem: The Academy of the Hebrew Language and the Shrine of the Book 1973); P.C. Beentjes, *The Book of Ben Sira in Hebrew: A Text Edition of All Extant Hebrew Manuscripts and a Synopsis of All Parallel Hebrew Ben Sira Texts* (VTSup 68, Leiden: Brill 1997).

Greek text editions: A. Ralfs, *Septuaginta. Id est Vetus Testamentum graece iuxta LXX interpretes* II (Stuttgart: Württembergische Bibelanstalt 1935 [repr. 1965]); H.B. Swete, *The Old Testament in Greek. According to the Septuagint* II (Cambridge: University Press 1922 [repr. 1930]); J. Ziegler, *Sapientia Iesu Filii Sirach* (Septuaginta. Vetus Testamentum Graecum auctoritate Societatis Litterarum Gottingensis editum XII/2, Göttingen: Vandenhoeck & Ruprecht 1965).

Syriac text editions: P. De Lagarde, *Libri Veteris Testamenti Apocryphi* (Leipzig: Brockhaus and London: William & Norgate 1861); N. Calduch-Benages, J. Ferrer and J. Liesen, *La sabiduría del escriba. Edicón diplomática del texto siríaco de Ben Sira según el códice Ambrosiano con traduccíon española e inglesa* (Biblioteca Midrásica 26, Estella: Verbo Divino 2003).

Latin text editions: *Biblia Sacra iuxta Vulgatam versionem adiuvantibus B. Fischer osb, I. Gribomont osb, H.F.D. Spartes, W. Thiele recensuit et brevi apparatu instruxit R. Weber osb* II (Stuttgart: Württembergische Bibelanstalt 1969); *Biblia Sacra, iuxta latinam Vulgatam versionem ad codicum fidem iussu Pauli PP. VI cura et studio monachorum Abbatiae Pontificiae Sancti Hieronymi in Urbe Ordinis Sancti Benedicti edita XII* (Rome 1964).

[10] The first mention refers to *Spr bn-syr'*, the second to Beentjes, *Text Edition*.

44:23d	44:23e / 23c	44:23d	44:23e	44:26c
44:23e	44:23f / 23d	44:23e	44:23f	44:26d

4. As compared with the Hebrew text of 44:21, the *Versiones* usually have a *plus*: vs. 21cd. At a closer look, however, the matter appears to be quite complicated. Sir 44:21cd is completely absent in Codex Sinaiticus (*prima manus*), as well as in minuscule 672, whereas 44:21d is not found in Codex 248, which is considered the main witness of the Lucian recension.[11] Since the vocabulary of all three *Versiones* (Greek, Syriac, Latin) on crucial points differ from the formulae that have been used in the obvious passages in the Book of Genesis (13:16; 15:18; 22:17), one may assume that the supposed Hebrew text of Sir 44:21cd did not reflect mere quotations from the Book of Genesis either.[12] Since, moreover, the Greek, the Syriac, and the Latin differ from one another in their rendering of 44:21b-d, as is shown in the *Appendix I*, it is impossible to reconstruct a reliable "original" Hebrew text of 44:21cd.

That such reconstructions are unsuccessful indeed can be demonstrated with the help of a few earlier scholarly attempts:

Peters:[13]   וכוכבים להרים זרעו   להרבות אותו כעפר הארץ
Smend:[14]   ולתת זרעו ככוכבים
Segal:[15]   ולתתו עליון על כל גוים   להרבות זרעו כחול הים

It is impossible, therefore, to establish the exact reason why the second Hebrew bicolon of 44:21 has been skipped. However, at least one solid argument can be adduced in favour of the existence of such a bicolon in Ben Sira's original Hebrew text. In the factual Hebrew text of 44:21 as handed down by MS B. the suffix in להנחילם is rather odd, since in that case the antecedent is גוים, which would give rise to an extreme theological view. It stands to reason, therefore, that the antecedent of להנחילם is the offspring of Abraham.

Syntactical and grammatical remarks

Though it is irrefutable that the collocation אב המון גוים (Sir 44:19a) has been adopted from Gen 17:4-5, it nevertheless remains obscure what exactly is its *grammatical* function. Ben Sira scholars hold different views as to this phrase; should it be considered an *apposition* to "Abraham" or be apprehended as a

---

[11] See Ziegler, *Sapientia*, 334; J.H.A. Hart, *Ecclesiasticus. The Greek Text of Codex 248* (Cambridge: University Press 1909).

[12] For a detailed analysis of 44:21b-d according to the *Versiones*, see Reiterer, *Urtext*, 102-06.

[13] N. Peters, *Der jüngst wiederaufgefundene Hebräische Text des Buches Ecclesiasticus* (Freiburg i. Br.: Herdersche Verlagshandlung 1902) 407.

[14] R. Smend, *Die Weisheit des Jesus Sirach erklärt* (Berlin: Georg Reimer 1906) 424.

[15] M.Z. Segal, *Spr bn-syr' hšlm* (2nd ed., Jerusalem: Biliak 1958) 306.

nominal clause?[16] As 44:19b does not open with a copulative *waw*, the most obvious option, therefore, appears to be that the collocation should be considered an *apposition*: "Abraham, father of a multitude of nations, set no blemish upon his glory."

There is also discussion relating to the status of the verbal form נתן in 44:19b. Both the Greek (εὑρέθη) and the Syriac (ܐܬܚܟܡ) have a passive rendering ("was given"), which might be the rendering of a *niph'al* (נִתַּן) in Hebrew which is indeed advocated by some scholars.[17] There are good reasons, however, to advocate an *active* voice ("he gave"). No doubt the most important argument would be that elsewhere in the Book of Ben Sira the collocation נתן מום בכבוד is always in the active voice (Sir 33:23; 47:20),[18] just as Sir 11:33b (נשא מום) and Sir 18:15a (μὴ δῷς μῶμον) have the active voice.

The marginal reading דופי in substitution for מום (Sir 44:19b) can only be understood properly if it has to do with the question of how to qualify the verbal form נתן. The collocation מום + נתן is attested two times in the Hebrew Bible, i.e. in Lev 24:19-20, the verb being used in the passive voice (*niph'al*). The noun דופי is used one more time in classical Hebrew, viz. in Ps 50:20, where it is accompanied by the verb נתן in the active voice (*qal*). We therefore cannot rule out the possibility that a copyist—in order to safeguard his conviction that the verbal form נתן in Sir 44:19b should be interpreted as an active voice—has deliberately exchanged דופי for מום, remembering Ps 50:20. This problem is not found in the other two passages in the Book of Ben Sira in which the collocation מום + נתן occurs, since it is obvious that the verb נתן there is in the active voice. Both the Greek (μῶμος) and the Syriac (ܡܘܡܐ) are solid proof that מום in Sir 44:19b is to be considered the original reading.[19]

---

[16] In favour of an *apposition* are, e.g., I. Lévi, *L'Ecclésiastique ou la Sagesse de Jésus, fils de Sira* I (Bibliothèque de l'École des Hautes Études, Sciences Religieuses 10/1, Paris: Leroux 1898), 91; R. Smend, *Die Weisheit des Jesus Sirach. Hebräisch und Deutsch. Mit einem hebräischen Glossar* (Berlin: Georg Reimer 1906) 79; W.Th. van Peursen, *The verbal System in the Hebrew Text of Ben Sira* (Studies in Semitic Languages and Linguistics 41, Leiden: Brill 2004) 320.

In favour of a *nominal clause* are, e.g., Peters, *Das Buch Jesus Sirach*, 380; G. Sauer, *Jesus Sirach/Ben Sira*, 303; R.C.T. Hayward, "El Elyon and the Divine Names in Ben Sira", in *Ben Sira's God. Proceedings of the International Ben Sira Conference Durham—Ushaw College 2001* (ed. R. Egger-Wenzel, BZAW 321, Berlin: De Gruyter 2002) 180-98 (187).

[17] "Die Punktuation נִתַּן verlangen Gr. und Syr;" Peters, *Der jüngst wiederaufgefundene*, 231; Segal, *Spr bn-syr'*, 306 also has the vocalization נִתַּן, just as *The Dictionary of Classical Hebrew* V (ed. D.J.A. Clines, Sheffield: Sheffield Academic Press 2001) 175.

[18] D. Barthélemy and O. Rickenbacher, *Konkordanz zum hebräischen Sirach* (Göttingen: Vandenhoeck & Ruprecht 1973) 274 consider נתן in Sir 44:19 as "3.m.sg.pf.qal"; the same is true for *Spr bn-syr'* (The Historical Dictionary) 225.

[19] Sir. 44:20b according to the *Vetus Latina* (= Sir. 44:19b H) has been rendered in the passive voice. One should specifically notice the rather curious translation of the Hebrew noun מום: "non est inventus *simili illi* in gloria." This rendering, however, is

As for the final line of the passage relating to the Patriarchs (44:23d-e), the Hebrew of this bicolon is quite a bit refractory, as is clearly demonstrated by how the Greek and Syriac have rendered their Hebrew parent text.[20] From a grammatical point of view it is especially puzzling in what way one has to translate the *lamed* of לשבטים. Although the verb נצב *hiph.* occurs several times in the Book of Ben Sira (3:14b; 47:13d; 50:12b), it has nowhere else been accompanied by a *lamed*. In the Hebrew Bible, however, one comes across a number of occurrences in which the construction of the verb נצב *hiph.* + ל is attested (1 Sam 15:12; 2 Sam 18:18; 2 Kgs 17:10; Jer 31:21). In all these cases the *lamed* functions as the preposition that has been linked with a pronomen personale: "to set up for oneself." It always affects tangible objects, such as a monument, an altar, a pillar, or cairns. As to Sir 44:23d, the *lamed* cannot possibly have a similar function, since here *the verb* has a suffixed pronomen personale: "He set him;" and there is no question of a tangible object. There is no other possibility, therefore, but to render: "He [God] set him [Israel] up as tribes."[21] The final colon (44:23e), then, should be considered an apposition: "as a portion of twelve."

Structure

On first acquaintance, the passage seems rather familiar. It deals with Abraham, Isaac, and Israel = Jacob. At a closer look, however, one should notice a striking difference between Ben Sira's portrayal of Abraham and the way he deals with Isaac and Israel/Jacob. In 44:19-20, it is *Abraham* who is exclusively the subject throughout, whereas in 44:21-23 the subject is constantly *God*, being defined, however, only as "He." The only *specific* reference to God in the entire passage is to be found in 44:20a, where the collocation מצות עליון ("the commandment[s] of the Most High") is found.[22]

Upon further investigation, another striking feature has to be mentioned. In a rather creative way, Ben Sira has deviated from the 'canonical' order in which major themes of the Abraham cycle are found in the Book of Genesis and has rearranged them in a quite surprising new composition. Fortunately, we have a fixed point to start with, since the collocation אב המון גוים ("Father of a multitude of nations") in Sir 44:19a can only refer to Gen 17:4-5, as it is found nowhere else in the Hebrew Bible.[23] This reference is a major key to some more lines in Ben Sira's presentation of Abraham.

During my research on the Book of Ben Sira, I have become more and more convinced that sometimes it is not appropriate to make up a "telephone-book-like" list of every possible connection between a Ben Sira pas-

---

due to the reading ὅμοιος which—as a substitution for μῶμος—is found in some Greek minuscules.

[20] See Appendix III.

[21] Hayward, "El Elyon," 187.

[22] See Hayward, "El Elyon," 180-98.

[23] For a detailed analysis of Gen 17:4-5, see: A. van der Kooij, *Abraham, vader van/voor een menigte volkeren* (inaugural address, Leiden: Leiden University 1990).

sage and the Hebrew Bible. Instead, one should foster quite *another* frame of reference that is called "structural use of Scripture" or "structural style." "Structural use of Scripture" or "structural style" is a phenomenon to the effect that a passage in a Jewish writing is structured to a high degree by a cluster of characteristic elements or notions from *one* or *two* biblical texts. It was Daniel Patte who introduced this notion and applied this literary feature exclusively to the structuring of apocalyptic texts.[24] He discovered such an application of "structural use of Scripture" only in Jewish writings that can be dated to about the second century BCE. I think this feature of "structural style" should not exclusively be restricted to *apocalyptic* texts, but broadened to other literary genres as well. Would it be mere coincidence that Ben Sira composed his book in exactly the same period as in which Patte discovered this literary phenomenon?[25]

To my conviction, there is solid proof that in his portrayal of Abraham, Ben Sira has indeed used the structural style of Scripture to focus upon a specific text. It is chapter 17 from the Book of Genesis which no doubt plays a crucial role in Ben Sira's presentation of this patriarch. The most important indication that the Jerusalem sage used such a structural style of Scripture is, of course, the unique collocation אב המון גוים ("Father of a multitude of nations") in the opening line (Sir 44:19a). But other references to Genesis 17 also confirm and strengthen my conviction that Ben Sira has deliberately given this specific passage from Genesis a prominent role in his text. Both Sir 44:20b ("He entered into a covenant with Him") and Sir 44:20c ("In his flesh he cut for Him an ordinance") undeniably refer to Genesis 17.[26] The former is reminiscent of Gen 17:4-7, whereas the latter has a bearing on Gen 17:12-27.[27]

Having determined that within the Abraham passage three cola (44:19a, 20b, 20c) are governed by a structural use of Scripture from Genesis 17, some further observations relating to the structure of the Ben Sira passage are in order now. The lines referring to Genesis 17, in fact, enclose two cola which can by no means be traced back to specific biblical passages and therefore should be considered Ben Sira's own creation:

---

[24] D. Patte, *Early Jewish Hermeneutic in Palestine* (SBLDS 22, Missoula: Scholars Press 1975) 171.

[25] Elsewhere I have argued that this phenomenon of structural style can be very useful for the study of the Book of Ben Sira. See P.C. Beentjes, "Canon and Scripture in the Book of Ben Sira," in *Hebrew Bible / Old Testament. The History of its Interpretation I/2: The Middle Ages* (ed. M. Saebø, Göttingen: Vandenhoeck & Ruprecht 2000) 591-605 [= idem, *Happy the One who Meditates on Wisdom. Collected Essays on the Book of Ben Sira* (CBTE 43, Leuven: Peeters 2006) 169-86].

[26] I do not understand why in P.W. Skehan and A.A. Di Lella, *The Wisdom of Ben Sira* (AB 39, New York: Doubleday 1987) 503 the text of Sir 44:20c has been rendered in a *passive voice*: "In his own flesh the ordinance was incised."

[27] Both themes (covenant, circumcision) are explicitly linked in Gen 17:9-11.

— "He set no blemish upon his glory" (Sir 44:19b);
— "It was he who kept the commandment[s] of the Most High" (Sir 44:20a).[28]

Such patterns in which structural use of Scripture alternates with the author's own formulae are found more than once in the Book of Ben Sira.[29]

It can hardly be coincidental that Ben Sira's portrayal of Abraham both *opens* (Sir 44:19a) with a literal quotation from the Hebrew Bible ("Father of a multitude of nations;" Gen 17:4-5) and *concludes* (Sir 44:21ef) with a phrase that has also been directly adopted from the Hebrew Bible ("From sea to sea, and from the river to the ends of the earth;" Ps 72:8; Zech 9:10). Later on, we will discuss in what way Ben Sira has reinterpreted this latter phrase for his own purpose.

The remaining lines (Sir 44:20d-21d) have only *allusions* to Biblical passages dealing with the Patriarchs:

— Sir 44:20d: the trial of Abraham (Gen 22:1);
— Sir 44:21ab: God's oath to bless the nations through Abraham's descendants (Gen 26:3-4);
— Sir 44:21c [Greek]: to increase him like the dust of the earth (Gen 13:16);
— Sir 44:21d [Greek]: to exalt his descendants like the stars (Gen 15:5).

Whereas the portrayal of Abraham (Sir 44:19-21f) has been shaped with the help of two biblical quotations which bind those lines together in a kind of sandwich structure, the verse lines dealing with Isaac and Israel lack such literary features. Just as in the Hebrew Bible, Isaac appears to be a mere copy of his father's vicissitudes, which in the Ben Sira text are summarized in the phrase "Also with Isaac he established thus, on account of *Abraham* his *father*" (44:22ab). The reading בֵן (Bm.) is to be preferred here. Firstly, for contextual reasons: in 44:19-21 there is no question of God's promise to Abraham to provide him a son; secondly, since all the Versiones have a rendering that suppose an original reading בֵן.[30] By the way, Sir 44:22b's use of the words "Abraham" and "father" creates an *inclusio* with 44:19a: "Abraham, father of a multitude of nations," whereas the opening ("Also with Isaac He *established thus;*" 44:22a) dovetails with 44:21a ("Therefore with an oath He *established* with him").

With regard to the structure of Sir 44:19-23, finally the question should be answered which patriarch is meant in Sir 44:22c ("The covenant of each

[28] Further aspects of these two cola will be discussed in detail in the section "Exegetical Notes."

[29] P.C. Beentjes, *Jesus Sirach en Tenach. Een onderzoek naar en een classificatie van parallellen, met bijzondere aandacht voor hun functie in Sirach 45:6-26* (Nieuwegein: Selbstverlag 1981) 53-55; 180-86; Beentjes, "Canon and Scripture," 600-02.

[30] The argumentation by Penar who refers to 1 Chron 17:13 in order to stand up for the reading בֵן (MS B), is not convincing; T. Penar, *Northwest Semitic Philology and the Hebrew Fragments of Ben Sira* (BibOr 28, Rome: Biblical Institute Press 1975) 78.

forefather He gave him"), since scholars hold different views in this respect.[31] Some maintain that both Sir 44:22c and 44:23a have a bearing on Jacob/Israel.[32] Other Ben Sira scholars, on the contrary, hold the view that Sir 44:22c touches upon Isaac, whereas Sir 44:23a refers to Jacob/Israel.[33] To my mind, the Hebrew text of 44:22c according to MS B. allows no other possibility but to have reference to Isaac, being the antecedent of נתנו ("He gave him").[34]

So we conclude that the lines in which Abraham is dealt with (Sir 44:19-21) are more pronounced than the lines relating to Isaac (Sir 44:22) and Jacob/Israel (44:23).

However, the portrayals of the three patriarchs have been intertwined. Abraham and Isaac are linked with each other in a fourfold way:

1. The name of "Abraham" (44:19a; 22b);
2. The noun "father" (44:19a; 22b);
3. The verbal form הקים (44:21a; 22a);
4. The noun ברית (44:20b; 22c).

The description of Jacob/Israel has in a twofold way been interrelated with Abraham, viz. with the help of:

(1) The root נחל (44:21e; 23c);
(2) The root ברך (44:21b; 23a; 23b).

---

[31] A quite remarkable rendering is offered by Smend, *Die Weisheit des Jesus Sirach. Hebräisch und Deutsch*, 79: "Der Bund aller Vorfahren wurde gelegt / und ihr Segen ruhte auf dem Haupte Israels." With regard of נתנו (44:22c) he not only suppressed the suffix, but also rendered a passive voice. Moreover, there is no Hebrew equivalent for "ihr" ("their") in 44:23a.

[32] E.g. N. Peters, *Das Buch Jesus Sirach oder Ecclesiasticus* (EHAT 25, Münster: Aschendorff 1913) 382; Peters, *Der jüngst wiederaufgefundene*, 233; Reiterer, *Urtext*, 108; R.A.F. MacKenzie, *Sirach* (OTM 19, Wilmington: Glazier 1983) 170; J. Marböck, "Die 'Geschichte Israels' als 'Bundesgeschichte' nach dem Sirachbuch," in *Der Neue Bund im Alten. Studien zur Bundestheologie der beiden Testamente* (ed. E. Zenger, QD 146, Freiburg: Herder 1993) 177-97 (185).

[33] E.g. G. Sauer, *Jesus Sirach/Ben Sira* (ATD Apokryphen 1, Göttingen: Vandenhoeck & Ruprecht 2000) 303; G. Sauer, *Jesus Sirach* (JSHRZ III/5, Gütersloh: Gerd Mohn 1981) 616; Skehan and Di Lella, *The Wisdom of Ben Sira*, 503; J.G. Snaith, *Ecclesiasticus* (CBC, Cambridge: University Press 1974) 218; Hayward, "El Elyon," 188.

[34] This verbal form, though, is not found in the Greek and the Syriac. For a comparison between the Greek, Syriac, and Latin translations of this verse, see *Appendix II*.

EXEGETICAL NOTES

1. Ben Sira's presentation of Abraham (44:19-21)

In the section dealing with the pericope's structure we have already shown that Genesis 17 is to be considered the main frame for Ben Sira's presentation of Abraham, to which he added some lines of his own.

Ben Sira's first creation of his own is found in 44:19b ("He set no blemish upon his glory"). Some scholars hold the view this colon is reminiscent only of Gen 12:10-20 and 20:1-18, the narratives about Abraham saying that Sarah is his sister.[35] There are some arguments, however, to uphold the position that Sir 44:19b should not be confined to these narratives, nor that it should refer to Gen 17:1 only.[36] First, the marked collocation בכבוד נתן מום is found more than once in the Book of Ben Sira (33:23 [30:31 Gr.]; 44:19 47:20), the first occurrence of which is a strong indication that the collocation should preferably be given a general meaning: "to behave as a wise man." Second, the notion "blemish" (מום/μῶμος) is a continuous thread throughout the Book of Ben Sira (11:31 [11:33 Gr.]; 18:15; 20:24; 33:23). Third, since in the "Praise of the Famous" this collocation is not only used with respect to Abraham (Sir 44:19b), but also has a bearing on King Solomon (47:20), one can hardly maintain that Ben Sira in 44:19b should only refer to the stories in Genesis 12 and 20. On the contrary, Ben Sira uses the notion to promote Abraham as a role model.

In 44:20a we come upon a remarkable phrase too: "It was he who kept the commandment[s] of the Most High."[37] Relating to Abraham, Ben Sira seems to emphasize that keeping the commandment[s] should be considered a condition for entering the covenant. In this context, the reader should come to a decision how to vocalize מצות.

(a) If מצות is interpreted as a plural, it must refer to the Mosaic Law, as is suggested by the Greek (νόμος) and Latin (lex) of Sir 44:20a.[38] In that case, Ben Sira would in fact present an *anachronistic* concept in which Abraham is portrayed as the perfect, *Torah*-devoted Jew, an image that to a high degree has affected Jewish thought in later time. At first it was propagated by

---

[35] E.g. Smend, *Die Weisheit des Jesus Sirach erklärt*, 423 (quoted by Peters, *Buch Jesus Sirach*, 381); Skehan and Di Lella, *The Wisdom of Ben Sira*, 505.

[36] Marböck, "Die Geschichte Israels," 184. That being the case, Ben Sira would undoubtedly have adopted the adjective תמים from Gen 17:1, a notion which he used both in 44:16a (Enoch) and 44:17a (Noah).

[37] The collocation מצות עליון is a *hapax legomenon*. Most probably, the Hebrew text of Sir 24:23, which has not be found till now, would have read otherwise; see Segal, *Spr bn-syr'*, 146.

[38] As to Ben Sira's concept of the Law and the Commandments, see E.J. Schnabel, *Law and Wisdom from Ben Sira to Paul. A Tradition Historical Enquiry into the Relation of Law, Wisdom, and Ethics* (WUNT II/16, Tübingen: Mohr Siebeck 1985) 29-42.

Jewish authors like Philo and Josephus; later on it achieved great popularity in Rabbinic literature.[39]

(b) If the noun, however, should be considered a singular, then it has a direct bearing on God's explicit demand of Abraham to carry out his circumcision (Gen 17:9-14). And since Ben Sira will explicitly mention this in the next verse line—"In his flesh he cut for Him an ordinance" (44:20c)—this latter option is to be preferred here.[40]

Ben Sira's creativity has not been confined, however, to the statements mentioned above that were undoubtedly his own inventions. The biblical references that without a shadow of doubt were adopted from Genesis 17 have also undergone a creative reworking by Ben Sira. It is quite remarkable, for instance, that it is *Abraham* who "entered into a covenant with Him" (44:20b), whereas in Gen. 17:2 it is "God Almighty" (אל שדי) who makes the covenant. This is the more striking since in 44:22c—where the term ברית ("covenant") is used again—it is *God* who gives a covenant to Isaac.[41] The plausibility that it is *Abraham* indeed who entered into a covenant with God (44:20b) is to a high degree confirmed by the use of the collocation בוא ברית elsewhere. Both in the Hebrew Bible (Jer 34:10; 2 Chron 15:14)[42] and in the Qumran documents (CD xv 5; 1QS ii 12.26; v 8.20; x 10)[43] it is almost exclusively used for human beings.

Sir 44:20c poses an interesting tradition-historical question: "In his flesh he cut for Him an ordinance," or: "In his flesh he cut for himself an ordi-

---

[39] See, e.g. *Midrash Rabbah* Genesis I, 42-44 (ed. H. Freedman and M. Simon, London 1961); b.*B.Mes.* 87a (ed. I. Epstein, London: Soncino Press 1961); *Tannaitische Midrashim Sifre Numeri* II and XII (ed. K.G. Kuhn, Stuttgart 1959).

[40] Several scholars have rendered מצות as a singular. The translation "das Gebot" is found in Peters, *Buch Jesus Sirach*, 380; Smend, *Die Weisheit des Jesus Sirach. Hebräisch und Deutsch*, 79; A. Eberharter, *Das Buch Jesus Sirach oder Ecclesiasticus* (HSAT VI/5, Bonn: Peter Hanstein 1925) 145. Cowley and Neubauer, *The Original Hebrew*, 23 has "the commandment;" the translation in Skehan and Di Lella, *The Wisdom of Ben Sira*, 503 reads "the … command."

[41] The noun ברית ("covenant") is found *seven* times in the first section of the *Laus Patrum*. The contention "*berit* occurs 11 times in chapters 44-49" by R.A.F. MacKenzie, "Ben Sira as Historian," in *Trinification of the World* (eds. T.A. Dunne and J.M. Laporte, Toronto: Regis College Press 1978) 312-27 (317) is incorrect. In the Greek translation of Sir 44-49 the noun διαθήκη is found there *twelve* times (44:11.18.20.20.22; 45:5.7.15.17.24.25; 47:11), but does repeatedly not render ברית (44:18. 20b; 45:5.7.17; 47:11). In fact, the history of Israel as presented in the first part of the *Laus Patrum* (Sir 44:1-45:25d) is described as a continuous chain of covenants, which will culminate in the High Priestly covenant with Aaron (45:15) and Phinehas (45:24). God's covenant with David is transferred to the High Priestly dynasty. This view has been expounded in: Beentjes, *Jesus Sirach en Tenach*, 188-92; see also P.C. Beentjes, "'The Countries Marvelled at You.' King Solomon in Ben Sira 47,12-22," *Bijdragen* 45 (1984) 6-14 [*Happy the One who Meditates on Wisdom*, 135-44]. See also Marböck, "Die Geschichte Israels," 177-97.

[42] Only in Ez 16:8 the collocation has a bearing on God.

[43] The reference to 1QS x 4 as found in *The Dictionary of Classical Hebrew* 2: 266 should be corrected into: 1QS x 10.

nance"?[44] Earlier, when dealing with the structure of this pericope, we have
seen that Gen 17:24 serves as the basis for Ben Sira's presentation of
Abraham's circumcision. The most striking difference between both texts is
undoubtedly that in Gen 17:24 the circumcision is described with a *niph'al*
(בְּהִמֹּלוֹ), which in nearly all Bible translations—except for Martin Luther's
and the *New English Bible*[45]—is rendered in a passive voice: "when he was
circumcised," whereas in Ben Sira's presentation it is an action by Abraham
himself ("he cut"). Ben Sira's presentation is the more intriguing since the
conception that Abraham circumcised himself is also found in the Samaritan
Pentateuch (בהמלו את בשר ערלתו),[46] in the Septuagint (περιέτεμεν) and the
Vulgate (*circumcidit*) as well as in Targum Pseudo-Jonathan / Jerushalmi I
(כד גזר ית בישרא דעולתיה).[47]

It is beyond doubt that Sir 44:20c (בבשרו כרת לו חק) refers to the circumcision of Abraham. This colon, however, has some special features that
deserve further attention. First, the collocation חק + כרת is unparalleled, not
only in the Book of Ben Sira, but in the entire Hebrew Bible as well. Second,
it is hard to clarify the exact meaning of חק here. I am of a different opinion
from those scholars who hold the view that חק is used here in a metony-
mical sense to denote either "circumcision" (Smend) or "foreskin" (Peters).[48]
Considering the previous cola, חק appears to be used as a synonym to both
"the commandment of the Most High" (44:20a) and "covenant" (44:20b). As
a consequence, this requires a rendering like "In his flesh he cut for Him an
ordinance."[49] This, in any case, seems more likely, since all ancient versions

---

[44] As I have argued earlier in this contribution, only Abraham is considered to be
the subject of 44:18-20. I therefore disagree with Reiterer, who proposed two more
possible renderings of 44:20c in both of which *God* is the subject. *Contra* F.V. Reiterer,
"The Hebrew of Ben Sira Investigated on the Basis of his Use of כרת: A Syntactic,
Semantic, and Language-Historical Contribution," in *Sirach, Scrolls, and Sages* (eds. T.
Muraoka and J.F. Elwolde, STDJ 33, Leiden: Brill 1999) 253-77 (esp. 268-74).

[45] "Und Abraham was neun und neunzig jar alt, da er die Vorhaut an seinem
Fleisch beschneidet;" D. Martin Luther, *Die gantze Heilige Schrifft Deudsch. Wittenberg
1545* (ed. H. Volz, München: Rogner & Bernhard 1972) 1: 51. "Abraham was ninety-
nine years old when he circumcised the flesh of his foreskin;" *The New English Bible*
(Oxford and Cambridge: University Press 1970) 17. In the next verse, however, *NEB*
has rendered *exactly the same* Hebrew verbal form as a *passive* voice: "Ishmael was thirteen years old when he was circumcised in the flesh of his foreskin."

[46] A. von Gall, *Der Hebräische Pentateuch der Samaritaner* (Giessen: Töpelmann 1918) 26.

[47] E.G. Clarke, *Targum Pseudo-Jonathan of the Pentateuch* (New York: KTAV 1984)
18. The text of Targum Neofiti I—במגזר ליה בשר ערלתיה ("in the circumcising to
him")—to my mind tends to the passive voice. However, M. McNamara, *Targum
Neofiti I: Genesis* (The Aramaic Bible 1A, Edinburgh: T&T Clark 1992) 102 advocates
the active voice: "when he circumcised the flesh of his foreskin."

[48] "...חק. bedeutet metonymisch die Beschneidung;" Smend, *Die Weisheit*, 423.
"חק meint die Vorhaut;" Peters, *Buch Jesus Sirach*, 381.

[49] For חק and ברית in parallel position, see Sir 45:25. For the Hebrew Bible, see e.g.
Ps 50:16; 105:10; 1 Chron 16:17. For חק and מצות in parallel position, see e.g. 1 Kgs 8:61;
Ezra 7:11.

tend to such a meaning: διαθήκη, ܩܝܡܐ, testamentum.[50] Referring to Abraham's circumcision, Ben Sira using the noun חק is undoubtedly playing here with the literal meaning of the verb חקק: "to engrave." He has linked it with the verb כרת, which literally means "to cut," but in the Hebrew Bible is usually used in a special sense: "to make a covenant." In the Book of Ben Sira, however, the collocation כרת ברית does not occur.[51] It is not far-fetched to assume that the author has deliberately avoided this collocation here in 44:20 in order to enable him to use the verb כרת in its literal sense. This possibility crossed my mind when reading another "covenant context," viz. Sir 50:24.[52] For here קום ברית hiph. is followed by the verb כרת in its literal meaning as well:

> May His faithfulness toward Simon be lasting; may He carry out for him the covenant with Phinehas, which may not be cut off [כרת] for him or for his descendants, while the heavens last.

By means of the stem נסה, the final colon of Sir 44:20 ("when put to the test, he was found faithful / steadfast") undoubtedly refers to the story of Genesis 22. The "trial motif" occurs several times elsewhere in the Book of Ben Sira.[53] And one would expect Ben Sira to have elaborated such an important theological stream in this particular text on Abraham. It is the more surprising, therefore, that the remainder of Sir 44:20d has no resemblance whatsoever with the famous text from Genesis 22.

Although in Jewish tradition the phrase "Abraham was found faithful/steadfast" occurs rather frequently (e.g. in *Jubilees* 17:17-18; 19:8), there are, however, some indications in favour of the view that the collocation נמצא נאמן in 44:20d might have some connections with Neh 9:8. First, it is the only occurrence of this collocation in the entire Hebrew Bible. Second, it is used in exactly the same context, viz. referring to Abraham. Third, it is also embedded in a summary of God's mighty deeds in the past.[54] That Neh 9:8 must indeed be the parent text can be deduced from the fact that Ben Sira did not adopt the wording from Gen 15:6, being the only text within the Abraham cycle where the verb אמן occurs, be it in the *hiph'il*: "Abraham put

---

[50] In the Book of Ben Sira חוק/חק is found twenty two times, of which ten times it is rendered διαθήκη (11:18 [Gr. 11:20]; 14:12, 17; 16:20 [Gr. 16:22]; 42:2; 44:20; 45:5, 7, 17; 47:11). This is the more surprising, because nowhere else in the Septuagint the Hebrew noun חוק/חק is rendered διαθήκη.

[51] Instead of it the author used: בוא ברית (Sir 44:20), קום ברית hiph. (Sir 45:24; 50:24), פרר ברית hiph. (Sir 41:19), הפך מברית (Sir 11:34).

[52] See Reiterer, "The Hebrew of Ben Sira," 274-77.

[53] See N. Calduch-Benages, "Trial Motif in the Book of Ben Sira with Special Reference to Sir 2,1-6," in *The Book of Ben Sira in Modern Research* (ed. P.C. Beentjes, BZAW 255, Berlin: De Gruyter 1997) 135-51.

[54] In classical Hebrew there is only one more occurrence of the collocation נמצא נאמן: 4QpsJubᵇ [4Q226] 7 1 — נמצא אברהם נאמן ל[א]ל[ו]הים] ("Abraham was found faithful / steadfast to God"); H. Attridge, *et al.*, *Qumrân Cave 4* VIII: *Parabiblical Texts* 1 (DJD 13, Oxford: Clarendon Press 1994) 165.

his faith in JHWH." It looks very much as if by using the participle *niph'al* נאמן, Ben Sira did not so much want to emphasize the aspect of faith as the aspect of firmness / reliability. For in all the seven occurrences of the participle *niph'al* נאמן in the Book of Ben Sira (30:17, 20; 31:2, 23, 24; 44:11, 20) the issue is not faith, but reliability.

Using the collocation נמצא נאמן in 44:20d, Ben Sira is not only referring to Neh 9:8, but in a subtle way has also created a parallel to 44:17a—נוח צדיק נמצא תמים. That this must be a *deliberate* reference appears from the fact that the collocation נמצא תמים is found nowhere in the Hebrew Bible, whereas תמים undeniably has been adopted from Gen 6:9.[55]

Relating to the *Greek* text of Sir 44:20d (καὶ ἐν πειρασμῷ εὑρέθη πιστός), it can hardly be coincidental that exactly the same phrase is found in 1 Macc 2:52, where it refers to Abraham too. Since Ben Sira's grandson, the translator of the Hebrew Ben Sira text, and the author of 1 Maccabees must have been contemporaries, it is impossible to determine who adopted this phrase from whom. It looks like a kind of a *topos* which was in the air at that time.

Does the causal adverb על כן ("therefore") at the opening of Sir 44:21a function in a limited or in a broad sense? In other words: does על כן only refer to the final colon of 44:20 ("when put to the test, he was found steadfast"), or does it have a bearing on *all* utterances about Abraham so far? The latter possibility should be preferred. On the one hand, since Ben Sira in his portrayal of Abraham lays stress upon the aspect that the patriarch is rewarded by God for his unbroken faithfulness, which has been demonstrated with the help of several remarkable expressions (44:19b-20d). And on the other hand, because the author is continuously at great pains to present Abraham in a very special way, which is expressed in many rare and unique collocations. Without interruption, this feature is continued in 44:21. For although the *content* of this verse undoubtedly bears upon Gen 22:16-18, the way in which Ben Sira has now worded it is a creation of his own again.[56]

The substance of the oath which God swore to Abraham (44:21a), being a reward for the patriarch's way of life, consists of five components—two of which are not to be found in the Hebrew text.[57] Referring to the first element of God's oath, Ben Sira has the formulation לברך בזרעו גוים ("to bless the nations through his descendants").[58] One would expect this wording to be directly adopted from one of the Abraham narratives in the Book of Genesis. This, however, is not the case, since Ben Sira—just as in many instances in 44:19-21—has created a new text of his own.

If we go through the Abraham cycle looking for vocabulary nearest to Sir 44:21b, two texts should seriously be considered, since they have more or less the same wording: Gen 22:18a / Gen 26:4b—והתברכו בזרעך כל גויי הארץ. As,

---

[55] See the contribution of M. Weigold in this volume.

[56] The combination of the verb קום *hiph'il* and the noun שבועה occurs only in Jer 11:5 and in Gen 26:3 (to Isaac!).

[57] See the final part of the paragraph entitled "Text."

[58] Cf. P.B. Payne, "A Critical Note on Ecclesiasticus 44:21's Commentary on the Abrahamic Covenant," *JETS* 15 (1972) 186-87.

moreover, the rare combination of שבועה and הקים in the preceding colon (44:21a) is reminiscent of Gen 26:3, it is not far fetched to assume it was Gen 26:3-4 that has inspired Ben Sira to formulate 44:21ab in this particular way. The most striking difference between these two texts would undoubtedly be that Ben Sira altered the collocation כל גויי הארץ into גוים. In my view, this is certainly to be considered a *deliberate* move, since so doing the author could explicitly refer back to the patriarch's epithet אב המון גוים in the *first* colon (44:19a), whereas the notion הארץ has been given a significant role in the *final* colon dealing with Abraham: ועד אפסי ארץ.

It is quite remarkable that in the final Hebrew bicolon of 44:21, Ben Sira did not adopt or rework one of the geographical formulae that are found in the Abraham cycle itself, such as Gen 13:15 ("all the land…"), 15:18 ("I give to your descendants this land from the river of Egypt to the Great River, the river Euphrates…") or 17:8 ("As a possession for all time I shall give you and your descendants after you the land in which you now are aliens, the whole of Canaan…"). Instead he has inserted a formula that occurs elsewhere in the Hebrew Bible (Ps 72:8; Zech 9:10) and is used both times in a specific sense:

> Ben Sira here quotes the standard expression of universal royal rule… and transfers it from the line of David to the entire posteriority of Abraham.[59]

Since it is the *final* bicolon of Abraham's portrayal by Ben Sira, this traditional royal statement now serves as a solemn conclusion of the first part of his presentation of the Patriarchs (44:19-21). One should not rule out the possibility that the shift from a royal to a nationwide, or even universal, background has something to do with the situation of the Jews in the Diaspora in Ben Sira's days. Whereas God's promises to Abraham in the Book of Genesis have a bearing only on the land of Israel, in Ben Sira's presentation the whole earth seems to be meant. Consequently the Diaspora is not longer presented as a punishment, but being the ultimate realisation of God's blessing to Abraham.[60]

2. *Ben Sira's presentation of Isaac (44:22)*

Considering the widely divergent renderings of this colon in the Versiones[61]—see *Appendix II*—it is advisable to stick to the Hebrew text of MS

---

[59] R.A.F. MacKenzie, *Sirach* (OTM 19, Wilmington: Glazier 1983) 170.

[60] "Die Diaspora erscheint damit nicht als Strafe, sondern als Verwirklichung des dem Abraham gegebenen Segens;" E. Janssen, *Das Gottesvolk und seine Geschichte* (Neukirchen: Neukirchener Verlag 1971) 18.

[61] The Greek not only has transposed the sequence of ברית and ברכה, it has also put these two nouns together into one colon (44:22c). Moreover, ἀνθρώπων is hardly to be considered an adequate rendering of ראשון and there is no equivalent of נתנו. In the Syriac both ברית and נתנו are missing. The text critical problems relating to Sir 44:22c have amply been discussed by Reiterer, *Urtext*, 109-11.

B.[62] As has been argued before, Sir 44:22c should have a bearing on Isaac. Ben Sira has selected a special vocabulary to mark Isaac's position. God makes Isaac participate in the covenant with "every ancestor" (כל ראשון). Within the context of the "Praise of the Famous" so far, the interpretation of this statement in 44:22c is that it not only has a bearing on God's covenant with Abraham (44:20b), but also on God's covenant with Noah (44:17d). The formulation as given in 44:22c is all the more striking because in the Hebrew Bible Isaac is said only to take part in God's oath to Abraham (Gen 26:3b). Upon a closer look, it is quite remarkable that Ben Sira in this colon has chosen the collocation נתן ברית, which in the Hebrew Bible is found only twice (Gen 17:2; Num 25:12). One cannot rule out the possibility that this might be a deliberate action again to lay emphasis on Genesis 17, the chapter that plays such a prominent role in the preceding lines relating to Abraham (44:19-21).

3. Ben Sira's presentation of Jacob/Israel (44:23)

Sir 44:23 has a number of special features. First, one should observe the rare combination of the verb נוח with the noun ברכה (44:23a), a collocation that in the Hebrew Bible is found only once (Ez 44:30). There is no reason whatsoever to assume Ben Sira adopted this wording from the prophet's book; it should be considered his own creation. Second, using the term "blessing" related to Jacob/Israel, the author is reminiscent of a crucial theme throughout the Jacob narrative (Gen 27:12, 35-36, 41; 28:4; 33:11). Third, it is hard to avoid the impression that Ben Sira plays upon words; there is a subtle pun between ראשון in the Isaac passage (44:22c) and ראש in that on Jacob (44:23a).

Special attention should be paid to the Hebrew text of Sir 44:23b and its marginal reading. The main text of this colon reads: ויכוננהו בברכה ("and He established him [כון polel] with a blessing"), whereas the marginal reading has ויכנהו בבכורה ("and He granted him [כנה pi.] with the title 'firstborn'"). The Hebrew of the main text of 44:23b is in fact a mere repetition or recapitulation of the preceding colon (44:23a) in which Jacob's blessing had already been topicalized. The Hebrew of the marginal reading, on the contrary, lays stress upon another theme that runs through the Jacob cycle as a major motif: בכורה, "the rank and rights as firstborn" (Gen 25:31-34; 27:36). It can hardly be a coincidence that earlier in his book, viz. in Sir 36:11, Ben Sira has explicitly broached this theme—ישראל בכור בינתה: "Israel, whom you granted the title 'firstborn'"[63]—in a prayer for deliverance (Sir 36:1-17).[64] The use of this theme is the more important, as it is found in a context which has some additional notions similar to the passage under discussion: "the tribes of Jacob;" the verb נחל (Sir 36:11-12). Therefore, there is solid proof

---

[62] "...muß die literarische Originalität Siras festgehalten werden;" Reiterer, Urtext, 111.
[63] See Exod 4:22.
[64] The verb כנה is also found in Sir 45:2a; 47:6b.

enough to advocate the marginal reading of Sir 44:23b as the more original and more theologically rich text.[65]

The phrase "He [God] gave him [Jacob/Israel] his heritage" (44:23c)—exactly the same phrase is found in Sir 45:20b with respect to Aaron!—must be considered Ben Sira's own interpretation of the Jacob narratives, as in the Book of Genesis the noun נחלה ("heritage") is nowhere used in respect of the patriarch.[66] That it is Ben Sira's hand indeed is the more likely since the author in the "Praise of the Famous" uses both the noun נחלה and the verb נחל rather frequently.[67]

The last question relating to Sir 44:23c-e that needs to be discussed here is whether these lines should be considered a thorough reworking of Deut 32:8-9, as is Hayward's contention.[68] He is absolutely right that there is a marked similarity of vocabulary between these two passages:

נחל	(Deut 32:8a / Sir 44:21d)
נחלה	(Deut 32:9b / Sir 44:23c)
חלק	(Deut 32:9a / Sir 44:23c)
נצב	(Deut 32:8c / Sir 44:23d)
עליון	(Deut 32:8a / Sir 44:20a)
כון	(Deut 32:6d / Sir 44:23b).[69]

Hayward argues:

> ...Ben Sira has subtly altered the general thrust of Deut 32:8-9. Whereas the latter speaks of the Most High making גוים inherit, and dividing up the sons of Adam, Ben Sira talks of the Most High making *Israel* inherit, and dividing *them* according to their tribes.[70]

I also do agree with Hayward's view that

> the inheritance of the twelve tribes is allotted by the Most High, but depends in the first instance on Abraham's obedience to the Most High's commandments.[71]

---

[65] Quite a few commentators are in favour of the marginal reading: Lévi, *L'Ecclésiastique* I, 92; Peters, *Der jüngst wiederaufgefundene*, 234; Skehan and Di Lella, *The Wisdom of Ben Sira*, 504; Sauer, *Jesus Sirach* (ATD) 304; Sauer, *Jesus Sirach* (JSHRZ) 616; Marböck, "Die Geschichte Israels," 185; J. Knabenbauer, *Commentarius in Ecclesiasticum* (CSS II/6, Paris: P. Lethielleux 1902) LXVI.

[66] In the Book of Genesis, the noun is found only once (Gen 31:14), where it has a bearing on Rachel and Lea.

[67] נחלה in Sir 44:8b, 11b, 23c; 45:20b, 22b, 22c, 25c, 25d; 46:8c, 9d; נחל in 44:21c; 45:22a, 23b; 46:1f.

[68] Hayward, "El Elyon," 188-90.

[69] This reference must be dropped if one favours the verb כנה (Bm).

[70] Hayward, "El Elyon," 189.

[71] *Ibid.*

Hayward's interpretation, however, that Abraham keeping the commandments of the Most High (44:20a) should be interpreted as paying the tithe to
the priest of the Most High[72] is rather far-fetched and should be dismissed,
not only because there is not a trace of evidence that Gen 14:20 was indeed
in Ben Sira's mind, but also because the noun מצות is to be considered a
singular, referring to Abraham's circumcision, as we have stated earlier.

CONCLUSION

However short Ben Sira's presentation of the Patriarchs in 44:19-23 may be,
time after time one is struck by the author's method to adopt, on the one
hand, traditional biblical concepts and notions and, on the other hand, to
link them in a creative way with fresh and stimulating views of his own.

---

[72] "...in all probability, we discover the rationale behind what he [Ben Sira] wrote
in 44:20, that Abraham kept the commandments of the Most High *specifically*,
inasmuch he paid tithe to the priest of God Most High;" Hayward, "El Elyon," 190.

APPENDIX I

Greek:

44:21b   that through his descendants nations should find blessing,
44:21c   that his family should be countless as the dust of the earth
44:21d   and be exalted as high as the stars (REB).

Syriac:

44:21b   that through his descendants all the nations of the earth would be
          blessed;
44:21c   that he would make his descendants numerous as the sands of the
          seashore,
44:21d   and that he would set his descendants above all other nations.[73]

Latin:

44:22b   that he would give him offspring[74] in his people,
44:22c   that he would make him numerous as a heap of earth[75]
44:23a   and would exalt his offspring as the stars.

APPENDIX II

Greek:

44:22c-23b The blessing of all men and the covenant
           he made to rest upon the head of Jacob.
           He acknowledged him in his blessings.

Syriac:

44:23a-c   and the blessing of all predecessors
           is resting on the head of Israel
           whom He named: my son, my first-born, Israel.

Latin:

44:25-26a The blessing of all nations He gave to him
           and He sanctioned the covenant on the head of Jacob.
           He acknowledged him in his blessings.

---

[73] Translation according to Skehan and Di Lella, *The Wisdom of Ben Sira*, 504.

[74] Codex *Metis*, however, reads *testamentum*, whereas a number of codices (e.g. *Amiatinus; Cavensis; Toletanus; Legionensis*) have *gloriam*.

[75] The text here has the word *cumulus* which is found nowhere else in the Vetus Latina or in the Vulgate.

APPENDIX III

Greek:
44:23c-e   and He gave him his inheritance;
            He determined his portions,
            and distributed them among twelve tribes.[76]

Syriac:
44:23d-e   and He gave him a heritage,
            and He established him as father for the tribes.
            They went out and divided themselves into twelve tribes.[77]

Latin:
44:26b-c   and He gave him a heritage
            and divided it for him among twelve tribes.

---

[76] Translation according to MacKenzie, *Sirach,* 170. Curiously, the *Revised English Bible* (1989) has all these sentences in the passive voice.

[77] The Syriac text according to Codex Ambrosianus reads: "and (when) he passed away, he was divided into twelve tribes;" Calduch-Benages, Ferrer and Liesen, *La sabiduría del escriba,* 244.

NOAH IN THE PRAISE OF THE FATHERS:
THE FLOOD STORY *IN NUCE**

Matthias Weigold
(University of Vienna, Institute for Jewish Studies)

In the Praise of the Fathers (Sir 44-50), Noah occurs as one—if not the first—of Israel's ancestors. So far, the brief portrayal of Noah in Sir 44:17-18 has not attracted a great deal of scholarly attention.[1] Commentators generally confine themselves to noticing some more or less evident connections with the

---

* I am indebted to Mr. Gerhard Haarmann and Dr. Volker Haarmann for improving the English of this article.

[1] T. Maertens, *L'Éloge des Pères (Ecclesiastique XLIV–L)* (LumVie 5, Bruges: Éditions de l'Abbaye de Saint-André 1956) 30-36, still provides the most extensive treatment; cf. now F.V. Reiterer, "Der Pentateuch in der spätbiblischen Weisheit Ben Siras," in *A Critical Study of the Pentateuch: An Encounter Between Europe and Africa* (eds. E. Otto and J. LeRoux, Altes Testament und Moderne 20, Münster: Lit 2005) 160-83 (168-73), as well as J. Schreiner, "Patriarchen im Lob der Väter," in *Textarbeit: Studien zu Texten und ihrer Rezeption aus dem Alten Testament und der Umwelt Israels* (eds. K. Kiesow and T. Meurer, AOAT 294, Münster: Ugarit-Verlag 2003) 425-41 (438); A.A. DiLella, "Ben Sira's Praise of the Ancestors of Old (Sir 44-49): The History of Israel as Parenetic Apologetics," in *History and Identity: How Israel's Later Authors Viewed Its Earlier History* (eds. N. Calduch-Benages and J. Liesen, DCLY, Berlin: de Gruyter 2006) 151-70 (159-60). The reference in Sir 44:17-18 is mostly neglected in studies on the ancient Jewish reception history of Noah and the Flood; cf. J.P. Lewis, *A Study of the Interpretation of Noah and the Flood in Jewish and Christian Literature* (Leiden: Brill 1968) 21; J.C. Vander-Kam, "The Righteousness of Noah," in *Ideal Figures in Ancient Judaism: Profiles and Paradigms* (eds. J.J. Collins and G.W.E. Nickelsburg, SBLSCS 12, Chico: Scholars Press 1980) 13-32 (15, 23-24); M.J. Bernstein, "Noah and the Flood at Qumran," in *The Provo International Conference on the Dead Sea Scrolls: Technological Innovations, New Texts, and Reformulated Issues* (eds. D.W. Parry and E. Ulrich, STDJ 30, Leiden: Brill 1999) 199-231 (203); D. Dimant, "Noah in Early Jewish Literature," in *Biblical Figures Outside the Bible* (eds. M.E. Stone and T.A. Bergren, Harrisburg: Trinity Press International 1998) 123-50 (125-26); G. Oberhänsli-Widmer, *Biblische Figuren in der rabbinischen Literatur: Gleichnisse und Bilder zu Adam, Noah und Abraham im Midrasch Bereschit Rabba* (Judaica et Christiana 17, Bern: Peter Lang 1998) 204-21, esp. 205; W. Uebele, "Der zweite Sündenfall und die Frommen der Urzeit: Kain und Abel, Henoch und Noach im Spiegel der alttestamentlich-frühjüdischen und urchristlichen Literatur," in *Alttestamentliche Gestalten im Neuen Testament: Beiträge zur biblischen Theologie* (ed. M. Öhler, Darmstadt: Wissenschaftliche Buchgesellschaft 1999) 40-53 (45); J. Ebach, *Noah: Die Geschichte eines Überlebenden* (Biblische Gestalten 3, Leipzig: Evangelische Verlagsanstalt 2001) 155 n. 108.

Book of Genesis.[2] In this article, I will provide a close examination of the portrayal of Noah in Sir 44:17-18, paying attention both to the perception of the figure of Noah and his story on the one hand, and to the purpose of the mention of Noah within the Praise of the Fathers on the other hand. In the final part, I will briefly address two major questions which bear on the placement of Sir 44:17-18 within the reception history of Noah and the Flood in ancient Jewish Literature.

THE PORTRAYAL OF NOAH IN SIR 44:17-18:
THE FLOOD STORY *IN NUCE*

The portrayal of Noah in Sir 44:17-18 is available in Hebrew in the Cairo Genizah MS B; v. 17a is also preserved in the Ben Sira scroll found at Masada (MasSir [Mas1h]). In both manuscripts the text is arranged in stichometric form. For the passage under consideration the Hebrew witnesses do not exhibit any major deviation:[3]

לעת⁴ כלה היה תחליף	נוח צדיק נמצא תמים	17
ובבריתו חדל מבול	בעבורו היה שארית	
לבלתי השחית כל בשר	באות עולם נכרת⁵ עמו	18

[17] Noah the righteous[6] was found blameless; at the time of destruction he became a renewer[7]. For his sake there was a remnant and with the covenant with him the deluge ceased. [18] With a lasting sign it was made with him, not to destroy all flesh.

---

[2] See, e.g., P.W. Skehan and A.A. DiLella, *The Wisdom of Ben Sira: A New Translation with Notes, Introduction and Commentary* (AB 39, New York: Doubleday 1987) 504-05; G. Sauer, *Jesus Sirach / Ben Sira: Übersetzt und erklärt* (ATD Apokryphen 1, Göttingen: Vandenhoeck & Ruprecht 2000) 304.

[3] The Text of Cairo Genizah MS B and MasSir (Mas1h) is presented according to *The Book of Ben Sira: Text, Concordance and an Analysis of the Vocabulary* (The Historical Dictionary of the Hebrew Language, Jerusalem: Academy of the Hebrew Language 1973) 54, with consideration of P.C. Beentjes, *The Book of Ben Sira in Hebrew: A Text Edition of All Extant Hebrew Manuscripts and a Synopsis of All Parallel Hebrew Ben Sira Texts* (VTSup 68, Leiden: Brill, 1997) as well as F. Vattioni, *Ecclesiastico: Testo ebraico con apparato critico e versioni greca, latina e siriaca* (Pubblicazioni del Seminario di Semitistica: Testi 1, Naples: Istituto Orientale di Napoli 1968) and Y. Yadin, *The Ben Sira Scroll from Masada: With Introduction, Emendations and Commentary* (Jerusalem: The Israel Exploration Society 1965). For the Greek text which slightly differs, see *Sapientia Iesu Filii Sirach* (2nd ed., ed. J. Ziegler, Septuaginta: Vetus Testamentum Graecum auctoritate Academiae Scientiarum Gottingensis 12.2, Göttingen: Vandenhoeck & Ruprecht 1980). The translation is my own.

[4] MasSir (Mas1h) may have read בעת.

[5] Cairo Genizah MS B has the marginal reading כרת.

[6] With attributes following a proper name the article can be left out, see GKC §126y.

[7] For the translation of the word תחליף, see below.

This poetic depiction consists of three bi-cola which may all be classified as synthetic parallelisms.[8] In the first bi-colon (v. 17a), Noah is introduced by name and, grammatically speaking, he is the subject. In terms of content, the portrayal of Noah opens with his characterisation (v. 17aα) and then indicates the setting of his story as well as Noah's particular role (v. 17aβ). This role of a lifetime is substantiated in the subsequent bi-cola (vv. 17b-18), referring back to Noah by the use of third-person singular suffixes (בעבורו, עמו ,ובבריתו).

On closer examination of the phraseology the generally recognised connection with the Book of Genesis can be specified. Indeed, the following terms and phrases link the description of Noah in Sir 44:17–18 with the text of Genesis:

To begin with, Noah's characterisation in v. 17aα נוח צדיק נמצא תמים ("Noah the righteous was found blameless") is entirely composed of different pieces from Genesis.[9] In Genesis, Noah is twice called righteous (צדיק) before the Flood (Gen 6:9; 7:1). However, the wording of Sir 44:17aα appears to combine Noah's designation as righteous (צדיק) and blameless (תמים)[10] in Gen 6:9 נח איש צדיק תמים היה בדרתיו ("Noah was a righteous man, blameless in his generation") with the root מצא found in Gen 6:8 ונח מצא חן בעיני יהוה ("But Noah found favour in the sight of the Lord."), rather than with Gen 7:1.[11] Unlike Genesis, a passive construction is used which implies God as the logical subject (*passivum divinum*).[12] It should be

---

[8] For the poetic pattern, cf. F.V. Reiterer, "The Hebrew of Ben Sira Investigated on the Basis of his Use of כרת: A Syntactic, Semantic and Language-Historical Contribution," in *Sirach, Scrolls, and Sages: Proceedings of a Second International Symposium on the Hebrew of the Dead Sea Scrolls, Ben Sira, and the Mishnah, held at Leiden University, 15–17 December 1997* (eds. T. Muraoka and J.F. Elwolde, STDJ 3, Leiden: Brill 1999) 253-77 (264).

[9] Irrespective of the fact that the phrase נמצא תמים also occurs in Sir 31:8.

[10] Cf. R. Egger-Wenzel, "Der Gebrauch von תמים bei Ijob und Ben Sira: Ein Vergleich zweier Weisheitsbücher," in *Freundschaft bei Ben Sira: Beiträge des Symposions zu Ben Sira, Salzburg 1995* (ed. F.V. Reiterer, BZAW 244, Berlin: de Gruyter 1996) 203-38, esp. 220-21.

[11] Cf. N. Peters, *Der jüngst wiederaufgefundene Hebräische Text des Buches Ecclesiasticus: Untersucht, herausgegeben, übersetzt und mit kritischen Noten versehen* (Freiburg: Herder 1902) 230; idem, *Das Buch Jesus Sirach oder Ecclesiasticus: Übersetzt und erklärt* (EHAT 25, Münster: Aschendorff 1913) 379. Schreiner, "Patriarchen im Lob der Väter," 438, stresses the difference in the portrayal of Noah: "Nach Gen 6,8 fand er Gnade in den Augen des Herrn, nach Sir 44,17 wurde er für vollkommen befunden." However, given the fact that תמים in Sir 44:17 is taken from Gen 6:9, the difference seems to be rather between Gen 6:8 and Gen 6:9 than between Gen 6:8 and Sir 44:17.

[12] This reference should be added to the examples given by C. Macholz, "Das 'Passivum divinum,' seine Anfänge im Alten Testament und der 'Hofstil,'" in *ZNW* 81 (1990) 247-53 (249-50).

added that Noah's righteousness is also prominent in Ezek 14:14, 20 as well as in ancient Jewish literature (e.g., 1QapGen vi 1-4, 6; xi 14; *Jub* 5:19; 10:17).[13]

Furthermore, the last three stichoi (Sir 44:17bβ-18) refer to the end of the Flood (מבול) and the covenant (בברית) with the bow in the sky as its sign (אות). One may wonder whether the phrase ובבריתו חדל מבול (v. 17bβ) implies a notion different from Genesis where the ending of the Flood is not directly related to a covenant.[14] Genesis rather relates how God announces his covenant with Noah *before* the Flood (Gen 6:18),[15] as well as the actual establishment of the divine covenant with all living beings *after* the Flood (Gen 9:8-17).[16] In the Praise of the Fathers, these two references seem to be conflated,[17] as becomes evident from two observations. On the one hand, the third-person singular suffix in ובבריתו, referring back to Noah, points to Gen 6:18 where Noah is addressed as the *sole* partner of the covenant, whereas in Gen 9:8-17 both Noah and his sons are addressed and the covenant itself includes all living beings. On the other hand, the covenant mentioned in Sir 44:17bβ is implied as the linguistic subject of נכרת in the subsequent bi-colon

---

[13] Cf. VanderKam, "The Righteousness of Noah;" J.L. Kugel, *The Bible as it Was* (Cambridge: Harvard University Press 1997) 116-17. For Noah's righteousness in the Genesis account, see also P.J. Harland, *The Value of Human Life: A Study of the Story of the Flood (Genesis 6-9)* (VTSup 64, Leiden: Brill 1996) 45-69.

[14] The verb חדל most likely denotes the ending of the Flood which is circumscribed by various other expressions in Genesis. By contrast, R. Smend, *Die Weisheit des Jesus Sirach erklärt* (Berlin: Reimer 1906) 422, claims that חדל expresses the absence of yet another Flood as explicated in the subsequent verse alluding to the postdiluvian covenant; cf. also E.S. Hartom, *Bn-syr' mtrgm bhlqw wmprš* (3rd ed., Tel Aviv: Yavneh 1969) 167. Although this interpretation is also attested by the Syriac translation, it hardly meets the meaning of חדל "to cease" (see *DCH* 3: 162 [s.v.]; *HALAT* 1: 280-81 [s.v.]); cf. Peters, *Das Buch Jesus Sirach*, 380.

[15] The future meaning of Gen 6:18a is clearly indicated by the inverted perfect והקמתי continuing the participle מביא (Gen 6:17) which also expresses the future; cf. Joüon, § 119n.

[16] It is a question in dispute, whether the covenant announced in Gen 6:18 is identical with the one established after the Flood (thus, e.g., O. Procksch, *Die Genesis: Übersetzt und erklärt* [KAT 1, 3rd ed., Leipzig: Deichert 1924] 471; S. van den Eynde, "The Missing Link: ברית in the Flood Narrative: Meaning and Peculiarities of a Hebrew Key Word," in *Studies in the Book of Genesis: Literature, Redaction and History* [ed. A. Wénin, BETL 155, Leuven: University Press 2001] 467-78 [471-73]) or whether Genesis has actually two distinct covenants in the Flood story (thus, e.g., C. Westermann, *Genesis* [BKAT 1.1, 3rd ed., Neukirchen-Vluyn: Neukirchener 1983] 1: 568; N.C. Baumgart, *Die Umkehr des Schöpfergottes: Zu Komposition und religionsgeschichtlichem Hintergrund von Gen 5-9* [HBS 22, Freiburg: Herder 1999] 226, 341–343). Most recently, E. Bosshard-Nepustil, *Vor uns die Sintflut: Studien zu Text, Kontexten und Rezeption der Fluterzählung Genesis 6-9* (BWANT 165, Stuttgart: Kohlhammer 2005) 63 n. 110, proposed to understand Gen 6:18-20 and 9:8-17 as "zwei Aspekte desselben umfassenden Bundesgeschehens" (cf. *ibid.*, 87).

[17] I am grateful to Professor Benjamin G. Wright for drawing my attention to this point at the symposium.

(v. 18),[18] which clearly alludes to the postdiluvian covenant, as will be shown in detail below.[19] Nevertheless, in contrast to Gen 9:8-17, but in accordance with Sir44:17bβ and Gen 6:18, the inflected preposition עמו singles out Noah as partner of this very covenant.[20] Thus it appears that Sir 44:17-18 presumes only one covenant which was established with Noah and which is somewhat connected with the end of the Flood. The exact nature of this connection depends on the meaning of the preposition ב (v. 17bβ) which is mostly defined as either causal or instrumental,[21] but might just as well introduce the covenant as a particular circumstance at the end of the Flood.[22] The latter interpretation is perhaps the one most close to Genesis, especially since the establishment of the covenant in Gen 9:8-17 marks the end of the Flood *story*, though not of the Flood itself. However, an additional clue can be found in Gen 6:17-18, where the announcement of the Deluge is immediately followed by the announcement of the covenant.[23]

---

[18] Reiterer, "The Hebrew of Ben Sira Investigated," 264-68, argues that an ellipsis of the feminine noun ברית is precluded by the verb נכרת because of both its passive and masculine form. Instead, he raises the possibility that אות is indicated as the subject by the preposition ב (*ibid.*, 264), but he finally favours a reflexive meaning of כרת *nip'al* implying God as subject (see *ibid.*, 266; cf. *idem*, "*Urtext*" *und Übersetzungen: Sprachstudie über Sir 44,16-45,26 als Beitrag zur Siraforschung* [Münchener Universitäts-schriften, Arbeiten zu Text und Sprache im Alten Testament 12, St. Ottilien: EOS 1980] 90-91, and already M.S. Segal, *Spr bn-syr' ḥšlm* [3rd ed., Jerusalem: Bialik Institute 1972] 308). Even though God is indeed implied as the logical subject, Reiterer's argument for a reflexive meaning of כרת *nip'al* is not convincing, particularly since in Sir 50:24 absolute כרת *nip'al* in a masculine form refers back to preceding ברית, although with a different (but still passive) meaning ("to be cut off"). Cf. also Smend, *Die Weisheit des Jesus Sirach erklärt*, 423, as well as the translation by W.Th. van Peursen, *The Verbal System in the Hebrew Text of Ben Sira* (Studies in Semitic Languages and Linguistics 41, Leiden: Brill, 2004) 372. See further *HALAT* 2: 476-77 (s.v.); *DCH* 4: 466 ("*with an eternal sign it was covenanted to him*"); GKC §145u.

[19] Unlike Sir 44:17-18, in Genesis (עם) כרת is not employed with respect to God's covenant with Noah. In Gen 9:11 כרת *nip'al* means "to be exterminated."

[20] It should be stressed, indeed, that Noah is perceived as *partner* of the covenant and not as its acting subject as could be inferred from an isolated reading of Sir 44:17bβ. However, the *passivum divinum* נכרת עמו (v. 18) leaves no doubt that בריתו in the previous colon has to be understood as God's covenant *with* Noah. Thus, the change from בריתי "*my* covenant" referring to *God* in Genesis (6:18; 9:9, 11, 15) to בריתו "*his* covenant" referring to *Noah* in Sir 44:17 can be explained as a mere matter of perspective.

[21] See, e.g., Peters, *Das Buch Jesus Sirach oder Ecclesiasticus*, 377 (causal); G. Sauer, *Jesus Sirach (Ben Sira)* (JSHRZ 3.5, Gütersloh: Gütersloher, 1981) 616 (instrumental).

[22] Cf. E. Jenni, *Die hebräischen Präpositionen* (Stuttgart: Kohlhammer 1992) 1: 329-48 ("Modalisation"); see also *HALAT* 1: 100-02 (s.v.).

[23] Likewise, a causal connection between the covenant as announced in Gen 6:18 and the ending of the Flood could be inferred from Gen 8:1, relating that God remembered (זכר; cf. Gen 9:15, 16) Noah and his fellow passengers, which marks the turning point in the course of the Flood; cf. Segal, *Spr bn-syr' ḥšlm*, 308; J. Marböck, "Die 'Geschichte Israels' als 'Bundesgeschichte' nach dem Sirachbuch," in *Der neue Bund im*

Turning to Sir 44:18, the "lasting sign" in v. 18a alludes to the bow in the sky which serves as a remembrance of the covenant (Gen 9:12-17).[24] Though the expression אות עולם does not occur in the Genesis account of the Flood, [25] both אות and עולם do occur in conjunction with the covenant, namely אות (ה) ברית "sign of the covenant" (Gen 9:12, 13, 17) and ברית עולם "everlasting covenant" (Gen 9:16).[26] Gen 9:12 even has both אות and עולם within one sentence (לדרת *עולם*... נתן אשר־הברית אני *אות* זאת "This is the sign of the covenant that I make... for all future generations."). The subsequent colon (v. 18b) finally provides the content of the divine covenant with Noah. Both the use of the infinitive construct to express negative purpose [27] and the vocabulary (שחת, כל בשר) particularly bring to mind Gen 9:15, where the negative stands at the beginning of the preceding clause (ולא־יהיה עוד המים

---

alten: Studien zur Bundestheologie der beiden Testamente (ed. E. Zenger, QD 146, Freiburg: Herder 1993) 177-97 (184). Whereas Smend, Die Weisheit des Jesus Sirach erklärt, 422; Hartom, Bn-syr', 167, reject this interpretation of Sir 44:17, Baumgart, Die Umkehr des Schöpfergottes, 343-44, even claims a similar interpretation for Genesis itself. Schreiner, "Patriarchen im Lob der Väter," 438, again emphasises the difference from Genesis, solely referring to Gen 9. However, he apparently ignores the preposition ב and turns בריתו into the subject ("hat der Bund [...] 'die Flut beendet'").

[24] The rainbow is mentioned explicitly in Sir 43:11 as well as in the praise of the High Priest Simon II in Sir 50:7. Whereas in the former passage the rainbow is introduced as a splendid work of God without the merest hint as to the postdiluvian covenant, with regard to the latter occurrence it is disputed whether the wording is adapted from Gen 9:14 (thus, e.g. O. Mulder, Simon the High Priest in Sirach 50: An Exegetical Study of the Significance of Simon the High Priest as Climax to the Praise of the Fathers in Ben Sira's Concept of the History of Israel [JSJSup 78, Leiden: Brill 2003] 132-33) or from Ezek 1:28 (thus, e.g., Skehan and DiLella, The Wisdom of Ben Sira, 552). The expression כל בשר in Sir 50:17 cannot easily be adduced as evidence for a reference to the postdiluvian covenant (thus Marböck, "Die 'Geschichte Israels' als 'Bundesgeschichte' nach dem Sirachbuch," 191; Mulder, Simon the High Priest in Sirach 50, 133), since unlike Gen 9:11, 15, 16, 17 and Sir 44:18 the animal world is not included here (pace E. Janssen, Das Gottesvolk und seine Geschichte: Geschichtsbild und Selbstverständnis im palästinensischen Schrifttum von Jesus Sirach bis Jehuda ha-Nasi [Neukirchen-Vluyn: Neukirchener 1971] 18; Egger-Wenzel, "Der Gebrauch von חמם bei Ijob und Ben Sira," 221).

[25] The same expression is used in Sir 43:6 with respect to the moon. Cf. also Isa 55:13 where it occurs in a negative sentence with כרת nip'al ("to be cut off").

[26] ברית עולם as in Gen 9:16 may have been the Vorlage of the Greek version of Sir 44:18a which reads διαθῆκαι αἰῶνος; cf. Reiterer, "Urtext" und Übersetzungen, 90-93; B.G. Wright, No Small Difference: Sirach's Relationship to Its Hebrew Parent Text (SBLSCS 26, Atlanta: Scholars Press 1989) 159. The reading of the Greek text is preferred, e.g., by Marböck, "Die 'Geschichte Israels' als 'Bundesgeschichte' nach dem Sirachbuch," 184 with n. 31.

[27] Cf. S.E. Fassberg, "On the Syntax of Dependent Clauses in Ben Sira," in The Hebrew of the Dead Sea Scrolls and Ben Sira: Proceedings of a Symposium held at Leiden University, 11-14 December 1995 (eds. T. Muraoka and J.F. Elwolde, STDJ 26, Leiden: Brill 1997) 56-71 (70); van Peursen, The Verbal System in the Hebrew Text of Ben Sira, 372. By contrast, Esther Yifrach, "The Construct Infinitive in the Language of Ben Sira," in Leš 59 (1995-1996) 275-94 (285) (Hebrew), regards the infinitive clause as an attribute to אות.

למבול לשחת כל־בשר "and the waters shall never again become a flood to destroy all flesh").[28]

These links with the Book of Genesis identified so far focus on the beginning of the Flood story and even more on its end. The event of the Deluge itself is, of course, present in the term מבול (v. 17bβ).[29] It is also implied in the expression עת כלה "time of destruction" (v. 17aβ), yet without echoing Genesis but rather Nah 1:8.[30] However, there is another possible allusion to the account of the Flood proper, i.e. the "remnant" (שארית)

---

[28] Cf. Wright, *No Small Difference*, 160. Gen 9:11 has כל בשר and שחת in two parallel negative clauses, whereas in Gen 6:17 the phrase לשחת כל־בשר occurs without the negative. The Samaritan Pentateuch in each case reads שחת *hip'il* instead of the *pi'el* in the Masoretic Text and thus provides a verbal parallel to Sir 44:18b in Gen 9:15 (and 6:17); cf. Macholz, "Das 'Passivum divinum', seine Anfänge im Alten Testament und der 'Hofstil'," 250 with n. 12. Strangely enough, B.L. Mack, *Wisdom and the Hebrew Epic: Ben Sira's Hymn in Praise of the Fathers* (CSJH, Chicago: University of Chicago Press, 1985) 239 n. 2 (to p. 206), claims concerning Sir 44:18b "that Ben Sira refers here to the Yahwist's account of the blessing on Noah (Gen 8:21) rather than to the priestly writer's account of the covenant with him (Gen 6:18-21)." Mack neither gives any reason for his claim nor does he even mention Gen 9:15!

[29] Based on the Genesis narrative (6:17; 7:6, 7, 10, 17; 9:11, 15, 28; 10:1, 32; 11:10), מבול is used almost exclusively as *terminus technicus* for the great Flood in the time of Noah in ancient Jewish literature; cf., e.g., 4Q252 i 3 (Gen 7:10); 4Q370 i 5, 8; 4Q422 ii 4, 11; 4Q577 4 1, as well as the Aramaic evidence in 1QapGen xii 9, 10; 4Q244 8 2; 4Q533 4 3.

[30] Admittedly, the Septuagint has καιρός in Gen 6:13, in place of קץ in the Masoretic Text. Although this equivalent is unique in the whole Pentateuch, it is unlikely that the Greek reflects a Hebrew variant (עת); cf. M. Rösel, *Übersetzung als Auslegung: Studien zur Genesis-Septuaginta* (BZAW 223, Berlin: de Gruyter 1994) 166. According to S. Schechter and C. Taylor, *The Wisdom of Ben Sira: Portions of the Book Ecclesiasticus from Hebrew Manuscripts in the Cairo Genizah Collection Presented to the University of Cambridge by the Editors* (Cambridge: University Press 1899) 28 with n. 6, the use of כלה "destruction" as a designation for the deluge alludes to Nah 1:8:
ובשטף עבר כלה יעשה. In the flood story of Genesis, the root כלה is only attested in Gen 6:16 referring to the construction of the ark as well as in Gen 8:2 where the Samaritan Pentateuch has ויכל instead of ויכלא in the MT. The latter passage refers to the subsiding of the flood as might be the case in the fragmentary 4QExposition on the Patriarchs (4Q464) 5 ii 3 which reads וכלון/יכלון שמ[י]הם (see E. Eshel and M.E. Stone, "464. 4QExposition on the Patriarchs," in *Qumran Cave 4.XIV: Parabiblical Texts, Part 2* [eds. M. Broshi, *et al.*, DJD 19, Oxford: Clarendon Press 1995] 215-30 [224]). Likewise, nothing can be inferred from the word כלם in 4Q370 i 5, a text that can be tentatively dated to the 3rd century BC (see A. Lange, "The Parabiblical Literature of the Qumran Library and the Canonical History of the Hebrew Bible," in *Emanuel: Studies in Hebrew Bible, Septuagint and Dead Sea Scrolls in Honor of Emanuel Tov* [eds. S.M. Paul, *et al.*, VTSup 94, Leiden: Brill 2003] 305-21 [311-12]), since it is uncertain whether this suffixed form derives from the verb כלה (thus C.A. Newsom, "370. 4QAdmonition Based on the Flood," in DJD 19: 85-93 [90-91, 94]), or rather from כל "all" (thus C.A. Newsom, "4Q370: An Admonition Based on the Flood," in *RevQ* 13 [1988] 23-43 [28, 36-37]; *The Dead Sea Scrolls Study Edition* [eds. F. García Martínez and E.J.C. Tigchelaar, Leiden: Brill 1998] 2: 732-33).

mentioned in v. 17bα, which is reminiscent of Gen 7:23 וישאר אך־נח ואשר אתו
בתבה ("Only Noah was left, and those that were with him in the ark.").[31]
Anyway, the "remnant" designates the human and animal survivors who
were spared in the destructive Flood.[32]

This survey, on the one hand, reveals a striking series of allusions to the
Flood story in Gen 6:5-9:17. Thus, in a few words focusing on Noah, the
whole Flood story is presented *in nuce*.[33] In comparison with the Genesis
account, significantly more attention is paid to the covenant with Noah
related to the end of the Flood than to the event of the Flood itself and its
motivation.[34] Not to mention the subsequent vineyard story (Gen 9:18-27)
which is entirely avoided in silence. On the other hand, it becomes clear that
the description of Noah in Sir 44:17-18 exhibits scarcely any independent
phrasing at all. In fact, the only stichos which appears to be phrased
completely independently, at least from the Book of Genesis, is found in
v. 17aβ לעת כלה היה תחליף.[35]

NOAH IN THE PRAISE OF THE FATHERS

Based on the examination of the relationship between the portrayal of Noah
in Sir 44:17-18 and its hypotext,[36] i.e. Gen 6:5-9:17, it is possible to grasp the

---

[31] Cf. Bernstein, 'Noah and the Flood at Qumran,' 203 n. 9. Likewise, this
observation applies to the Greek versions of Sir 44:17 (κατάλειμμα) and Gen 7:23
(κατελείφθη); cf. M. Harl, *La Genèse* (La Bible d'Alexandrie 1, Paris: Cerf 1986) 136. The
notion of a "remnant" is sometimes interpreted as reflecting an etymology of the
name "Noah" from נוח *hip'il* "to leave behind" (cf. *1 En* 83:8; 106:16, 18; *2 En* 35:1;
4 Ezra 3:11); see Lewis, *A Study of the Interpretation of Noah and the Flood*, 21 n. 2, 27 n. 2;
J.C. VanderKam, "The Birth of Noah,' in *idem, From Revelation to Canon: Studies in the
Hebrew Bible and Second Temple Literature* (JSJSup 62, Leiden: Brill 2000) 396-412 (404) (=
Intertestamental Essays in Honour of Józef Tadeusz Milik, ed. Z.J. Kapera, Qumranica
Mogilanensia 6, Kraków: Enigma Press 1992) 213-31 (222-23); Dimant, "Noah in Early
Jewish Literature," 125-26. As far as Sir 44:17 is concerned, it should be borne in mind,
after all, that the root employed is שאר rather than נוח.

[32] Cf. Segal, *Spr bn-syr' hšlm*, 308, as well as the pointed translation "survivors" by
Skehan and DiLella, *The Wisdom of Ben Sira*, 503.

[33] Cf. Dimant, "Noah in Early Jewish Literature," 126. Janssen, *Das Gottesvolk und
seine Geschichte*, 18, arbitrarily states with regard to Sir 44:17-18: "Bei Noah fällt auf,
daß die Sintflutgeschichte fehlt. Nur die Rettung wird genannt."

[34] The motivation of the Flood is betokened in the Greek version which has ὀργή
"wrath" in place of the Hebrew כלה "destruction" (Sir 44:17). Note that in Sir 40:10
כלה is rendered by κατακλυσμός (cf. Sir 21:13; 39:22); for the Hebrew of Sir 44:10, cf.
H.P. Rüger, "Zum Text von Sir 40 10 und Ex 10 21," in *ZAW* 82 (1970) 103-09.

[35] According to T.R. Lee, *Studies in the Form of Sirach 44-50* (SBLDS 75, Atlanta: Scholars
Press 1986) 77, "Sirach uses the new term תחליף as a way of expressing Gen 6:9." However,
on the linguistic level there is not the merest evidence for this claim; cf. also Marböck, "Die
'Geschichte Israels' als 'Bundesgeschichte' nach dem Sirachbuch," 184.

[36] For the term hypotext, see G. Genette, *Palimpsests: Literature in the Second Degree*
(trans. C. Newman and C. Doubinsky, foreword by G. Prince, Stages 8, Lincoln: University of Nebraska Press 1997).

role which is intended for Noah within the Praise of the Fathers. For this purpose, it seems advisable to have a closer look at (a) the independent stichos in Sir 44:17aβ and (b) the context of the Noah passage within the Praise of the Fathers.

First of all, it stands to reason that the very stichos shaped independently from Genesis (לעת כלה היה תחליף) betrays the author's own perception and is thus crucial for the picture of Noah in the Praise of the Fathers. The inventive contribution culminates in the new word תחליף, which is not attested as a noun in Hebrew or Aramaic before Ben Sira. However, the meaning of this key term, which also occurs in Sir 46:12 and 48:8,[37] is difficult to define.[38] Whereas in Sir 48:8 תחליף most probably designates the prophet Elisha as Elijah's "successor,"[39] this meaning seems inappropriate in the passage about Noah, simply because there is no predecessor whosoever whom Noah could follow.[40] In the Greek text of Sir 44:17, תחליף is rendered by ἀντάλλαγμα "that which is given or taken in exchange".[41] Although the two notions of substitution as well as of succession generally fit in with the range of meanings of the root חלף,[42] in the context of Noah another nuance of תחליף is suggested by the use of חלף hip'il in Job 14:7; 29:20.[43] In Job 14:7 the verb is used of a tree which is said to be cut down and means "to sprout afresh."[44] The connotation of "renewal" is further articulated in Job 29:20,

---

[37] In both cases it is disputed whether תחליף is a noun or a hip'il of חלף. A verbal interpretation is preferred, e.g., by *The Original Hebrew of a Portion of Ecclesiasticus (XXXIX.15 to XLIX.11) Together with the Early Versions and an English Translation, Followed by the Quotations from Ben Sira in Rabbinical Literature* (eds. A.E. Cowley and A. Neubauer, Oxford: Clarendon Press 1897) 31, 37; S. Krauss, "Notes on Sirach," in *JQR* 11 (1899) 150-58 (156-57). Peters, *Das Buch Jesus Sirach oder Ecclesiasticus*, 396, 398, only takes it as a verb in Sir 46:12, whereas Sir 48:8 is recorded as a verbal form in *Konkordanz zum hebräischen Sirach: Mit syrisch-hebräischem Index* (eds. D. Barthélemy and O. Rickenbacher, Göttingen: Vandenhoeck & Ruprecht 1973) 126.

[38] A thorough philological analysis of "The Word תחליף in Ben Sira" by Wido van Peursen is forthcoming in the proceedings of the *Strasbourg Colloquium on the Hebrew of the Qumran Scrolls and Ben Sira*, Strasbourg, 29-30 May 2006 (ed. J. Joosten, STDJ, Leiden: Brill). I am obliged to Professor van Peursen for providing me a pre-publication version of his contribution. I also want to express my gratitude to Mr. Kevin Trompelt for his helpful philological remarks.

[39] The interpretation of תחליף as "successor" is corroborated by the Greek equivalent διάδοχος, in spite of its plural form against the Hebrew singular.

[40] Pace M. Hengel, *Judentum und Hellenismus: Studien zur ihrer Begegnung unter besonderer Berücksichtigung Palästinas bis zur Mitte des 2. Jh.s v.Chr.* (WUNT 10, 3rd ed., Tübingen: Mohr Siebeck 1988) 249.

[41] See LSJ, s.v.; J. Lust, *et al.*, *A Greek-English Lexicon of the Septuagint* (2nd ed., Stuttgart: Deutsche Bibelgesellschaft 2003) s.v.

[42] Cf. *DCH* 3: 238-39 (s.v.); *HALAT* 1: 308 (s.v.); S. Tengström and H.-J. Fabry, "חלף," in *ThWAT* 2: 999-1001.

[43] As van Peursen, "The Word תחליף in Ben Sira," points out, it is disputed whether the *taqtil* pattern is particularly related to the *hip'il* or not.

[44] Interestingly enough, Sir 44:17-18 and Job 14:7 have not only the root חלף in common, but also the verbs חדל and כרת. Job 14:7 has already been adduced by D.

where חלף *hip'il* parallels חדש "new." Especially the notion expressed by the tree imagery in Job 14:7 offers an apt interpretation of the role attributed to Noah in Sir 44:17: like a fresh sprout arising from a stump, Noah provides a recommencement after destruction which implies renewal and continuation at the same time.[45] Accordingly, "renewer" might be a reasonable translation of תחליף in Sir 44:17, provided that it also comprises the aspect of continuation.[46] This latter aspect is underscored by the subsequent appraisal of Noah's merit that there was "a remnant" surviving the flood (Sir 44:17bα).[47]

Thus, the Praise of the Fathers credits Noah with the continuity and renewal of life on earth. Taking into account that v. 17aβ continues the opening stichos and that the subsequent stichoi refer back to it, this pivotal function of Noah is clearly based on his righteousness emphasised from the outset. Whereas in this way, Noah's performance is effectively related to the past, the divine covenant extends his role into the future, pledging to the

Kaufmann, "Das Wort תחליף bei Jesus Sirach," in *MGWJ* 41 (1897) 387-40 (339), though in favour of the meaning "substitution" ("Ersatz" or "Stellvertretung").

[45] Following I. Lévi, *L'Ecclésiastique ou La sagesse de Jésus, fils de Sira: Texte original hébreu édité, traduit et commenté* (Bibliothèque de l'école des hautes études: Sciences religieuses 10, Paris: Leroux 1898) 1.89, van Peursen, "The Word תחליף in Ben Sira," arrives at the conclusion that "Noah was the shoot that came up from the stump of the human race." With respect to Sir 46:12, he argues for the interpretation of תחליף as "shoot, offspring."

[46] Apparently, it is not only difficult "to cover the three usages" of תחליף in Ben Sira "by a single translation equivalent," as van Peursen, "The Word תחליף in Ben Sira," concludes, but even to render its complex usage in one and the same place by one word. With regard to Sir 44:17, this latter difficulty is reflected, e.g., in the combination of "renewer" with "procreator" (V. Ryssel, "Die Sprüche Jesus', des Sohnes Sirachs," in *APAT* 1: 230-475, 451) or "continuator" (Mack, *Wisdom and the Hebrew Epic*, 46; Marböck, "Die 'Geschichte Israels' als 'Bundesgeschichte' nach dem Sirachbuch," 184).

[47] Cf. Smend, *Die Weisheit des Jesus Sirach erklärt*, 422. Prompted by the catchword "remnant" (שארית), time and again stress is laid on this point as the alleged focus of the entire portrayal of Noah in Sir 44:17-18, linking it with the idea of a remnant either in the prophetic literature (thus, e.g., Maertens, *L'Éloge des Pères*, 30-36, esp. 33-35; R.T. Siebeneck, "May their Bones Return to Life!—Sirach's Praise of the Fathers," in *CBQ* 21 [1959] 411-28 [422-23]; R.A.F. MacKenzie, *Sirach* [Old Testament Message 19, Wilmington: Glazier 1983] 169; Uebele, "Der zweite Sündenfall und die Frommen der Urzeit," 53 n. 9; Di Lella, "Ben Sira's Praise of the Ancestors of Old," 159-60) or in the Qumran literature (thus Dimant, "Noah in Early Jewish Literature," 125-26). However, the mere occurrence of שארית does not provide sustainable evidence of such far-reaching claims, because this word can derive from the text of Genesis (cf. above with n. 31), as opposed to the preceding stichos. In fact, one might think of singling out another element in Sir 44:17bα which seems to be independent on a linguistic level and might therefore reveal an innovative notion, namely the word בעבורו. Rather than שארית, the inconspicuous בעבורו also carries the stress within this stichos, as is indicated by the suffix referring back to Noah as well as the parallel ובבריתו in the subsequent stichos. Cf. the comparable emphasis on Noah's merit in *Jub* 5:19.

righteous survivor of the flood "not to destroy all flesh" (v. 18b), that is in positive words: to maintain life on earth.[48]

Beyond this passage about Noah in Sir 44:17-18, its context sheds light on Noah's role within the Praise of the Fathers, all the more so, as a closer examination reveals a striking correspondence with the emphasis on particular details from the Genesis account in the portrayal of Noah itself. To begin with, it is still a matter of debate whether or not the reference to Noah was originally preceded by a mention of Enoch (Sir 44:16) who (re-)emerges in Sir 49:14. In view of the substantial disagreement between the Hebrew MS B and the Greek text on the reference to Enoch in Sir 44:16, as well as its absence from MasSir (Mas1h)[49] and the Syriac translation, textual evidence suggests considering the entire verse as an interpolation.[50] If so, Noah was indeed the first individual introduced by name in the Praise of the Fathers.

In any case, Noah is the first link in a chain of figures distinguished as recipients of a covenant (ברית), ranging to the chronologically premature covenant with David (Sir 44:17-45:26).[51] This sequence is introduced before,

---

[48] Reiterer, "Der Pentateuch," 168-73, 179, reaches a similar conclusion although his leading point of Enoch and Noah as "'vorisraelitisches' Paar, das eine relativ in sich geschlossene Botschaft transportiert" (p. 171) stands on shaky grounds; see below.

[49] Judging from Yadin, *The Ben Sira Scroll from Masada*, pls. 5 and 8, Yadin's placing of a small fragment to the beginning of col. vii 24 (cf. *ibid.*, 38) seems accurate, although it has been doubted by D. Lührmann, "Henoch und die Metanoia," in *ZNW* 66 (1975) 103-16 (108). However, as Lührmann himself admits (*ibid.*, n. 14), the letter following נמצא תמים can be read as a ב according to Sir 44:17, but certainly not as a ו which should be expected in Sir 44:16.

[50] Cf. T. Middendorp, *Die Stellung Jesu Ben Siras zwischen Judentum und Hellenismus* (Leiden: Brill 1973) 53-54, 109-10, 112, 134; Mack, *Wisdom and the Hebrew Epic*, 199-200, as well as on literary and theological grounds P.C. Beentjes, "The 'Praise of the Famous' and Its Prologue: Some Observations on Ben Sira 44:1-15 and the Question on Enoch in 44:16," in *BTFT* 45 (1984) 374-83 (380-82). The argument is followed by Marböck, "Die 'Geschichte Israels' als 'Bundesgeschichte' nach dem Sirachbuch," 183 with n. 29.

[51] For the concept of covenant as a structural feature in the Praise of the Fathers, see especially Marböck, "Die 'Geschichte Israels' als 'Bundesgeschichte' nach dem Sirachbuch." Cf. J. Haspecker, *Gottesfurcht bei Jesus Sirach: Ihre religiöse Struktur und ihre literarische und doktrinäre Bedeutung* (AnBib 30, Rome: Päpstliches Bibelinstitut 1967) 85 n. 94; Beentjes, "The 'Praise of the Famous' and Its Prologue," 379, 382; Mack, *Wisdom and the Hebrew Epic*, 20-21, 38-39, 76; Schreiner, "Patriarchen im Lob der Väter," 436-437. A. Goshen-Gottstein, "Ben Sira's Praise of the Fathers: A Canon-Conscious Reading," in *Ben Sira's God: Proceedings of the International Ben Sira Conference, Durham, Ushaw College 2001* (ed. R. Egger-Wenzel, BZAW 321, Berlin: de Gruyter, 2002) 235-67 (246-47), also includes Enoch (Sir 44:16) as well as Moses (Sir 45:1-5) in this chain of covenants, although the term ברית does not occur in the respective passages, arguing that אות is used as an equivalent of ברית. However, apart from the questionable equivalence as inferred from Sir 44:17-18, the particular designation of Enoch as אות דעת "sign of knowledge" does not hint at any covenant whatsoever. By the same token, the "signs" mentioned in Sir 45:3—where the Hebrew word is not even preserved—

in the Prologue (Sir 44:12),[52] and finally culminates in the praise of Simon the High Priest which explicitly recalls the covenant with Phinehas (Sir 50:24).[53] The linking theme of covenant within the Praise of the Fathers corresponds to the emphasis on the covenant in the portrayal of Noah in Sir 44:17-18 as described above. Hence, the covenant established with Noah turns out to be crucial for Noah's mention within the Praise of the Fathers.

Compared to the subsequent covenants, the peculiarity of the covenant with Noah consists in its universality. Admittedly, according to the overall perspective on the "Fathers," Noah is singled out as partner of the covenant, leaving aside his descendants as well as the animals mentioned in Gen 9:8-17. Nevertheless, the universal scope of the covenant with Noah is clearly indicated by its "perpetual sign" (אות עולם) and its content, i.e. the divine promise "not to destroy all flesh (כל בשר)."[54] Noah, to whom man and beast owe their survival of the flood, is granted that life on earth will henceforth be spared global destruction.[55]

THE PRAISE OF THE FATHERS
WITHIN THE RECEPTION HISTORY OF NOAH AND THE FLOOD

Having analysed the portrayal of Noah in the Praise of the Fathers, at least two questions should be addressed which bear on the placement of Sir 44:17-18 within the broader reception history of Noah and the flood in ancient Jewish literature. The following considerations solely aim at raising the scholarly awareness of these questions which have far-reaching consequences for the study of both the Noah traditions and Ben Sira, much too far-reaching to be explored here.

The first question which has been previously touched on by Moshe Bernstein arises from the observation that Noah takes the first place in a chain of figures with whom covenants were established.[56] Within this chain, Noah is particularly linked to the patriarchs in Sir 44:19-23.[57] In addition to

refer to Moses' activity in Egypt, i.e. before the giving of Torah which is *not* referred to as ברית.

[52] The Hebrew text of Sir 44:12 is only partly preserved in MasSir (Mas1h). Cf. P.A.H. de Boer, "Sirach xliv 12a," in *Hebräische Wortforschung: FS W. Baumgartner* (VTSup 16, Leiden: Brill 1967) 25-29.

[53] According to the Hebrew MS B. In the Greek, Latin and Syriac versions of Sir 50:24 the covenant with Phinehas is not mentioned.

[54] Cf. A. Jaubert, *La notion d'alliance dans le judaisme aux abords de l'ère chrétienne* (Patristica Sorbonensia 6, Paris: Seuil 1963) 56; Marböck, "Die 'Geschichte Israels' als 'Bundesgeschichte' nach dem Sirachbuch," 184, 197.

[55] Cf. Mack, *Wisdom and the Hebrew Epic*, 27; Jean Louis Ska, "L'Éloge des Pères dans le Siracide (Si 44-50) et le canon de l'Ancien Testament," in *Treasures of Wisdom: Studies in Ben Sira and the Book of Wisdom, FS M. Gilbert* (eds. N. Calduch-Benages and J. Vermeylen, BETL 143, Leuven: Peeters 1999) 181-93 (186).

[56] See Bernstein, "Noah and the Flood at Qumran," 203 n. 9.

[57] Cf. R.J. Coggins, *Sirach* (Guides to Apocrypha and Pseudepigrapha, Sheffield: Sheffield Academic Press 1998) 80. For the patriarchs in Sir 44:19-23, cf. Schreiner,

the term ברית which recurs in Sir 44:20, 22, the verb נמצא is used analogously in the Abraham section (Sir 44:20) as is the case for the emphatic בעבור in the Isaac section (Sir 44:17, 22). Furthermore, both כרת and בשר recur in Sir 44:20, designating circumcision as the sign of the covenant with Abraham (cf. Gen 17).[58] Finally, the reference to "the covenant with every forebear" (ברית כל ראשון) in Sir 44:22 is likely to include the covenant with Noah.[59] Notwithstanding the respective peculiarities,[60] the incontestable linking of Noah and the subsequent recipients of a covenant, especially the patriarchs, raises the question in how far this placing of Noah in the chain of Israel's ancestors simply follows the Book of Genesis or whether there is more behind it. On the one hand, in Ez 14:14-20 Noah appears together with Daniel and Job, whereas in somewhat comparable outlines like 1 Macc 2:51-60 or CD ii 14-iv 12 he is absent.[61] Later on in rabbinic tradition, Noah is primarily perceived as the father of the *nations* (גוים) which are stereotypically called "sons of Noah" (בני נוח), but *not* a representative of *Israel*.[62] On the

---

"Patriarchen im Lob der Väter," esp. 438-41, as well as the contribution of Pancratius C. Beentjes in the present volume. For the figure of Abraham, see also G. Sauer, „Die Abrahamgestalt im 'Lob der Väter:' Auswahl und Intention," in *Wiener Jahrbuch für Theologie* 1 (1996) 387-412, esp. 401-12.

[58] Cf. Reiterer, "The Hebrew of Ben Sira Investigated on the Basis of his Use of כרת," 268-74

[59] Thus Skehan and Di Lella, *The Wisdom of Ben Sira*, 505; cf. Marböck, "Die 'Geschichte Israels' als 'Bundesgeschichte' nach dem Sirachbuch," 185. According to Janssen, *Das Gottesvolk und seine Geschichte*, 19, even Enoch is included, whereas A. Kahana, "Dbry šm'wn bn syr'," in *Ltwrh lnby'ym lktwbym wš'r sprym hyswnym bšny krkym 'm mbw'wt wpyrwšym hsprym hhyswnym* (ed. *idem*, Jerusalem: Makor 1978) 2.2.435-530, 520, points to the covenants with Abraham and Isaac which, then, Jacob receives. In fact, it is disputed whether the mention of the covenant in Sir 44:22 belongs to the following portrayal of Jacob as is the case in the Greek translation, or rather to the preceding portrayal of Isaac. The parallelism seems to argue in favour of the former (thus, e.g., Peters, *Der jüngst wiederaufgefundene Hebräische Text*, 233; Marböck, "Die 'Geschichte Israels' als 'Bundesgeschichte' nach dem Sirachbuch," 185), yet the verb נתנו is more likely to refer back to Isaac (thus, e.g., Wright, *No Small Difference*, 179; Sauer, *Jesus Sirach / Ben Sira*, 303). If so, the links between Noah and the patriarchs would focus on Abraham and Isaac only.

[60] Thus, Mack, *Wisdom and the Hebrew Epic*, 42-43, 53, points out a contrast between the negative promise to Noah and the positive promise to Abraham.

[61] In the *Damascus Document*, Noah's absence is particularly remarkable since CD ii 16-iii 1 refers to the wicked generations of the flood and of Noah's sons, followed by Abraham, Isaac, and Jacob.

[62] A similar view is claimed for the Praise of the Fathers by Goshen-Gottstein, "Ben Sira's Praise of the Fathers," 248 n. 33, arguing that up to the covenant with Abraham God is only implied "as the hidden subject" by the use of *passivum divinum*, whereas thereafter he "becomes the linguistic subject," which according to Goshen-Gottstein indicates a distinction of "status" between the pre-Israel heroes and "Israel's heroes" who are credited "true covenantal divine action." However, the alleged turning point from the passive to the active voice stands on shaky grounds, since it is more than questionable whether God—rather than Abraham—is indeed the subject of

other hand, in somewhat more contemporary[63] texts, Noah is also linked with the patriarchs. Thus, in 4QPrFêtes[b] (4Q508) 3 2-3 the covenants with Noah as well as Abraham, Isaac and Jacob seem to be associated.[64] Moreover, in Tob 4:12 those four are adduced together as paradigms of endogamous marriage: "Remember, my son, that Noah, Abraham, Isaac, and Jacob, our ancestors of old, all took wives from among their kindred." Furthermore, the *Aramaic Levi Document* and the *Book of Jubilees* attest to a chain of transmission, in particular of halakhic teachings, in which Noah figures as a kind of "bridge" over the deluge in order to preserve the original knowledge.[65] However, coming back to Noah the Praise of the Fathers, the notion seems to be closer to the Book of Genesis: Noah is perceived as the progenitor of postdiluvian humankind, including both Israel and the nations.[66]

When speaking about contemporary texts, a second question should be approached. Armin Lange has recently made a case that the Praise of the Fathers in Sir *44-49 represents an older composition dating from the third century BC which was incorporated by Ben Sira and enlarged with the paean to the high priest Simon II in Sir 50.[67] According to Lange this

---

the phrase ובא בברית עמו (Sir 44:20). Moreover, the *passivum divinum* נמצא is used analogously for both Noah (Sir 44:17) and Abraham (Sir 44:20); cf. Macholz, "Das 'Passivum divinum', seine Anfänge im Alten Testament und der 'Hofstil,'" 249-50. Cf. also the critical remarks of DiLella, "Ben Sira's Praise of the Ancestors of Old," 153. For Noah in rabbinic tradition, see Lewis, *A Study of the Interpretation of Noah and the Flood*, 121-55; Oberhänsli-Widmer, *Biblische Figuren in der rabbinischen Literatur*, 201-58, esp. 222-41; cf. also W.J. van Bekkum, "The Lesson of the Flood: מַבּוּל in Rabbinic Tradition," in *Interpretations of the Flood* (eds. F. García Martínez and G.P. Luttikhuizen, Themes in Biblical Narrative: Jewish and Christian Traditions 1, Leiden: Brill 1999) 124-33.

[63] The Book of Ben Sira was composed in the first quarter of the second century BC See, e.g., Skehan and Di Lella, *The Wisdom of Ben Sira*, 8-16; Coggins, *Sirach*, 18-20; J. Marböck, "Das Buch Jesus Sirach," in Erich Zenger, *et al.*, *Einleitung in das Alte Testament* (6th ed., Stuttgart: Kohlhammer 2006) 408-16 (413). For the Praise of the Fathers as a possibly earlier work, see below.

[64] Cf. Bernstein, "Noah and the Flood at Qumran," 220. For the dating and provenance of the work, see D.K. Falk, *Daily, Sabbath, and Festival Prayers in the Dead Sea Scrolls* (STDJ 27, Leiden: Brill 1998) 61-63, 156-57. In light of this passage, Bernstein, "Noah and the Flood at Qumran," 220-21, suggests a similar reading in 4Q405 124 4-6.

[65] Cf. M.E. Stone, "The Axis of History at Qumran," in *Pseudepigraphic Perspectives: The Apocrypha and Pseudepigrapha in Light of the Dead Sea Scrolls, Proceedings of the International Symposium of the Orion Center for the Study of the Dead Sea Scrolls and Associated Literature, 12-14 January, 1997* (eds. E.G. Chazon and M.E. Stone, STDJ 31, Leiden: Brill 1999) 133-49. In *Jub* 7:38-39; 21:10, this tradition is traced back as far as Enoch.

[66] Cf. A. Niccacci, "La Lode dei Padri: Ben Sira tra passato e futuro," in *Initium sapientiae. Scritti in onore di Franco Festorazzi nel suo 70. compleanno* (ed. R. Fabris, Supplementi alla Rivista Biblica 36, Bologna: Dehoniane 2000) 199-225, speaking of "una galleria di personaggi della storia biblica, Padri dell'umanità, non solo di Israele" (202).

[67] See Lange, "The Parabiblical Literature of the Qumran Library," 307-08; *idem*, "From Literature to Scripture: The Unity and Plurality of the Hebrew Scriptures in

accounts best for the well-known facts of 1) the disproportionately accentuated praise of Simon II, 2) the supposedly second mention of Enoch in Sir 49:14 (cf. 44:16), and 3) the chronologically inappropriate praise of Joseph, Shem, Seth, Enosh and Adam in Sir 49:15-16. Indeed, the assessment of the Praise of the Fathers as well as other textual units in the Book of Ben Sira as originally independent compositions has long since been a matter of scholarly debate.[68] Broadly speaking however, most of the scholars who actually hold this view still adhere to the authorship of Ben Sira, arguing that the book has been compiled of what he had written in the course of time, whether by Ben Sira himself[69] or by one of his students.[70] There are only few dissenting voices assuming that the Book of Ben Sira includes earlier works which were not composed by Ben Sira, but rather taken up.[71] As for the Praise of the Fathers, it has indeed been previously asserted that Ben Sira depends on a poetic description of the history of Israel ranging from Adam to Nehemiah and dating from the second half of the third century BC.[72] Leaving aside the minor differences between Fuss and Lange, the basic suggestion regarding Ben Sira's Praise of the Fathers as a reworked version of an older composition deserves a detailed examination, which goes far beyond the scope of the present article. Generally speaking, this suggestion seems particularly attractive because it adequately explains the very inclusion of the Praise of the Fathers within the Book of Ben Sira, a fact which in any case requires an explanation in view of the clear differences

Light of the Qumran Library," in *One Scripture or Many? Canon from Biblical, Theological, and Philosophical Perspectives* (eds. C. Helmer and C. Landmesser, Oxford: Oxford University Press 2004) 51-107 (80 with n. 65).

[68] See, e.g., J. Marböck, "Structure and Redaction History in the Book of Ben Sira: Review and Prospects," in *The Book of Ben Sira in Modern Research: Proceedings of the First International Ben Sira Conference, 28-31 July 1996, Soesterberg, Netherlands* (ed. P.C. Beentjes, BZAW 255, Berlin: de Gruyter 1997) 61-79 (76-79).

[69] Thus, e.g., Peters, *Das Buch Jesus Sirach oder Ecclesiasticus*, XXXIX-XL; Skehan and Di Lella, *The Wisdom of Ben Sira*, 10; Marböck, "Structure and Redaction History in the Book of Ben Sira," 76-79; idem, "Das Buch Jesus Sirach," 412-13, following the pioneering work of J.G. Eichhorn, *Einleitung in die apokryphischen Schriften des Alten Testaments* (Leipzig: Weidmann 1795) 50-54, and O.F. Fritzsche, *Die Weisheit Jesus Sirach's: Erklärt und übersetzt* (Kurzgefasstes exegetisches Handbuch zu den Apokryphen des Alten Testaments 5, Leipzig: Hirzel 1859) XXVII-XXXIII, esp. XXXII.

[70] Thus particularly L. Schrader, *Leiden und Gerechtigkeit: Studien zu Theologie und Textgeschichte des Sirachbuches* (BBET 27, Frankfurt: Lang 1994) 58-68, 303.

[71] To my knowledge, the first one to raise this assumption was H.G.A. Ewald, "Über das Griechische Spruchbuch Jesus' Sohnes Sirach's," in *Jahrbücher der biblischen Wissenschaft* 3 (1850-1851) 125-40 (131-39); idem, *Geschichte des Volkes Israel* (3rd ed., Göttingen: Dieterich 1864) 4: 340-47, though referring to Sir 1:1-16:21 as well as 16:22-36:22 and just ascribing Sir *36:23-51:30 to Ben Sira.

[72] See Werner Fuss, *Tradition und Komposition im Buche Jesus Sirach* (Diss., University of Tübingen, 1963) 252-59, 288, basically reckoning Sir 44:16-45:5; 46:1-49:13 to this work. Cf. the abstract of Fuss's dissertation in *ThLZ* 88 (1963) 948-49.

between the Praise of the Fathers and the rest of the Book, be it in terms of form, content, or scope.

CONCLUSION

In the Praise of the Fathers, Noah appears as the first of Israel's ancestors to be extolled by name. Noah's portrayal in Sir 44:17-18 includes a series of allusions which evoke the substance of the whole Flood story in Gen 6:5-9:17. Thus, on the one hand the brief praise of Noah presents the entire Flood story *in nuce*. On the other hand, the sparse independent phrasing indicates the author's own understanding of Noah, which culminates in his designation as "renewer" (תחליף). Taking into account the broader context of the Praise of the Fathers, the accentuation of the covenant with Noah corresponds to his role at the beginning of a sequence of covenants (Sir 44:17-45:26). All in all, Noah is not only presented as the righteous survivor of the flood to whom man and beast in general owe their survival, but he is also granted the divine promise that life on earth will be spared global destruction.

INDEX OF MODERN AUTHORS

INDEX OF CITED PASSAGES

SUPPLEMENTS

TO THE

JOURNAL FOR THE STUDY OF JUDAISM

50. YARBRO COLLINS, A. *Cosmology and Eschatology in Jewish and Christian Apocalypticism.* 1996. ISBN 90 04 10587 5

51. MENN, E. *Judah and Tamar (Genesis 38) in Ancient Jewish Exegesis.* Studies in Literary Form and Hermeneutics. 1997.
ISBN 90 04 10630 8

52. NEUSNER, J. *Jerusalem and Athens.* The Congruity of Talmudic and Classical Philosophy. 1996. ISBN 90 04 10698 7

54. COLLINS, J.J. *Seers, Sibyls & Sages in Hellenistic-Roman Judaism.* 1997. ISBN 90 04 10752 5

55. BAUMGARTEN, A.I. *The Flourishing of Jewish Sects in the Maccabean Era: An Interpretation.* 1997. ISBN 90 04 10751 7

56. SCOTT, J.M. (ed.). *Exile: Old Testament, Jewish, and Christian Conceptions.* 1997. ISBN 90 04 10676 6

57. HENTEN, J.-.W. VAN. *The Maccabean Martyrs as Saviours of the Jewish People.* A Study of 2 and 4 Maccabees. 1997. ISBN 90 04 10976 5

58. FELDMAN, L.H. *Studies in Josephus' Rewritten Bible.* 1998.
ISBN 90 04 10839 4

59. MORRAY-JONES, C.R.A. *A Transparent Illusion.* The Dangerous Vision of Water in Hekhalot Mysticism: A Source-Critical and Tradition-Historical Inquiry. 2002. ISBN 90 04 11337 1

60. HALPERN-AMARU, B. *The Empowerment of Women in the* Book of Jubilees. 1999. ISBN 90 04 11414 9

61. HENZE, M. *The Madness of King Nebuchadnezzar.* The Ancient Near Eastern Origins and Early History of Interpretation of Daniel 4. 1999.
ISBN 90 04 11421 1

62. VANDERKAM, J.C. *From Revelation to Canon.* Studies in the Hebrew Bible and Second Tempel Literature. 2000. ISBN 90 04 11557 9

63. NEWMAN, C.C., J.R. DAVILA & G.S. LEWIS (eds.). *The Jewish Roots of Christological Monotheism.* Papers from the St. Andrews Conference on the Historical Origins of the Worship of Jesus. 1999.
ISBN 90 04 11361 4

64. LIESEN, J.W.M. *Full of Praise.* An Exegetical Study of Sir 39,12-35. 1999.
ISBN 90 04 11359 2

65. BEDFORD, P.R. *Temple Restoration in Early Achaemenid Judah.* 2000.
ISBN 90 04 11509 9

66. RUITEN, J.T.A.G.M. VAN. *Primaeval History Interpreted.* The Rewriting of Genesis 1-11 in the book of Jubilees. 2000. ISBN 90 04 11658 3

67. HOFMANN, N.J. *Die Assumptio Mosis.* Studien zur Rezeption massgültiger Überlieferung. 2000. ISBN 90 04 11938 8

68. HACHLILI, R. *The Menorah, the Ancient Seven-armed Candelabrum.* Origin, Form and Significance. 2001. ISBN 90 04 12017 3

69. VELTRI, G. *Gegenwart der Tradition.* Studien zur jüdischen Literatur und Kulturgeschichte. 2002. ISBN 90 04 11686 9

70. DAVILA, J.R. *Descenders to the Chariot.* The People behind the Hekhalot Literature. 2001. ISBN 90 04 11541 2

71. PORTER, S.E. & J.C.R. DE ROO (eds.). *The Concept of the Covenant in the Second Temple Period.* 2003. ISBN 90 04 11609 5

72. SCOTT, J.M. (ed.). *Restoration.* Old Testament, Jewish, and Christian Perspectives. 2001. ISBN 90 04 11580 3

73. TORIJANO, P.A. *Solomon the Esoteric King.* From King to Magus, Development of a Tradition. 2002. ISBN 90 04 11941 8

74. KUGEL, J.L. *Shem in the Tents of Japhet.* Essays on the Encounter of Judaism and Hellenism. 2002. ISBN 90 04 12514 0

75. COLAUTTI, F.M. *Passover in the Works of Josephus.* 2002. ISBN 90 04 12372 5

76. BERTHELOT, K. *Philanthrôpia judaica.* Le débat autour de la "misanthropie" des lois juives dans l'Antiquité. 2003. ISBN 90 04 12886 7

77. NAJMAN, H. *Seconding Sinai.* The Development of Mosaic Discourse in Second Temple Judaism. 2003. ISBN 90 04 11542 0

78. MULDER, O. *Simon the High Priest in Sirach 50.* An Exegetical Study of the Significance of Simon the High Priest as Climax to the Praise of the Fathers in Ben Sira's Concept of the History of Israel. 2003. ISBN 90 04 12316 4

79. BURKES, S.L. *God, Self, and Death.* The Shape of Religious Transformation in the Second Temple Period. 2003. ISBN 90 04 12954 5

80. NEUSNER, J. & A.J. AVERY-PECK (eds.). *George W.E. Nickelsburg in Perspective.* An Ongoing Dialogue of Learning (2 vols.). 2003. ISBN 90 04 12987 1 (set)

81. COBLENTZ BAUTCH, K. *A Study of the Geography of 1 Enoch 17-19.* "No One Has Seen What I Have Seen". 2003. ISBN 90 04 13103 5

82. GARCÍA MARTÍNEZ, F., & G.P. LUTTIKHUIZEN. *Jerusalem, Alexandria, Rome.* Studies in Ancient Cultural Interaction in Honour of A. Hilhorst. 2003 ISBN 90 04 13584 7

83. NAJMAN, H. & J.H. NEWMAN (eds.). *The Idea of Biblical Interpretation.* Essays in Honor of James L. Kugel. 2004. ISBN 90 04 13630 4

84. ATKINSON, K. *I Cried to the Lord.* A Study of the Psalms of Solomon's Historical Background and Social Setting. 2004. ISBN 90 04 13614 2

85. AVERY-PECK, A.J., D. HARRINGTON & J. NEUSNER. *When Judaism and Christianity Began.* Essays in Memory of Anthony J. Saldarini. 2004. ISBN 90 04 13659 2 (Set), ISBN 90 04 13660 6 (Volume I), ISBN 90 04 13661 4 (Volume II)

86. DRAWNEL, H. *An Aramaic Wisdom Text from Qumran.* A New Interpretation of the Levi Document. 2004. ISBN 90 04 13753 X

87. BERTHELOT, K. *L'«humanité de l'autre homme» dans la pensée juive ancienne.* 2004. ISBN 90 04 13797 1

88. BONS, E. (ed.) *«Car c'est l'amour qui me plaît, non le sacrifice ...».* Recherches sur Osée 6:6 et son interprétation juive et chrétienne. 2004. ISBN 90 04 13677 0

89. CHAZON, E.G., D. SATRAN & R. CLEMENTS (eds.). *Things Revealed.* Studies in Honor of Michael E. Stone. 2004. ISBN 90 04 13885 4

90. FLANNERY-DAILEY, F. *Dreamers, Scribes, and Priests.* Jewish Dreams in the Hellenistic and Roman Eras. 2004. ISBN 90 04 12367 9

91. SCOTT, J.M. *On Earth as in Heaven.* The Restoration of Sacred Time and Sacred Space in the Book of Jubilees. 2005. ISBN 90 04 13796 3

92. RICHARDSON, P. *Building Jewish in the Roman East.* 2005. ISBN 90 04 14131 6

93. BATSCH, C. *La guerre et les rites de guerre dans le judaïsme du deuxième Temple.* 2005. ISBN 90 04 13897 8

94. HACHLILI, R. *Jewish Funerary Customs, Practices and Rites in the Second Temple Period.* 2005. ISBN 90 04 12373 3

95. BAKHOS, C. *Ancient Judaism in its Hellenistic Context.* 2005. ISBN 90 04 13871 4

97. NEUSNER, J. *Contours of Coherence in Rabbinic Judaism.* 2005. ISBN 90 04 14231 2 (Set), ISBN 90 04 14436 6 (Volume I), ISBN 90 04 14437 4 (Volume II)

98. XERAVITS, G.G. & J. ZSENGELLÉR (eds.). *The Book of Tobit: Text, Tradition, Theology.* Papers of the First International Conference on the Deutero-canonical Books, Pápa, Hungary, 20-21 May, 2004. 2005. ISBN 90 04 14376 9

99. ROSENFELD, B-Z. & J. MENIRAV (Translated from the Hebrew by Chava Cassel). *Markets and Marketing in Roman Palestine.* 2005. ISBN 90 04 14049 2

100. COLLINS, J.J. *Jewish Cult and Hellenistic Culture.* Essays on the Jewish Encounter with Hellenism and Roman Rule. 2005. ISBN 90 04 14438 2

101. NEUSNER, J. *Rabbinic Categories.* Construction and Comparison. 2005. ISBN 90 04 14578 8

102. SIVERTSEV, A.M. *Households, Sects, and the Origins of Rabbinic Judaism.* 2005. ISBN 90 04 14447 1

103. BEYERLE, S. *Gottesvorstellungen in der antik-jüdischen Apokalyptik.* 2005. ISBN 90 04 13116 7

104. SIEVERS, J. & G. LEMBI (eds.). *Josephus and Jewish History in Flavian Rome and Beyond.* 2005. ISBN 90 04 14179 0

105. DAVILA, J.R. *The Provenance of the Pseudepigrapha.* Jewish, Christian, or Other? 2005. ISBN 90 04 13752 1

106. BAKHOS, C. (ed.) *Current Trends in the Study of Midrash.* 2005. ISBN 90 04 13870 6

107. FELDMAN, L.H. *Judaism and Hellenism Reconsidered*. 2006.
ISBN 90 04 14906 6

108. BRUTTI, M. *The Development of the High Priesthood during the pre-Hasmonean Period*. History, Ideology, Theology. 2006. ISBN 90 04 14910 4

109. VELTRI, G. *Libraries, Translations, and "Canonic" Texts*. The Septuagint, Aquila and Ben Sira in the Jewish and Christian Traditions. 2006. ISBN 90 04 14993 7

110. RODGERS, Z. (ed.) *Making History*. Josephus and Historical Method. 2006. ISBN 90 04 15008 0

111. HEMPEL, C. & J. M. LIEU (eds.) *Biblical Traditions in Transmission*. Essays in Honour of Michael A. Knibb. 2006. ISBN 90 04 13997 4

112. GRAPPE, Ch. & J.-C. INGELAERE (éds.) *Le Temps et les Temps* dans les littératures juives et chrétiennes au tournant de notre ère. 2006. ISBN 90 04 15058 7

113. CAPPELLETTI, S. *The Jewish Community of Rome*. From the Second Century B. C. to the Third Century C.E. 2006. ISBN 90 04 15157 5

114. ORLOV, A.A. *From Apocalypticism to Merkabah Mysticism Studies in the Slavonic Pseudepigrapha*. 2007. ISBN-13: 978 90 04 15439 1,
ISBN-10: 90 04 15439 6

115. MACASKILL, G. *Revealed Wisdom and Inaugurated Eschatology in Ancient Judaism and Early Christianity*. 2007. ISBN-13: 978 90 04 15582 4,
ISBN-10: 90 04 15582 1

116. DVORJETSKI, E. *Leisure, Pleasure and Healing Spa Culture and Medicine in Ancient Eastern Mediterranean*. 2007. ISBN-13: 978 90 04 15681 4,
ISBN-10: 90 04 15681 X

117. SEGAL, M. *The Book of Jubilees Rewritten Bible, Redaction, Ideology and Theology*. 2007. ISBN-13: 978 90 04 15057 7, ISBN-10: 90 04 15057 9

118. XERAVITS, G.G. & J. ZSENGELLÉR (eds.). *The Books of the Maccabees: History, Theology, Ideology*. Papers of the Second International Conference on the Deuterocanonical Books, Pápa, Hungary, 9-11 June, 2005. 2007. ISBN-13: 978 90 04 15700 2, ISBN-10: 90 04 15700 X

119. LIDONNICI, L. & A. LIEBER (eds.). *Heavenly Tablets*. Interpretation, Identity and Tradition in Ancient Judaism. 2007.
ISBN-13: 978 90 04 15856 6, ISBN-10: 90 04 15856 1

120. ASSEFA, D. (ed.). *L'Apocalypse des animaux (1 Hen 85-90): une propagande militaire?* Approches narrative, historico-critique, perspectives théologiques. 2007. ISBN 978 90 04 16267 9

121. BOCCACCINI, G. & J.J. COLLINS (eds.). *The Early Enoch Literature*. 2007. ISBN 978 90 04 16154 2

122. HILHORST, A., É. PUECH & E. TIGCHELAAR (eds.). *Flores Florentino*. Dead Sea Scrolls and Other Early Jewish Studies in Honour of Florentino García Martínez. 2007. ISBN 978 90 04 16292 1

123. COHEN, N.G. *Philo's Scriptures: Citations from the Prophets and Writings*. Evidence for a *Haftarah* Cycle in Second Temple Judaism. 2007.
ISBN 978 90 04 16312 6

124. TROXEL, R.L. *LXX-Isaiah as Translation and Interpretation*. The Strategies of the Translator of the Septuagint of Isaiah. 2008. ISBN 978 90 04 15394 3

125. ADAMS, S.L. *Wisdom in Transition*. Act and Consequence in Second Temple Instructions. 2008. ISBN 978 90 04 16566 3

126. VOITILA, A. & J. JOKIRANTA (eds.). *Scripture in Transition*. Essays on Septuagint, Hebrew Bible, and Dead Sea Scrolls in Honour of Raija Sollamo. 2008. ISBN 978 90 04 16582 3

127. XERAVITS, G.G. & J. ZSENGELLÉR (eds.). *Studies in the Book of Ben Sira*. Papers of the Third International Conference on the Deuterocanonical Books, Shime'on Centre, Pápa, Hungary, 18-20 May, 2006. 2008. ISBN 978 90 04 16906 7

ISSN 1384-2161